ALL THE GREAT REASONS TO TUNE IN TO . . .

GLUED TO THE SET

"An opinionated crash course in the medium that
has influenced virtually every aspect of American life."
—*The New York Times*

"PROVOCATIVE."
—*People*

"GREAT FUN . . . A MUST-READ FOR ANYONE
INTERESTED IN TV, HISTORY, AND SOCIAL STUDIES."
—*The Indianapolis Star*

"ENTERTAINING . . . AUTHORITATIVE . . .
COMPULSIVELY READABLE."
—*Seattle Post-Intelligencer*

"A COMPULSIVELY READABLE ANTHOLOGY . . .
[STARK'S] research is impressive, providing insights
that are often disturbing."
—*The Boston Globe*

"A REFERENCE GUIDE OF DIVERSE PLEASURES."
—*Newsday*

"A MUST-READ . . . giddy blend of highbrow intellectualism
mixed with an affection for lowbrow entertainment.
Stark's arguments are so cogent that his analyses sound
not only possible, but even linked, fated, and prophetic."
—*Contra Costa Times,* Walnut Creek, Ca.

GLUED TO THE SET

The 60 Television Shows

and Events That Made Us

Who We Are Today

STEVEN D. STARK

Delta
Trade Paperbacks

To Sarah and Harry,
who make it all worthwhile

A Delta Book
Published by
Dell Publishing
a division of
Bantam Doubleday Dell Publishing Group, Inc.
1540 Broadway
New York, New York 10036

ISBN: 0-385-32411-1

Reprinted by arrangement with The Free Press

Manufactured in the United States of America
Published simultaneously in Canada

July 1998

10 9 8 7 6 5 4 3 2 1

BVG

Contents

Acknowledgments xi

Introduction 1

Part I. The Forties

1. What's So Funny About Milton Berle? The Unacceptable
   Ethnicity of *The Texaco Star Theater* 9
   (NBC: 1948–53)

2. *Howdy Doody* and the Debate Over Children's Programming 18
   (NBC: 1947–60)

3. *Meet the Press*: Television's Anachronism 25
   (NBC: 1947–Present)

Part II. The Fifties

4. *I Love Lucy:* The Woman as TV Superstar 35
   (CBS: 1951–57)

5. *Dragnet* and the Policeman as Hero 42
   (NBC: 1951–59)

6. Bishop Sheen's *Life Is Worth Living* and the New American
   Religion of Television 51
   (DuMont and ABC: 1952–57)

7. Resistance to Reality: Why Edward R. Murrow's
   See It Now Didn't Change Television More 57
   (CBS: 1951–58)

8. *Today,* Barbara Walters, and TV's Definition of News 63
   (NBC: 1952–Present)

9. *Disneyland* and the Creation of the Seamless
   Entertainment Web 70
   (ABC, CBS, and NBC: 1954–90)

10. The Secret of *The Lawrence Welk Show*   76
    (ABC: 1955–71; Syndication: 1971–82)

11. *The Ed Sullivan Show* and the Era of Big Government   79
    (CBS: 1948–71)

12. *Gunsmoke* and Television's Lost Wave of Westerns   84
    (CBS: 1955–75)

13. *American Bandstand* and the Clash of Rock and TV   92
    (ABC: 1957–87)

14. *Twenty-One*, the Quiz Scandal, and the Decline of Public Trust   99
    (NBC: 1956–58)

15. *Leave It to Beaver* and the Politics of Nostalgia   109
    (CBS and ABC: 1957–63)

16. *The Twilight Zone:* Science Fiction as Realism   115
    (CBS: 1959–64)

Part III. The Sixties

17. The Rise and Fall of the Televised Presidential
    Press Conference   123
    (All Major Networks: 1961–93)

18. *Perry Mason* and the Criminal Lawyer as Brief Television Hero   129
    (CBS: 1957–66)

19. *The Dick Van Dyke Show* and the Rise of Upscale Television   134
    (CBS: 1961–66)

20. Space Television   139
    (All 3 Networks: 1961–69)

21. *The Beverly Hillbillies* and the Rise of Populist Television   143
    (CBS: 1962–71)

22. Assassination Television   148
    (All 3 Networks: 1963)

23. *Mister Ed:* How Real Were TV's Escapist Comedies?   154
    (Syndication and CBS: 1961–66)

24. *The Dating Game,* Game Shows, and the Rise of
    Tabloid TV   159
    (ABC: 1965–73)

25. Walter Cronkite, the *CBS Evening News,* and the Rise of News on
    Television   165
    (CBS: 1963–Present)

26. *The Monkees* and TV's Subversion of the 1960s   173
    (NBC: 1966–68)

27. *Mission: Impossible* and Its Cold War Fight to Save America   177
    (CBS: 1966–73)

28. *The Smothers Brothers Comedy Hour* and the Fate
    of Controversy on TV   183
    (CBS: 1967–69)

29. *Rowan and Martin's Laugh-In* and Acceleration as a TV Style   190
    (NBC: 1968–73)

Part IV. The Seventies

30. *Sesame Street:* The Last Remnant of the Counterculture   199
    (PBS: 1969–Present)

31. TV's Biggest Show: The Super Bowl   205
    (ABC, NBC, Fox, and CBS: 1967–Present)

32. *The Brady Bunch* as Television Icon   212
    (ABC: 1969–74)

33. *All in the Family* and the Sitcom "Revolution"   216
    (CBS: 1971-83)

34. *The Mary Tyler Moore Show* and America's Newest "Families"   223
    (CBS: 1970–77)

35. *Masterpiece Theatre* and the Failure of PBS   228
    (PBS: 1971–Present)

36. Television's Biggest Scandal: The Local News   235
    (All Major Affiliates: 1970–Present)

37. *The Tonight Show* and Its Hold on America   243
    (NBC: 1954-Present)

38. *60 Minutes* and the Evolution of News to Entertainment   251
    (CBS: 1968–Present)

39. TV's Most Self-Congratulatory Hit: *Saturday Night Live*   258
    (NBC: 1975–Present)

40. The Miniseries as History: Did *Roots* Change America?   265
    (ABC: 1977)

41. *All My Children,* Soaps, and the Feminization of America   270
    (ABC: 1970–Present)

42. The Oddly Winning Dark Sensibility of *M*A*S*H*   278
    (CBS: 1972–83)

Part V. The Eighties

43. The Hostage Crisis as Metaphor   289
    (All Major Networks: 1979–80, 1985)

44. *Dallas* and the Rise of Republican Mythology   292
    (CBS: 1978–91)

45. Debating Our Politics: The Ronald Reagan Show   298
    (All Major Networks: 1967–89)

46. CNN and the Changing Definition of News   310
    (1980–Present)

47. *Hill Street Blues* and TV's New Elite Style   318
    (NBC: 1981–87)

48. What MTV Hath Wrought   325
    (1981–Present)

49. Bob Newhart as the Embodiment of TV Culture   331
    (CBS: 1972–78; 1982–90; 1992–93)

50. *Entertainment Tonight* and the Expansion of the Tabloid,
    Celebrity Culture   334
    (Syndication: 1981–Present)

51. The Forgotten Promise of *The Cosby Show*   340
    (NBC: 1984–92)

52. The *Star Trek* Galaxy and Its Glimpse of TV's Future   346
    (NBC: 1966–69; Syndication: 1987–94; Syndication:
    1993–Present; UPN: 1995–Present)

53. How *Roseanne* Made Trash TV Respectable   351
    (ABC: 1988–97)

Part VI. The Nineties

54. How *America's Funniest Home Videos* Tore Down Our Wall   359
    (ABC: 1990–Present)

55. Hill–Thomas and the Congressional Hearing as Miniseries   364
    (All Major Networks: 1991)

56. *The Oprah Winfrey Show* and the Talk–Show Furor   370
    (Syndication: 1986–Present)

57. A Tale of Two Sitcoms   378
    (*Home Improvement* [ABC]: 1991–Present; *Seinfeld* [NBC]:
    1990–Present)

58. Home Shopping: Commercialism as Salvation   384
    (QVC: 1986–Present)

59. The Innovations of *ER* and the Fight for Health–Care
    Reform   389
    (NBC: 1994–Present)

60. How *Wheel of Fortune* Won the Cold War   395
    (NBC, CBS, Syndication: 1975–Present)

    Appendix: How I Came Up With the 60 Shows   403

    Bibliography   409

    Index   449

Acknowledgments

A lot of people helped me with this book and deserve thanks. First, there are all the editors and producers at various publications or places where I initially worked through some of these ideas in other forms: Bob Malesky at National Public Radio; Bill Whitworth, Jack Beatty, and Cullen Murphy at *The Atlantic Monthly;* Allison Silver at the *Los Angeles Times;* Connie Rosenblum and Margot Slade at the *New York Times;* Jodie Allen at the *Washington Post;* Marge Pritchard, David Greenway, Loretta McLaughlin, and the late Kirk Scharfenberg at the *Boston Globe;* Don Forst at *Boston Magazine;* Richard Gaines at the *Boston Phoenix;* and the editors at the *University of Miami Law Review* in the fall of 1987. My agent, Gail Hochman, was extremely helpful in formulating the idea and organization for the book, and all the editors at The Free Press—from my current "team" of Bruce Nichols, Norah Vincent, and George Rowland to Peter Dougherty and the late Erwin Glikes—offered terrific suggestions throughout. Ralph Whitehead's telephone exhortations were a source of constant amazement and, through the years, Brian Rose has always offered choice insights. My friend Alex McNeil (whose *Total Television* is still the best encyclopedic source for program information on the medium) read a draft of the entire manuscript and his copious comments and corrections were invaluable. Finally, my wife Sarah Wald reviewed every chapter: I never knew when we met and married that I had chanced upon the second coming of Maxwell Perkins.

Introduction

No one talks about literature without making distinctions between Shakespeare and Tom Clancy. It is impossible to evaluate music without putting Mozart and the Temptations in different categories. Yet many writers and critics seem to have no problem always treating television as an utter abstraction. "TV has dumbed down America," they will say, or "Television encourages violence."

Most Americans, however, look at the medium more perceptively. When they think about television, they draw on memories of something that's fun and they think about individual shows—the *Ed Sullivan, Gunsmoke,* and *Tonight* shows. When they talk about the small screen—and they talk about it constantly—they don't discuss the history of broadcast regulation (who would?) but rather their recollections of Lucy on the assembly line, O.J. on the highway, or Seinfeld and his friends in his apartment.

In such a diverse country as the United States, television has supplied everyone with common reference points and a shared culture. Could this be because TV is, in effect, a drug? Maybe. A necessity? That too. But mostly we watch because we choose to, and then we watch some more. We love television because of what it has brought us through its vast array of presentations.

But do Americans really understand what TV has in fact brought forth upon this nation? Television may be influential, but its influence has hardly been as monolithic as that of, say, the automobile industry. The car changed America too, but it would be hard to make the case that Cadillacs changed it in different ways from Buicks. In contrast, *Life Is Worth Living,* Bishop Fulton J. Sheen's popular TV show, had a far different audience and influence on the country than a series like *The Twilight Zone.* Television is a medium with over 5,000 series in 50 years, not to mention all the specials and news events made into programs. To try to understand this medium, you have to try to understand its key shows.

In the 1950s, *Dragnet* permanently altered our view of the police and crime control, and *I Love Lucy* helped change our national sense of humor. In the sixties, shows like *Mission: Impossible* made it easier for the United States government to spy on its perceived adversaries— whether at home or abroad. In 1976, Barbara Walters asked Jimmy and Rosalynn Carter if they slept in single or double beds, eroding the presidency to such an extent that less than two decades later, a future president would volunteer on MTV his underwear preferences.

Some of the changes have been less discernible, but are no less significant. In writing this book, I was struck again by how much *Howdy Doody* helped create a class of child consumers, how central a role *Leave It to Beaver* played in the rise of the fifties nostalgia which continues to grip our culture, and how CNN helped change the definition of news itself. Similarly, everyone talks about the television skills of Ronald Reagan and John F. Kennedy, but I never realized until I wrote this book how consistently news events like the space program become important television shows in themselves, conforming to television's dictates of entertainment. That's one reason why, for example, the Iranian hostage crisis in 1979–80 was such a big deal in the culture, but the bombing of a marketplace in Sarajevo in the early nineties hardly raised a flicker of interest. The first made a great miniseries, full of Americans; the second did not.

Just as our affection for television comes from the shows themselves, the essence of this book is in the chapters about the shows which follow this introduction. Yet it may be helpful to readers to understand the context in which I view individual shows.

In many ways over the past half-century, the history of television has become the history of America, and not just because we all now experience everything from moon landings to wars via the tube. Television's ubiquity makes it a pop-culture version of the air we breathe. It is hardly news that this medium's programming has been influential—superseding school, and sometimes even the family, as the major influence on our social and moral development. It is fair to say that there have been two eras in America: Before Television (BT) and After Television (AT). Popular culture has been around for centuries, but never so persistently, to the exclusion of so much else and with so much influence, as now. Futurists in previous centuries wrote about how horseless carriages and electric lighting might change our lives, but no one—not even the medium's earliest pioneers—saw what television might become. It certainly wasn't just radio with pictures; and in influence, structure, and content it isn't much like the movies, either. From the Kennedy assassination to the last episode of *M*A*S*H,* television has unified us and shaped us at key moments far more than other forms of popular culture. TV series have been the engine of consumerism, telling us what to buy, how to dress, and which toys we should ask our parents to purchase. TV programming first defined certain news events for us; then it defined "the news" itself. Finally, television has utterly changed our civic life—from the types of speeches and candidates we hear to the deterioration of certain forms of public life itself, as the small screen has drawn everyone indoors, sometimes for days at a time.

Yet, when looking at television, it is always important to remember the following two basics. *First:* American television is almost always commercial TV, and advertisers have crafted this form of entertainment to suit their own purposes. That's significant because it means we almost never get more than a few minutes of programming without being interrupted by ads, and because Americans are now addressed in their public lives primarily as consumers—a state of affairs which affects everything from the way we define ourselves as a nation to how much money we save compared with past generations.

Critics constantly complain about TV's conversion of everything into a form of entertainment, as if popular culture had never done that before with folk tales or penny magazines. Where American TV shows differ from presentations in other media, and where their sponsored influence matters most, are *in the way* they change reality into entertainment. Because advertisers sponsor the shows, they tend to want only entertainment that puts audiences in a mood to buy. For example, *The Day After* (the made-for-TV 1983 movie about a nuclear holocaust) posted some of the highest ratings in the history of television. Yet some sponsors were reportedly afraid to touch the show because its message might make the home audience feel "bad"—a feeling which, they suspected, would infect the commercials surrounding the movie, and put that audience in no mood to buy their products. So television history has had very few *Day Afters.*

The upshot is that most American TV shows conform to a changing yet powerful ethos to make the advertising look good. This complex ethos is so ingrained in our culture that we hardly notice it any-more. On one level, it simply means that shows which implicitly dampen the spirit of consumerism—say tragedies—have less of a chance of making it to television. Yet it also means that because tele-vision is a powerful force that changes anything it touches, the adver-tising ethos has affected almost everything in our lives, from movies and politics to novels and rhetoric. The world we inhabit AT (as op-posed to BT) is structured far more like a giant commercial—or at least a promotion.

Second: Americans may talk about television engagingly, but most don't watch it with much engagement. Studies have shown that up to 20 percent of all TVs play to an empty room. While this may be changing a bit in the nineties because of the influence of cable pro-gramming (which tends to create niche audiences who watch with more intensity) prime-time network entertainment still tends to be designed for a tired, stressed-out audience watching at home without paying close attention. That, too, has dictated a certain type of enter-tainment throughout the life of the medium: simple, repetitive, and low-key programming that can be understood even if you leave the room now and again for a few minutes, or do something else while only vaguely watching. There's nothing patently wrong with that, but many TV critics (and also a fair number of influential intellectuals) want their television as absorbing as the movies they see or the nov-els they read. This often puts them in the position of viewing this medium in a far different fashion from that of the masses. One per-son's wasteland, after all, is another person's oasis.

Beyond these two attributes, most analysts make a mistake when they analyze television in broad terms as, say, liberal or conservative. American TV programming is as diverse and contradictory as the country itself, and many of the criticisms people make of the medium are what was said about American culture long before television. Many critics have also mistaken the effects of network television for television itself. TV was controlled by three networks (ABC, NBC, and CBS) for roughly the first 40 years of its existence. Thus, some of the characteristics we commonly attribute to it—from types of shows which are popular, to scheduling maxims—are not really inherent in the medium itself, but in the fact that three corporations controlled that medium for decades via something of a monopoly. As cable has changed the face of television, many of those supposedly inherent attributes have begun to disappear.

In writing this book, I learned that there isn't much being debated about television today that hasn't been discussed before. For all the recurrent talk about television's being a window on the world, realism has never been the strength of this medium's programming, and indeed TV executives have usually gone to almost any length to avoid controversy. Television has obviously changed in key ways since people went over to a neighbor's house in the late 1940s to watch Milton Berle. Yet whether it's the nature of children's programming, the propensity for this medium to feature violence, or the question of whether New York or Los Angeles elites will control broadcasting, most issues surrounding the tube haven't changed very much over the past 50 years.

So this book is less a history of how television changed than it is the story of how its presence and programming changed us and therefore the world. Commentators often talk about how the export of American values helped end the Cold War. Yet when the Poles or Ukrainians look to emulate America, they're usually thinking more of J. R. Ewing and Doug Ross than of Jefferson and Madison. Because television democratizes experience, it leads to a certain type of democratic zeitgeist in culture and government. More important, when foreigners think "freedom," they tend to think "freedom to acquire"—an ideology straight from the world of television. If this medium never gives us anything else, we should still be grateful for political successes it has helped to support, if not create.

But enough blabbering: I should have learned from watching so much television that if there's anything audiences can't stand, it's talking heads. There are scores of wonderful books and articles on the medium, many mentioned in these pages. Yet while histories of broadcast regulation, treatises on the economics of the industry, and academic criticism all have their place, what we watch, talk about, and make our companions through life are the likes of *The Dick Van Dyke Show, All in the Family, The Brady Bunch*—and even *The Monkees*. Their histories have, in a very real way, become part of our history. What follows herein are the stories of the 60 shows and TV events that I think shaped us the most, molding us into the nation that we are today.

Part I

THE FORTIES

Milton Berle and *The Texaco Star Theater*
Howdy Doody • *Meet the Press*

The dawn of the medium. Even by the end of the decade, fewer than 10 percent of American homes had television, and the TV industry was still in the red. Since all TV was live and relied heavily on the styles of radio or vaudeville, most types of programming from this decade are virtually absent from today's television. The same holds true of the era's stars—from the vaudevillian Milton Berle to the puppet Howdy Doody. Demonstrating which network got out of the blocks the fastest, all three shows in this section appeared on NBC.

1

What's So Funny About Milton Berle?
The Unacceptable Ethnicity of *The Texaco Star Theater*
(NBC: 1948–53)

When viewing a megahit from a prior era, one can usually understand why the movie, recording, or television show was so popular. Some TV hits, such as *I Love Lucy* and *The Honeymooners*, transcend their era, becoming permanent sensations in reruns. Others, such as *Gunsmoke* and *The Beverly Hillbillies,* might not be popular today, but it's still possible to appreciate what caused audiences to flock to the small screen in their time. Despite sweeping societal changes, the formulas that have tended to sell in popular culture haven't changed so much over the decades, that their appeals have become indiscernible to the modern eye.

Then there's Milton Berle.

It is impossible to watch tapes of Berle—hailed as "Mr. Television" and universally acknowledged as the medium's first superstar—without experiencing a severe sense of displacement: How could millions of Americans have stayed home to watch *that*? As critic Robert Lewis Shayon wrote then, Berle was the king of "the yak, the blacked-out teeth, the idiot's wig, the lisp, the swagger, the falling pants." It was said that Berle would do anything for a laugh, but watching his tapes today, it's hard to see why people were laughing at all at a man columnist Walter Winchell called "the thief of badgags." It's certainly true there have been other products of popular culture—19th-century melodramas, Frank Merriwell stories, silent movies—which had no staying power, outside their own eras. It's also true that television historians have come up with plenty of reasons why Berle's brand of humor appears so anachronistic today. But the bottom line is that in television history, Milton Berle stands alone—not as a pioneer, but as one of those rare superstars whose persona and brand of entertainment were to become as extinct as the dinosaur.

What made the transformation all the more striking was that it came so fast. In 1947, Berle was a minor vaudeville and radio comic. By 1949, his *Texaco Star Theater* was watched each week by 75 percent of the television audience—figures never again attained for an entertainment program. In the wake of his popularity, sales of television sets went through the roof ("Since I've been on television they've sold a lot of sets. My uncle sold his, my father sold his . . . ," Berle joked), while the networks rushed to schedule almost any vaudeville comedian or variety show they could find. Yet by 1953, Texaco had dropped its sponsorship of the show, and only a few years later, the vaudeville-variety format Berle had made the rage of television had just about disappeared for good from the medium.

Berle was an odd figure for the role of "Mr. Television." Derided by the critics and distrusted by many of his peers, his career before television had been a 35-year series of virtual one-night stands. Born in Harlem in 1908, Berle entered the entertainment world at age five, pushed by his mother into performing in silent movies. From there, he went into vaudeville as part of a kid act in which he would sing, dance, and imitate Eddie Cantor. In his autobiography, Berle described an opening night on the road, when his mother ordered him to mess up a group dance routine so he could draw laughs and attention to himself. Though he infuriated the producer, the audience loved his innovations, and Berle never forgot the lesson.

He also never forgot vaudeville, even as it faded from the American scene during the Depression and the rise of talking movies. "The vaudeville theater belongs to the era of the department store and the short story," a critic once wrote. "It may be a kind of lunch-counter art, but then art is so vague and lunch is so real." An American invention, vaudeville mirrored the democratic culture from which it sprang. In its appeal to the broadest audience possible, its merging of high and low culture, and the way it took ordinary people seriously, vaudeville foreshadowed the values and role that television would later assume in the culture. A typical show had something for everyone—animal trainers, comedians, jugglers, magicians, acrobats, pantomimists, dancers, and singers—all presented in rapid-fire succession. Yet despite the variety of acts, vaudeville's fundamental core was comedy—often corny visual jokes, such as pie-throwing or dressing in drag, presented in exaggerated fashion so they could be seen anywhere in a large theater.

With the collapse of vaudeville theater, Berle spent the thirties and forties bouncing from nightclubs to grade-B movies to radio—never staying in one place long enough to make a lasting impression. His visual gags were obviously unsuited for radio, and he was too overstated to be of much use to Hollywood. After the war, few foresaw that television would soon wipe out network radio, so network stars such as Jack Benny and Fred Allen initially avoided the tube. Thus, when Texaco decided to sponsor a TV variety show on Tuesday nights at 8:00, beginning on June 8, 1948, it turned to a rotating group of what might be called second-tier MC's for audition—a group including Berle, Henny Youngman, Morey Amsterdam, and Jack Carter.

There were still only about a half-million sets in the country. With television in its infancy, the networks were broadcasting only in prime time, featuring a schedule heavy with series such as *The Village Barn* (square dancing from Greenwich Village), *Author Meets the Critics,* and *The Nature of Things,* an early science show. Texaco's first variety show, aired on NBC's New York affiliate and broadcast via seven other stations on the East Coast, reassembled the old vaudeville format with a seven-act show, featuring Berle hosting Señor Wences (a ventriloquist), Bill "Bojangles" Robinson, Pearl Bailey, harmonica player Stan Fisher, and a Spanish trampoline team called Rosario & Antonio. The next week, under the headline "Vaudeo Comes of Age in Texaco Show; Seen Outlet to Vast Talent Pool," *Variety* went wild, proclaiming the show a "milestone in television" and the "greatest single hypo" yet given the medium. *Variety* also praised Berle. "His better qualities, still to be captured in a radio script, are given complete play through the sight medium," it wrote.

By September, the show had been given to Berle permanently. No wonder: By November, he was being watched by 86.7 percent of all TV households; 97.4 percent of all sets in use in that time slot were tuned to his show. NBC delayed broadcasting election returns of the 1948 Dewey-Truman race on November 2 until Berle's program was over. By then, the comedian's seemingly informal format had been formalized. Each hour began with the four Texaco service men, singing the jingle which began:

Oh, we're the men of Texaco.
We work from Maine to Mexico.
There's nothing like this Texaco of ours.

After that came Berle, usually in some outlandish guise—that of a
caveman, a bride, Cleopatra—with the help of which he delivered his
routine. This was followed by the usual succession of vaudeville acts
(introduced of course by Berle) interrupted only for the obligatory
funny commercial, which was delivered live by sober-faced comedic
actor Sid Stone; Stone would open up a briefcase full of sales items
and turn his pitch for Texaco into a fast-talking spiel, beginning with
the phrase "Awright—I'll tell ya what I'm gonna do!" It would become the first of many phrases that television would add to the language through advertising.

Though the show attracted some of the biggest names in show
business (Frank Sinatra, Phil Silvers, Martin & Lewis), Berle was really
the singular attraction. "Anything for a laugh" was his motto. By modern standards his jokes were terrible, though often they were topical:

I love Thanksgiving, because that's the time of the year you have
turkey stuffed with chestnuts. Of course, with the high taxes this
year, you'll be lucky to have chestnuts stuffed with turkey!

He delivered his material at a breathtaking pace—first the bad jokes
("I wanna tell you, marriage helps the sale of Texaco. It really does,
'cause when you're married, you wind up taking gas"); and then the
routines (snapping off ties and pie-throwing were popular items); and,
finally, the changing of costumes, often up to five or six times an
evening (from a Pilgrim to Cupid to Carmen Miranda). Audiences
were simply overwhelmed with his energy. "I think he ought to be investigated by the Atomic Energy Commission," quipped Bob Hope.

Still, for four years it all worked. "The only ones who like Milton
Berle," Walter Winchell once wrote, "are his mother—and the public." Beginning a trend, the other pachyderms in broadcasting grabbed
the tail of the elephant in front of them: The networks started copying the vaudeville-variety format extensively, with weekly all-star re-
vues hosted by Jimmy Durante (*All-Star Revue* on NBC), Ed Sullivan

(*Toast of the Town* on CBS), Ed Wynn (*The Ed Wynn Show* on CBS), and Sid Caesar and Imogene Coca (*The Admiral Broadway Revue* on NBC). The William Morris Agency ran an ad in *Variety:* "Vaudeville is back . . . . Wanted: Variety artists from all corners of the globe." By the 1950-51 season, two years into Berle's reign, prime-time television was mostly an odd assortment of these shows, a few easy-to-televise sports programs such as boxing and the roller derby, the old public-affairs genre left over from TV's infancy (*The Marshall Plan in Action* or *Old Fashioned Meeting*), and some serious drama.

Yet only two years later, the medium had changed. For the 1952–53 season the sports shows, live-drama shows, and variety shows hosted by once-loud comedians remained, but public-affairs programming had virtually disappeared from prime time. In its place, television had begun to televise a new set of weekly series—often situation come-dies similar to those done on radio—with names like *Our Miss Brooks* and *I Love Lucy*. Even variety shows were changing, with many now hosted by soft-spoken singers like Dinah Shore and Perry Como. Be-tween January and June of 1952, Berle slid from Number 1 to Num-ber 20 in the ratings.

So even Berle changed during that September, scrapping the vari-ety format and replacing it with a show-within-a-show concept. Fea-turing his secretary and other regular crew members, the new Berle show was built each week around the tribulations of putting out a weekly television program. Though critics praised the changes, Berle disliked them. "The truth was that while the show . . . certainly had jokes and funny situations," he would later write, "you could listen to it without looking—like too much of today's television—and get most everything that was going on." Contrast that attitude toward the sitcom genre with a comment of Jackie Gleason's a few years later: "Situation comedy is based on honesty," he said. "On the other hand, the [standup] monologue is predicated chiefly on a succession of lies. You can bet that the 'honesty' factor will win out with the audience in the long run." At the end of that 1952–53 season, Texaco termi-nated its sponsorship of Berle's show, even though it finished the year at Number 5. (Buick, however, picked it up.) Three years later, Berle was pretty much out of television, returning over the years only to host a bowling show, an occasional special, and a few failed variety series—though the 30–year contract he had signed with NBC in 1951, guaranteeing him $200,000 a year whether he worked or not, undoubtedly salved his feelings somewhat. (The contract was renegotiated in 1965 to allow Berle to appear on other networks.)

Why did Berle rise so high so quickly, fade so fast, and never return? As television historian Arthur Frank Wertheim has detailed in his bellwether history of the show, part of the reason was the changing way in which people began to watch television. In its infancy, when there were few TV sets, viewers tended to gather in bars or in groups at friends' houses to watch the small screen as if in a theater. With groups of interested "audiences" so assembled, as in vaudeville, Berle's brand of humor worked—particularly since his outrageous visual gags could be appreciated when seen from a distance on a fuzzy screen. His trademark entrance in an endless series of make-you-want-to-laugh costumes, for example, was a brilliant idea: People often gathered around the set each week simply to see what he'd be wearing. Berle realized earlier than most that TV was a visual medium, and capitalized on that—unlike say Fred Allen, or even Edward R. Murrow. *Meet the Press* didn't make you want to go out and buy a television set, but Berle did because you had to *see* him to enjoy him.

Yet by a bare few years later, sales of televisions had skyrocketed: The number of households owning sets went from around 2 percent in 1948 to over 70 percent in 1956. Most viewers now watched TV in the quiet of their own home, where Berle's behavior seemed out of place and exaggerated. Television could no longer attract audiences simply by presenting something "live." Home-based viewers also began to look for a tighter narrative structure to their programming. Berle was in fact attacked from the beginning by critics who complained that his shows lacked "show-wise continuity" while lauding competing shows that displayed the "smoothness" that sitcoms would come to provide. "I like the spontaneity of live television," Berle once said. "You never knew what was going to happen." Yet that's precisely what bothered sponsors and home audiences alike.

What's more, the networks came to like sitcoms better because they could be rerun, bringing in additional profits. In contrast, variety shows featuring "hot" performers were both complicated to produce—since acts had to be hired each week—and quickly dated. Narrative shows also had a longer life, since they burned up jokes and wore out performers at a far slower pace. Berle, unsurprisingly, collapsed from overwork during his run, as did several of his vaudeville contemporaries. "Back in the old days, you would do one sketch for five years," said Bob Hope, who resisted the initial plunge into weekly television. "But if you use that sketch on TV, in one night it's used up." Needless to say, audiences would quickly come to find the sitcom format so conducive to the style of television that it soon replaced virtually every other form of comedy in the culture. Television had quickly changed the definition of what was funny in America, and Berle no longer qualified.

As Wertheim noted, Berle's decline was also due to demographics. When he began in 1948, television reached into only a few major cities, with New York dominating the audience (35 percent). Berle's brand of ethnic vaudeville humor—peppered with yiddishisms—sold well mainly in New York, just as Sophie Tucker's rendition of "My Yiddisha Mama" had attracted wide audiences in New York's vaudeville houses a generation before. "On the show, Milton loved to do Jewish schtick," Mel Diamond, a television writer, told Jeff Kisseloff for his TV oral history, *The Box*. "He would use words like *hamentashen* that you wouldn't understand if you weren't Jewish."

By 1952, however, television had spread to 108 stations; two years later, it was 354. Less-urban audiences couldn't stand Berle's brand of humor, as measured by a 1954 survey, published in *Variety*, which showed Berle's program drawing a 1.9 rating in Charlotte, North Carolina, compared to a 56.3 there for *Death Valley Days*. Ironically, Berle had helped sell televisions to viewers who couldn't stand him. Though no one expressed it in quite these terms in those days, Berle was too fast, too urban, and too Jewish to be broadly acceptable. His demise thus foreshadowed an important development: As television's soul moved from New York to Hollywood, the medium began to portray the typical American as conforming to a suburban, white-bread ideal.

As Al Smith might have said, "Let's look at the record." Though the early fifties did feature a few carryover series from radio which featured first-generation Americans, such as *Life With Luigi* and *The Goldbergs*, television quickly came to disdain ethnic and racial differences, in both program content and the look of its performers. This was a noticeable difference from the programming style of radio, which—perhaps because the audience couldn't see the performers—more frequently relied on what would now be recognized as a more New York, urban, and ethnic form of humor. After Berle, such shows of the 1950s as *Leave It to Beaver, Father Knows Best,* and *Gunsmoke* usually were inhabited by men and women who sounded and looked like they had stepped off of either the beaches of Malibu or the front porches of Dubuque. Carl Reiner's original scripts for *The Dick Van Dyke Show* were written with Reiner as the lead. By the time the show appeared in 1961 it had been, in one executive's words, "midwesternized"—with Van Dyke now in the lead.

As TV grew in the sixties, those few immigrants who appeared in starring roles often came from solid Saxon countries whose immigrants had an easier time assimilating: England *(The Patty Duke Show)* or Scandinavia *(The Farmer's Daughter)*. On dramas and news programs the actors, reporters, and anchormen usually looked the same—emanating from the heartland and from places like Port Charles, Mayberry, or Pine Valley, where immigrants and New York Jews are rare. Sure performers could be culturally distinctive and make it on television, but to do so they often had to suppress the elements that emphasized how distinctive they were. Michael Landon seemed a suitable star for *Bonanza* and *Highway to Heaven*. But what if he hadn't changed his name from Eugene Maurice Orowitz?

There are many reasons why television presented such a picture of homogeneity until the late eighties, when the rise of cable helped make TV programming and performers alike more diverse. In its appeal to the masses, television usually seeks consensus—a set of cultural values and assumptions that can be shared as widely as possible. As cultural critic Benjamin Stein has suggested, perhaps the southern California producers who control television are so out of touch with other parts of America that they produce programming that reflects only their own lives. It may be, as in the movies before, that even though there is a high percentage of Jewish writers and producers in the entertainment business, these Jews are extremely sensitive to anti-Semitism, and overcompensate in their portrayals of "reality." Or it may be that television programming reflects and supports its advertising, always seeking to assimilate its viewers so the national products it peddles find a broader and more receptive audience.

Whatever the reasons, Milton Berle's early ethnic brand of entertainment left practically no mark on television. In the world of network TV, leading-character portrayals of blacks, by Bill Cosby and others, would find acceptance before those of Jews. To the extent that the remnants of vaudeville remain, they do so only on late-night programs such as *Saturday Night Live* and *The Tonight Show,* whose audience demographics are closer to what the demographics for *The Texaco Star Theater* were. Even there, however, television has usually conspired to produce a subtler, lower-key, and less-visual form of humor than Berle's.

Thus in the end, as TV historians would note, Berle signified more by his fall than his rise. For television to become successful, programmers decided that they had to bleach diversity out of mass culture. For a few decades, with so few choices reaching so many people, television helped build America's consensus culture of the fifties and early sixties. Yet in its move from New York to Hollywood, Times Square to Main Street, and urban to suburban, television also created a certain monolithic view of America. The lesson of Milton Berle would be that there would be little room for diversity in the Brave New World of network programming. After a while on television, everyone came to look alike, act alike, and sound alike—even the politicians—a point which would later prove to be of great concern to the electorate. A casualty of the new American cultural juggernaut he helped establish, the legacy of Uncle Miltie was that he left none, as he disappeared without reruns, and thus even from memory.

2
Howdy Doody and
the Debate Over Children's Programming
(NBC: 1947–60)

No matter how you measure its worth, there have clearly been better series in the history of television than *Howdy Doody*. But there may never have been any as relentlessly unrespectable and, not coincidentally, with such a devoted following. For 2,543 episodes, on more than 200 NBC stations, often five times a week, over almost 13 years from December 27, 1947 to September 30, 1960. *Howdy Doody* systematically alienated the Establishment—which, by and large, meant parents—while becoming the darling of their children, which meant baby boomers. In 1948, Howdy received more write-in votes for president than did independent candidate Henry Wallace, by running on this platform: Two Christmases and one schoolday a year, more pictures in history books, double sodas for a dime, and plenty of movies. No wonder ABC analyst Jeff Greenfield would later credit the show for the rise of the sixties counterculture and generational war, calling Clarabell the original Yippie and likening Mayor Bluster to a puppet version of then-president Dwight Eisenhower.

There was more to *Howdy Doody*, however, than subtle generational politics, or the fact that in the wake of its success, other live children's shows soon followed, including *Kukla, Fran and Ollie, Rootie Kazootie,* and even *Ding Dong School*. Howdy's was the first children's show on NBC; the first program of any sort to hit the 2,000-show mark; the first regular network series in color; and the first TV presentation to generate a major mail response from viewers (about 1.5 million pieces annually during the show's first eight years). Howdy Doody changed the way "kids were entertained," Burt Dubrow, a TV producer, once said. "He changed the way kids were taught, and even sold to, forever."

Howdy Doody also presaged the beginning of a never-ending debate about children's programming on television—though the debate was essentially settled virtually the moment Howdy became a national phenomenon, V-chip or no-chip. By the time this show became a hit, it had already become clear that if a series helped move an advertiser's merchandise, TV was going to find a way to disregard any moralizing about content or suitability.

For half a century, Americans have argued about the merits and demerits of children's programming: *Howdy Doody* vs. *Romper Room; Captain Kangaroo* vs. *Sesame Street; G.I. Joe* vs. *Mister Rogers.* Well into the nineties, Congress was once again debating whether television was serving the needs of its younger viewers, and whether *The Jetsons* could be considered educational fare. Of course, by now the question doesn't matter any longer, no matter what Congress or the Federal Communications Commission (FCC) decides. The success of *Howdy Doody* as far back as five decades ago decreed that children could watch the same types of shows that adults could—even if adults looked into this mirror of their own programming and were appalled by the quality of what they saw.

What's striking at first about watching *Howdy Doody* a generation or two later is how similar it is to so much else that was popular on television among adults in those early days. That's hardly surprising when one considers that most households had only one television, and that if Sally or Bobby wanted to watch *Howdy Doody,* somebody who was older had to watch it, too. If Milton Berle had designed a kids' hour in 1947, it would have been *Howdy Doody.* Like Berle's program, this show was loud, boisterous, and out of control. "Long on action, short on coherence" was the way *Time* described it, with a phrase that would neatly sum up much of television's future.

Howdy Doody had a master of ceremonies (i.e., an MC) about Berle's age, one "Buffalo Bob" Smith—who also liked to dress up in costumes and shill for products, only in this case especially for kids: Welch's grape juice, Wonder Bread, and Colgate "with Gardol." There were skits, songs, and a noisy audience. Critics called it a "circus," which made it virtually indistinguishable from variety shows like Berle's, wherein the entertainment was always designed to reach the broadest audience possible.

Yet the makers of *Howdy Doody* eventually learned from Berle's demise—or at least knew their young audience and new medium better than Mr. Television did. It is to the credit of everyone associated with this show that it managed to stage such madness five days a week, with no repeats; and that it began before Berle's hit show, and kept going for almost six years longer. For starters, *Howdy Doody* had a far larger cast of regular characters, including host Buffalo Bob, the puppet Howdy, and Clarabell—the mute, Harpo Marx-like clown with the spraying seltzer container. Clarabell originally was played by future Captain Kangaroo Bob Keeshan, who had been recruited from the NBC page staff. (The real reason he didn't say anything was that the original studio rules made it cheaper to pay a nonspeaking performer, but the silent-partner ploy caught on anyway.) These characters were joined by Cornelius Cobb, Princess Summerfall Winterspring, puppets Phineas T. Bluster, Flub-a-Dub (a composite of eight different animals), and Dilly Dally (the incompetent carpenter), as well as the human Chief Thunderthud, who first uttered the now immortal "Cowabunga!" later stolen as a slogan by the Teenage Mutant Ninja Turtles.

The show had an ongoing series of predictable stories, often involving attempts to foil the stern Mayor Bluster. There was the mystery of the Lucky Leg of a Lima Llama, and the adventure of the Mangle Wurzel. "Slapstick alone will not hold kids," Buffalo Bob once said. "You have to have a story line." *Howdy Doody* thus developed into an early kind of situation comedy. That evolution was something Berle could never manage to pull off.

Howdy Doody also involved its audience to a far greater degree than most other shows, beginning with the opening, "Say, kids, what time is it?" and the shrieks back, "It's Howdy Doody time!" That made the show the medium's first major venture into interactive programming; this "peanut gallery" feedback was an essential element in the telecast's appeal. Kids were a real part of the action, which is why demand for studio tickets was so strong that expectant mothers were said to ask for tickets for their unborn children. Where Howdy Doody trod, Phil Donahue and Larry King one day followed as television eventually became ever more interactive.

There were other innovations, too. Practically anybody born between 1941 and 1955 still knows the words to the show's theme song (to the tune of "Ta-ra-ra Boom-der-e":

It's Howdy Doody time!
It's Howdy Doody time!

Bob Smith and Howdy, too
Say "Howdy do!" to you.

Let's give a rousing cheer,
'Cause Howdy Doody's here.
It's time to start the show—
So, kids, let's go!★

Nothing so unusual there, except this was the new medium's first theme song to sweep the culture, beginning a tradition that would lead to similar occurrences with such shows as *Bonanza, Secret Agent, The Patty Duke Show,* and even *Cheers.* Theme songs, originated on radio, are catchy—causing (if nothing else) viewers to want to hear them over and over again, thus creating something of a Pavlovian reaction. It's difficult to establish a connection between the quality of a theme song and that of a show, except to say that theme songs with words (such as the *Cheers* song with the refrain "Sometimes you want to go where everybody knows your name") often give viewers a sense of a program's themes. In Howdy's case, that theme was noise and disorder.

Like just about everyone else on television in those early days, Howdy had begun as a radio character when he appeared on a children's quiz show. His name then was Elmer, and his greeting was "Howdy doody, kids!"—the first two words of which soon stuck as the name. When *Howdy* debuted as a weekly show in 1947 (it went to five days a week in 1948), parents and critics had nothing but good things to say about it; the carping came later.

The first review in *Variety* praised the show's function more than its content, yet another preview of the shape of television in decades to come. The role of TV as a baby-sitter was emerging. "In the middle-class home," *Variety* wrote, "there is perhaps nothing as welcome to the mother as something that will keep the small fry intently absorbed and out of possible mischief. This program can almost be guaranteed to pin down the squirmiest of the brood." NBC also let it be known that conductor Arturo Toscanini watched the show with his grandchildren—implying, of course, that Howdy appealed to the whole family,

---

★Copyright © 1949, 1974 Kean-Smith Publishers, ASCAP.

however cultured. "Youngsters like to identify themselves with [Howdy's] jaunty, invincible, personality," wrote *Life* in 1950.

True, the program would evolve over the years, but not enough to account for the change in tone that would characterize reviews only a short time later. "After witnessing it once," wrote New York's influential *Herald Tribune* columnist John Crosby in 1951, "the exasperated parent is likely to head for the cellar or the roof to escape the darned thing." When assessing programming during the fifties, the self-styled National Television Review Board condemned *Howdy Doody* as "loud," "confused," and "senseless," and even criticized Clarabell's role as "too feminine."

What happened? Essentially, *Howdy Doody* became a metaphor used to describe the effect of *all* television on the culture. Short of those debates that followed a certain well-publicized quiz-show scandal, or an on-air shooting, most Americans have never been terribly excited by the ongoing discussions that address the effect of television on their lives. The exceptions have of course been those concerning children's programming, which means that debates about its quality have often been a way for intellectuals to talk to the masses about TV's overall effect on everybody.

So it went in the early fifties when such magazines as *Better Homes and Gardens, House Beautiful, Saturday Review,* and *Ladies' Home Journal* made the influence of television one of their abiding preoccupations, through articles like "Is Television Good or Bad for My Children?" and "Should You Tear 'em Away from TV?" Critics charged television with everything from encouraging violence to undermining the structure of the family itself. This tone of anguish was in marked contrast to the days only a few years earlier when the reaction to the introduction of television had been much different. Then, the prevalent view was expressed in an ad which promised: "Tomorrow's children, through the great new medium of Television, will be enrolled in a world university before they leave their cradles."

There have from its inception been those who claimed that *Howdy Doody* really did prove somewhat educational—given for example Chief Thunderthud's "do's and don'ts," the show's avoidance of the word "war," and the way the program favorably treated Indians and women. Nice try.

The real import of *Howdy Doody* in American culture was the opportunity it offered for a vast expansion of marketing to children. This show sparked the real beginning not only of children's advertising, but also of the explosion of products designed to fuel the demand the ads created. If this show were on today, there would be tie-in figurines of everyone on it, and Clarabell might well appear on Burger King cups. Years later children's shows would constitute their own "ghetto" of continuous programming on Saturday mornings, and the commercial tie-ins would become so explicit that characters who began as figurines (like G.I. Joe) would get their own TV shows.

As for this program, children flocked to *Howdy Doody* in the early fifties rather than to more "educational" fare like *Romper Room* for the same reason that their parents were apt to watch Milton Berle rather than CBS's *Dione Lucas Cooking Show:* It was far better television. Putting aside the important issues surrounding violence on the tube, through the years the debate over the quality of children's programming would always hinge on whether adults would permit their children to see pretty much the same type of programming that they did, since—given the choice between something educational and something entertaining—it was obvious which one kids would pick. Even on PBS there would be compromises: There wasn't that much on *Sesame Street* that *Laugh-In* hadn't tried first, just as *Where in the World Is Carmen Sandiego?* was a paler version of *Jeopardy!,* and Mister Rogers a moralistic clone of the television style of Arthur Godfrey. There were even network crossovers, such as *The Flintstones, Rocky and His Friends,* and *The Simpsons,* which presented adult entertainment in a juvenile form in prime time.

Like anything else on the small screen, *Howdy Doody* couldn't last forever. The culprit in this case was Walt Disney, whose *Mickey Mouse Club* premiered in 1955 with an hour show on ABC, beginning at 5:00, a half-hour before *Howdy Doody.* Within a year, *Howdy Doody* had been exiled to the new children's programming ghetto of Saturday mornings, where it remained for another four years.

The difference between these two shows offered a vision of television's past versus its future. *Howdy Doody* was New York, live, with adult performers and a studio audience. *Mouse Club* was Hollywood, on film, with child performers but no studio audience. Because *Howdy*

Doody was live (which meant no repeats) it was less profitable. Though both "named" characters weren't real, one was a marionette, the other a cartoon character. The future belonged to the mouse: Forty years later, the Disney empire would be all over the globe and own ABC, while cartoons still retained their cultural currency. On the other hand, America is still waiting for the Howdy Doody Theme Park and the Marionette Network.

In September 1960, the same month as the first Kennedy-Nixon debate, NBC killed *Howdy Doody* with a simple announcement: "In this special one-hour show, everybody in Doodyville is packing up and getting ready to leave town. And Clarabell has a secret." Then came an additional reminder: "Last show of the series." The finale was notable for Clarabell's finally speaking, if that's what it could be called. "Goodbye, kids" was all he said. No clowning around this time: The painted frown turned real.

Because it isn't in syndication, *Howdy Doody* exists today mostly as a memory. For that reason, its legend has grown over the years, so that people romanticize the show as more than it was. In later years, Buffalo Bob toured college campuses on nostalgia tours, and was fond of quoting the magazine which wrote that Doodyville was "the only paradise never lost: the children's paradise. Howdy Doody has become as famous as Pinocchio or as any of the fiction characters who inhabit the golden world of television." Yet Bob was being hyperbolic, as usual. Despite its innovations, *Howdy Doody* was schlock. This was the Golden Age of television, however, and *Howdy Doody* at least offered better schlock than most. And, in doing so, it offered glimpses of interactive television; the coming counterculture; the self-absorption of baby boomers; and the importance of TV theme songs. Watch *The Oprah Winfrey Show* or *Seinfeld* today, and you can still see faint traces of the *Howdy Doody* influence. The difference now is that the strings are attached to us.

3

Meet the Press: Television's Anachronism
(NBC: 1947–PRESENT)

On Thursday, November 6, 1947, at 8:00 P.M., New York television station WNBC premiered a half-hour public-affairs show that had become something of a success in its two years on network radio. Moderated by Martha Roundtree, an independent radio producer, the program introduced a format in which a prominent public figure—in this case former Roosevelt cabinet secretary James Farley—was questioned by four reporters. Two weeks later, *Meet the Press* was picked up by the NBC national network (which then included all of two stations), and through three wars and ten American presidents, through all the *Gunsmoke* and *Home Improvement* shows, through the fall of black-and-white television and the rise of cable, the program persevered.

It should be no surprise that television's longest-running series is also its most anachronistic—a throwback to the primitive days when TV was little more than radio with pictures, it was live, "public affairs" meant only formal affairs of state, and the news was still a lot more about the world than about the reporters covering it. The significance of *Meet the Press,* however, lies not just in its longevity, or in the way it still reminds us of the ghosts of television past. The show was instrumental in defining the early nature of political talk on television, as each week a guest answered a series of questions from the journalist-panel.

That question-and-answer (a.k.a. Q & A) format would later be widely imitated, not only in the TV press conferences that would help make John F. Kennedy a living room idol, but also on such erudite panel shows as *I've Got a Secret* and *What's My Line?* with hosts like newsman John Charles Daly. Moreover, since it was also one of the earliest TV programs to feature politicians regularly, *Meet the Press* helped introduce the American public to the now well-accepted notion that our leaders were to be evaluated by a new standard—one which allowed viewers to judge their leaders firsthand for themselves, without the journalistic screening that had always been provided by the print press. Where *Meet the Press* trod, the Kennedy-Nixon debates, Ronald Reagan, and others ultimately followed, and therein lay many consequences.

While television was seemingly dispensing with journalists as middlemen or gatekeepers, however, it was also catapulting them into celebrity status. Though this show never transformed itself into the kind of promotional vehicle for journalists that *The McLaughlin Group* or even *This Week With David Brinkley* became, it did, after all, call itself "Meet the *Press*," not "Meet the Celebrity" or "Meet the Newsmaker." In 1995, the show even allowed viewers in Russell, Kansas—invited to sit in on a live broadcast featuring Senator Bob Dole—to ask personal questions of the panel journalists themselves, thus giving new meaning to the show's name.

After *Meet the Press* and its considerable progeny over five decades, the voters would have a very clear picture of how journalists did their job, and as public-opinion surveys would document, they would dislike the press intensely for it. Moreover, it would never again be possible to think of Washington reporters as anything more or less than the people they covered. As early as 1956, *New Republic* critic David Ebbitt was complaining that the purpose of the panel show was to bait and embarrass. "As far as I've been able to make out," he complained, "it doesn't even pretend to take an interest in the significant ideas or activities of the people it examines. . . ." *Meet the Press,* more than most such programs, has always rejected the notion that it is anything more than news programming. Still, it is a TV "show"—meaning, inevitably, that it is sometimes hard to tell where the news stops and the entertainment begins.

Today it seems quaint that it was once considered an open question whether television should make room for anything as free-wheeling as *Meet the Press.* NBC originally hesitated over converting the radio version to TV because it was considered too showy. "Drama-plus-news," *Reader's Digest* sniffed, and some publications even forbade their reporters from appearing on the program. Still, through the years, in its choice of setting, guests, and questioners, the show made fewer concessions to show business than almost everyone else on television. Only in recent years did the program join other shows in putting the guests and questioners around a common table, scrapping the distant desks that had made *Meet the Press* look like the competitive *G.E. College Bowl.*

For better or for worse, the message given by the new arrangement is that journalists and politicians no longer see themselves as the adversaries they once were, perhaps because the country has united in disliking anyone from inside the Beltway. Otherwise, not much has changed. *Meet the Press* even now portrays the world largely as print news defined it five decades ago. The guests are still almost always Washington politicians—though occasionally a foreign leader is thrown in. Whereas Robert Frost, Jane Fonda, and Jackie Robinson each appeared on the show to talk about public affairs, people like Bob Dole (who has had well over 50 appearances) have been guests far more often. (Hubert Humphrey was also a frequent visitor.)

"America's Press Conference of the Air," as *Meet the Press* likes to bill itself, will never be confused with *Entertainment Tonight,* a Barbara Walters special, or even the late Edward R. Murrow's *Person to Person,* which used to feature the likes of Marilyn Monroe and Humphrey Bogart. The show has thus tended to marginalize itself over the years, as modern public affairs and news have increasingly focused on the tabloid "up close and personal." Tim Russert, who took over the show in 1992, once said about his choice of guests: "I'd take Dole over Simpson"—presumably referring to O.J., not Alan.

Through the decades, the show has also tended to stick with journalist-questioners known more for their accomplishments in the print world than on television. Perhaps that's a reflection of the show's original radio mission in 1945—largely to promote *American Mercury* magazine, of which longtime moderator Lawrence Spivak was editor and publisher. *Meet the Press* has always favored sober questioners who are pillars of the Washington press establishment—Jack Bell of the Associated Press, Peter Lisagor of the *Chicago Sun-Times,* David Broder of the *Washington Post,* and R. W. Apple, Jr. of the *New York Times.* Contrast those selections with the more flamboyant Sam Donaldson and even George Will for the comparable *This Week With David Brinkley,* or the participants on *The McLaughlin Group* and *Capital Gang.* Only in its selection of May Craig of the *Portland Press-Herald,* known for her wild hats and persistent questioning, did the program ever seem willing to acknowledge that journalists might someday want to become the stars of the series, and thus of the news as well.

That isn't to say, however, that—over time—*Meet the Press* was able to avoid making its moderators household names. The bespectacled

and laconic Spivak—the founder of *Ellery Queen* magazine who began as a panelist and took over as moderator in 1965, serving for a
decade in that position—became a bit of a TV folk hero, even if he
had to sit on two pillows to reach the desk. *The Economist* labeled him
"a scowling pessimist." "Sit up straight!" he once barked at a guest
while on the air.

Nor could the show avoid changing the culture in ways that television in general would later make familiar. This series had its origins
in the radio panel program, most notably NBC radio's weekly *The
University of Chicago Roundtable,* which featured academics and politicians discussing the leading issues of the day. *Meet the Press* narrowed
that focus entirely to governmental affairs, and originated from Washington.

Though television would continue to produce its national newscasts out of New York, *Meet the Press* thus gave Washington and its
journalists their first dose of consistent TV publicity. With the growth
of the federal government after World War II, it was probably inevitable that our news would become more Washington-centric—
with a corresponding growth in the power of the Washington press
corps. Still, *Meet the Press* led the way. Some 40 years later, it would be
left to some savvy sitcom creators to acknowledge the obvious when
they made Murphy Brown a glamorous TV journalist inside the Beltway. In this sense, Murphy was Spivak's spiritual stepdaughter.

In its heyday, the show had many imitators. In the early days, when
live talk shows were one of the few things TV could produce easily,
Meet the Press spawned a whole series of clones, including *Town Meeting of the Air, Meet the Professor, Meet the Congress,* and *Meet the Veep,* starring Alben Barkley, Harry Truman's vice-president. *Author Meets the
Critics,* hosted by John K. M. McCaffrey, featured authors and critics
debating works with such ferocity that fights sometimes broke out.
(Or other faux pas: Eugene O'Neill once passed out drunk on camera.)

Today's Sunday-morning imitators—CBS's *Face the Nation* and
ABC's *This Week* (first called *Issues and Answers,* then *This Week with
David Brinkley* until Brinkley retired in 1996)—premiered in 1954
and 1960 respectively, though CBS started an unsuccessful program in
the early fifties with Walter Cronkite called *Man of the Week,* which

enraged Spivak because he thought it was such a close copy of his show. (Perhaps it bothered Cronkite, too: "Thank you, Senator, for being on *Meet the Press*," Cronkite once said mistakenly.) Unlike its competitors at the time, the Brinkley series was notable in the eighties for allowing a regular set of journalists (usually Brinkley, Will, and Donaldson) to editorialize about the week's events and thus make themselves the centerpiece of the morning's infotainment.

It was that shift to journalists as commentators—implied but resisted by *Meet the Press* until recently—that has marked the genre in the past decade. From *The McLaughlin Group* to PBS's *Washington Week in Review*, reporters are now constantly called upon to analyze and advocate. They thus blur the line between fact and opinion, or truth and fantasy, in ways similar to what docudramas and historical miniseries do. This genre is, of course, supposed to be the *real* news—or at least a branch thereof. Still, to be popular, television requires both conflict and personalities: As news shows have fallen prey to the demands of the marketplace, they have gone the way of sitcoms and police shows in developing and promoting their "stars."

Thus, today's panel-show participants and plots often seem as scripted as those of any other TV show, offering stereotypical liberal-vs.-conservative debate in sound-bite doses. Television news talk now has its clichéd bad guys (Sam Donaldson or Robert Novak) versus the good guys (Mark Shields or George Will); *Crossfire* even packaged the formula into a nightly CNN series. It is probably no coincidence that as journalists have been portrayed across the dial making themselves the focus of stories and arguing more but revealing less, public confidence in the media has plummeted.

In the process, the original purpose of these news shows—to give the public a view of its political leaders—has been either obscured or left to C-Span. Thus it's only on Sunday mornings, the last time slot left in American life when the public seems able to resist television (and the networks can't make money), that old-fashioned, leisurely paced shows such as *Meet the Press* and CBS's *Sunday Morning News* flourish. (*Meet the Press* was moved out of prime time in 1965.) "It's the most serious time on television," *Face the Nation* host Bob Schieffer once said—which means that ad rates for these shows are said to go for around 10 percent of the price in prime time. The ratings for a show such as *Meet the Press* average about a third of that for a nightly network newscast. This actually sounds better than it is because so many people are at home on Sunday mornings that the potential audience is positively huge.

Thus the heyday for these shows—such as when Whittaker Chambers first publicly accused Alger Hiss of being a communist on the August 27, 1948, radio edition of *Meet the Press*—has clearly passed. It's true that Russert, a savvy political analyst who does his homework, has valiantly tried to enliven the show: His questions to H. Ross Perot were so tough in a 1992 appearance that the flustered Perot left the campaign trail for a time afterwards to study up. Yet, while even a mere decade ago this show might have provided a lead story for the Sunday-night news, or Monday's newspapers, which would then dominate public discussion for a day, not many people watch network newscasts or even read newspapers anymore.

What former TV producer Jon Katz calls the Old News—mainstream papers, network news, and such "serious" discussion shows as *Meet the Press*—have gradually been replaced in American culture by the New News: a rough amalgam of today's talk TV and radio, local tabloid news, rock music, movies *(Thelma and Louise),* and television shows *(Murphy Brown).* Americans now receive an increasing amount of their information from these new sources, and many consider them more important and even more reliable than the old ones. By the late eighties, a New News show like *America's Most Wanted* was affecting American culture far more than something like *Meet the Press,* as it led to the actual arrest of over 400 fugitives in its run on the Fox network.

Thus the *Meet the Press* innovations—celebrity journalists, the live and unfiltered exposure of politicians, and the interjection of entertainment into news—have sown the seed of its irrelevance. David Broder has given way to Don Imus; Dan Rather to Larry King. The Old News is *Time* and *Newsweek;* the New News is MTV and *A Current Affair.* The Old News is a documentary hosted by Bill Moyers; the New News is a *Rescue 911* reenactment hosted by William Shatner. The Old News is Dan Quayle talking about Murphy Brown; the New News is Murphy Brown talking about Dan Quayle. *Meet the Press* helped define the news for almost anyone born before 1955; there is now simply no such thing as a traditional newscast for almost anyone born since.

The Old News system was orderly and established: The *New York Times* and other major dailies set a strict agenda for what constituted proper news, and the network news followed it. In contrast, the New News deals as much with personality and emotion as fact, and it has no hierarchy. In our current culture, *Meet the Press* is thus a true artifact—the closest thing the revisionist culture of television still has that reflects its slow-moving, print-based past. If you want to know what America was like before television changed it, watch *Meet the Press* and pretend that what's going on really means something significant to anyone beyond a few hundred staffers in the executive and legislative branches, and the reporters and pundits who cover them. Then turn back to the world of today.

Part II
THE FIFTIES

I Love Lucy • *Dragnet* • **Bishop Sheen** and *Life Is Worth Living* • **Edward R. Murrow** and *See It Now* • *Today* **and Barbara Walters** • *Disneyland* • *The Lawrence Welk Show* *The Ed Sullivan Show* • *Gunsmoke* **and TV's Westerns** *American Bandstand* • *Twenty-One* **and the Quiz Scandal** *Leave It to Beaver* • *The Twilight Zone*

This is the decade during which television became an American habit and a virtual necessity. In 1950, 9 percent of all American households had television; by 1959, the number was 86 percent, and the average American was watching the small screen more than five hours a day. In 1951, the industry was financially in the black for the first time, and TV revenues passed those of radio in 1954. In this decade, television institutionalized its scheduling, programming, and many of the genres we recognize today—the sitcom, the taped adventure series filmed in Hollywood, and its morning and afternoon features. Unlike shows of the forties, most of the series described in this section remain remarkably popular today, even if surviving mostly in reruns. Yet there are popular facets of fifties television which have become virtually extinct—the network documentary, the prime-time quiz show, the variety show, live theater, and the Western—and whose disappearance reveals a lot about both the peculiar evolution of this medium and America's infatuation with it. CBS has as many shows in this section as the other two major networks combined, which demonstrates how its programming during this era tended to set the standard for the industry.

4

I Love Lucy: The Woman as TV Superstar
(CBS: 1951–57)

"Television," comedy writer Larry Gelbart once said, "was the box they buried vaudeville in after it died." What replaced vaudeville on the small screen, by and large, was a genre borrowed from radio: the situation comedy. *I Love Lucy* was the show that cemented the transformation. Its contributions to television history are legendary: First sitcom to be a hit. First show to be Number 1 three years in a row. First show to reach an audience of 10 million households. First major hit show to be produced in Hollywood. First show to use the innovative three-camera technique. First show to be filmed live before a studio audience.

In fact, calling *I Love Lucy* the most popular television show of all time is hardly an overstatement. For four of its six seasons, it was first in the ratings, and in the other two it was second and third. In the decades since it left the air, it has enjoyed phenomenal success in reruns. For years, dozens of local stations ran the show in syndication, and the cable channel Nickelodeon does now, making it the most enduringly loved fixture in the history of television. *TV Guide* had it right when it once wrote that Lucy had "a face seen by more people, more often, than the face of any [other] human being who ever lived."

Above everything else, however, *I Love Lucy* stands out because its superstar was a woman. Rarely, if ever, in the history of entertainment had a female attained a following far beyond that of any man's, and rarely—again, if ever—has one gained it since. In movies, perhaps only Garbo or Marilyn Monroe reached such heights. In popular music, only Madonna did the same. On television (a medium notorious for copying any formula that works) it took almost 40 years before Roseanne Barr took *Roseanne* to a marginally comparable place in the culture. In the 33 years and 15 Number 1 shows between Ball and Barr, only one Number 1 series—the eminently forgettable *Laverne and Shirley*—even made women the major leads. Certainly no other superstar, much less a woman, made the cover of *TV Guide* 29 times. What's more, Lucy's popularity has lasted through perhaps the greatest change in the status and perception of women in history.

What kind of woman had this kind of hold on the public? Why did television not attempt to replicate her success? And what does it tell us about television that perhaps its greatest and longest-lasting star—its Elvis or Chaplin—was a woman?

There was little in Lucille Ball's background to suggest she would play this role. From 1933, when she left New York for Hollywood, to 1951 when *I Love Lucy* went into production, Ball appeared in over 50 movies, acting in both dramatic and comic roles. Though she occasionally reminded audiences of wisecracking Katharine Hepburn or Carole Lombard, she was never considered a breakthrough star, and was given the nickname "Queen of the B's." Married to Cuban bandleader Desi Arnaz, Ball had pretty much left the movies to become the 1948 colead of a popular weekly radio series, *My Favorite Husband,* whereon she played the wacky wife of a Minneapolis banker. As both television and the radio series gained popularity, CBS approached Ball and asked her to transfer the show to TV. Lucy and Desi had lived apart for a decade—she in Hollywood, he on the road—and their marriage was on the rocks. In what has become a well-known piece of TV allegory, Lucy refused to do the new TV show unless her husband was cast in the lead, thus bringing him back home. What gave *I Love Lucy* much of its original and honest sentiment was that it was grounded in its costars' attempt to save their own marriage.

As the story goes, CBS refused to hire a Cuban, so Ball and Arnaz went on the road in 1950 as a vaudeville act to prove their popularity. When CBS remained adamant, the duo formed their own production company and began producing scripts loosely based on their own lives. Lucille Ball would become housewife Lucy Ricardo, married to Cuban bandleader Ricky Ricardo. As with *My Favorite Husband,* the plots would revolve around the antics of Lucy. The cast would include another "older" couple—the Mertzes, their best friends and landlords, who lived in their mutual Manhattan apartment building. CBS finally went along with the idea, though only after struggles over the following: the name of the show (CBS wanted *The Lucille*

Ball Show); whether it would be filmed or live (filming prevailed, even though it cost four times as much); the filming location (CBS wanted New York, not Hollywood, and lost again); the timing (ad agencies wanted the show to be weekly rather than biweekly, and won); and sponsorship (Philip Morris backed the show only after the most prominent sitcom sponsor of the time, General Foods, turned it down). In the late summer of 1951, *I Love Lucy* finally went into production, with Lucy and Desi assuming most of the financial burden and risk through their own company, Desilu Productions. The show premiered on CBS on October 15, 1951, running on Monday nights at 9:00, and within four months it was Number 1.

The history of *Lucy* by itself, however, doesn't tell us much about the television persona that this 40-year-old woman quickly created which became such a durable sensation. Even publications at the time had a hard time understanding it. "When 'Lucy' went on the air last October," wrote *Time* back then, "it seemed to be just another series devoted to family comedy." Who, then, was Lucy Ricardo? She was, first, what most married women were in those days—a housewife who went on in celebrated fashion to bear a child in an era when many of her contemporaries were doing the same. "I wanted our characters to have problems," said Ball much later. "I wanted to be an average housewife. A very nosy but very average housewife. And I wanted my husband to love me."

Still, Lucy was hardly the average "contented matron of the house" as portrayed in the popular press of the time. Long before Betty Friedan gave voice to the restless aspirations of a generation of housebound women, *I Love Lucy* was doing something similar. Looking back, it's striking how many of the shows were about Lucy's attempts to begin her own show-business career, get out of the house, change into men's clothes, or make her husband appreciate her more. On this show, the women bonded against the men: *I Love Lucy,* said the title, but who really loved her more—Ricky or Ethel?

I Love Lucy was both of and ahead of its time; one only has to look at the satisfied, conformist mothers on *Father Knows Best* or *Leave It to Beaver* a few years later to see that Lucy—by contrast—was in unending revolt against the conventions of her age. Moreover, by defying her "place," she symbolically rebelled against all middle-class norms.

Though these crises were portrayed humorously, they were often not laughable subjects, perhaps the reason why Ball once said, "I never thought that I was funny." "It's got warmth and sympathy," her manager, Don Sharpe, was once quoted as saying. "And people believe in her, even while they're laughing at her."

And they *were* laughing, despite what Ball thought, because she was hilarious. The 1952 episode "Lucy in the Candy Factory," where Lucy and Ethel have to wrap bonbons on an accelerating candy production line, remains one of TV's classic episodes, and it's only one of many from this show. That brand of humor was a key component of Lucy's appeal. It is one of the best-known secrets of television that it always presents its most radical ideas in the form of comedy, the better to beguile the masses while preaching to them. The racial message of *The Cosby Show* was subsumed by its comedic tone; *All in the Family* and *M*A*S*H* never could have gotten away with what they had to say, had they been strictly dramatic shows.

According to TV scholar Lynn Spigel, the persona of Lucy had its roots in the female characters introduced into vaudeville in the late 19th century. Those performers developed "a set of conventions by which women's humor was deemed more respectable" to a mass audience: Women always had to be the butt of jokes; they had to downplay their good looks, or act scatterbrained, to appear less threatening to the audience; and they always had to be linked in the public eye with a man. Thus costar Vivian Vance was forced to gain 20 pounds to look more frumpy for her role, and the glamorous Ball would frequently dress down and tie her hair up in a kerchief for performances. ("Beauty Into Buffoon," *Life* called its 1952 profile of Lucy.) The antifeminine persona of Lucy would be followed by such others in TV history as Imogene Coca, Phyllis Diller, Joan Rivers, and Roseanne Barr—all comediennes who could never be accused of making it in the allegorical "traditional show-biz way"—that is, on their looks.

Lucy's rebellion was also less threatening because its target was a Cuban immigrant. It's one thing to make fun of a supermacho Hispanic bandleader who can't even speak English very well; it would have been quite another to take shots at white pillars of the Establishment, such as Jim Anderson or Ward Cleaver. Though CBS officials may have originally rejected the show because they thought mass audiences wouldn't accept a Cuban, it may be that audiences would have accepted nothing but. Everyone—including men—could identify with Lucy; few in the audience ever mistook themselves for a Desi.

So it worked, for over 180 episodes over six seasons as the Ricardos had a baby—just as Lucy did in real life, with Lucy and child gracing the first cover of *TV Guide*. The Ricardos moved to Hollywood, went to Europe, moved back to New York, and then relocated to suburban Connecticut. At the end of that sixth season in 1957, with both Desi and Lucy exhausted from having to film so many shows a year and run the production company, the principals decided to call it quits. Though the couple would return for a few *Lucy-Desi Comedy Hour* stints, their departure from *I Love Lucy* would mark only one of two times in television history that a show left the air while it was still Number 1. Lucy would go on to star in three other TV sitcoms, though none approached the original.

The odd thing, of course, is that in one essential sense, the show's success was never really replicated. On a medium notorious for shamelessly copying any formula that works, television rarely returned to Lucy's slapstick-rebellious form of situation comedy. That break in custom was due both to the uniqueness of Lucy's talent for comedy, and to a network shift in the 1950s to softer story lines—away from the vaudeville slapstick method still occasionally employed by Lucy. Early TV sitcoms were far closer to stand-up comedy than they are today; series such as *The Jack Benny Program* and *The Burns and Allen Show* constructed only the finest of lines separating the TV characters of these stars from their actual personas. It was hard to tell where Lucy and Ricky stopped and Lucy and Desi started—they even had babies at the same time. That style of comedy, bordering on realism, soon disappeared from television, though it would reemerge decades later on such vehicles as *Seinfeld*.

There was something else to television's failure to replicate the Lucy formula, however, and the clues were there even when the show was the hit of the nation. Advertisers and network executives never really seemed to like *I Love Lucy*—no small irony, since Desi's business innovations (filming, syndication, establishment of the sitcom as a genre) paved the way for much of the medium's financial success. In fact, one of the more enduring *I Love Lucy* legacies was the way it demonstrated to television producers how you could make *real* money with the new medium:

1. You film your show, not do it live.
2. You do well on network television, so you have enough episodes in the can for successful syndication.
3. You retain the distribution rights.
4. You sell the reruns in syndication.

Every producer wants to replicate this kind of success.

Yet, finding an original sponsor for this show proved difficult. At least six agencies turned it down cold, and CBS was forced to place newspaper ads seeking help before Philip Morris signed on. After the first show, a company executive wanted to cancel the contract, calling the effort "unfunny, silly, and totally boring." In fact, after the 1955 season, Philip Morris did abruptly drop its sponsorship. Though surprised and pleased by the show's success, network executives weren't that much more supportive—at least before *Lucy* helped push CBS into first place in the ratings.

To be sure, there have been other instances in television history where ratings alone weren't enough to please the network and sponsor superiors. Yet this was different, and more subtle: Despite the concessions made to conform Lucy's persona to female stereotypes, the show—at bottom—still revolved around a woman's attempts to rebel against the middle-class mold. Lucy was often portrayed displaying her independence: She smoked; she screamed; she constantly challenged Ricky's authority; she also clearly had sex because we saw her pregnant. As television analyst Gerald Jones has noted, TV censors even allowed Lucy and Ricky the unusual step of sharing the same bed, since the audience knew they were married in real life.

It's noteworthy that by the time *Lucy* left the air, TV had already domesticated and desexualized its women, either by moving them happily back into homemaker roles on programs such as *The Donna Reed Show* and *Ozzie and Harriet,* or by removing from their arsenal the weapon of sharp humor. It is no coincidence either that after *Lucy,* the networks abandoned the idea of making major sitcoms starring women—or at least ones that realistically resembled half the audience at home. In the sixties, TV had two hit sitcoms that starred women other than Lucy: *Hazel,* a show about a maid, and *Bewitched,* a sitcom about a housewife-witch. Neither could be seen as threatening the status quo in any such way as *I Love Lucy.*

This obviously mattered to advertisers (and therefore to the networks), and not just because Lucy's mild rebelliousness might offend their social conventions. As several TV scholars have noted, advertisers saw television as a powerful medium that could teach housewives, with the benign acquiescence of their husbands, how to become better consumers of the sponsors' products—indeed, to be the queens of the culture of consumption. To be a consumer *par excellence,* a woman had to buy into a whole series of assumptions which went well beyond the rather quaint notion that money buys products, which in turn buy happiness. She also had to invest herself in the entire complicated set of social arrangements between the sexes which evolved in postwar America and dictated that a woman's proper place was at home (where she watched television), bearing and raising kids (who watched more television), and spending money (for products she heard about from television). As a real professional actress and restless sitcom housewife, Lucy was an implied threat to that order.

Over time, as everyone—male and female, young and old, black and white—eventually become acculturated by the consumer ethic that television institutionalized, programmers could afford to become more cavalier about such matters. And, though Lucy's kind were banished from the home screen for some time, no one could ever get rid of *I Love Lucy,* thanks to the new rerun process envisioned by Desi. If the show continued to draw viewers decade after decade, it was a tribute to the fact that she was one of the few women on TV (at least until the nineties) whose conflicts and aspirations seemed to parallel those of the audience. Even in the seventies and eighties, despite surface changes indicating otherwise, the Lucy of the fifties was still as much in tune with her audience as was a Mary Richards of *The Mary Tyler Moore Show* or a Clair Huxtable of *The Cosby Show.*

As a woman, Lucy also illustrated something important about the medium of television which made it different from anything that had come before. You don't have to be a devotee of scholars Carol Gilligan or Deborah Tannen to know that women express themselves in ways different from those of men: They tend to focus on emotions; they seek consensus, not conflict; they disclose more of themselves in conversation; they emphasize the personal, not the impersonal.

These attributes are well-suited to television. Because it doesn't arrive via a public sphere—like the theatre or film—but comes directly into the home (the traditional domain of women), TV tends to rely on female forms of expression, such as narratives and self-disclosure. The medium's strength is going "up close and personal"; from *Person to Person* to *The Oprah Winfrey Show*, its ultimate promise has often been the disclosure of intimacy. What's more, despite a multitude of changes brought on by the feminist movement, women remain the primary consumers in the culture, and television's principal audience in prime time, as anyone knows who watched NBC's production of the 1996 Summer Olympics—which revolved around diving and gymnastics rather than more traditional "male" sports like boxing.

Thus, it was no accident that television stumbled upon a woman as its premier mega-superstar. Nor was it happenstance that the woman happened to be Lucy. Confined yet liberated, acquisitive yet generous, she was ambivalently enough at the center of American life to appeal to everybody. *I Love Lucy* was a leader in using the new medium of television to disclose to us what we really were. But like any work of genius, its rare gift lay also in the power to reveal what we would become.

5

Dragnet and the Policeman as Hero
(NBC: 1951–59)

Despite the success of *I Love Lucy*, there was more to prime-time entertainment than comedy. There was also drama, or better yet action melodrama—a genre which, in contrast to sitcoms, tends to have stronger appeal to men. With its corny lines and stilted action, *Drag-*

net—just such a melodrama—would top no one's list of the most well-done shows of all time. Yet it was among the most influential. In its original years on NBC on Thursday nights, this series both defined the concept of the police drama on television, and redefined the image of law enforcement in the culture at large.

In the years since, television has rarely challenged Jack Webb's view of the police, while continuing to share his utter obsession with crime. Almost one-third of all prime-time entertainment shows since *Dragnet* have concerned law enforcement and crime, and nearly a third of the characters on prime time have been involved in either the enforcement or the violation of the law. It has been estimated that the average child will see 18,000 television murders by the time he or she becomes an adult. In fact, from the time this show premiered until now there has rarely been a TV season which hasn't featured at least one show "starring" the Los Angeles Police Department.

When television first came on the scene, it looked to the familiar for its story lines. Both Westerns and private-eye stories, two genres with proven track records in radio, the movies, and fiction, became the basis for much of its dramatic programming. "Criminality is still the backbone of broadcasting," wrote critic Charles Morton in the *Atlantic Monthly* in 1951, and he was right. Thirty or 60 minutes is not much time for dramatic complexity, and crime shows and Westerns offered proven formulas. With little time for character development, TV drama demanded that problems be solved through action, and crime shows offered an abundance of excitement without requiring much in the way of special effects.

Because they were often presented as mysteries, crime shows also required tubeside audience engagement—an important attribute for advertisers who want to keep viewers involved. Once, when network chief Fred Silverman was asked why all of his series characters were policemen or doctors, he replied, "What are they going to be? Architects? What will happen to them?" Finally, both genres provided an acceptable opportunity to show violence—a traditional calling card of TV entertainment because it forces audiences to stop doing other things and watch.

Until the advent of television, however, popular culture had traditionally romanticized crime, with the police (or their equivalents) often treated as villains, not heroes. A strong antiestablishment distrust of formal legal authority used to run through our popular culture. Even in the early days of Anglo-American popular culture, in the ballads, songs, and tales of medieval and Elizabethan England, wrongdoers often were depicted as romantic and heroic figures—the people's "Robin Hoods." Many American colonists, themselves the subject of religious or political oppression in their native lands, brought to the New World a similar distrust of legal authority. According to many scholars, this ambivalence toward the law helped make the subject of crime America's great imaginative obsession. "If the United States could be said to have a national literature," critic Martin Williams once wrote, "it is crime melodrama."

However, traditional pop-culture crime-solvers before television— Edgar Allan Poe's Auguste Dupin (America's first literary detective), Sherlock Holmes, Sam Spade, and Philip Marlowe—were often private detectives tracking down criminals while outwitting the police. Westerns, too, retained this ideology, with justice often carried out by a single, highly individualistic sheriff or cowboy who disdained the traditional mechanisms of the law. The most celebrated policemen in movie history are still probably the bumbling Keystone Cops from the silent era. Though the medium of radio changed their images somewhat in the 1930s and 1940s through such shows as *Homicide Squad* and *Treasury Agent,* it didn't change them much.

Then, in December 1951, with a preview on *Chesterfield Sound Off Time* (a weekly variety show), came television's first great crime sensation, *Dragnet.* Its hero was a hard-working cop, which made the show so different from traditional private-eye dramas that CBS executives originally turned the series down on radio because it "didn't resemble Sam Spade enough." Jack Webb played the prime *Dragnet* hero, Sgt. Joe Friday, who at the top of each show would intone, via "voice-over": "This is the city. Los Angeles, California. I work here. I carry a badge. My name's Friday." He would make the cover of *Time* in 1954, a year that saw 38 million viewers tune in on him each week.

Unlike the traditional private eye, who usually chased alcohol, women, and wrongdoers (in roughly that order), Friday seemed to have no personal life and interests other than police work. He even announced to the audience the exact time of day he undertook certain tasks: "It was 3:55 P.M. . . . We were working the day watch out of homicide." He served the public, not private clients; and there were other changes, too: Unlike most private detectives, Friday worked as part of a team, setting the model for scores of TV sleuths to follow.

To add realism, the show was filmed basically outdoors and presented like a documentary based on actual police-department files. Beginning each week with the terse announcement "The story you are about to see is true. Only the names have been changed to protect the innocent," *Dragnet* featured frequent close-ups accompanied by such deadpan police lingo as "Book him on a 390." Check forgers were called "paper hangers"; a "heel-and-toe job" was robbing a cash register. Over half of each show involved the painstaking routine questions Friday would ask of up to 10 rather ordinary-looking potential witnesses. "People should look like people," Webb once said. "Who's to say who's a killer?" *Dragnet* was the precursor to today's *COPS* and *Rescue 911*.

It was that pseudorealism which immediately caught the eyes of the critics. It "has become the best of the TV crime shows by tossing overboard TV clichés from incendiary blondes and comic stooges to roaring gunfights and simple-Simon detection," wrote *Time*. There was also little violence: In the first 60 shows, Webb once said, there were only three brawls, and 15 shots fired. Yet what got imitated in series to follow was not so much this show's "realism" as its ideology. As David Thorburn, a professor at MIT, would later note, Webb's show promulgated a series of "themes and preoccupations, of visual and even musical styles," including "an arthritically pompous camera that's so worshipful toward buildings and representatives of official authority that it hardly moves. . . ."

As with other pop-culture sensations, the show's impact was immediate; even the series' "Dum-da-dum-dum-da" theme song made the Hit Parade. But the ideological impact was even more striking. "The flood of *Dragnet* fan mail suggests that the U.S. completely forgets that it is a nation of incipient cop-haters," wrote *Time* in their 1954 cover story. "[I]t [the country] has gained a new appreciation of the underpaid, long-suffering, ordinary policeman, and [has gained] its first rudimentary understanding of real-life law enforcement."

Why was television improving the image of the policeman? The reasons help explain a lot about the evolution of programming over the subsequent decades. Like so much else in television history, the popularity of *Dragnet* was partly a case of Jack Webb's being in the right place at the right time: Sympathetic to the work of the police, he filled a programming vacuum with a well-directed, compelling series, which could be moved from radio. Part of the show's success was also due to time constraints imposed by the broadcast industry. Private eyes—as typecast as they had become—tended to be more complicated heroes than your stereotypical policemen, and thus harder to depict in a 30- or 60-minute show.

Yet clearly the status of television as a commercial medium played a major role in the crime-fighting genre's shift in emphasis. Most companies that do business in pop culture, such as film and record companies, understand that they are primarily in the business of responding directly to popular taste—no matter where those sentiments lead. In broadcasting, however, there is a key intermediary, the sponsor, who controls all air time, either directly or indirectly. The *Dragnet* portrayal of the police undoubtedly warmed the hearts of advertisers, who found a pro-establishment sentiment more in keeping with their political views.

Far more important than politics, however, police dramas offered a sense of security to their audiences. In theory, that made the viewers better consumers, which from a sponsor's view is the real purpose of all programming. Think about it: A private-eye show, no matter how admirable its hero, often leaves the audience with the impression that the system, police included, is corrupt and incompetent. An audience who believes that message is often in no mood to buy. Television cop shows, however, rarely leave such loose ends. Police shows and commercial television were a match made in heaven, because, beginning with Jack Webb, the cops always got their man.

As it turned out, the sense of security fostered by these shows was not well-founded: The crime rate actually increased while *Dragnet* was on the air. Moreover, by 1954 one researcher had already found that the depiction of crime and crime fighters on television was frequent and highly stereotyped: Already 20 percent of all TV characters were lawbreakers; and nonwhites, rarely appearing as law-enforcement officers, almost always were featured as criminals. By the end of 1952 there were 29 cop shows on the air, and in January 1954, *Time* could already assert: "More people are killed each year on TV's crime shows than die annually by murder and non-negligent manslaughter in the six largest cities of the U.S. But in one respect, television has a better record than the nation's police: every TV lawbreaker pays the penalty for his crime."

One other thing was clear: These shows drew audiences. And, like other successful television shows, *Dragnet* spawned immediate imitators, slowly adding to popular culture's new celebration of traditional law enforcement. There was *Mr. District Attorney,* the former radio hit, who was "champion of the people, defender of truth, guardian of our fundamental rights to life, liberty, and the pursuit of happiness." There also was Broderick Crawford as Capt. Dan Matthews in *Highway Patrol* ("Ten-four and out"), which preached traffic safety on our Western highways; *Harbor Command,* billed as "true-to-life stories of America's Harbor Police"; and *Treasury Men in Action.* These were followed in the late 1950s by *Naked City* ("There are eight million stories in the Naked City. This is one of them.") and the violent and popular *The Untouchables,* narrated by Walter Winchell and glorifying the exploits of G-man Eliot Ness.

These improved depictions of the police were, at least in part, a reflection of reality. In the years following World War II, police departments across the country had undergone major reforms. In reaction to scandals, public criticism, and their own desire to uplift their social standing, the police had become more professionalized, placing a higher priority on fighting crime, as opposed to keeping the peace. Yet it is also true that these reform efforts were not all that was responsible for improving the public's image of the police; television played a role, too. In 1947, according to the National Opinion Research Center, the public ranked the police 55th out of 90 occupations in esteem, above mail carriers and carpenters but right below insurance agents and traveling salesmen. By 1963 the police had moved up to 47th—now ahead of reporters, insurance agents, and managers of small stores. A small leap, perhaps, but one of the biggest gains for any occupation. More important, it was a move which would be repeated in the 1970s and 1980s.

In the rebellious sixties, police shows briefly fell out of favor: Think of how cops were depicted in *Car 54, Where Are You?* or *Batman*. Yet successive waves of these shows in the late sixties, seventies, and eighties proved to be the true progeny of *Dragnet*. Joe Friday himself came back for three seasons of workmanlike law enforcement in the form of *Dragnet '67* (though the number changed each year)—this time aiming his deadpan ire at sixties undesirables, like the LSD pusher caught in the first episode, and the stoned couple who let their baby drown in the bathtub.

By 1971, there were almost twice as many law-enforcement characters on television as the number appearing just two years earlier. From *Ironside* and *Hawaii Five-O* to *Kojak* and *The Streets of San Francisco,* these police shows came to dominate television drama during the seventies and early eighties. Beyond their glorification of cops, they had other obvious and pervasive effects. For example, one empirical study of television in that era found that:

Almost two out of every three shows on TV featured at least one crime.

Over half the crimes were violent.

Almost all TV crime was premeditated.

The overwhelming majority of TV murder victims were young and white.

More than half of all TV criminals were the victims of violence usually inflicted by law-enforcement officers.

Like Jack Webb, the producers of these crime and police shows often made no secret of their sympathies. "Let me put it in a very corny phrase," Quinn Martin, producer of *Barnaby Jones* and *The FBI* said. "I am a patriot. In the police shows that I do, I show the police in an idealized way. Without respect for the police, I think we'd have a breakdown in our society."

"We were close to chaos, close to suspicion of institutions in the early 1970s," said David Gerber, producer of *Police Story*. "The blue line was there to preserve what was left, what was the semblance of what used to be a helluva government when it served the people."

ABC executive Jonathan Axelrod didn't put it much differently: "I like shows that are about institutions that we look up to. In a country where crime is exploding, things like the FBI become more important to people. When you think of the amount of kidnapping that's going on, and murder, it's very important."

Kojak regularly preached that unshackling the police from legal restraints would reduce crime. (In fact, studies showed that the infamous *Miranda* decision had virtually no adverse impact on the real work of the police.) Almost all shows implicitly endorsed the notion that crime was always the product of deranged or greedy professional criminals; social factors were never mentioned. Every show also taught viewers that the criminal-justice system was working well. One study showed that 90 percent of all television crimes were solved by police making successful arrests. If viewers knew that the real figure was around 10 percent, they might have felt a bit different about "law and order."

And the effect on the public? According to James Carlson, author of a 1985 study, "[T]hose who spent the most time viewing crime shows were the least disposed to support civil liberties for those who were accused of crimes." Moreover, he found that:

> [H]eavy crime-show viewing contributes to support for the legal system and the norm of compliance. . . . Crime-show viewing appears to play a role in the inhibition of the natural growth of cynicism regarding the legal system that comes with cognitive maturation.

That's a fancy way of saying that if in fact these police shows were about law and order, they were light on the law and heavy on the order. On television, at least until very recently, the police always won unless "the system" stopped them; "due process" is not a term heard frequently on prime time. And, if nothing else, these police shows gave legitimacy to a process that didn't really warrant it, while changing the public's entire conception of legal reality. "If you can control the storytelling," TV scholar George Gerbner, former dean of the Annenberg School, once said, "then you do not have to worry about who makes the laws."

Even the police series of the early eighties did their best to romanticize police work, though, at the time, shows such as *Hill Street Blues* and *Cagney and Lacey* were being hailed for their realism. In their own way, these shows portrayed the police as gallant as any heroes in history; only the nuances were different. These cops had become eighties heroes—less macho, more compassionate, and more upscale.

Beginning in the late eighties, however, with the rise of "reality" television, extended local news, and such docudramas as *COPS* and *Rescue 911,* the public began to be given a more realistic vision of what was happening in the streets. The police still tended to receive heroic treatment, but it was impossible anymore to mask their often futile efforts to contain crime. This sentiment eventually would find its way into commercial programming on shows such as *Homicide* and *NYPD Blue*. By then, however, views about crime-fighting had changed for good.

In fact, when Webb died in 1982, the Los Angeles Police Department flew its flag at half-staff. He thus didn't live to see the image of his beloved LAPD begin to unravel in the nineties—beginning with the Rodney King beating and spilling into the O.J. Simpson trial a few years later. Yet even if the image of the LAPD began to suffer, viewer-voters still never wavered in their support for a certain type of crime-fighting which Joe Friday had made respectable. Over the past 40 years, save for a brief period in the sixties, voters have moved in an almost direct line to the right on crime issues—favoring tougher crime-fighting measures, more freedom for the police, and less spending on the social causes of crime. Jack Webb and *Dragnet* deserve at least a share of the credit.

6

Bishop Sheen's *Life Is Worth Living* and the New American Religion of Television

(DuMont and ABC: 1952–57)

American rhetoric has been shaped by many sources, but few have been more influential than the church and television. Our rhetoric has always had strong religious roots, in part because until recently, many Americans heard their most stirring speeches as participants in a religious assembly. One only has to think about how many of our most famous political speeches—the Gettysburg Address, Kennedy's inaugural address, Martin Luther King's "I Have a Dream" speech—have invoked God, or otherwise have had something of the perorational quality of a sermon. Television, on the other hand, has dramatically altered the definition of what constitutes memorable rhetoric, even for those speeches we don't hear via a TV set. Because we now watch and listen to so much of our rhetoric in bedrooms and living rooms, we expect our public speakers almost everywhere to act and talk the way others do in those private sanctuaries. Thus the demonstrative, hyperbolic styles of a William Jennings Bryan or a Milton Berle have largely been superseded by the low-key, conversational, story-telling tone of a Ronald Reagan or a Mister Rogers.

With these influences at work, it should be no surprise that those at the vortex of these forces—TV preachers—should have had something of a role to play on television. Billy Graham used television specials to make himself one of the best-known and most admired figures in the country. Names like Jerry Falwell, Pat Robertson, Oral Roberts, and Rex Humbard are familiar to everyone, despite the low ratings of their shows.

Yet television's first religious broadcaster to become a star may well have been the biggest: Bishop Fulton J. Sheen. From 1952 to 1955, he had his own popular prime time show on the soon-to-be-defunct DuMont Network, *Life Is Worth Living* (which later became *Mission to the World* on ABC). As a Catholic cleric rather than a fundamentalist Protestant, Bishop Sheen was an odd forerunner of the televangelists who followed him. Nevertheless, his early popularity revealed something about both the evolution of the medium and the role that religion would play in its constellation of programming.

Because it didn't have the resources to compete with the "Big Three," DuMont, the ill-fated fourth network, was known for turning out inexpensive entertainment—though it did televise the first NFL championship game in 1951, and gave Jackie Gleason his first show. In the early 1950s, NBC's Milton Berle was still king of the early Tuesday-night schedule, demolishing competitors like Frank Sinatra, who had a musical variety show on CBS. In early 1952, DuMont turned to Sheen, the auxiliary bishop of New York who had been broadcasting sermons on radio for over two decades on NBC's *The Catholic Hour.* His job was to fill a half-hour opposite Berle at 8:00 P.M. on Tuesdays, a post politely called an "obituary spot" in the trade. After being convinced that a studio living-room set was a better broadcasting venue than a church, Sheen debuted with a 20-minute talk followed by questions from the audience. ("Why does God permit evil in the world?") Unexpectedly, something clicked: DuMont's ratings rose, as NBC's and CBS's ratings dropped almost five points each within a month.

DuMont's coup may be one of the first examples of successful counterprogramming: Sheen was nothing if not different from Uncle Miltie, the principal competitor in his time slot: It was in effect the Catholic versus the Jew. Sheen was able to tap into a whole Catholic subculture in the early fifties, including parish papers and close-knit neighborhood parochial schools. The Church would become well-known in this era for its condemnation of rock and roll. In contrast, by appearing on this new medium soon after it hit the scene, Sheen legitimized TV in the eyes of his followers—an important development in the history of television, if not also in the election of the nation's first Catholic president, thanks to television less than a decade later.

Yet there was more to Sheen's success than that. Decked out in his finery (replete with a classy skull cap, a gold cross hanging down on his chest, and a cape), he was a commanding television presence with, *Life* wrote, "one of the most remarkable pair of eyes in America." "[H]e not only looks at people, but through them and at everything around them," it wrote. Sheen worked without notes, prompting *Time* to send a reporter to investigate fruitlessly what tricks he used to get through the broadcast. The star of the show began by emerging from offstage to polite applause: After all, the Archdiocese had turned down requests for any tickets from what looked like girls' schools. "We don't want any squealing," said a spokesman. "First thing you know, he'd turn into a clerical Sinatra." Sheen then stood in what appeared to be a living room with a fireplace and a blackboard, and basically told stories straight into the camera. Almost 40 years later, some Sheen fans were reminded of that style when General Norman Schwarzkopf gave his blackboard briefings during the Gulf War.

Peppered with anecdotes, Sheen's "messages" about love and humor were less religious than psychological; this was religion meets Norman Vincent Peale, whose *Power of Positive Thinking* had been published only a year earlier. The program began with the announcer's dictum "A program devoted to the everyday problems of all of us," and Sheen was careful to tell interviewers that, unlike Billy Graham's appearances, his own were not specifically religious. "I am talking as a . . . lecturer," he said. With talks that decades later would be packaged as videos given titles like "Stop the World—I Want to Get On" and "Are We Neurotic Today?" Sheen became an anachronistic forerunner of Phil Donahue and Oprah Winfrey.

Politics—particularly Red Scare propaganda—played a role, too. Sheen's most celebrated show may well have been on the evening he turned the burial scene from Julius Caesar into a denunciation of Stalin and his government. (When Stalin suffered a stroke less than a week later and then died, Sheen's show about him became a topic of conversation for months.) "Liberty," Sheen once said, "has become doing as you please, and that is not freedom. Freedom is the right to do what you ought to do." On another occasion he told the audience:

> America, it is said, is suffering from intolerance. It is not. It is suffering from tolerance: tolerance of right and wrong, truth and error, virtue and evil, Christ and chaos. . . . The man who can make up his mind in an orderly way, as a man might make up his bed, is called a bigot; but a man who cannot make up his mind, any more than he can make up for lost time, is called tolerant and broadminded.

Critics would charge that Sheen had a definite political agenda—as he attacked labor unions, agitation for social reform, and universities which "house agents of Satan." Yet whatever he was doing was working. Loretta Young called him "the greatest actor of our time," and Sheen even made the cover of *Time*. "If he came out in a barrel and read the telephone book," said a spokesman for the Archdiocese of New York, "they'd love him." When criticized for being on TV at all, Sheen said Christ might do the same if he lived today. "It would be just as acceptable as his entrance into Jerusalem on a donkey," Sheen said. "He used the best means available." As Mary Ann Watson noted much later in a wide-ranging study of Sheen's show for *Television Quarterly,* unsolicited charitable contributions came in by the thousands—illuminating the way for the televangelists who followed. Milton Berle of *The Texaco Star Theater* responded to the new star in his time slot with a joke: "We both work for the same boss—Sky Chief!" And a certain Hispanic Hollywood actor named Martin Estevez was so taken with the Bishop that he asked if he could change his own last name to Sheen—and did.

By the end of 1952, "Uncle Fultie" found himself up against Jimmy Durante, Edward R. Murrow, Lucille Ball, and Arthur Godfrey for the Emmy for TV's Most Outstanding Television Personality. Sheen won, accepting the award with the quip "I wish to thank my four writers—Matthew, Mark, Luke, and John." By 1957, Billy Graham had followed Sheen to ABC television (still in third and willing to try almost anything) with the first live telecast of his New York crusade. *Variety* called it a "surefire click" and "tremendous box office" as that show went up against Perry Como and Jackie Gleason.

Yet Graham and Sheen, the latter of whom died in 1979 at the age of 84, would turn out to be the last religious figures to make a real impact in prime time on a regular basis, notwithstanding *Crossroads,* an ABC series of the mid-fifties which dramatized the experiences of clergymen; *Going My Way,* a one-season flop in the early sixties; and the adventures of a young Sally Field in *The Flying Nun* for three seasons in the late sixties on ABC. Even Tennessee Ernie Ford's closing gospel number and salutation, "May the good Lord take a likin' to you," was unusual on this medium. The truth is that, for all the attention paid to televangelism, religious shows have almost always been relegated to "ghetto" time periods like Sunday morning, when television can't draw much of an audience, or to cable and syndication, where intensity of following is as important as numbers.

It's certainly true that shows such as Pat Robertson's *700 Club* or Robert Schuller's *Hour of Power* have reached millions with their messages, though Robertson is a good example of how television has modulated the old fire-and-brimstone style of evangelists, and turned the successful modern telepreachers into theistic Arthur Godfreys. Still, religious broadcasting remains a form of fringe programming: Just as Pat Robertson fell flat as a presidential candidate in 1988 when he had to appeal to the masses, so too has religious and fundamentalist programming failed to draw a diverse audience. Moreover, unlike MTV or the Home Shopping Network, two forms of concentrated programming which have greatly influenced the mainstream, religious broadcasting has had little effect on anything the major networks produce. For all the importance that religion tends to have in the daily lives of many Americans, its absence from television is striking.

In one sense, though, it's easy to see why. Religious shows tend to be full of talking heads and short on visuals—the very definition of uninteresting television. Like the religions they represent, they tend to deal in abstractions rather than personalities. They often stress a hierarchical community, not an audience of individualized listeners and consumers. Churches and synagogues have also been understandably reluctant to turn their places of worship into studios, and subject matters into dramatic presentations, for fear that religion will inevitably become just another "show," and thus just another form of entertainment on a medium which takes pride in believing that nothing is sacred. TV programming from *Mister Ed* to *ER* thrives on irony, not faith—on suspended belief, not belief itself.

Yet there's even more to it than all this. Commercial television is ruthlessly secular. Its emphasis is on the immediate, the here-and-now, the accumulation of goods, and the denial that there is any higher experience than consuming and watching TV. The reason why television pays so little attention to religion, and features so few religious figures—even on fictional shows—is that, ultimately, conventional religion is heretical to television's very notion of itself.

Thus, the whole zeitgeist of television is a kind of antireligion that has become its own religion, even if Michael Landon got to play an itinerant angel for several seasons on *Highway to Heaven* (a theme revisited in the mid-nineties' CBS hit *Touched By An Angel*), or shows like *Picket Fences* occasionally have touched on religious themes. Media analysts such as Tony Schwartz have written how the modern media have become a kind of "second God"—invisible but everywhere, all-knowing, and working in mysterious ways. After all, Saint Augustine's definition of God was one of a Being whose center is everywhere and whose borders are nowhere—something akin to television. George Gerbner, former dean of the Annenberg School, has described the medium as the "new state religion" of the modern age—the major dispenser of our current allegories, gospels, and parables. "The sitcom has taken the place of church, of religious training," Susan Borowitz, a TV comedy writer once said. "Sitcoms work better if they're little sermons or parables." Television has even established its own new "religious" holidays, like the Super Bowl; its own set of new rituals, like watching the O.J. chase; and its own new set of saints, who are honored at countless televised awards banquets.

In this atmosphere, it is no surprise that practically the only denominations that have been able to survive on the small screen are those that have been willing to suborn themselves to television's own conventions and theology. It's been written before how fundamentalism—based on the individual's interpretation of "the word"—has always been drawn to the individualism inherent in broadcasting. Fundamentalist preachers have often been far more willing than other religious leaders to allow themselves to be transmogrified into a kind of game-show host selling a vision little different from television's ideal materialistic lifestyle.

Thus, in retrospect, it is clear that television looked into those haunting eyes of Bishop Sheen in the mid-fifties and decided that, as good a performer as he was, his kind of religion wasn't really in its cards. Yet perhaps religion thrives in America now precisely because it is absent from the corrosion of prime-time television. After all, TV loves politics, and viewers now detest Washington. Even those traditional broadcast heroes, the police, have faded in favor somewhat, and no reasonable person would maintain that the subject matter of shows about them (crime control) is actually in better shape today than it was before television arrived on the scene. If television has avoided religion, that abstinence may only go to show that the Lord works in mysterious ways indeed.

7

Resistance to Reality:
Why Edward R. Murrow's *See It Now*
Didn't Change Television More
(CBS: 1951–58)

It is impossible to write a book about the most influential shows in television history without examining the role of Edward R. Murrow, the patron saint of television news. Murrow pioneered the television documentary on *See It Now* and confronted Senator Joseph McCarthy in one of the medium's more celebrated moments; his insights and predictions about television are still treated as gospel. Whenever anchors or newsmen bemoan the state of the medium, they frequently invoke his name—especially if they work for CBS, his network. "Edward R. Murrow said sometimes the news is dull," Bob Schieffer once told the *Washington Post's* Howard Kurtz, as if in order to justify the fact that his Sunday morning talk show could also be boring and ignored by the masses. Peter Boyer begins his book about the demise of CBS News *(Who Killed CBS?)* with a scene from correspondent Charles Collingwood's funeral in 1985, when the participants realized that the Murrow tradition "had really come to a terminal point."

This is one case, however, where the true import of a legendary television show was not in its popularity, but in the unforeseen resistance of the public to its message and format. Despite the accolades, the Murrow "tradition" never really existed on television: Murrow's distinguished radio career, by and large, went the way of many silent film stars' careers when talkies invaded the marketplace. While Murrow was a central character in several of television's defining moments, and has subsequently been canonized, he had a negligible impact on the overall course of the medium and its news coverage.

True, the exceptions are well worth noting. Murrow bravely took on McCarthy on a 30-minute *See It Now* broadcast on March 9, 1954, generating 15,000 letters and an equal number of phone calls to CBS and the show's sponsor, Alcoa Aluminum. (Almost all were in favor of Murrow.) That show featured clips of the senator using his own words against himself. Murrow concluded:

> The actions of the junior senator from Wisconsin have caused alarm and dismay amongst our allies abroad and given considerable comfort to our enemies. And whose fault is that? Not really his. He didn't create this situation of fear. He merely exploited it, and rather successfully. Cassius was right: The fault, dear Brutus, is not in our stars, but in ourselves.

Still, as reporters like Paul Fahri have pointed out, Murrow's broadcast came years after McCarthy had begun destroying the reputations of his foes. Others had taken on McCarthy before Murrow, including the *Baltimore Sun* and the *New York Times,* though Murrow's courageous broadcast undoubtedly reached far more people with greater impact. What's more, television historians now tend to agree that the 35-day Army-McCarthy hearings later that year—which included the famous confrontation between McCarthy and Joseph Welch ("Have you no sense of decency, sir, at long last?")—did more to bring down the senator than Murrow did, though only the two minor networks, DuMont and ABC, televised the hearings. Murrow's CBS refused because it didn't want to lose the commercial profits from soap operas; the upstarts had little or no daytime programming, and thus could afford the gamble.

Where Murrow was a really instrumental media figure was on radio, through which he permeated the country's consciousness on an almost daily basis with his reporting from World War II London during the Blitz. "This . . . is . . . London" was his trademark, and his personal reportage was notable. "The small incendiaries were going down like a fistful of white rice thrown on a piece of black velvet," he once said with his typical eloquence. In contrast, his telecasts were less memorable, less frequent, and less popular—that is, when they were watched at all.

See It Now, Murrow's first TV public-affairs program, premiered on Sunday afternoons in 1951, to high praise. On the first show he sat at a table, looking at live individual shots of the Statue of Liberty and San Francisco Bay, as the two coasts were now linked by the new coaxial cable. "We are impressed," he said, "by a medium through which a man sitting in his living room has been able for the first time to look at two oceans at once." "Television's best and liveliest show," *Time* called it, confirming Murrow's reputation even then as the print journalist's journalist.

Yet this was a medium in which words counted for far less than images, and Murrow's ratings soon reflected that fact. By the following year, his show had been moved from Sundays to Tuesday nights at 10:30 P.M. After three years, the documentary news show appeared only about eight times a year, leading critics to dub it "See It Now and Then." Similarly, Murrow's moving and celebrated documentary about migrant farm workers, "Harvest of Shame," barely registered with the general public because CBS ran it on November 25, 1960—the night after Thanksgiving, and one of the worst television viewing nights of the year. The real shame is that so few viewers were there to pay attention to its eloquent portrayal of the disadvantaged. "The people you have seen have the strength to harvest your fruit and vegetables," Murrow concluded. "They do not have the strength to influence legislation. Maybe we do. Good night, and good luck."

Murrow did the kind of tough documentaries that commercial television today will seldom touch. *See It Now* not only went after McCarthy, but highlighted the Red Scare in "The Case Against Milo Radulovich." The show also investigated the refusal of the Indianapolis American Legion to permit its hall to be used by the American Civil Liberties Union, and produced a two-part report on the relationship between smoking and lung cancer, presaging the much later Surgeon General's Report. Murrow's unusual take on the Korean War was to spend time with the soldiers, digging foxholes on "Christmas in Korea."

It says something further about Murrow's integrity—and that of his producer, Fred Friendly—that for a number of the more controversial broadcasts, the two had to pay out of pocket for advertisements in the *New York Times,* promoting the shows without the CBS logo. Murrow also withstood enormous sponsor pressure, which was far more typical at that time than today because one advertiser usually sponsored an entire program. After Murrow ran a piece on a small Texas paper which had won a Pulitzer Prize for exposing a land scandal, Alcoa dropped him. The paper's report had upset state officials—and Alcoa had state contracts for piping.

Many of Murrow's shows, however, were not at all controversial. In fact, they often were terribly boring, not only by today's standards but even by those of the time. Murrow spent evenings on subjects with titles like "Interview with Marshal Tito" and "Burma, Buddhism and Neutralism."

Meanwhile, *Person to Person,* Murrow's other show, was a far stronger television offering—a forerunner of Barbara Walters' celebrity interviews, as Murrow sat down live with John and Jacqueline Kennedy, Zsa Zsa Gabor, Liberace, and Marilyn Monroe. In contrast to *See It Now, Person to Person* ran a full seven years in its time slot—usually on Fridays from 10:30 to 11:00 P.M., as it battled shows like *Gillette Cavalcade of Sports* and *77 Sunset Strip* in the ratings. "To do the show I want to do," Murrow once said, "I have to do the show I don't want to do." Yet that series on people—far better suited to the strengths of the television medium—ended up as the offering that actually influenced the direction of future television programming.

It may be true, as the *Saturday Review* once noted, that Murrow pulled TV and radio "to their limits." And it may be true, as Murrow himself once warned, that TV was being used "to insulate the citizenry from the hard and demanding realities." Yet it's also clear that audiences rarely flocked to his shows—a near-fatal flaw on what is, after all, a mass commercial medium. "If I were in charge of CBS," Murrow once told a friend, "I am sure it would go broke." This was a man who campaigned against commercials during newscasts, and probably would have been far happier with the model of television developed by the hierarchical, elitist, and ad-free BBC, which had dropped wrestling from its entertainment lineup because the sport was "undignified for television."

Yet that misfit wasn't the interpretation, either then or now. "Murrow . . . [has] devised a formula for TV news that seems to many to be so far unbeatable," wrote *Newsweek* in a cover profile in 1954. The magazine was wrong, however, because, like Murrow, it fundamentally misunderstood this new medium—which would almost always engender high mass-audience resistance to news. After all, the highest-rated regularly scheduled news segment in TV history is still the one-minute NBC News update which appeared in the middle of the first TV showing of *Gone With the Wind* in 1976.

Moreover, the tendency in TV's early days was to treat television as radio with pictures; *See It Now* had originally been a radio show called *Hear It Now*. Television, however, was not radio—and not simply because, in Marshall McLuhan's words—one was "hot" and one was "cool." For starters, television pieces demanded more narrative in order to engage audiences. "[F]ifteen minutes of a radio news analyst, plus a camera, add up to something less than television," Quincy Howe admitted, in a 1957 *Saturday Review* piece lamenting how old radio commentators such as Murrow and H.V. Kaltenborn were having a tough time adjusting to television. That's why one of the more popular CBS news-based shows of the fifties featured a young Mike Wallace and Walter Cronkite covering restaged historical events, such as Lee and Grant at Appomattox, on a show called *You Are There*. Over the years, American rhetoric would follow the same path, forsaking the old Lincoln-Douglas discussion of serious themes and issues for the kind of storytelling that Ronald Reagan did best.

More importantly, television seemed to promote its own unique kind of personality—warm, easygoing, and amiable—not only in news but in other contexts, including politics. Ironically, that's one of the reasons why the medium so successfully broke McCarthy. If there was ever a soul not made for TV, it was the sweaty, darty-eyed, balding, and frumpy senator from Wisconsin.

Yet Murrow had his problems with the medium, too. "Murrow's stuff always had that sharp edge," his "Harvest of Shame" editor John Schultz once said. Just as extraordinary talents like Frank Sinatra and Judy Garland never really made it on television, leaving the field to inferior musical artists such as Dinah Shore and Perry Como, so too did television news demand its own personalities. "Did you see Perry

Como last night?" went the joke. "No, I fell asleep." "That's funny, so did he," went the rejoinder.

That tendency would have consequences for the whole culture. Over the decades, pollsters would note how voters often demanded that their politicians be as likable as their favorite TV personalities. The voters would complain constantly if politicians were too confrontational, or failed to stress the upbeat. So it went here as well: The anachronistically intense Murrow—Bogart-like, cigarette in hand— never fit the new icon, so he was replaced, in much the same way that recording companies in the same era took rock-and-roll hits by black artists and gave them to Pat Boone to "cover." Even by the early sixties, *Newsweek* had shifted course, complaining that CBS was strangled "with an air of doom and gloom, a hangover from the Ed Murrow era."

For better or for worse, the advocacy documentaries that Murrow produced never really suited the medium or its viewers either, at least as network television was now defining it. Perhaps it's true, as journalist David Halberstam once wrote, that "there is an unwritten law in American journalism that states that the greater and more powerful the platform, the more carefully it must be used and the more closely it must adhere to the norms of American society." Network television is a mass medium, and it tends to avoid offending even the few in order to preserve its standing with the many. "Once you take a stand," Joseph Wershba, a *See It Now* producer once explained, "you lose the viewers who don't agree with you." Certainly, in a country where broadcast licenses are distributed by the government, there is an incentive to be extravagantly nonpartisan—if only to avoid alienating the wrong party.

Yet even though some critics might object, it's not impossible to do documentaries on television and make them popular. Producers like David Wolper, who produced *Roots,* and Don Hewitt, who developed *60 Minutes,* and Ken Burns, who produced PBS's *The Civil War,* would do a better job discovering American television's unique take on genre—which usually demanded high drama, actors, music, and that the reporter take no point of view which could be identified as politically partisan. In the ultimate irony, HBO did just such a "docudrama" on Murrow himself in 1986, which former CBS newsman Daniel Schorr promptly labeled "Harvest of Sham."

If Murrow rarely seemed to understand television, the fault (to paraphrase the line from *Julius Caesar* he used with McCarthy) was not in his stars, but in himself. A great journalist? Undoubtedly. But Murrow was a *radio* star who, like the Fred Allens and Ed Wynns, could never quite accommodate the transition to a new technology and also make it suit his talents the way Lucille Ball—or even Walter Cronkite—could. Despite what many critics say, there is such a thing as good journalism that TV viewers will watch. The Murrow tradition, however, was rarely much a part of it.

8

Today, Barbara Walters, and TV's Definition of News
(NBC: 1952–PRESENT)

For the *Today* show, January 14, 1952, was not an auspicious beginning. At the time, television scheduling was much like the movies: There were prime-time and weekend shows broadcast when everybody was home, but there wasn't much else on at other times of the day, and there was nothing at all on early in the morning. This was also a full decade before the news became a significant TV institution. As conceived by Sylvester "Pat" Weaver, the NBC executive who also created *The Tonight Show* (and the father of Sigourney), *Today* would fill this early-morning dead-air time by mimicking radio, and thus steal its audience with a mixture of news, light comedy, conversation, and music—while exploiting television's ability to give the public a "window on the world." The program was originally supposed to be called *The Rise and Shine Revue*.

Running on 26 stations, the first *Today* show went according to plan—more or less. Host Dave Garroway, a low-key former Chicago radio personality, called London and Frankfurt, played some records, reviewed the weather, showed scenes of the New York skyline, displayed a few newspaper headlines, had someone review the day's news, and chatted up some guests. ("How's the Navy going these days,

Admiral?" "Guess it's all right. It was there last night all right, when I left it.") "I really believe this begins a new kind of television," said Garroway as he introduced the show, though it wasn't readily apparent what kind that was. "We tried to do pure television as against translating vaudeville to television," Garroway would say later.

He was right, of course. The program had its roots in a garrulous style known as "Chicago talk." In the very early days of television, local Chicago TV had *Garroway at Large* on one station, writer and interviewer Studs Terkel on another, and the kids' show *Kukla, Fran and Ollie,* as well as Hugh Downs. Terkel described the unscripted, easy-going, conversational style as "nonformula." "It was as fresh as jazz," he once said. "It had an air of improvisation to it."

Yet the New York critics—used to formal theatrical scripts and vaudeville—reacted with scorn to that style on *Today,* a response that was ratified by early advertisers and audiences. *Today* premiered with only one sponsor, the Kiplinger newsletter, while John Crosby, in the *New York Herald Tribune,* described *Today* as "an incredible two-hour comedy of errors, perpetrated as 'a new kind of television.'" "Do yourself a favor, NBC," wrote another critic. "Roll over and go back to sleep." The problem for the network wasn't simply that the show's concept was so new. This was an era when most households had only one television, so a program like *Today* had to offer something for everyone in the house in order to gain an audience in the early morning. That problem was solved a year later when the show added to its cast of regulars one J. Fred Muggs, a chimpanzee owned by two former NBC pages. Muggs appeared in skits, and pretended to read the morning papers. It was said that he was added to the cast in order to appeal to children, but the undeniable effect was to convert *Today* almost overnight from an iffy proposition into a network institution. "His charm," said Garroway, "is his unpredictability—same as any animal's." To his credit, Muggs did once bite Martha Raye.

And so, by and large, the show has remained true to its conversational origins—"[A]s American as Frosted Flakes," *Newsweek* once wrote. The show's cast has been a kind of "Who's Who" of television, or at least of the various types of personalities who have populated what passes for television news. From Jack Lescoulie, Garroway, and Muggs (who stayed four years, leaving—as the network's release put it—to "extend his personal horizons"), to Frank Blair, Betsy Palmer, Hugh Downs, former Miss America Lee Ann Meriwether, John Chancellor, Barbara Walters, Frank McGee, Tom Brokaw, Joe Garagiola, Jim Hartz, Gene Shalit, Jane Pauley, Bryant Gumbel, weatherman Willard Scott, and on to Katie Couric, *Today* has always represented television's uneasy attempt to balance journalism and entertainment, public service and ratings.

This, let it be remembered, was the show famous for presenting an interview with a senator, next to a scene from *Caesar and Cleopatra,* next to a kidney-transplant operation, next to the filmed sinking of the *Andrea Doria,* next to the recitation of 100-year-olds' birthdays, next to consumer and health news, next to the once-ubiquitous ads for Alpo and other products that often were presented by *Today* personalities such as Willard Scott—a former Bozo clown.

Forty-odd years later, some things are different: Women obviously have more of a role on the show than in the days when they were allowed only limited appearances on camera. The evolution from the quirky Garroway—with his famous daily goodbye, "Peace"—to the pugnacious Gumbel and the perky Couric is a story of how TV talk moved from true conversation to an exchange of sound bites. The comic skits were eliminated in 1961, when the newly formed news division took over the program. And, over the years, the show has been allowed to travel more from its New York base: The show's first out-of-studio trip was to Miami Beach in 1954, and it's been just about everywhere else since, becoming a kind of *Wide World of Sports* of news.

Yet the wonder of the show, and its clones, like *Good Morning America,* is not that they have changed so much, but that they have changed so little. Television is a visual medium, but *Today*—designed to be heard more than watched, and at that in sound bites and snippets, by people on their way to work or school—has always been essentially a radio show with a few pictures, making its influence and continued appeal all the more astonishing. In the end, it may only prove that the distance between J. Fred Muggs and Willard Scott is smaller than one might think.

The show's significance in television history is not merely that it had an almost virtual lock on its time slot for almost 25 years, a rare enough occurrence in the annals of television. (CBS certainly tried to challenge it in the fifties, with shows hosted by Walter Cronkite, accompanied by a puppet lion, and Dick Van Dyke.) Nor is it merely that this show ended up defining practically the only type of programming that the networks will try during the morning hours, not just here, but abroad, too. "The package of news, culture, and entertainment is like the first cup of coffee," *Chicago Sun-Times* radio-TV critic Paul Molloy once said. "The hardest part was getting stations to start in the morning," Weaver told a reporter, but once they did, they never broke the habit.

Instead, the show's principal contribution to television was its style, which became a paradigm. There were the bite-size programming chunks with the repetition of news and weather every half-hour: *Today* set the country on a road that led to its current case of attention deficit disorder. Moreover, by giving the locals five minutes every hour to insinuate their own news, and thereby sell more local ad time, the show's producers provided many markets with their very first taste of local news—an institution which would change the country markedly, beginning in the 1970s.

This was also the show that made the world safe for news chitchat (the hosts all sitting around a mock living room, joking and drinking coffee), thus launching the format that would come to dominate the local news in the seventies and beyond. The show's mingling of news and entertainment—later dubbed "infotainment"—soon became the model for virtually all TV news except the staid evening variety, and even that would eventually fall prey to some of its charms. Indeed, from *Entertainment Tonight* and *Larry King Live* to *Prime Time Live* and *The Oprah Winfrey Show*, it's hard to think of a television newslike show which doesn't have its roots somewhere in *Today*. It's not an exaggeration to contend that perhaps no show in the history of TV news has ever been so influential.

"You had to make it entertaining," Weaver once said. Describing the show's origins, he continued:

> I was trying to make the news department do it, but I finally threw them off the show because they yelled and screamed at me for putting on people who were not totally newsmen. Jack Lescoulie did sports, but he was there to be funny.

This was the show that had Lescoulie wear a certain famous New York baseball Giants hurler's uniform and demand that the real pitcher, Sal Maglie, interview him; the show also, à la David Letterman, once put a $20 bill in a glove, then dropped it onto a New York sidewalk, to see what would happen when people picked it up. "Weaver didn't like the news department, and the news department hated the *Today* show with a venom," Gerald Green, the show's news editor once said—and that Weaveresque zeitgeist lived long and prospered, even after the news division took over *Today* in the early sixties.

The program's influence even spread far beyond television. Consider the one person who best symbolizes the *Today* definition of news, Barbara Walters—who is to TV news what Lucille Ball was to TV entertainment. Edward R. Murrow didn't change television, but Walters did big-time—taking the *Today* approach of mingling the personal and the political, hard news and showbiz news, and turning it all into a prime-time institution. The perennially underestimated Walters joined *Today* in 1961 as a writer-assistant, and by 1964 had made it onto the show. Soon she joined host Hugh Downs in interviewing guests, and she went on to cohost the show for years with Downs, Frank McGee, and Jim Hartz.

Walters' dual trademark was her preparation and persistence—*Variety* called her "a victory of brains over mannequin beauty." (Her speech impairment would have certainly prevented her from becoming a superstar on radio, but it became almost endearing on the small screen.) Walters soon became known for asking the kind of impertinent, personal questions that viewers at home (particularly women) really had on their mind: whether Mamie Eisenhower had heard the rumors that she drank too much; whether Lady Bird Johnson knew the stories about her husband's infidelity. "Were you made fun of as a child because you were different?" Walters inquired of Truman Capote, while Ingrid Bergman was asked, "What's it like for great beauties to grow old?"

Walters, with television's first million-dollar news contract in hand, left *Today* in 1976 to coanchor *The ABC Evening News,* amid a flurry of charges that network news had sold out to the entertainment division. "When I first heard the offer," said CBS's Morley Safer, "a wave of nausea was my first reaction—with my second reaction being a spasm of nausea." Yet, as a news anchor, Walters wasn't allowed to act much different from other news anchors, and her talent was hidden. "The days of the Olympian commentator are over," she said (mistakenly), and she ended up holding the anchor job for only several years.

Walters' contract, however, also called upon her to do four prime-time specials a year, and they ended up, in one ABC executive's words, as "the tail that wagged the dog." In her first ABC prime-time appearance, Walters interviewed the reclusive Barbra Streisand ("Why don't you get your nose fixed?") and the newly elected Carters—thereby invoking the old *Today* formula of mingling hard news with entertainment. She made TV and political history of a sort by asking the Carters if they slept in single beds or a double. "Double bed," Carter replied, opening the way some 15 years later to another president to reveal his underwear preferences. "Be wise with us, governor. Be good to us," she implored at the end of the show—a kind of mirror image of Edward R. Murrow's old salutation, "Good night and good luck." (Now she ends every *20/20* broadcast with "We're in touch—so you be in touch.") Critics lambasted the show for its "banality," but as the ratings showed, the show had garnered an unbelievable-for-a-news-show 36 rating in prime time.

Neither television nor public life would be the same, as Walters helped lead the way in personalizing our politics—intermingling the status of its stars with those of the show-business celebrities with whom they shared top billing on her specials. First ladies, like Eleanor Roosevelt, had been political figures in their own right before Walters, but by giving these women such prominence and exposure, Walters helped push them to the forefront. By 1996, Elizabeth Dole and Hillary Clinton were the virtual stars of their husbands' political conventions, assuming roles that no one would have predicted before Walters arrived on the scene.

For her part, Walters went on to host more than 75 specials and display her brand of journalism on *20/20*—one of the first of the successful magazine shows. Over the years, she would become the queen of the celebrity interview, racking up every big Hollywood star imaginable, as well as Boris Yeltsin, Desiree Washington (the victim in the Mike Tyson rape case), Fidel Castro, and the Shah of Iran.

Obviously Walters wasn't everyone's cup of tea. Over time, in fact, a number of interviewees and critics alike gave her strong feedback. The Russian poet Yevgeny Yevtushenko once described her as "a hyena in syrup." And critic Mark Crispin Miller would come to dub Walters' shows "The Theatre of Revenge" for the way she would abuse the stars, acting out an elaborate hostility play which embodied the jealousy and occasional loathing with which Americans view their entertainment and political royalty. "Can you have sex?" she asked singer Teddy Pendergrass, severely disabled since an auto accident. She inquired of Katharine Hepburn what kind of tree she would choose to be. One of her favorite questions, according to *TV Guide,* was this: "If you had to spend three weeks in a hospital, who would you want in the bed next to yours?" ("The best damned doctor in town," said Johnny Carson.)

Walters' success in prime time helped convince the networks that the *Today* approach to news could sell to the masses, in the evening, on a scale which morning TV, with its limited audience, never could. Until recently, news and public affairs had been television's loss leaders. Except for *60 Minutes,* prime-time documentaries and news shows were almost always at the bottom of each week's ratings until the networks stopped doing them. Once Walters proved otherwise— with an approach which was far less expensive than the average dramatic show (no actors or crews to hire; no exotic settings to stage)—it was only a matter of time before TV became overrun with news magazines in prime time that aped both the *Today* format and approach. Conventional newscasts took note of her ratings success as well, and became Waltersized. "As this society becomes the celebrity society, she is the progenitor of that," journalist David Halberstam once told a reporter.

Thus, as time went by, the inherent values of *Today* would come to overrun the culture. News would virtually eliminate the separation between the personal and political as politicians saw the most graphic details of their sex lives paraded before the public. The line between the worlds of Hollywood and Washington would gradually erode as politics increasingly became a business in which the image of what happened grew to be far more important than what actually transpired. It's now a nation where leaders are measured almost solely by popularity polls, where candidates are judged by how well-groomed and glib they appear in TV debates, and where David Letterman and Jay Leno are the Walter Lippmanns of their day.

Barbara Walters was hardly responsible for all of these changes, just as *Today* was not solely the reason for the notion that television could expand to fill the whole day with programming. But watching the early-morning chitchat beginning at 7:00 A.M. daily, you can still just about begin to see the whole procession unfold before your eyes.

9

Disneyland and the Creation of the Seamless Entertainment Web

(ABC, CBS, AND NBC: 1954–90)

When you think of the name Disney, you still more than likely think primarily of movies and theme parks—of films like *The Lion King* and *Aladdin,* and of Walt Disney World, the country's major tourist attraction. Few think of "Disney" in terms of television, even though it now owns ABC through its holding company Capital Cities, offers the Disney Channel on cable, and in the nineties produced such TV shows as *Home Improvement*.

Yet Disney was a pivotal company in the history of television almost from the beginning—not so much for what it broadcast, but for what it accomplished from a business standpoint. Virtually alone among Hollywood executives who tended to shun the new medium because of the threat it could pose to movie box offices, Walt Disney embraced TV in the 1950s with two popular shows: the daily daytime *The Mickey Mouse Club* and the Wednesday evening offering, *Disneyland,* hosted by Walt himself. Through its episodic films on *Disneyland* (most notably the *Davy Crockett* series), Disney pioneered the concept of the miniseries, paving the way for *Roots* and *The Thorn Birds.* "We're selling corn," Walt Disney once said, "and I like corn."

Disney also shamelessly used his television shows to plug his theme park and movies, pioneering the idea of merging advertising with programming in one seamless presentation. "Never before have so many people made so little objection to so much selling," said one ABC executive at the time. And where Disney trod, the infomercial one day followed. So, too, did Disney's conquest of the entertainment world—from theme parks to movies to television. By the mid-nineties, media critics such as Mark Crispin Miller would document the rise of the "national entertainment state"—in which corporate giants such as Disney, General Electric, Time Warner, and Viacom now controlled a vast interlocking network of broadcast, publishing, and entertainment ventures. These monopolies, Miller wrote, produced "the true causes of those enormous ills that now dismay so many Americans: the universal sleaze and 'dumbing down,' the flood-tide of corporate propaganda, the terminal inanity of U.S. politics." And it all began, on television at least, with *Disneyland*.

Even in the fifties, Disneyism was pervasive. As TV historians like Christopher Anderson have noted, the marriage of promotion and entertainment guided Disney's first steps into television. Early in that decade, Disney was planning his amusement park of the future in southern California. "I saw that if I was ever going to have my park," he said, "here, at last, was a way to tell millions of people about it—with TV." He went to General David Sarnoff at NBC, offering him the Disney cartoon library in return for financing and the chance to publicize the park with a show. Sarnoff told Disney that TV was inevitably a "live" medium with little use for film, and turned him down. So did CBS.

Leonard Goldenson, head of upstart ABC, however, made a deal—and the TV show *Disneyland* was launched. Describing his efforts as "total merchandising," Disney planned to devote roughly a third of each episode to the promotion of either the park or an upcoming Disney film. As Anderson has noted, the show was divided into segments roughly corresponding to Disneyland's worlds—Fantasyland, Adventureland, Frontierland, and Tomorrowland. Many of the segments took viewers behind the scenes as a new Disney film was made or the new park went up. Needless to say, the promotion worked, though it also didn't hurt that ABC, as part of the deal, helped provide a $500,000 loan for the park.

Disneyland opened in July 1955, in a made-for-TV ceremony (another novelty then) cohosted by Ronald Reagan and Art Linkletter.

Meanwhile, rather pedestrian Disney films of the era, such as *20,000 Leagues Under the Sea,* gloried in the TV-show promotion too, setting Disney records for initial box-office grosses.

In retrospect, *Disneyland,* which premiered on October 27, 1954, didn't offer viewers much: Beyond the carefully constructed shilling, Disney mostly recirculated old cartoons and movies. Yet, even then, critics knew a hit when they saw one: "It is hard to see how 'Disneyland' . . . can miss," wrote *Newsweek* after the show's premiere. *Disneyland* was among the top six rated shows during the 1954–55 season, and again in the following year. That made it the first ABC show ever to crack the Top 20—a notable feat because ABC then still had fewer local affiliates than the larger NBC and CBS. Thus *Disneyland*—a slickly produced film show—became a centerpiece of upstart ABC's strategy of countering the live shows and big-name stars on the other two networks with the filmed or taped weekly series, which would eventually become television's mainstay.

Almost no one recalls today the bitter enmity that existed between TV and the movies in the early 1950s. Many Hollywood stars were contractually prohibited from appearing on television, and "LaLa-Land" also owned the film rights to most important literary and dramatic works. Moreover, CBS and NBC were run by New Yorkers with radio backgrounds. When Goldenson took over ABC in 1953, he succeeded in bringing a Hollywood mentality to that network, and the deal with Disney was a first step. "Disney got the place off the ground, and nobody is going to laugh at Mickey Mouse ears on that network," critic John Crosby wrote of ABC then.

Yet the deal eventually changed the medium, too, as the other networks followed the upstart. By the end of the decade, all of the studios had made peace with television; all were producing filmed TV series; and the era of live, dramatic broadcasting was over. Not only that: With more freedom of production, television could now largely usurp the myth-making and comic roles of movies in the culture. Before television, films like *Gone With the Wind* and *The Wizard of Oz* had helped define America, and genuinely funny films by the Marx Brothers and Frank Capra filled the theaters. After television became established in Hollywood, comedy was virtually transferred to television, as the new medium redefined the definition of humor in the culture via variety shows and sitcoms. "There has been more comedy on television in 20 years than the civilized world has seen since the first caveman took the first pratfall for the tribe," a critic in the *New York Times* wrote once. Moreover, with few exceptions (principally in the area of children's movies), the magic moments in mass culture emigrated from the big screen to the small one.

When Disney turned to original programming in his initial seasons on television, he hit it big. That first season of 1954–55 saw the premiere, beginning on December 15, of a three-part saga on Davy Crockett starring Fess Parker—"Davy Crockett, Indian Fighter"; "Davy Crockett Goes to Congress"; and "Davy Crockett at the Alamo"—whose units were presented a month apart. The series ended up sparking television's first cult craze, as coonskin caps sold by the thousands. In the seven months that followed, over $100 million worth of "Crockett" items were sold (many of them, of course, licensed by Disney), accounting for about 10 percent of all domestic children's product sales at the time. It was also the beginning of a heritage craze that would sweep the nation, beginning with the Alamo shrine itself, now elevated from a local San Antonio monument to a major tourist destination. (By the eighties, San Antonio—once a sleepy town—would be considered one of the hotspots of America.) Eventually every major American city would do its best to sell its own historical sites, even if Disney hadn't plugged them.

For all the criticism Disney would receive in the nineties for attempting to build a Civil War theme park in Virginia (which never got off the ground), the "Crockett" series did a lot on its own to alter traditional views of history. In the fifties, critics had a field day pointing out that the real Davy Crockett "would bear any hardship to escape a routine day's work," couldn't have shot 105 bears in nine months because he "couldn't count that high," and "was never king of anything except maybe the Tennessee Tall Tales and Bourbon Samplers Assn." Yet it didn't matter: Kids now revered him. In future years, Disney would follow with miniseries about Zorro, the Swamp Fox, Johnny Tremaine, and the adventures of Texas John Slaughter—many of which placed children at the center of historical events.

The Mickey Mouse Club, which ran from 1955 to 1959 on weekday afternoons, also played a role in the conversion of Disney into a household TV name. Unlike much of the children's programming that preceded it, *The Mickey Mouse Club* wasn't presented before a studio audience, and it featured taped serials, such as "Spin and Marty" and "The Hardy Boys," which could be repeated for more profits. The show was obviously used to popularize Disney attractions and products, like those mouse ears that the Mouseketeers wore. It also featured more ads than any show up to that point—22 an episode. In 1955, Mattel bought 15 minutes of those ads a week—half the amount that the entire toy industry had put into television only the year before. This was another step in a process which culminated years later when marketers of children's toys (through tie-ins featuring G.I. Joe and the Transformers) virtually controlled Saturday morning programming.

The Mickey Mouse Club also converted its young stars into miniversions of Davy Crockett—celebrities in their own right. Long before there were Davy Jones, *The Partridge Family, The Brady Bunch,* New Kids on the Block, and even the Lion King characters, there were Annette, Doreen, Karen, Cubby, and Bobby. The show's theme song, like Howdy Doody's, even became a national battle cry ("M-I-C-K-E-Y M-O-U-S-E!") for budding baby boomers.

In the decades that followed, Disney's television offerings never reached that influence again, though they did continue to embody the values that parents would hold dear. Disney shows never had much violence, and they professed a nostalgic optimism which eventually became so much a part of the culture that it would someday be hard to tell where Disneyism stopped and Reaganism began. *The Wonderful World of Color,* one of the first TV shows to expand the tint spectrum, created a splash when it premiered in 1961 ("The world is a carousel of color," went the theme song), but it was more notable for the way that it, too, merged the values of commercialism and entertainment. Since NBC was owned by RCA and was anxious to have a show that hyped the value of owning a color set, Walt helped do for color TV what he'd done for Disneyland. Over the next 29 years, the show changed names five times, and networks twice—making it one of the few series in the medium's history to eventually land on all three major networks. Like its predecessor, this show ended up relying on the 1950s routine of recycling old movies and cartoons, and occasionally presenting a new miniseries—although Disney did manage to introduce one new cartoon character in Ludwig Von Drake, an uncle of Donald Duck. When the show left network television in 1990, virtually no one complained.

By then, Disney's preoccupation with using all media forms to create "an image in the public mind," as Walt once put it, had led the company into the cable programming and video business earlier than most competitors. The Disney Channel premiered in 1983, and became one of the more solid cable networks. It essentially combined the standard Disney formula of traditional values with a new one of no commercials (Who needed them? Disney was one big commercial!), along with the recirculation of old cartoons and movies, an updated *Mouse Club,* and soft documentaries (aimed at baby-boom parents) on subjects like the rock band Fleetwood Mac.

As for videos, Disney understood earlier than most that children will watch a home-use tape again and again, making cassettes one of the hotter new media markets of the eighties and nineties. Thus, the Top Ten best-seller video list is still often dominated by several Disney titles at any one time. In the summer of 1994, the Walt Disney Company had the rare distinction of having the Number 1 movie, record, and video in the country, while producing the nation's top-rated TV show, *Home Improvement.* And then it bought the most powerful network of its time, ABC—an appropriate move, since it was ABC that helped get Disney established in the medium.

Once, when a reporter asked Disney what he was proudest of, he replied, "The whole damn thing." Acquiring or assembling that "whole damn thing" became the future of the industry. By weaving together the worlds of television and movies, programming and advertising, and adult programming and children's programming, Walt Disney made his TV offerings part of a seamless mesh of entertainment. Today, we are all ensnared in Walt's web.

10

The Secret of *The Lawrence Welk Show*
(ABC: 1955–71; SYNDICATION: 1971–82)

Perhaps the best way to assess *The Lawrence Welk Show*—and the critical questions about television that it has always sparked—is to go back to 1991, when Congress became embroiled in a dispute as to whether it should appropriate $500,000 to Welk's hometown of Strasburg, North Dakota, for a German-Russian settlers' museum. The indirect tribute to Welk (whose homestead did later become a museum, thanks to private contributions) was perhaps that year's leading symbol of pork-barrel politics as congressmen and editorialists rushed to attack both Welk and the appropriation. "We can no longer afford projects that have little or no merit," said Rep. Cliff Stearns of Florida, in a typical comment during the debate. "Can anybody in this body argue that restoring the birthplace of Lawrence Welk is absolutely essential?"

Absolutely essential? Obviously not. But commendable, appropriate, and worthy of support? Most definitely. It's hard to tell whether the members of the 102nd Congress had no sense of history, were out of touch, or were just being ornery. But "the Champagne Music Man" and his birthplace deserved better. Few Americans have been as popular with as many for as long as the Guy Lombardo of the Corn Belt. Welk was one of TV's first and most lasting superstars—the Geritol set's Elvis. At one point in the 1950s he hosted two national shows a week, helped pitch Dodge cars, had records near the top of the charts, and was the subject of profiles in *Life* and *Look,* not to mention on TV's *This Is Your Life*. In that unique era, Welk was ubiquitous in a way few achieve, a Michael Jordan for the Eisenhower era.

Of course, trashing Welk has never been anything new. "What has Welk got?" asked *Time* in 1957. "According to the critics, nothing," it answered. But audiences loved him, beginning in the 1920s, when he pioneered the musical variety format on radio in the Dakotas. For decades he led one of the most successful dance bands in the nation. In the summer of 1955, ABC put him on at 9:00 on Saturday nights, and within a year his audience had grown from 7.1 million to 32.5 million on a show called *The Dodge Dancing Party*. (To be sure, ABC got carried away a bit when they also had Welk host—unsuccess-fully—a show aimed at teenagers: *Lawrence Welk's Top Tunes and New Talent*.)

By 1957, *Life* was calling Welk "the most popular musician in U.S. history." By that time, the 53-year-old Mr. "Wunnerful, Wunnerful" was drawing television audiences of 40–50 million, or roughly one-fifth of the nation's population. Despite cancellation by ABC in 1971 (not because the show's audience was too small, but too old, and therefore unattractive to advertisers), Welk's show continued in syndi-cation for 11 years—one of the earliest shows to take that route in first run successfully. The Welk program was, even in the nineties, among the most watched PBS shows in the nation: A 1991 count revealed that over 200 stations ran repeats of the Liberace of the Accordion's shows each week.

What was Welk's secret? Perhaps it was the way he took the en-semble format and applied it to musical variety. Welk was not Ed Sul-livan introducing you to New York's hottest acts. He was instead a proud midwestern immigrant father letting you spend an hour each week with his extended family. Each episode, viewers were treated not only to Welk, but also to "da luffly Lennon Sisters" (whom he discov-ered when his son dated one of them), accordionist Myron Floren, singer-pianist Larry Hooper, violinist Aladdin, dancers Barbara Boylan and Bobby Burgess (a former Mouseketeer), and the chanteusey Champagne Lady (originally Alice Lon, and later Norma Zimmer). Decades before the producers of *ER* and *L.A. Law* discovered that it's easier to hold an audience if you give them a number of sympathetic characters, Welk was doing the same.

Or maybe the key to Welk's success was his low-key personality. Kathy Lennon once called him "a constant in the constantly changing world." In an era when the more boisterous Jackie Gleasons and Sid Caesars drew most of the critical acclaim, Welk plodded along with his predictable "an' a one, an' a two." The pictures weren't any better: "You can turn your TV set upside down while we're on the air," Welk once said. But much of his appeal came from his very reliability. Welk understood earlier than most that the personalities who would tend to last on the medium were those that tread softly. "He makes us feel comfortable; we feel we know him so well; he's just like we are; he's right in our living room," were comments *Life* attributed to his TV fans in its 1957 profile. Years before Walter Cronkite or, indeed, Ronald Reagan discovered what sort of persona it took to survive and prosper in the world of television, Welk was paving the way.

Or it could be that Welk just understood a significant portion of his audience better than most, which means he understood that part of America once called the Silent Majority. "If we have a comedian who just once says or does anything out of line, then that's a danger point for the children," he once said. "It makes for an unhealthy atmosphere and it will show up on the program. The mothers who watch our show are just not going to like it." Welk was said to keep a "fever chart" of performers, listing the ratio of their positive to negative mail, and what types of music his audience liked or hated. And he *really* knew what they liked, playing the kind of mainstream, polka-type music that rock was driving right off the charts and out of the stores.

Welk's "rules" sometimes caused problems for the performers. "There was a dress code that everyone had to live up to," his manager, Sam Lutz, once said. "And that got to be a problem when he started working with a younger generation of people in the music business." No one would confuse the Lennon Sisters with Janis Joplin, but even they left the show in 1968. "[H]e wanted to give people music he thought they could understand, and he didn't think they could understand Beatles songs or Stevie Wonder songs," Kathy Lennon was once quoted as saying.

Politically correct he wasn't: The Italian people are "a musical race always wid a song in dare heart," Welk once said. Yet clearly he was on to something: Long before there were Super Bowl halftime shows, or *Hee Haw,* or televised visits to flag factories by politicians, Welk was practically inventing TV corn pone. And his audiences ate it up. He was among the first to teach marketers—political and commercial— that a wide schism had developed between the urban coastal cultures and the more-populous "other America." It was a lesson lost on many elites as, beginning in the 1960s, intellectuals began bashing John Wayne films regularly and, on a larger scale, lauded growing government bureaucracies that took power out of the heartland and put it in the hands of "experts" who supposedly knew better. Yet others learned their lesson from Welk, including those with such names as Wallace,

Nixon, Reagan, and (eventually) H. Ross Perot—the lattermost of whose 1992 rallies often seemed to include a Welk-like entertainer or two.

That was the really surprising thing about the way in which political Washington a few years ago turned on Welk and, by implication, on his old neighbors. It's not as if both parties, for example, still don't need to woo the constituency he represented. When asked to explain his popularity, Welk once said, "There seem to be a lot of midwesterners everywhere." For a group of leaders considered to be wholly out of touch with mainstream America, you'd think congressmen would be lining up to sing Welk's praises. The Bubble King doesn't deserve a museum? Maybe not according to the denizens of Manhattan, Washington, and the west side of Los Angeles. But anywhere else—it would be an honor.

11

The Ed Sullivan Show and the Era
of Big Government
(CBS: 1948–71)

Once a CBS fixture on Sunday nights at 8:00 Ed Sullivan is worth recalling for both what he changed and what he represented in American culture. As the country's leading TV impresario—and thus the national arbiter of taste—Sullivan sold the masses on everyone from Martin & Lewis to Elvis to the Beatles. More importantly, Sullivan symbolized an era in American life when large institutions and larger-than-life figures created a national culture in the midst of our diverse disunity. From John Glenn to Walter Cronkite to Jack Kennedy, Sullivan presided over a bygone era of Really Big Heroes, Really Big Networks, and Really Big Government. Not to mention 1,087 Really Big Shows—a.k.a. "Rilly Big Shews."

Life once called him television's "only institution." Yet he was an odd man for the job of national emcee, a job he assumed almost from the moment he hosted *Toast of the Town* on June 20, 1948, with a show introducing that new comedy team of Martin & Lewis, until he left the air on June 6, 1971. A sportswriter who became a gossip columnist for New York's *Graphic* as well as the *Daily News,* Sullivan couldn't sing, act, dance, joke, or juggle, even though he had hosted some vaudeville in the 1930s, and some of the first telethons. One writer called him "cod-eyed and cement-faced." A certain suspicious viewer thought Sullivan, with his hands continually in his pockets, must have been suffering from a disease. "You're a real inspiration to us all," said yet another, upon meeting him. "It takes a real man to get up there week after week—with that silver plate in your head." Asked *New York Herald Tribune* TV critic John Crosby: "One of the small but vexing questions confronting anyone in this area with a television set is: 'Why is Ed Sullivan on it every Sunday night?'"

As *TV Guide* once noted, Sullivan was legendary for his botched introductions, such as when he shouted, "Let's hear it for the Lord's Prayer!" after Sergio Franchi sang it on the air; and when he introduced some New Zealand natives as "the fierce Maori tribe from New England." "Please welcome to our stage José Feliciano," he said one night. "He's blind, and he's Puerto Rican!" Milton Berle he was not. But Sullivan was, in the McLuhanesque sense, very cool, and he fit the new style of television more than people then realized. "I was on the ground floor of radio and dropped out of it like a dope," he once said. "Now I'm on the ground floor of TV, and I'm not giving up my lease until the landlord evicts me."

His show featured stars every week, but they were always sandwiched between acts like the West Point glee club, tumblers from behind the Iron Curtain, bullfighters, ventriloquists, an actor reading the Bible, puppet shows, and Albert Schweitzer on the organ. Booked on a $375 talent budget, that first *Toast of the Town* in 1948 featured Martin & Lewis, Oscar Hammerstein, a pianist, a ballerina, a singing fireman, and the referee of the Joe Louis-Jersey Joe Walcott fight. "I don't think there's anything that, expertly done, the public won't go for," Sullivan once said—and he was generally right about that.

Sullivan was known to make occasional new-talent finds—and not just because Bob Hope, Dinah Shore, Walt Disney, and Victor Borge made their television debuts on his show. A 17-year-old Liza Minnelli appeared on Ed's stage, as did 10-year-old Itzhak Perlman. It is said that Sullivan "discovered" Richard Pryor, as well as the Singing Nun. In an era when black performers had trouble getting on TV, he head-lined Ella Fitzgerald, Duke Ellington, and Lena Horne. On the other hand, Rickie Layne appeared 40 times, and Myron Cohen 41, and Wayne and Shuster made 46 trips to the Really Big Show. (The all-time leader was the amazingly convincing Italian puppet mouse, Topo Gigio, with 50.) In 1954, Will Jordan became the first of many im-pressionists to imitate Sullivan. Then came Jackie Mason, whom clock-watching Sullivan thought flipped him "the bird" upon being shown a finger signal of time left, thus precipitating a decades-long feud.

Still, Sullivan's influence on popular culture was enormous, begin-ning in the 1950s when he first caught on. "Ed Sullivan will be a suc-cess," the acerbic comedian Fred Allen once said, "as long as other people have talent." It's fair to say that by putting his version of the *Good Housekeeping* seal on Elvis Presley and the Beatles, Sullivan in-stantly made them national icons, thus helping them to sell millions of records. It's difficult to recall how far removed rock music was from the mainstream—and, not coincidentally, from prime-time TV—be-fore Sullivan pushed it to center stage.

There was a price meted out to the performers, of course: The Rolling Stones appeared six times, but had to change "Let's spend *the night* together" to "Let's spend *some time* together," and network exec-utives objected to Bob Dylan, who walked out after a rehearsal when informed he couldn't sing "Talkin' John Birch Society Blues" because of its overt politics. Jim Morrison of the Doors was told he couldn't sing the line "You know we couldn't get much higher" during "Light My Fire," ignored the edict, and was never invited back.

Few now remember that Elvis had actually been on television more than a half-dozen times before Sullivan was persuaded to feature him on three Sundays, beginning in September 1956. Still, when Elvis fi-nally appeared on the show on September 9, after Ed had spent months hyping his performance while simultaneously encouraging critics in private to attack him for obscenity, around 60 million Americans tuned in, the largest audience in TV history to that point. Those millions who watched Elvis perform "Don't Be Cruel," "Ready Teddy," "Hound Dog," and "Love Me Tender" made up a phenomenal 82.6 percent of the viewing audience, the largest in TV history to that point. (Sullivan had been in a car wreck, and missed the show. Host Charles Laughton introduced Elvis as "Elvin Presley.")

By the third and final show on January 6, 1957, with the audience diminishing, Sullivan announced that he was ordering his cameramen to shoot Elvis only from the waist up, an obvious attempt to rekindle a publicity spark that nonetheless worked so well that most Americans still don't remember that Sullivan had already shown Elvis full-figure twice before. By the time it was over, of course, Elvis had been transformed into a cultural icon, and even Sullivan had been impressed. On air, he said:

> This will be the last time we'll run into each other for a while. . . . And I wanted to say to Elvis Presley and the country that this is a real decent, fine boy. And wherever you go, Elvis . . . we want to say that we've never had a pleasanter experience on our show with a big name than we've had with you. You're thoroughly all right—so let's have a tremendous hand for a very nice person!

That process of transformation would be repeated endlessly on TV—not the least with the Beatles, whom Sullivan "discovered" when his plane landed at London's Heathrow Airport in the fall of 1963 and was overrun by screaming fans waiting for the rock group. When the Fab Four appeared, on February 9, 1964, for the first of three consecutive appearances, they too attracted the largest audience for a show in the history of the medium up until that point—around 70 million viewers. ("Next week, the Beatles and the Pietà!" Sullivan once announced.)

The variety show, of which Sullivan was undisputed king, was a revamped descendant of vaudeville—the entertainment of "the people." It was so popular in the late forties and fifties that it even flourished on daytime TV, on shows such as *The Arthur Godfrey Show* and *Art Linkletter's House Party*. Thus Sullivan's thorough success helped solidify television as a democratic medium through which the pursuits of the lower classes would triumph over the opera, symphony, and theater alike. Today, even if its democratic ethos still pervades television, variety shows no longer exist, having fallen victim to the move long ago toward multiple-set ownership within families (which ended "one thing for everybody" programming) and to taped shows which could run in syndication for years. Now, with cable television and its specialized niches, anyone can watch rock-and-roll 24 hours a day. To the extent that the excitement of live performances still exists on television, it does so on the likes of *Saturday Night Live,* award shows, late-night talk shows, and—ironically—such news-programming specials as the O.J. Simpson trial. When Ronald Reagan used to introduce American heroes to the audience during his State of the Union speeches, he, too, was in a fashion only following in Sullivan's footsteps.

There is a pervasive nostalgia today for Sullivan, as for the simpler time he personified—when the whole country gathered around TV sets and shared experiences preselected by someone else. His show has become perhaps the best symbol of an era when television provided a national and cohesive culture in the midst of our disunion. Which raises the question: Has anyone taken Sullivan's place?

The answer, of course, is that *we* have. In the cable age, we don't need benign autocrats such as Sullivan or Cronkite telling us who is really big, or that's the way it is. Flipping channels, we judge for ourselves. In the postmodern era, Sullivan's New York is no longer the center of the universe, just as the three major networks aren't at the epicenter of broadcasting anymore, and Washington's big government is no longer the focus of voters' lives. In the diversity that comes with freedom, the trend in this country is to decentralization and choice, even at the risk of some disorder.

That movement, in fact, is consistent with the drift of American history. As Alexis de Tocqueville noted over 150 years ago, America is a fragmented, atomized nation whose people have usually been free to pursue their own varied interests. "It isn't easy to imagine America without the Big Networks," media analyst Barbara Matusow once wrote—but that's only true if you refuse to crack open a history book that covers the period 1781–1932. The cohesiveness and national sense of unity that the networks offered for so brief a period were the historical aberration—not the other way round.

That means there may even be a trenchant political lesson in the saga of Ed Sullivan. Really Big Shows have gone the way of the New Deal, the central city, the labor union, and, not coincidentally, the old Democratic Party of LBJ and Tip O'Neill. The ordered, simpler, "bigger is better" past that the Sullivan show recalls might be a really nice place to revisit for an evening. But like a lot of aspects of our past, you can't go home again.

12

Gunsmoke and Television's Lost Wave of Westerns
(CBS: 1955–75)

"You could almost say the history of television was written in Gunsmoke," Cecil Smith, a television critic, once wrote in the *Los Angeles Times;* and it was true, perhaps, for television's first quarter-century. The show, after all, was TV's longest-running prime-time series with continuing characters: 640 episodes for almost 20 years to the day, from September 10, 1955 to September 1, 1975. It was the Number 1 rated show in the country for four years in a row (1957–61), and sat tall in the Top Ten saddle for a dozen of its 20 seasons on the air.

The popularity of *Gunsmoke* helped trigger a wave of Westerns which came to dominate television in its early days. The year before it premiered, there were only a handful of Westerns, like *The Lone Ranger,* on the air, but only four years later, six of the top seven rated shows were Westerns: *Gunsmoke, Wagon Train* (which itself went to Number 1 for the 1961–62 season), *Have Gun Will Travel, The Rifleman, Maverick,* and *Tales of Wells Fargo.*

In the next year, there were 30 Westerns on the networks in prime time (the broadcast equivalent of 400 feature films), and horses were being paid more than actors. Some cost-conscious observer figured that it set producers back $3,000 every time a wagon burned on one of these shows, and *Wagon Train* alone burned more than a hundred. Things got so crowded, hero-wise, that, in the 1958–59 season, two different shows were set in Dodge City that featured different lawmen—Wyatt Earp and Matt Dillon. So Earp moved to Tombstone for the following season. In 1961, actor Barry Sullivan stated emphatically: "If Shakespeare were alive today, he'd be writing Westerns."

Many of those Westerns did turn out to be memorable, as did their stars. This is, after all, the genre that launched Clint Eastwood, James Garner, Michael Landon, Steve McQueen, Chuck Connors, and Gene Barry. Westerns sat atop the year-end ratings for eight of the 10 years between 1958 and 1967. None of these shows, however, turned out to be as notable or enduring as *Gunsmoke*—which ran on Saturday nights on CBS at 10:00 for its first 13 years, then moved to Tuesdays, and eventually to Mondays, much earlier in the evening. A carryover from radio (on which William Conrad, later the star of *Jake and the Fatman,* had assumed the role of Marshal Matt Dillon), the show already had a history to build on which gave it greater range than the rest. It was designed to be an "adult Western" focusing more on character than on action—a trend which would be picked up by shows such as *Maverick,* and by a Shakespeare-quoting Paladin on *Have Gun Will Travel.*

TV Guide had originally described *Gunsmoke* as a "Western Dragnet," but it didn't turn out that way. Introduced for the first episode by John Wayne, CBS's original choice for the role of Dillon, *Gunsmoke* starred the six-foot-six James Arness as the loner who was to keep order in Dodge City. (Raymond Burr, later to play Perry Mason, was turned down for the role because he was "too big.") Arness was joined by Dennis Weaver as his deputy, Chester Goode, who left the show in 1964 ("Muster Dellon," he always said); Amanda Blake as Kitty Russell, the softhearted owner of the Long Branch Saloon, who finally got to kiss her lawman after 70 episodes; Milburn Stone as grumpy "Doc" Adams; and a supporting cast which featured Burt Reynolds for four years (as the half-Indian blacksmith, Quint Asper), and Sam Peckinpah as a writer.

The keys to success for *Gunsmoke* were the sophistication and subtleties it brought to its characters. "We worked on the character of Matt Dillon," CBS vice-president Hubbell Robinson once said. "We made him a man with doubts, confused about the job he had to do." Like many other popular shows of the era, the stars also did commercials which blended in with the show. "Live modern: Change to L&M," Arness shilled.

With the characters presented as a large, extended Western family, the shows became a kind of weekly morality play. "I think primarily the reason for *Gunsmoke*'s longevity . . . was the *Gunsmoke* family," Weaver once said. "The people were very likable, very human, very believable." "This is the only show on TV where the characters sit around a barroom and say hello for half an hour," Amanda Blake said. And the stories were consistent: "The words that can kill this show," producer John Mantley once said, "are 'Let's do it differently!' "

In one typical episode, Matt faced down a crooked farmer who failed to provide for his family. In another, Matt protected from angry citizens of Dodge City an Indian woman who needed medical help. The show won an award with an episode about two bounty hunters who raffled off shares in an outlaw they wanted to kill. There was, of course, the usual residue of violence. "What is *Gunsmoke* without gunsmoke?" asked one critic—and in fact the show may be best remembered for its weekly infamous opening-credit scene of Matt walking onto Main Street for a showdown that some critics later compared to Kennedy's faceoff with Khrushchev during the Cuban Missile Crisis.

Still, the broader issues that *Gunsmoke* raises concern the entire Western genre itself on TV: What did it reflect and teach to Americans—and could it be popular again? Hollywood, of course, has always been attracted to Westerns—the mythic epics of American pop culture. Throughout this century, they have almost always appealed to us, and indeed the history of the country is a Western, in that it is the story of heading west and bringing civilization to the frontier.

The movie industry began at about the same time the Western began to gain readership popularity: Owen Wister's *The Virginian,* published in 1902, singularly defined the cowboy hero for decades to come, and within a matter of months the big screen had its first definitive Western too. The two developments neatly complemented each other. The Western novel offered this new industry action, violence, and easily recognizable villains and heroes. Many of the founders of the film business were also Westerners, conversant with the myths they were creating. Thus, as the entertainment industry grew, so did the number of cowboy films. Indeed, until 1960 more than a quarter of *all* American movies were Westerns. Audiences liked the action, the simplicity, and the symbolism. And they loved William S. Hart, Tom Mix, Gary Cooper, John Wayne, and Gene Autry (the "singing cowboy"). Even radio—a medium that could never convey the proper sagebrush setting—cashed in on the craze, with shows like *The Lone Ranger.*

As popular as movies were, however, they didn't reach into living rooms. Television did, and its infatuation with Westerns really began in 1955, even though the genre had been on the tube since the late forties. In 1955, William Warner produced the first one-hour filmed TV series, *Warner Brothers Presents,* featuring three shows in rotation—one based on *Casablanca,* another on *King's Row,* and a third on *Cheyenne.* Given its experience with the movies, Warner thought the first two series would succeed best, but *Cheyenne* became the favorite of viewers.

Once Westerns began catching on, there were as many explanations as there were Westerns. "The Western story offers us a chance to return to the soil, a chance to redefine our roots," said Ernest Dichter, a motivational researcher. "The Western is just the neatest and quickest type of escape entertainment, that's all," said ABC's program director, Tom Moore.

Yet there was more to this early marriage than those explanations. A TV show has little room for dramatic complexity or character development, *Gunsmoke* and its "adult" brethren notwithstanding. With its simple formulas and constant action, the Western fit the medium's requirements perfectly. Standup comedians complained that they were being driven off television, but Hubbell Robinson noted that, whereas the same Western story could be told in three different ways, the same joke was always the same joke. Besides, said a writer for Phil Silvers, "A man can wear himself out more easily than a horse." Moreover, TV was new: The Western helped place this strange medium in a traditional context which made audiences feel comfortable. It's a "taproot in the American tradition, a meaning beyond the moment," theorized *Time* during the TV Western's heyday. And the studios obviously knew how to make them.

Yet Westerns changed the focus of television drama—then mostly live—from conflicts concerning inner life to those on the outside. Once the change was made, TV never looked back until the nineties.

These outer-directed stories also appealed to advertisers, because they were often allegories of the ads themselves: A problem (outlaws or clogged drains) can be solved in a short period by someone or something with know-how (a sheriff or Drano).

Politicians in this era also loved the conservative values embodied in the Western, with its emphasis on individualism, small government, and traditional values. In TV Westerns, the message was clear: It's not the law or big government which can make America a great place to live in, but the basic decency of the good man. One night in 1953, President Dwight Eisenhower, "the man from Abilene," threw away his prepared text and told a civil-rights dinner crowd:

> I was raised in a little town of which most of you have never heard, but in the West it's a famous place. It's called Abilene, Kansas. We had as marshal for a long time a man named Wild Bill Hickok. If you don't know him, read your Westerns more. Now, that town had a code—and I was raised as a boy to prize that code.

The Western's "Us Versus Them" mentality also reflected and reinforced the Cold War paranoia of the fifties. "When Eisenhower described the world as 'forces of good and evil arrayed as never before,' he was offering a picture viewers could recognize," TV historian Eric Barnouw has written.

Ralph and Donna Brauer have described the procession of Westerns on television as "the horse, the gun, and the property." The "horse" Westerns of the early and mid-fifties defined the first wave. These shows tended to be for children (*The Lone Ranger, Roy Rogers, Hopalong Cassidy, Annie Oakley*), with Trigger or Silver, the horses, playing leading roles. The shows displayed little sophistication, often featuring good guys in white hats for hire, usually assisted by a humorous sidekick, such as Andy Devine (Jingles, the sidekick to Wild Bill Hickok).

The second wave of Westerns flourished in the late fifties: the adult "gun" Westerns, like *Gunsmoke*. If they caught on, it was in no small part because it was easier to get away with violence if you put it in a Western context—though by today's standards the violence was relatively benign. Wyatt Earp, for example, didn't kill his first man until he'd been on the air almost three years. Still, with gunfights often the principal attraction, many of these shows featured guns, or at least portended violence, in their titles: *The Restless Gun, Gunsmoke, Colt .45, Have Gun Will Travel, Yancy Derringer, Wanted—Dead or Alive,* and *The Rifleman,* which featured former baseball player Chuck Connors as a cowboy who could twirl his weapon like a baton. "You know what differentiated them?" former CBS programming chief Mike Dann once asked. "The size of the gun. Steve McQueen had a sawed-off shotgun. Chuck Connors had a rifle. Paladin put a revolver in a holster with a chess knight on it."

By 1960, the "property Western" had begun to emerge, drawn from shows like *Rawhide* ("Head 'em up, move 'em out!"). On shows such as *Bonanza* and *The Big Valley,* the emphasis was less on violence and more on family management of real estate. Often the heroes went from being individualists to members of a group—no surprise, given the oncoming collectivism of the sixties. For some, *Bonanza* was nothing more than suburbia transferred to the Ponderosa, and Ben Cartwright was only another version of Ward Cleaver, or Jim Anderson of *Father Knows Best.* To others the popular show's three young brothers—Adam, Hoss, and Little Joe—recalled the Kennedys. "Women used to be the big stars," Michael Landon, who played Little Joe, said then. "But these days, it's men. So *Bonanza* has four of them in a supermarket setup. You don't have to turn on four different channels to get the father type; the big, lovable bear type; the handsome, brooding type—and me. . . ."

In its mid-sixties heyday, *Bonanza* proved to be one of the most popular shows in TV history, eventually anchoring NBC's Sunday-night coverage. The show had come to NBC in 1959 because the network was anxious to promote another big series in color, and thereby help sell more color sets. Yet the initial critical reaction to the show—then running early on Saturday nights—often was negative. Jack Gould of the *New York Times* called the series "disastrous," while another critic called the show "early-Autry at its most advanced . . . a terrible waste of color."

The series prospered, however, once it moved to Sundays at 9:00 P.M. two years later, in the fall of 1961, as the replacement for Dinah

Shore. "You know exactly what's going to happen in most 'Bonanza' scripts," a writer for the show once said in trying to account for its popularity. "And in this uncertain world, stability is comfort devoutly to be sought." At least one of the stars, Pernell Roberts (who played Adam and eventually left the show), was more cynical. "Look at the setup of the show. Strange man," he once said. "The Ponderosa is a little kingdom of very rich people, with Ben Cartwright as absolute monarch. No women to speak of, three of the four men troubled as adolescents. . . ."

By the mid-sixties, however, the Western had virtually disappeared from television screens; *Bonanza* was finally toppled in the ratings by CBS's *The Smothers Brothers Comedy Hour,* which premiered in 1967. Overexposure was clearly a problem. So, too, was the Western's appeal to a predominantly rural audience now less attractive to advertisers. President Kennedy's "New Frontier" had helped make the Old West begin to seem obsolete; his presidency helped begin the shift of television's allegories from Westerns to spy and outer-space shows, as cowboys exchanged their six-guns for ray guns.

The emerging restlessness and violence of the rest of the decade clearly played a major role, too. In the wake of the Kennedy assassination in 1963, and the turbulence of the civil-rights movement and the counterculture, the whole premise of the traditional Western began to seem suspect. American values were in doubt. Loners began to be viewed as questionable. Tombstone seemed to resemble a police state. Rugged masculinity was out of favor. Persecution of Indians seemed racist. And there was Vietnam. By the seventies, when a national concern about crime might have triggered a rebirth of the Western, Tombstone had become New York, and the "urban cowboy" fought muggers rather than desperadoes. Kojak was the new cowboy.

Given that rapidly eroding taste for TV Westerns, it is a tribute to *Gunsmoke* that it lasted as long as it did. Slated for cancellation in 1967, the show was continued at the urging of CBS president William Paley, whose wife liked it, and survived for eight years longer by concentrating even more than before, in its new 8:00 P.M. time slot, on children and family issues: Festus visits his relatives or Doc seeks a home for orphaned triplets. Shows about the rights of minorities began to appear more frequently, as did guest stars. The opening sequence changed, too, as the old violent showdown was discarded for shots of Dillon riding across the plains. Yet by 1975, the show had fallen out of the Top 20 for the first time since 1967, and its audience was still demographically unappealing—predominantly old and rural. That finally killed it.

The decline of the Western would presage the decline in popularity of television drama in general. Between 1972 and 1995, only two other dramas—*Dallas* and *Dynasty*—would lead the ratings again for a season, and their plots and locales owed a fair amount to the Western. From 1970 to the early nineties, prime-time TV would become primarily a medium of comedy.

Yet even as drama returned in popular force to television in the nineties, Westerns did not. Despite the enduring appeal of John Wayne—still the top-rated star in many polls, past and present—the TV Western is dead, and for more than just stylistic reasons. Westerns were the embodiment of a cultural sense that America's rough decency made it a great country. That notion is no longer universally shared by the viewing audience. Moreover, movies can still be for "guys" or "girls"; television, a mass medium, cannot be. Very little today can succeed on TV without appealing to women (even the Olympics), and Westerns seldom did, what with their loner, outer-directed male leads and suppliant women. The psychological and gender revolutions of the past 30 years have made the emotionless Western virtually obsolete. The same fate has met heroes in the Western mold—including a taciturn Kansan from near Dodge City named Bob Dole, whose persona would have fit right into the Westerns of the 1950s, but fell flat in 1996. It is now the age of feelings, and it's hard to imagine Matt Dillon, the sheriff on TV's ultimate adult Western, feeling anybody's pain in the way that Bill Clinton could.

13

American Bandstand and the Clash
of Rock and TV

(ABC: 1957–87)

Rock music and television. Though both arose at nearly the same time in American culture, they appealed to vastly different audiences through vastly different means. Television's strength lay in its visuals; rock in its sound. Television was a mass medium; rock, at least in its early days, appealed to only one demographic group—teenagers. You watched TV in those days in the living room; you listened to rock on the radio in your bedroom. Television gave us *Circus Boy Show* and *The Real McCoys;* rock offered up "Be Bop-a Lula" and "Great Balls of Fire."

Compare Kookie on *77 Sunset Strip* to Little Richard and you begin to understand the early gulf between television and rock that *American Bandstand,* hosted by Dick Clark, tried to bridge. By presenting daily sanitized doses of rock music, Clark ended up influencing the music industry more than anyone else in the history of television. He sought to take the rebellion out of rock so as to guide it into the mainstream, forever recasting the music in television's middle-of-the-road image. And 40 years later, who is to say he didn't succeed?

In one sense, it came down to demographics. On average, teenagers constitute only about 10 percent of the TV audience. They also tend to form an insular audience, usually watching shows or buying products, like Clearasil and Juicy Fruit gum, that are directed at them. That's why the major networks pitch them few shows, leaving them even now, to cable. Look, for example, at what happened to the critically acclaimed *My So-Called Life* on ABC in the mid-nineties: a massive hit among teenagers but a flop among everyone else. Until recently, with the growth of cable, teenagers stood alone in American culture in their allegiance to media other than television. For all the attention now paid to "seminal" baby boom shows like *Leave It to Beaver,* the influence of those programs actually came much later, in a nostalgic afterglow. In the fifties and sixties, radio and music were the principal molders of the teenage boomers—creating for that generation its own early voice and sense of identity.

In the early 1950s, television considered rock way too far out of the mainstream to present to the general public. What with the melange of early fifties variety shows, only a few performers like Bo Diddley and Elvis Presley made appearances on the Steve Allen and Milton Berle programs. It wasn't until Ed Sullivan booked Presley for three appearances beginning in September 1956 that things began to change. On the strength of Elvis's Sullivan-show performances, upstart ABC decided to begin running a national version of an afternoon rock show that had been drawing strong ratings in the Philadelphia area for almost five years, on local station WFIL.

Hosted by a popular local disc jockey, Bob Horn, *Bandstand* had begun in Philadelphia by featuring a group of local teenagers who gathered daily in what looked like a high-school gym, to dance and spin records. "It [*Bandstand*] was invented to use up some afternoon time," Dick Clark once told a reporter in describing the origins of the local predecessor to his hit TV show. He went on:

> Somebody asked, "What can we do to fill up a couple of afternoon hours?" The guys in the studio got together and decided to play games, show short films of musical stars and persuade people to telephone in and request their favorite recordings. They also thought it would be a good idea to invite an audience to watch them. The only audience conveniently located were high school kids on their way home from school.

In the spring of 1956, however, Horn was arrested for driving while intoxicated, right in the middle of a local campaign against drunk driving. He was fired, and the station turned to the genuinely young Dick Clark, then a fairly accomplished radio DJ doing a similar show on Philadelphia radio. Clark had actually already been on TV, reading the Tootsie Roll commercials on *Paul Whiteman's TV Teen Club*, a prime-time ABC show from Philadelphia which had begun in the late forties. On July 9, 1956, Clark took over Horn's local TV show. By August 5, 1957, *Bandstand* had gone national—or "American"—to 67 stations every weekday, and neither rock nor TV would ever be exactly the same.

It could only have happened on ABC. NBC and CBS already had a profitable daytime lineup of soaps, game shows, and talk shows. ABC, however, was still a pathetic third in the competition in 1957, without daytime programming until *Bandstand*. This was a classic example of counterprogramming: While the NBC and CBS shows were geared primarily to housewives, Leonard Goldenson at ABC offered a dirt-cheap show aimed at teens—at just the moment the burgeoning masses of baby boomers were beginning to enter that demographic group. "I once tried to peddle a talk show for kids called *Teenage America* but there was no interest," television writer Mel Diamond once told author Jeff Kisseloff. "They said, 'Who gives a shit about kids? They don't have any buying power.' Elvis proved they were wrong."

Rock, however, was still enormously controversial, and television, of course, hated controversy. Pablo Casals would speak for many when he wrote an essay calling rock an "abomination," "a terrible convulsive sound," and a musical form "against art, against life." Yet Clark's show was not the only regular rock series to be presented on national television during the summer of 1957. *Bandstand* was joined by ABC's *The Big Beat*—which ran on Fridays at 10 P.M. hosted by famed disc jockey Alan Freed, the man said to have coined the term "rock and roll."

Freed presented a far better array of performers than Clark typically did: In four shows his guests included the Everly Brothers, Chuck Berry, Frankie Lymon and the Teenagers, Fats Domino, and Jerry Lee Lewis. Freed, however, was intent on re-creating his successful "live" stage shows directly on TV. They didn't transfer—either to the evening audience or to television's demands. They were too loud, too frenetic, and far too controversial, particularly after Frankie Lymon, a black, was shown dancing with a white girl.

With Clark's help, *Bandstand*—a toned-down version of a rock show—became a better fit for TV and middle America. Unlike Freed, Clark not only highlighted the performers but also established a regular cast of student dancers with whom audiences could identify: Over time, regulars such as Arlene Sullivan, Myrna Horowitz, Carmen Jimenez, and Denny Dzienza became household names, as did Frani

Giordano who made the cover of *Teen* posing with Alvin of the Chipmunks. Clark put the emphasis on dancing, with its visual attraction, rather than on music; it was no coincidence that, over the years, *Bandstand* would start or popularize a number of dance crazes, such as the stroll and the mashed potato.

Clark stressed "lip synching" to recorded music, and sometimes even "air concerts" (featuring performers pretending to play the instruments) ostensibly to improve the sound quality. Yet faking it was also cheaper and easier than doing it live, and solo acts didn't have to bring a backup band. Clark also introduced a segment in which records were rated ("It's got a great beat, and you can dance to it")— thus creating a segment which encouraged a kind of participation at home.

Most important, Clark focused on safe, noncontroversial music and artists alike. Freed—like a lot of early rock disc jockeys—saw his role as introducing black rhythm and blues (R & B) to predominantly white audiences. Clark, who always wore a coat and tie, featured just about everybody at one point or another, but tended to promote more telegenic, white, "teen idols," often from Philadelphia, like Fabian, Frankie Avalon, and Bobby Rydell—teenage versions of such popular TV singers as Perry Como. This had the effect both of making rock more acceptable to parents (still an important point in the days when most households had only one TV set) and of turning early rock into a less rebellious and thus more mainstream product. "We don't try to preach to anybody, but we help to set a good example for the people watching at home," Clark once told *TV Guide*. Even then, however, the show was considered cutting edge for its time. "Some adult squares get the feeling that they are peeking at a hotbed of juvenile delinquency," wrote *Time* in 1958. Clark reassured the nation: "We've never had an incident," he said.

Because television attracted much larger audiences than radio, the show's influence on rock was both enormous and immediate. When rock went through a fallow period in the late fifties—as Buddy Holly died, Elvis went into the army, and Chuck Berry was arrested—there was a vacuum in the industry. Dick Clark, now affectionately known as the "Czar of the Switchblade Set," helped fill it with his *Bandstand* stars and music.

After all, a gold record—a million seller—is the record industry's traditional measure of success. Yet even the lowest rated television shows in the fifties drew audiences several times that size, which meant that TV exposure could weave virtually any song into gold. Nothing illustrated that process better than the story of the decade's biggest hit, "The Ballad of Davy Crockett," which sold over 10 million copies. First aired in December 1954, as the theme song for Walt Disney's popular Crockett "miniseries," the tune was put on record as an afterthought when Disney suggested to the producers that the show could use a narrative song to tie the plot together.

That's why *TV Guide* could write that TV "can sell a new song just as effectively as it sells a sponsor's product." "When appearances are set on any of these shows," wrote *Variety,* "distributors and field men are alerted in order to get full exploitation value out of the appearance and to make sure records are ready to roll. . . ." Even before *Bandstand* premiered nationally, producers were asking scriptwriters of dramatic shows if they could construct entire plots around new releases. "Few songs are written, much less recorded, unless they first satisfy the question, 'What can we do with it on TV?' " *TV Guide* asked. "Let Me Go Lover" became a Number 1 hit in 1954 after being featured on *Studio One. Mr. District Attorney* devoted a script to the pirating of recordings so it could introduce Nat "King" Cole's new hit, "Someone You Love," which promptly shot to Number 1 after the show aired.

It had been widely predicted when *Bandstand* premiered nationally that it wouldn't last: The show was too easy for local stations to replicate—and, in fact, many did. Few at the time, however, figured on how valuable a national show with around eight million viewers (mostly female) could be to the record industry in promoting products and artists, as *Bandstand* spun around 65,000 records and featured 10,000 performers over the years. Buddy Holly, Chuck Berry, Johnny Cash, the Doors, Otis Redding, and the Jefferson Airplane all made their first national TV appearances on *Bandstand,* and Berry even immortalized the show in "Sweet Little 16": ("They'll be rockin' on Bandstand . . . ."). *Bandstand* eventually turned out to be the second longest-running series in ABC history (1957–87)—though the show did go to once-a-week on Saturday afternoons in 1963 and moved to Los Angeles a year later.

Clark's influence was greatest during the "teen idol" period from roughly 1959 to 1963, when his "purified" view of teen culture coincided with the watered-down music of the era. The "love" portrayed in rock during that period was love as seen through the eyes of a 15-year-old on *Bandstand*—going steady, attending the Hop, cruising Main Street in a Chevy. Feelings were not expressed except in the most shallow ways. Girls, for example, had as a role model none other than singer Shelley Fabares of the *Donna Reed Show*, whose dedication to her boyfriend caused her to turn down dates, the better to sit home and contemplate her Johnny Angel. In fact, rock music became so sedately mainstream and removed from the aspirations of youth that when uninfluenced-by-TV British rock hit in 1964, its musical and spiritual authenticity captured the culture completely. At that point, Clark's and television's influence over rock dissipated.

Thus for the rest of the sixties and into the seventies, the youth culture and rock reverted to their status as countercultural forces, nurtured primarily by media geared less to the mainstream. That left Clark on the sidelines, as *Bandstand* became something of a joke, lost on many of the teenagers to whom it was supposedly pitched. Clark tried another afternoon show then, *Where the Action Is,* a kind of outdoor, on-the-beach *Bandstand* featuring Paul Revere and the Raiders. Its influence was negligible too, however, as the musical energy on TV, what little of it there was, shifted to *The Ed Sullivan Show, Hullabaloo,* and *Shindig* in primetime; late-night shows such as *Don Kirshner's Rock Concert;*and the immortal *Soul Train,* the self-described "hippest trip in America" and the black clone of *Bandstand. Soul Train,* which previewed in 1971, had dancing that not only put *Bandstand* to shame, but helped inspire the street dancing craze.

Nonetheless Clark more than survived: Over the years, he ended up producing over 180 shows, and became a pioneer in creating TV's slew of ritual award shows, once even proposing an award show for award shows. He also hosted, among other things, an annual New Year's Eve show, *The $25,000 Pyramid, The Krypton Factor, The Challengers,* and *Inside America* (an early clone of *Entertainment Tonight*), and cohosted with Ed McMahon *TV's Bloopers and Practical Jokes,* another show popular with teenagers. In the mid-1990s, repeats of some of the later *Bandstand* shows could be seen on the cable channel VH-1.

Clark made a lot of hits and a lot of groups through his under-standing of "the business." He once told Creem's Lester Bangs:

A lot of the whole world [that] kids don't understand is politics and money. When you learn politics, money, the advertising world, where the skeletons are buried, you have then matured enough to stay alive. . . . [O]ne must learn to screw the system from within.

To succeed on TV, however, Clark had to present to the world a false image of rock, and therefore of teenagers themselves. "I don't make culture. I sell it," he once admitted. "I'm the storekeeper." To get rock past the censors and sell it to the mainstream—and a much bigger po-tential audience—Clark had to try to domesticate it. His portrait of rock and roll purported to represent youth and their ideals, but instead he portrayed the youth culture mostly in the trivial way that adults wanted to see it. In the sixties, that youth culture ended up as the cyno-sure of the world's eyes—whether in the streets protesting the Vietnam War or in the fields at Woodstock—and authentic rock and roll was its soundtrack. To those who had relied on *American Bandstand* to keep them up to date, it must have all come as an awfully big surprise.

Yet the irony is that rock did eventually follow the trail Clark blazed. When TV and rock were effectively linked again in the eight-ies—this time on a new product called MTV—the taming and com-mercialization of the music as practiced on *American Bandstand* would appear, in contrast, as only so much child's play.

14

Twenty-One, The Quiz Scandal, and the Decline of Public Trust

(NBC: 1956–58)

"It," said President Dwight Eisenhower, "was a terrible thing to do to the American people."

"It" was not the selling of atomic secrets to the Russians. Nor was "it" Ike's pal and adviser, Sherman Adams, improperly accepting a vicuna coat for his wife and embarrassing the Eisenhower administration. "It" was the television quiz-show scandal of 1959—a phenomenon dramatized in Robert Redford's 1994 film *Quiz Show* and analyzed extensively in Kent Anderson's book, *Television Fraud.* In the mid-fifties, television quiz shows such as *Twenty-One, The $64,000 Question,* and *Name That Tune* were among prime time's hottest items, attracting some of the largest audiences in the short history of the medium. The revelation that some of these popular shows had been rigged shocked America, causing a national reappraisal not only of that new phenomenon, television—but also of that older one, the American character. After all, only three months after *The $64,000 Question* premiered on CBS in June 1955, almost half the TV sets in the country were regularly tuned to the show; and its sponsor, the Revlon Corporation, found its sales soaring by more than 50 percent. *The $64,000 Question* ended up being the only game-type show ever to hit Number 1 for a season (1955–56).

So for months after Charles Van Doren confessed to a Senate committee on November 2, 1959 that his victories on the show, NBC's *Twenty-One,* had been fixed, editorial writers asked their readers what had gone wrong with America. "Are we a nation of liars and cheats?" queried the *Christian Century. New York Times* columnist James Reston wrote, "There is an overwhelming feeling here that somehow we have lost our way. Nobody seems to know just how or why, but everybody feels that something's wrong."

Today, the quiz-show scandals hardly seem to qualify as an event worthy of provoking a reexamination of either TV or our national character. At best, they appear to be a footnote in the history of popular culture, a cause for nostalgia. Yet, months later, Ike himself was caught lying about the U-2 spy-plane incident in which American pilot Gary Powers was shot down by the Russians and, for a time, imprisoned. In the following decade came a presidential assassination, complete with charges of conspiracy; and then, almost every week, false reports of "successes" in Vietnam. In 1974, President Nixon was forced to resign amidst the coverup of the Watergate break-in—and the decades since have seen scandals (and the search for them) become a virtual way of life for millions of Americans, as well as the media. The quiz-show scandals didn't only change television history: In many ways, they became a portent of things to come in a now thoroughly skeptical America.

The quiz scandal was the first crack in the facade of its era—a time of affluence, optimism, and the growth of the television habit. In 1950, less than 10 percent of American homes had a TV set. By 1960, the figure had grown to almost 90 percent. The 1950s was the decade of Nixon's "Checkers" speech, live TV drama, and Molly Goldberg. It was also an age of conformity and confidence that bordered on narcissism. "In the West, therefore, there is today a rough consensus among intellectuals on political issues," wrote Harvard sociologist Daniel Bell in *The End of Ideology.* "Egghead" became a populist epithet, while a Monsanto recruiting film glorified the common man: "No geniuses here: just a bunch of average Americans working together."

The quiz shows thrived in this atmosphere. Convinced that good packaging could make knowledge attractive and entertaining, television producer Lou Cowan envisioned the quiz show as an antidote to Joseph McCarthy's anti-intellectualism. Similar shows, such as *Pot O'Gold,* had been popular on radio before—though never for such high dollar stakes. "I've never subscribed to the belief that the average American radio and TV listener has a 12-year-old intelligence," Cowan once said. "The average American has a brain and an integrity that's really wonderful. You just have to look for it. Everybody's smart at something." Because these shows were cheaper to stage than other types, they also became a source of enormous profit to both the networks and the advertisers.

Premiering on June 7, 1955, *The $64,000 Question*—the first big-money, prime-time quiz show—was the prototype. Sponsored by Revlon ("Keep your lips looking luscious longer. . . .") and hosted by the good-looking Hal March, this CBS show, which ran on Tuesdays at 10:00 P.M., was aimed at a female audience. To heighten the program's drama, the contestants, wearing headphones, attempted to answer difficult questions from within isolation booths. ("For $32,000, name the six players besides Ty Cobb who accumulated 3,000 career hits.") To convince home players that the show wasn't rigged, the producers kept the questions under lock and key in a New York bank. Each week, the cameras dutifully showed banker Ben Feit of Manufacturers Trust holding the questions while sitting in the studio at a desk surrounded by armed guards.

The contestants were said to be average Americans who displayed expertise in traditionally American subjects. ("Last week our grand-mother-housekeeper from Buford, Georgia, whose category is base-ball, Mrs. Myrtle Power, answered the $16,000 question.") And, in keeping with the tenor of the times, the show displayed a populist air—and not simply because audiences could participate at home by trying to answer the questions themselves. When Hal March asked Mrs. Power why she would risk her winnings by going for the $32,000 question, she said "So many people have told me that they have confidence in me, and believe I can do it, and have told me so many times, that I've gotten to the point that I believe I can." Norman Vincent Peale couldn't have said it any better. Or, as Max Lerner wrote in the *New York Post:* "It is Huey Long's 'Every man's a king' put into TV language, but altered to say that even ordinary people can become high-bracket taxpayers—at least for one year."

Today we take instant celebrity for granted. Back then, it was new, and the nation fell in love with quiz winners of all types like Van Doren and Mrs. Power, as well as Joyce Brothers (subject: boxing), Gino Prato, Elfreda Von Nardroff, and Mr. and Mrs. Steve Rowland—whose prize was $100 a week for 14 years, after participating on *Do You Trust Your Wife?* Even Ben Feit, the banker, became something of a celebrity and was promoted to vice-president of his bank. The nation also debated the morality of the shows themselves. Some asked why the prizes had to be so lucrative, if the nation valued brains so much.

"It is my idea," wrote John Lardner in the *New Yorker*, "that the producers of these programs concluded long ago that intelligence per se is fundamentally repulsive to the so-called mass audience." Opined *Newsweek:*

> It was probably natural that modern Americans be the first to combine on a grand scale the ancient institution of the giveaway with the ancient institution of the question and answer, their paths smoothed by possession of the world's greatest mass communication system, their appetites for rich sport whetted by the traditional national disapproval of such giveaway diversions as lotteries.

It was *Twenty-One* and its hero, Charles Van Doren, however, that became the nation's conversation piece. Hosted by Jack Barry, who previously was emcee of the kiddie show *Winky Dink & You, Twenty-One* made its prime-time debut on Wednesday, September 12, 1956, on NBC at 10:30 P.M. (It moved to Mondays at 9:00 P.M. in the next season, and then to Thursdays at 8:30 P.M.) Its format was slightly different from that of *The $64,000 Question:* Contestants competed against each other, and stayed on the show, until they lost. This made the winners' personalities crucial to the ratings, because an "unlikable" winner could turn viewers off for months. The show also seemed to go against the populist image of some of the other quiz shows by featuring well-educated professionals who, the show's producers later explained, displayed "poise."

As Redford's movie related, the show's first big winner was Herbert Stempel, who was then working his way through New York's City College. For almost two months Stempel defeated all opponents, winning nearly $100,000. Yet, despite the show's initial success, it still lagged in the ratings. "It was just plain dull," said producer Dan Enright.

On November 28, 1956, Stempel faced a new opponent: Charles Van Doren, who came from one of the country's most famous intellectual families. Van Doren's father, a poet, was an English professor at Columbia; his mother also was a writer. Twenty-nine years old and an instructor at Columbia, the good-looking, six-foot-two-and-a-half-inch Van Doren was later described by a critic as "so likable that he comes to be a 'friend' whose weekly visits the whole family eagerly anticipates."

On their first show together, Van Doren and Stempel earned equal scores. The following week, Van Doren broke the tie and defeated the reigning champion when Stempel missed a key question. Here's how it went:

JACK BARRY: The toughest question of them all. One of the most revered names in American journalism is that of a Kansas newspaper publisher who died in 1944. Tell us this man's name, the name of his newspaper, and the title of the editorial he wrote which made him and his paper nationally known.

HERB STEMPEL: The name of the editor is William Allen White.

BARRY: That is right.

STEMPEL: His paper was the *Emporia Gazette*.

BARRY: That is right. Finally, for 11 points.

STEMPEL: I'll have to think a little bit about the third.

BARRY: Herb, you can take a little time—you go right ahead. It's the title of the editorial we want which he wrote. It made his paper nationally famous, and well known.

STEMPEL: I don't know.

BARRY: No idea?

STEMPEL: Just a moment . . . [mumble].

BARRY: I beg your pardon.

STEMPEL: Just won't help to guess. I don't know.

BARRY: I'm afraid I'm going to have to give it to you then, Herb. The editorial—the title was: "What's the Matter with Kansas?"

Because Van Doren correctly identified Joseph Medill's grandsons, Robert R. McCormick and Joseph Patterson—who had owned the *Chicago Tribune* and *New York Daily News,* respectively—and Henry VIII's last five wives and their fates, he became the new champion.

As Van Doren kept on winning, week after week, the show's ratings rose. By February 19, 1957, he had won $143,000 and was a national hero. According to a *Time* cover story, his persona on the tube was:

Like a boxer staying down for a count of nine he takes all the time he can. . . . When trying to identify the character in *La*

Traviata who sings the aria "Sempre Libera," he half-whispered: "She sings it right at the end of a party given by . . . what's her name? Soprano. Her name is like . . . Violetta. Violetta!"

"Just by being himself," said the *Time* cover story, "he has enabled a giveaway show, the crassest of low-brow entertainments, to whip up a doting mass audience for a new kind of TV idol—of all things, an egghead." Some critics likened the show to Sophoclean drama; others saw Van Doren as a modern Horatio Alger.

On March 11, Van Doren was defeated by a young lawyer, Vivienne Nearing, when he failed to name the king of Belgium. Van Doren "retired" with $129,000. Yet, in the months that followed, *Twenty-One* continued its phenomenal success. By that July, television's Top Ten included five quiz shows—*The $64,000 Question, I've Got a Secret, Twenty-One, What's My Line?,* and *The $64,000 Challenge.* The craze was still on a year later, as the networks introduced six new quiz shows to fill out the day and evening—*Lucky Partners, Bid 'n' Buy* (first prize was the Scottish island of Stroma), *For Love or Money, Anybody Can Play, Play Your Hunch,* and *Haggis Baggis.*

Van Doren, for his part, continued to live the life of a celebrity. Though still teaching at Columbia, he wrote an article for *Life* on what it was like to live in the limelight, and signed a five-year contract with NBC for a reported $50,000 a year (his duties included a daily spot on the *Today* show with Dave Garroway). "I think I may be the only person who ever read 17th-century poetry on a network television program," he said.

Then the rumors began. In 1957, *Time* had asked, "Are the quiz shows rigged?" Van Doren and others had denied the charges, however, and *Time* believed them—though it reported that many of the shows were planned "far more effectively than most viewers suspect." Slowly, however (as Redford's movie has documented), a different story began to emerge. Herb Stempel, who had become increasingly bitter about Van Doren's mounting fame and fortune, told two New York newspapers that *Twenty-One* had been fixed, but the newspapers refused to print the story, for fear of a libel action. In August 1958, CBS abruptly cancelled *Dotto*—a show on which contestants answered questions in order to connect dots that revealed the face of a celebrity—when one *Dotto* contestant revealed he had accidentally found backstage an opponent's notebook containing answers to forthcoming questions. New York County impaneled a grand jury, and in the fall of 1959 a U.S. House of Representatives committee began its own investigation.

What the nation learned during that October was that many quiz shows, including *Twenty-One,* were planned down to the last detail. Stempel told the House committee that he, and by implication Van Doren, had been told not only when to win or lose, but also when to pause, mop his brow, and smile. (The investigation showed, however, that the program's emcee, Jack Barry, had never been aware of the fix.)

Despite Stempel's testimony, Van Doren continued to deny all charges. But in early November he answered a subpoena from the committee, and began to tell his story. In later years, and especially during the Watergate hearings, the public would grow accustomed to public confessions. In 1959, as Van Doren began to spill the beans, it was not. Here's how he began:

> I would give almost anything I have to reverse the course of my life in the last three years. I cannot take back one word or action; the past does not change for anyone. But at least I can learn from the past.
>
> I have learned a lot in those three years, especially in the last three weeks. I've learned a lot about life. I've learned a lot about myself, and about good and evil. They are not always what they appear to be. I was involved, deeply involved, in a deception. The fact that I, too, was very much deceived cannot keep me from being the principal victim of that deception, because I was its principal symbol.

Van Doren went on to explain to the committee that he had been persuaded to join in the fix, as had many other contestants, because he was told that "the show was merely entertainment and that giving help to quiz contestants was a common practice and merely part of show business." In addition, Van Doren said he was told his participation "would increase public respect for the intellectual life and for the teaching profession."

He [the show's producer] took me into his bedroom, where we could talk alone. He told me that Herbert Stempel, the current champion, was an unbeatable contestant because he knew too much. He said that Stempel was unpopular, and was defeating opponents right and left, to the detriment of the program. He asked me if, as a favor to him, I would agree to make an arrangement whereby I would tie Stempel and thus increase the entertainment value of the program.

It's worth noting that at the time, fixing game shows was *not* illegal. The only potential crime committed by any participants was perjury. Yet the nation still reacted with shock to both the revelation of the scandal and the confession of its fallen hero. TV's Dave Garroway burst into tears while discussing the event on the *Today* show. And the *New Republic* reprinted a letter John Steinbeck had sent to Adlai Stevenson, in which he had written: "If I wanted to destroy a nation, I would give it too much and I would have it on its knees, miserable, greedy, and sick. . . . I am troubled by the cynical immorality of my country."

Comedians predictably found humor in the situation. Red Buttons said he finally understood why no one laughed at his jokes: "The audience was fixed." Bob Hope quipped that contestants would now be asked one more question: "How do you plead?" For some more-serious observers, it was simply a tale of greed. For others, it was grounds to censure television in general. "The moral squalor of the quiz mess reaches through the whole industry," wrote one critic. "[Almost] nothing is what it seems on television. . . . The feeling of high purpose, of manifest destiny that lit the industry when it was young . . . is gone." Critics at *Life* thought the scandal "exposed a nation's sagging moral standards." And yet, when asked by pollsters about the incident, many Americans forgave Van Doren. In fact, 54 percent of those questioned still approved of quiz shows. Thus, to the majority, it appeared, what was most important was that the show go on.

But it didn't—at least not as it had before. Most of the quiz shows, even the honest ones, were pulled off the air. (A notable exception was the Mark Goodson-Bill Todman stable of shows that included *What's My Line?* and *I've Got A Secret,* neither of which ever paid big money or exuded a whiff of scandal.) Congress passed legislation banning similar fraud. Yet the networks went even further: Stung by the criticism, they went to extraordinary lengths to draw a clear line between entertainment and reality—on a "purity kick," as one critic described it. CBS even began running a disclaimer before comedy shows, stating that the laughter accompanying the programs wasn't real. At another point, network president Frank Stanton went after *Person to Person* because the guests each week were "vaguely rehearsed." But such measures were short-lived. Television depends on its ability to exploit the thin line between truth and fiction. "Does [CBS president] Mr. Stanton want me to believe that Rochester really works for Jack Benny? Will they use real bullets for Westerns?" asked scriptwriter Goodman Ace.

Needing something to replace the quiz shows, the networks turned away from live production in prime time, to take advantage of the emerging technology of what historian Eric Barnouw has called *telefilms*—the modern filmed television series. The purported justification given by the networks was that filmed productions could be more easily reviewed for any improprieties. The real reason, however, was that filmed "series" television was more profitable because syndication and rerun rights could provide extra returns.

Filmed or taped series were also more predictable than live TV, and thus safer for sponsors—whom the networks now took out of the production business, forcing them to buy individual spots rather than entire programs, as they had frequently done before (*The Texaco Star Theater* or *The General Electric Theater*). Early TV had been modeled on old network radio. There, the networks viewed themselves mainly as "carriers" which sold time to sponsors who, in turn, hired an agency to create a show for them. It would seem ludicrous to us today if the articles in, say, *Time* or *Newsweek* were prepared by advertisers, subject to some vague approval by the publisher. Yet that's exactly how network TV operated through much of its early days.

This scandal changed it all as the networks concluded that, with so much control over production, advertisers had polluted quiz shows. In some cases the charge was true, though the shift to selling spots ultimately allowed the networks to charge far more for their ad time, and thus greatly increase profits. However, the programming hardly improved, and in some cases even got worse. Under the old system, a corporation would frequently sponsor a public-affairs show with low ratings merely for the prestige involved. Now, attracting a mass audience was all that mattered.

There were other consequences, too. The quiz-show scandal led to a formal network division between news and entertainment, and thus to the creation of large, permanent news divisions. The first product of these branches was a set of documentaries, including CBS's study of migrant workers, "Harvest of Shame." Within four years, the networks established their 30-minute nightly national-news shows, and Cronkite, Huntley and Brinkley (along with the others who followed) became household names.

The quiz-show scandal occurred over a generation ago—an eternity in TV time. Yet the doubts and issues that it raised have persisted as, one by one, other American institutions have fallen in esteem. With the rise of docudramas and tabloid news, the boundary between entertainment and reality has become more ambiguous than ever.

Yet the quiz-show scandals illustrated still another quirky fact: People don't mind being taken in—at least for long. As quickly as the Van Dorens rose they fell, and the reaction of most viewers was to suspend disbelief and watch even more television, not less. We watch a Letterman today and understand that nearly everything around him is "rigged"—the ad-libs, the conversations, the stunts. Yet we accept it all without blinking. We are told that we live in an age of skepticism and distrust, and no wonder. Through the quiz-show scandal, we learned two truths of the age. First: When you cannot trust the mirror, you can no longer trust anyone or anything. Second: We could no longer resist the mirror.

15

Leave It to Beaver
and the Politics of Nostalgia
(CBS AND ABC: 1957–63)

It's no secret that *Leave It to Beaver* is an icon in American culture. Each year, it is mentioned close to a thousand times in various articles—as in:

It's a wholesome, "Leave It to Beaver" existence.

By age 17, I was living the "Leave It to Beaver" TV-show life, being a Cub Scout den mother, doing PTA—all these things.

Are you stuck in the dregs of "Leave It to Beaver"?

The commission gave notice Wednesday that it was banishing six rules that probably made a lot of sense to the "Leave It to Beaver" generation but now seem pretty silly.

The show has come to symbolize an entire era and state of mind. And no wonder: *Leave It to Beaver,* which ran for six seasons, premiered on October 4, 1957, the day the Soviets launched *Sputnik,* and ended two months before the Kennedy assassination of November 1963. Its tenure thus spanned what many Americans now remember as the country's last Golden Age—a time of remarkable economic growth and social stability.

The show has also lasted in the public imagination because of the underrated cast, as well as the memorable supporting characters who surrounded the adorable and well-loved Beaver. There was—first and foremost, of course—the patient, understanding family head, Ward, a forerunner of today's new father (even if he often is mistakenly caricatured as a distant fifties patriarch). Then there was June, the anticipant mother, always waiting in high heels for her men at 211 Pine Street, Mayfield, USA. "Ward," she would say in one of television's classic lines, "I'm worried about the Beaver." Brother Wally followed—five years older than the Beaver, compliant but cool, the ideal role model for a younger kid. Right along with Wally came his greasy friend Eddie Haskell, who called Beaver "squirt" but always tried to butter up his victim's parents: "That's a lovely dress, Mrs. Cleaver," he would say, even while trying to get Wally to go astray: "This is vacation: Your parents aren't allowed to make you work all the time. It's a state law!"

Then there chimed in the whole gang of Whitey, Gilbert, Lumpy, and Larry—although, as Gerald Jones pointed out in his book *Honey, I'm Home,* many seemed to come from families far less functional than the Beave's. Finally, there was the theme song, and opening that practically every baby boomer can recite by heart: "*Leave It to Beaver,* starring Barbara Billingsley, Hugh Beaumont, Tony Dow—and Jerry Mathers as the Beaver."

Yet, looking back at the series (which actually shifted from CBS to ABC after just one season), two eye-opening things stand out: *Beaver* was never really popular in its own time. And, for a situation comedy of the 1950s, it was never very humorous.

Take that second surprise: *Beaver* is cute and heart-warming, but, unlike such memorable shows of its era as *I Love Lucy* and *The Honeymooners,* it wasn't really funny. The show followed Beaver from ages 7 to 12, but stopped just before he became a teenager—when it might have had to tackle more difficult issues. Barbara Billingsley once recalled:

[O]nce he grew up and became self-conscious, it all left. If an actor cannot concentrate and is not relaxed, the juices aren't there. When this happened to Jerry, Joe Connelly said, "We have to stop the show. What are you gonna do with a big, clunker kid like that?"

Yet, on the air, this was a new and different type of situation comedy because the situations—Beaver smashes a car window and tries to keep the news from his father; attempts to give himself a haircut after losing his money; or breaks down in the dentist's chair—were too realistic to be humorous. "Beaver eschews slapstick to concentrate on humorous realism," *Look* warned its readers in 1958. This show tried to tell the truth, even in impossible situations like when Beaver fell into the soup cup on the billboard, or tried to raise a baby alligator in the toilet. He washed his hands only to his wrists because he knew the dirt wouldn't show under his sleeves. "My name's Beaver," he told his teacher on the first day of school. "Is that your given name?" she asked. "Yeah, my brother gave it to me," he answered.

It was, in part, the lack of belly humor that caused television historian David Marc to dub shows like *Beaver* "WASP-coms"—visions of suburbia which provided reassurance to the new, unsure middle class of the 1950s, as fathers left home for long periods in their corporate jobs. (On television, in contrast, no one could ever quite figure out what Ward Cleaver, Jim Anderson, or Ozzie Nelson did for a living, since they were always hanging around the house.)

In fact the verisimilitude of *Leave It to Beaver* was so powerful that it is now widely assumed that the fifties were *exactly* the way this show portrayed them. That sort of schtick makes this show an odd forerunner, not only of *The Wonder Years* but of the whole wave of shows ranging from *The Mary Tyler Moore Show* to *M*A*S*H* which attempted to bring a new level of seriousness to television comedy in the seventies. That's one reason why *Leave It to Beaver* didn't really catch on until that era.

Credit for the innovations should go primarily to the show's creators and writers, Bob Mosher and Joe Connelly, whose prior stints included scripts for *The Amos and Andy Show*. By the mid-1950s, television had begun to follow up on the surprise success of *The Adventures of Ozzie and Harriet*. That show had premiered in 1952 on ABC, where it became TV's longest-running sitcom, and was notable for its portrayal of family life—as opposed to that of either couples or single people on *Our Miss Brooks, I Love Lucy,* and *The Honeymooners.* When *Father Knows Best* followed the formula two years later (though not to particularly great success in the ratings), others soon followed, so that by 1957 TV also had *Bachelor Father* and *Make Room for Daddy.*

Mosher and Connelly wanted to do something different. Unlike the other family shows, *Beaver* was presented from the star kid's point of view. Even decades later, that would be unusual on a medium where wisecracking six-year-old characters usually sound more like the adults who create them than anyone real. The *Beaver* writers also were careful to use their own families as models. When Connelly's son was sent to school in short pants and felt humiliated, a similar episode soon showed up on *Beaver*. Too, Connelly's own car window had been broken by his son, who had tried to cover it up by rolling it down. (In the show, Ward slams the door and thinks he has broken the window.) Even Eddie Haskell was modeled on one of Connelly's son's friends. That child's-eye view permeated the show all the way down to how it was put together in Hollywood. "We've asked both kids' parents not to talk about the show when the boys are around," Mosher once said. "The minute they turn into kid actors, the show is dead."

No doubt the child-centeredness of *Leave It to Beaver* is one of the reasons it never achieved high ratings: In the days when most households had only one TV set, a show had to appeal to everyone—and *Beaver* didn't offer much to the Wards and Junes of the world. That same "children only" quality, however, is what gave *Beaver* its niche with the baby boomers, that generation born between 1945 and 1959. This was a view of their mores, one of the first building-blocks in what would become their culture and eventually, because of their numbers, our culture.

The baby boomers would eventually make the world safe for nostalgia, which goes to the show's other surprise. Because *Beaver* has enjoyed phenomenal success in reruns, few recall that it failed to make much of an impression in its own time. *Beaver* premiered on Fridays at 7:30 P.M., but also ran on Wednesdays, Thursdays, and Saturdays during its run, too. The show never landed in the Top 25, and in its six seasons it was regularly and substantially outdrawn by such similar and lesser lights as *My Three Sons, The Donna Reed Show,* and *Dennis the Menace*—in which an only child, about Beaver's age, grows up in a far more indulgent household. It was only long after *Beaver* had left the air that it became an icon.

This is not an unprecedented development in popular culture. The Western only came to prominence largely after the West had already been won, and novels glorifying the "Old South" only became popular after the antebellum period. Similarly, *Leave It to Beaver*—the sitcom that glorified the traditional, paternalistic, middle-class family of the 1950s—only began to gain mass popularity as that family model, and the era it represented, disappeared and the nation longed for both it and the stability it represented. As such, *Beaver* may be the best symbol of contemporary pop culture's obsessive longing for the past—exemplified by everything from the pervasiveness of today's radio's "oldies" stations, which play fifties and sixties music; to the ways in which old television series like *The Brady Bunch* or *Mission: Impossible* are made into hit movies; and even to the manner in which the funerals of fifties and sixties luminaries like Jackie Kennedy and Richard Nixon become instant causes for national days of mourning.

Or—put another way—several years ago a New York newspaper polled its readers and asked, "If you could live in any time period, which would you select?" Not one chose the present.

There are many reasons for the current pervasiveness of nostalgia—particularly on television. With the networks having to produce thousands of hours of programming a year, good ideas get recycled again and again, sometimes as sequels or spinoffs, but often as pure nostalgia. According to television historian Ron Simon, reruns themselves—which are nostalgia incarnate—began in 1953 when CBS began putting repeats of ABC's popular *The Lone Ranger* on its Saturday afternoon schedule, and picked up even further in 1957 when CBS put repeats of *I Love Lucy* on five times a week during the day.

It was the rise of independent stations without an affiliation to a network, and with no programming of their own, however, which really created the need for the rerun—and a permanent market for constant trips to the past. By the late seventies, in fact, nostalgia for the fifties as portrayed in reruns had already become so suffusive that the Number 1 prime-time shows for three years running were new sitcoms set back in that time period. And the title of one of them—*Happy Days*—told it all. (The other was its spinoff, *Laverne and Shirley.*)

"No immigrants; less-bitter class divisions; a benign federal government; utter domination of the world economy," was the way Michael Elliott described the fifties in his history, *The Day Before Yesterday.* "America had *never* been like that before, yet, in our addled national memory, we think of such exceptional times not only as the way that America has always been, but as it should be in the future." Thus it was no surprise that when times turned tough in the late seventies and early eighties, a kind of spokesman for the fifties—Ronald Reagan, the host of old TV shows like *General Electric Theater* and *Death Valley Days*—became president.

Reagan's rise highlighted how the optimism of eighties and nineties conservatism tended to be established in the vision of a reclaimable past often rooted in the world of the fifties. In his own way, Reagan was a figure from the vanishing world of Ward Cleaver's paternal authority; and other Republicans were always trying to join him. "To those who say it was never so, that America has not been better, I say 'You're wrong,' and I know because I was there," said Bob Dole in his 1996 convention acceptance speech.

These Republicans were helped by the fact that, in an age of deficits and budget balancing, policy debates often focused on the best way to move backwards, not ahead. The collapse of the political Left removed a traditionally forward-looking force from the culture, too. A yearning for the rapid economic growth and social stability of those prior decades played a role, as did some traditional American longings. "There is a peculiarly compulsive American effort to recapture our past," Stanford University historian David Kennedy once told a reporter. "We are an invented nation; we made ourselves up—so uneasiness about our identity is a facet of the American character."

No doubt, viewers today watch *Leave It to Beaver* with a bit of irony: Do we really care whether Beaver can learn the clarinet well enough to play in the school band? Still, it would be a mistake to assume that the culture's obsession with the Beavers of its past is simply a way of lampooning the squares of ages gone by. If the baby-boom generation has made a narcissistic kind of nostalgia into the national religion, Beaver is the patron saint. "The very numbers of the baby-boom generation—the pig in the python bulge, as demographers once called it—always meant that it would speak with a loud voice," Michiko Kakutani once wrote in the *New York Times.* "It's just that no one expected the pig to use that voice to lip-synch its own past."

Leave It to Beaver didn't cause any demographic changes itself, but by offering a child-centered show for a youthful boomer generation, it led the way into the soon-to-be-pervasive boomer culture. More importantly, the show's after-the-fact popularity symbolized our new and pervasive belief that progress is no longer our most important product. For a country that always prided itself on its exuberant optimism, this turnaround represented a radical shift of opinion, affecting our politics, and not just our taste for remakes. The continued affection for the Beaver is a sign that America is still heading forward. Forward, that is, into a past it can never reclaim.

16

The Twilight Zone: Science Fiction as Realism
(CBS: 1959–64)

The Twilight Zone is another of those rare shows, like *Leave It to Beaver,* which stands far taller in memory than it did in the time during which it ran. In the five seasons that it was on the air from 1959 to 1964, its 154 episodes never cracked the Top 20 in the ratings, and the show didn't receive the critical plaudits that one might now expect. Yet this weird science-fiction anthology show, which ran on CBS on Friday nights at 10:00 for its first three years, before being moved considerably around the schedule, somehow permeated the consciousness of the entire culture. In 1993 alone, the Nexis research index cited over two thousand references to *The Twilight Zone,* in everything from politics ("caught in the political twilight zone between insider and outsider") to sports ("it really would have been a time warp, a *Twilight Zone* episode"). The clipped introductions of creator Rod Serling, who wrote more than half the episodes, continue to be fodder for commercials, comedians, and impersonators; the show's indelible, repetitious eight-note theme is still synonymous with eeriness, as is the spoken introduction (begun in the second season and changed a bit over the years):

> You're traveling through another dimension—a dimension not only of sight and sound, but of mind; a journey into a wondrous land whose boundaries are that of the imagination. Next stop: The Twilight Zone!

Scratch a few male baby boomers and you're likely to find more than one follower who can recite the show's episodes practically verbatim. There was, for example, the airliner that went back in time to the dinosaur age. And the woman who kept seeing the same hitchhiker every few miles as she traveled. And the aliens who landed on Earth claiming the possession of plans to help humanity, though armed with only a tome titled *To Serve Man,* which turned out to be a cookbook. Or the man allowed to live forever, who then decides to murder for murder's sake and is sentenced to life in prison. According to a viewers' poll taken by the Science Fiction Channel (which ran the show in the nineties), the most popular episode was "I Shot an Arrow Into the Air," about a group of astronauts who crash in what looks like a barren alien desert, and start killing each other off over short supplies—only to discover that they landed in Nevada.

Like O. Henry, Serling's specialty was the plot twist at the end—and his preoccupation, as TV analysts Harry Castleman and Walter Podrazik once put it, was the often fuzzy line between reality and illusion. Was that a creature the mental patient saw on the plane's wing, or was everyone right that he was having another breakdown? Perhaps you believed the stewardess—until you saw the damage to the wing at the end of the episode, as the patient was carted away.

Those themes may not have had much mass appeal: This was, as show chronicler Mark Zicree once wrote, the only series to deal regularly with existential concepts like alienation. Such notions, however, would prove to be particularly resonant ones for baby boomers. Remember that this was the generation whose poets would sing "Strawberry fields/Nothing is real," and which insisted that beneath the sheen and hypocrisy of "the system" lay a deeper and often darker secret. Rod Serling never said "The issue is not the issue," as they did at Berkeley—but his shows did, unlike anything else on television. Like Hermann Hesse and Kurt Vonnegut, two other poets laureate of the baby boomers, *The Twilight Zone* combined elements of science fiction, surrealism, and mysticism to get at a higher truth.

Remarkably, this occurred on a medium where the urge to turn everything into lowest-common-denominator entertainment usually made the "search for truth" impossible. Thus, in TV terms, *The Twilight Zone* was notable for being almost everything that prime-time series television was not. It was a cerebral show: What other program promised to enter "a dimension of *mind*"? And its domain was science fiction—a relative rarity for television until the cable age 30 years later.

Too, it was an anthology show—each episode standing on its own—which meant not only that viewers had no regular characters or actors with whom they could identify, but also that Serling had less than 30 minutes each week on TV to turn out a complete story. (The show ran for an hour during one season.) The series also featured ambiguous, often downbeat endings, with plots far removed from TV's tendency to tie up all the loose ends. This often left studio executives pondering the real meaning of the episodes. According to one story, one of the show's sponsors called up CBS each Monday to ask for an explanation of the previous Friday's show. "And then," said Serling, "he demanded an explanation of the explanation."

The most important characteristic of *The Twilight Zone* was its grounding in psychological truth. Despite its plunge into fantasy, the show referenced reality—far more, in fact, than reality-based shows do today. Presenting a psychologically sophisticated show in a new era for the discipline, Serling had turned to science fiction primarily because it offered him more freedom to make statements about politics and social conditions.

This came about for two reasons. From 1947 to the mid-fifties, television presented hundreds of quality live dramas on shows such as *Playhouse 90* and *Kraft Television Theatre*. After all, film was very expensive; TV had few other ways to tell noncomedic stories, and television audiences were disproportionately from New York and the east coast where the live stage was still a viable model for programming. Moreover, the film studios owned the rights to many Broadway plays and major literary works, which meant that the TV plays usually had to be original.

Yet there was still the problem of sponsor and network pressure. As one of the medium's outstanding writers during this "golden age of television," Serling had experienced firsthand how television tended to shy away from both controversy and anything else that made a sponsor look bad. In this atmosphere, the Chrysler Building had to be painted out of the skyline of New York because the sponsor was Ford; and the word "lucky" had to be removed from a script because the sponsor was a rival cigarette company. As *Newsweek* quoted Serling in 1959:

> If you're doing a controversial script, you perform the stage rit-
> ual of track-covering. If you want to do a piece ("A Town Has
> Turned to Dust") about prejudice against Negroes, you go in-
> stead with Mexicans and set it in 1890 instead of 1959 . . . . If
> you want to do a play about a man's Communist background as

a youth, you have to make him instead a member of a wild teen-age group. . . .

Concerning the Serling play "Noon on Doomsday," whose script was based roughly on the death of Emmett Till, a black 14-year-old murdered in Mississippi, *Newsweek* related how "a victim was changed from a Negro to a Jew, then to an unnamed foreigner. The locale was changed from the South to an unnamed place in New England." "I finally suggested Alaskan Eskimoes as a way out," Serling said. Once he was heard to exclaim: "The troops can't even ford a stream if Chevy is the sponsor." Yet it could be even worse: In a drama about the Nuremberg Trials, a gas company deleted all references to the fact that poison gas had been used to kill Jews. And a certain variety show sponsored by Studebaker reportedly fired band singer Joey Nash because his last name was the same as that of a rival car.

When another Serling play for *Studio One* dealing with the U.S. Senate was similarly subverted, Serling made a decision. "In retrospect, I probably would have had a much more adult play had I made it science fiction, put it in the year 2057, and peopled the Senate with robots," he said. "Things which couldn't be said by a Republican or Democrat could be said by a Martian." Thus was born the idea for *The Twilight Zone,* though television luminaries could never quite figure out the point. "You've given up writing anything important for television, right?" Mike Wallace asked Serling shortly before the show premiered. Serling is "forsaking the glory trail of live TV drama for the gory trials of a filmed series," wrote *Newsweek.*

Turning to science fiction also allowed Serling to retain his roots in literate live drama, even as it disappeared from television screens. There is only the finest of lines between the ideology of some of Serling's earliest teleplays, such as "Requiem for a Heavyweight" (telecast in 1956 on *Playhouse 90*), and many of his *Twilight Zone* pieces which display a similar Norman Rockwellesque empathy for the "little people," and reflect the social realism then in vogue on the Manhattan stage. Serling knew that after the film studios "made peace" with TV in the mid-fifties, the need for original plays was evaporating as TV went for the regular plots, schedules, and characters that allow producers, advertisers and—ultimately—audiences to set their expectations and viewing habits accordingly.

Yet when those live plays disappeared from television, a writer like Serling soon became subservient to everyone else on the production line. The programming became less ambitious—and, with the emphasis on crime shows, Westerns, and parable sitcoms, it soon became far less dependent on words. This was death to a serious playwright. Moreover, in the world of episodic series television, virtually all crimes are solved, all family crises inevitably resolve themselves, and all heroic figures remain heroic. Prime-time TV has little sense of sadness, and no tragedy; it is almost entirely a world of resolved, happy endings—even in the nineties and the age of the "nitty gritty." That, too, meant the end for a serious playwright like Serling. So, to attain realism, he turned to—of all things—science fiction.

Thus *The Twilight Zone* presented an alternate universe which, as fantastic as it was, ultimately proved more authentic than almost anything else in the teleculture. That's why the show lasted. In some episodes the politics are obvious, as when a dealer sells Soviet leader Khrushchev a car whose owners must tell the truth. In others they are more guarded, such as in the episode where a neighborhood faced with an invasion of "aliens" ends up destroying itself through fear before the unwanted visitors can even arrive. Yet, as America headed into the unknown of space in the late fifties, this series was about the only thing available on TV that confronted the uncertainty of such a quest. Where it trod, *Star Trek* one day followed—though that was to prove far sunnier in outlook than this show.

As many would note, the 1950s and early 1960s were also a time of national propaganda and paranoia—Communists could be lurking anywhere! *The Twilight Zone* implicitly dealt with our newfound national inability to trust anyone or anything—even reality itself. Beneath the facade of fifties unity there were doubts, after all. This show for unbelievers helped form the ethos of skepticism that would someday rule an age when no one believed anyone in authority anymore—whether the authorities were American presidents or L.A. cops gathering evidence against O. J. Simpson. By the mid-nineties, television would be able to build an entire *Zone*-like series—*The X-Files*—around the notion that government agencies knew all about the supernatural and paranormal, but kept it hidden away.

Yet—back in Serling's heyday—this skepticism was new, and rarely acknowledged openly. And its roots lay not only in the lies of government, but also in the lies of television. From quiz shows to cop shows, the medium had used the decade of the fifties to institutionalize itself as a weaver of myths, not a monument of realism—the better to indulge the fantasies of the viewing public. By the time *The Twilight Zone* left the prime-time schedule, Americans inhabited a true world of mirror images—and the next stop, as the Serling introduction used to indicate, was up ahead. Everyone now knew that the world of television—which was increasingly the only world we knew—was the *real* Twilight Zone.

Part III
THE SIXTIES

The Presidential Press Conference • *Perry Mason*
The Dick Van Dyke Show • The Space Program as TV
Show • *The Beverly Hillbillies* • Assassination Television
Mister Ed and TV's Escapist Comedies • *The Dating Game*
Walter Cronkite and the *CBS Evening News* • *The Monkees*
Mission: Impossible • *The Smothers Brothers Comedy Hour*
Rowan and Martin's Laugh-In

By now, almost everyone had a television set, and the medium's schedules and genres were firmly established. This then became the decade in which the networks greatly expanded their efforts in the areas of sports and news, with a corresponding double effect on our public life. Though presented as reality, these events came to be packaged as shows with attributes like other TV programming—drama, stars, supporting casts, and exotic locations. How a medium wedded to the noncontentious could possibly deal with the turmoil of the era became an unspoken theme of other programming. Continuing the trend from the past decade, better than two-thirds of the shows in this section appeared on CBS—the early network flagship for news, just as it had been for entertainment.

17

The Rise and Fall of the Televised
Presidential Press Conference

(ALL MAJOR NETWORKS: 1961-93)

At 6:00 P.M. on January 25, 1961, John Kennedy, inaugurated as president only five days earlier, strode into the State Department Annex to face a battery of 11 TV and movie cameras, 418 reporters, and an estimated 60 million Americans watching via the tube. Though Kennedy was already known as a president who had laid claim to the office through a series of superb television performances—four televised debates with Richard Nixon several months before—his scheduled live appearance here was still considered a terrible political risk, if only because he might blurt out something that could cause a foreign crisis. Columnist James Reston of the *New York Times* labeled the exercise "the goofiest idea since the Hula Hoop."

Yet Kennedy went ahead. He made a brief opening statement, and then with impeccable ease fielded 31 questions in 39 minutes as 34 percent of the potential viewing audience tuned in via all three networks. "'Kennedy and Press' seems a Hit," read a headline in the *New York Times* the following day, as reporter Russell Baker called the president "a new star with a tremendous national appeal, the skill of a consummate showman."

The event marked a shift, beginning what would become an institution for 30 years—the live televised presidential press conference. First covered by all three major networks, and eventually also by newcomer CNN, this "roadblock" across the dial in prime time guaranteed a rare mass audience for such "news." That made these events enormously important in cementing impressions of our chief executives, in some cases even replacing the function that presidential speeches had once held.

In the following decades, viewers were treated to the jabbing forefinger and spontaneous wit of Kennedy, the pained defensiveness of

Lyndon Johnson, the "I am not a crook" denial by Nixon, and the amiable ramblings of Ronald Reagan—not to mention the ever-present hordes of screaming reporters shoving to get the president's attention, and the high drama inherent whenever Dan Rather or Sam Donaldson asked a question. (When he left office, Jimmy Carter said he wished only two things on his successor: Menachem Begin and Donaldson.) In many ways, the live televised presidential press conference launched a new age of politics and communication for presidents, journalists, and viewers. The question, in retrospect, is "Who is better off for the change?"

And a change it was. According to historians, the modern presidential news conference probably began with Teddy Roosevelt, who used to summon groups of favored reporters to his barber's chair every Tuesday at 1:00 P.M. and Friday at 4:00 P.M. while he was shaved, though no direct quotation was allowed. Woodrow Wilson refined the custom further by allowing reporters to set the agenda and ask him questions. Presidents Warren Harding and Calvin Coolidge averaged two informal press briefings a week, though both men required that questions be submitted in writing, in advance. Coolidge used to go through the stack of questions and, on coming to one he didn't like, place it at the bottom. In 1927, on a special experimental broadcast, Herbert Hoover became the first president-to-be to appear on TV— whereon, in much the same sort of juxtaposition that television would later impose on the whole culture, he was followed by an Irish comedian in blackface.

Franklin Roosevelt, who met privately with the press almost every day in his office during his first two terms, thereafter dropped the requirement of submitting questions in advance—though he still set careful ground rules, and retained the custom of speaking "off the record" whenever he wanted—which was quite often. Dwight Eisenhower was the first president to allow his sessions to be taped completely for radio or TV (the first televised presidential press conference was held on January 19, 1955), though they could be played only on a delayed basis in order to give the White House a chance to correct any mistakes.

Convinced of his television prowess after his debate performances several months earlier against Nixon, Kennedy reversed that practice as soon as he took office. Yet Kennedy was hardly a natural to television. When he was younger, he had not been particularly good before the cameras, pausing long seconds to think of answers to questions. "He was so frigid at the beginning," Fred Friendly, Edward R. Murrow's old producer, once recalled. "Most people were scared of television, *are* scared of television. . . ." According to Jeff Kisseloff's book *The Box,* Kennedy improved only after getting feedback from comedian Morey Amsterdam, later of *The Dick Van Dyke Show,* who told Kennedy how he himself dealt with a vocal, raucous audience:

> I start talking and as I'm talking the wheels are grinding. . . . You've got to do the same thing. Let's say someone asks you about civil rights and up to that moment you've never heard of civil rights, you can still start saying things like "It's the number-one thing on my agenda" or "I've got men working on it."

Besides, Kennedy was convinced, as he told informal adviser James Rowe, "that the press will turn against me sooner or later while I am president, and I must have a way to get to the American people." It's a sentiment which has driven every president since—including Bill Clinton, who revealed to a citizen-MTV questioner 30 years later that he wore briefs, not boxer shorts.

So, from a president's standpoint, were televised press conferences a blessing? Not really. Because Kennedy was such an appealing off-the-cuff figure on TV, and the conference was a novelty, his 64 White House press gatherings undoubtedly did much to enhance his image. But history never repeated itself in this area, even though pundits have been forever complaining that the press is easy to control. Lyndon Johnson actually started out giving press conferences more frequently than Kennedy, but by the middle of his second term they had become so combative (because of the Vietnam War) that they were considered a disaster for him.

In response, Richard Nixon reduced the frequency of press conferences by around 80 percent, but some of the more embarrassing moments of his presidency still occurred there—his defenses during Watergate, and his celebrated fights with Dan Rather. Jimmy Carter came to Washington determined to revive the press conference as a means of direct communication with the people, but in large part because of Donaldson & Company left four years later having held press conferences almost as infrequently as Nixon did—and with similar success.

As to the Great Communicator Reagan, he treated the institution of the press conference with disdain, since other speaking forums were so much easier to orchestrate. Perhaps that's one reason why he left office with some degree of public respect. George Bush revived the institution somewhat, giving unscheduled press conferences almost biweekly, but only because he could use the press briefing as a substitute for making a speech—which he did poorly. In any event, no one can recall much of anything Bush ever said at these briefings, and eventually no one but CNN would cover most of them. ("Well good morning, and I'm back again," Bush said at the introduction of one, as the press laughed.)

As for Bill Clinton, his presidency has seemed to be one perpetual news conference, a kind of political telethon—meaning that the practice has become a virtual irrelevancy. By 1996, in fact, Clinton's press secretary was dismissing the whole exercise as "a kind of dinosaur," which is why Clinton (who never met a microphone he didn't like) had only around a dozen formal televised conferences in his entire first term.

Then how about the viewing public? Outside the benefits of the occasional special press conference during a crisis or scandal, it's hard to see what viewers gained out of the arrangement, either. True, voters did get to see their president "in action," or "being held accountable," but we're dealing with rather odd definitions of action and accountability here. Answering questions impressively may be a prized attribute for a contestant on *Jeopardy!* but its relevancy to the presidency is less clear. Robert Pierpoint, a former CBS White House correspondent, once rated presidential press conferences in a magazine survey and found Kennedy did the best, primarily because he outshone his rivals in "combative skill" and "humor." Interestingly, in the categories of "candor" and "informative value," Kennedy was rated near the back of the pack.

And what about the press? With good reason, the print press never particularly liked televised press conferences. Television, after all, quickly disseminated what little hard news came out of the sessions. And, predictably, the medium turned what had been a somewhat useful spontaneous exchange of information into a highly artificial staged performance—otherwise known in the world of television as a "show." That left print reporters frequently functioning as little more than stenographers, bit players in the audience, or third-rate drama critics. Even when they attempted to point out mistakes or "misstatements" (as they frequently did during the Reagan years), they found that few Americans cared about that kind of thing anymore. "Reagan is really a very electronic-age person," *Washington Post* columnist Richard Cohen once told the *Los Angeles Times.* He went on:

> He's not literal-minded. He offends people who are, who read, who are careful about words and think that logic is important and all of that. He knows that none of that is important. A lot of us write, after press conferences, where he was wrong, and the people who were watching him say, in effect, "I know what he meant," and they do.

After all, who's the real hero of *To Tell the Truth*—the honest contestant, or the actor whose misrepresentations stump the panel?

Television journalism, however, was another story. Like everything it touched, TV made the press conference conform to the dictates of its own forms of entertainment. Part game show, part miniseries, and yes, even part sitcom (otherwise, why would Kennedy score so high for laughs?), the press conference evolved into one of our longest-running series. Each episode was supposed to last exactly a half-hour. The plot line was simple: Can the press trip up the president?

And the stars? Presidents came and went, but through the years it was the TV reporters—the Rathers, Donaldsons, Stahls, and Blitzers—whose confrontations with power supplied this series with its magic moments and ongoing drama. "Are you running for something, Mr. Rather?" President Nixon had asked Rather at one press gathering held before members of the public. "No, Mr. President," shot back Rather. "Are you?" "Don't get the impression that you arouse my anger," Nixon lectured Rather at another press conference, as the nation cringed. "You see, one can only be angry at those he respects."

Eyebrows were raised when Donaldson asked Carter if he thought himself competent enough to be president—though, to balance the scales (so to speak), he also suggested to Reagan that his presidency was "failing." The careers of TV newscasters fairly rocketed as a result of such performances, but the prestige of the targeted presidents was left on the launching pad. Humiliate the Chief of State: Win Valuable Prizes!

Thus, times of crisis excepted, the televised press conference—like so much else in American life—became a vehicle that did little but promote the culture, values, and stars of television. It's thus no surprise that any candidate or president with sense now prefers to schedule these sessions in the afternoon, when few are watching—or, better yet, to take some questions in another context from the home viewers.

What's more, these events increasingly have meant less because the importance of the presidency itself has diminished—in part, again, due to changes in television itself. The rise of presidential power in the era during and after World War II coincided with the growth of the major broadcast networks. From Franklin Roosevelt to John Kennedy to Ronald Reagan, the history of the past 60 years was often the story of how presidents tried to use the megaphone of the mass media to become our prime political movers, appropriating roles once held by Congress and the parties. Today, of course, there are far more stations—and still only one beleaguered president.

Thus the era of the TV press conference has for all intents and purposes drawn to a close, as the ability of a president to draw a mass audience has been dramatically diminished by cable television. Where once the very machinery of television built up the chief, now it tears him down. Sixty percent or more of all households with television sets watched the first televised addresses of presidents Nixon, Carter, and Reagan. In the cable age of atomized audiences (when a network-and-CNN "roadblock" only covers four of 50 odd stations on the dial), President Bush never even broke 40 percent, except with one speech announcing the Gulf War. In the cable age, the spotlight has all but disappeared: Just about everyone agrees that there are now more-useful—and dare we say more-entertaining—ways for viewers to spend their time.

18

Perry Mason and the Criminal Lawyer as Brief Television Hero

(CBS: 1957-66)

On June 13, 1966, Chief Justice Earl Warren delivered his opinion in a case that Justice William Brennan declared "one of the most important . . . of our time." The case was *Miranda* v. *Arizona,* and its insistence that the police advise criminal suspects in custody of their rights to be granted counsel and to remain silent signaled the peak of the Warren Court's efforts to ensure that the police treat defendants more fairly in the future.

Less than a month earlier, on May 22, 1966, a lawyer with similar concerns about police practices had argued his last case in court. For the better part of a decade, this attorney had skillfully exposed the police as a group of well-meaning buffoons who—procedural niceties notwithstanding—were so incompetent that they continually arrested the wrong suspects. But there was a key difference between Chief Justice Warren and his litigating counterpart. Whereas Warren delivered his judgments only a few times a year to a small audience of lawyers and reporters, who then carried his message to others, Perry Mason spoke directly to millions of Americans each week.

Did *Perry Mason* pave the way for the Warren Court's liberal criminal-procedure decisions? Though it would be preposterous to suggest that this program did it singlehandedly, it would be equally foolish to pretend that it played no role at all. In 271 cases over 10 years (from 1957 to 1966), before audiences of millions, *Perry Mason* presented a view of police and lawyers that did more to give people the verdict on how the legal system operates than any grade-school civics course or news article ever could. And that verdict was "Guilty!"

The show made its debut in 1957 on CBS on Saturdays at 7:30 P.M., and its launch and achievements are now part of television lore. Perry Mason, a creation of author Erle Stanley Gardner, had been featured in over 50 novels, four movies, and a popular radio show before CBS brought him to television. Gardner himself selected the actor to play Mason. Originally, the part was to go to Fred MacMurray, later the star of *My Three Sons.* (Rod Serling was also tested for the role.) MacMurray, however, didn't want to appear in a weekly series, so the producers kept testing actors for the part until Gardner saw Burr—who had come by ostensibly to try out for the prosecutor's role—and shouted "That's him. He's Perry Mason!"

When the show debuted, the critics were typically harsh. *Variety* called Burr merely a "wholesome resident of suburbia on his way up the executive ladder" and forecast that the show "would not offer serious competition for Mr. [Perry] Como" in its time slot. Yet the show rose as high as Number 5 in the ratings, attracting over 30 million viewers a week—and became the longest-running and most popular lawyer show in TV history. A poll conducted some 10 years after the series left the air found it to be the favorite show of those working in the television industry. Back in the 1980s, the show spawned a series of made-for-TV movies reuniting Burr with Barbara Hale, who played Della Street, his secretary. In a 1993 survey, Mason even finished second on a list of the lawyers Americans admired most—behind F. Lee Bailey (this was pre-O.J.) but ahead of anyone on the Supreme Court, much less on TV. Today, *Perry Mason* is still syndicated all over the country.

In his nine seasons on the air, Mason never really lost a case—though, to be fair, in "The Case of the Deadly Verdict" the jury did find Mason's client guilty, so TV's most able lawyer had to find the real culprit later. ("We got 35,000 letters from the public saying 'Please don't do that again,'" Burr once recalled.) The portly actor, who won an Emmy for Best Actor in a Dramatic Series in 1959, was surrounded by a superb supporting cast (particularly William Talman, as hapless prosecutor Hamilton Burger), as well as given one of the medium's memorable theme songs.

To describe the show as formulaic in its 49 minutes and 40 seconds of action each week is an understatement. Burr had to deliver so many lines during each episode that this was one of the first shows to use a TelePrompTer on the set. According to one report, creator Gardner instructed Hollywood that Mason should never lose a case, the client must always be innocent, Mason must never be violent, and the star's character must never be associated with the "innuendo of flirtation."

Even when Bette Davis and others took over for Burr for four weeks when the star underwent minor surgery, the scenario wasn't allowed to change. Davis claimed that she stepped in for Burr without even reviewing a script. "It's a formula show," she said, "and I know the formula."

Though as an attorney he was a member of the legal establishment, Mason combined the private eye's distrust of established institutions with a few Joe Friday (of *Dragnet* fame) traits—persistence, lack of interest in women, and a regular job. Each episode opened with a crime—often a murder—which was then usually investigated by Lieutenant Arthur Tragg and the Los Angeles Police Department. The clues invariably would point to one frightened suspect (always a middle-class white person), who claimed to be innocent and inevitably became Mason's client. Through a series of investigations, Mason— aided by able secretary Della Street ("It's for you, Perry") and detective Paul Drake—would gradually unearth a web of motives that could have led any of several characters to commit the crime.

At the preliminary hearing, which always constituted the last half of the show, earnest prosecutor Hamilton Burger would appear to be on his way to yet another easy conviction of a Mason client. Then Perry would produce a string of witnesses (Robert Redford once, and on another occasion Dustin Hoffman) whose testimony would eventually force the real culprit to confess in the courtroom while Burger objected ("Mr. Mason is turning the courtroom into a circus!"). In the final scene, Mason would sit in his office with Street, Drake, and the grateful client, and explain how he had solved the crime.

Star Raymond Burr would claim that the show promoted "the true meaning of the law." Perhaps. Yet, while the show presented an odd vision of L.A.'s finest, it created an even odder picture of an attorney's job, since he acted more as a private eye—doing no actual library research or formal discovery. Occasionally, Mason was not above violating the law himself, illegally breaking into houses in the zealous pursuit of some client's interest. In one episode, Mason even bought an apartment building so he could change the locks on the doors and fool his adversaries. Outside of court, this lawyer spent about half his time investigating crimes, and half reassuring his client (he seemed to represent only one at a time). Thus Mason was not only the lawyer as detective, but also the lawyer as friend, displaying a kindly demeanor that until then had been missing from other crime-fighting heroes.

Mason was also one of TV's first heroes with a postgraduate degree, a role model for the highly educated baby boomers growing up on television. In the world of Perry Mason, crime-fighting was not only heroic; it was respectable work for the upper middle class. It apparently paid well, too—though money was rarely mentioned: Mason had a secretary, drove a Cadillac, and had well-furnished offices in downtown L.A. Contrast that with the sleazy headquarters of Sam Spade, or even Joe Friday—who worked in a crowded police station.

The show's uplifting effect on the image of defense lawyers came at the expense of the public's perception of law enforcement, for Mason's implicit ridicule of the police had an effect on both television programming and viewers. "This show presents problems in the field of law enforcement—and I'm the first to admit it," creator Gardner once said. It's thus no surprise that what followed Mason were not only lawyer shows glamorizing the defense, such as *The Defenders,* but offerings such as *Car 54, Where Are You?* (incompetent police in New York); *The Fugitive* (police arrest wrong man); and *Batman* (campy spoof of traditional crime dramas). For much of the decade of the sixties, television continually mocked the wayward ways of the crime-fighting establishment and even of the law itself. These shows, *Time* would observe, "seem to suggest that (1) any citizen would be stupid to leave an important matter to the police, and (2) a little misdemeanor can be a good thing if applied in a good cause."

It was a complete turnaround from the world of *Dragnet.* In a sense, these brief and negative portrayals of the police were a reflection of public sentiment: The well-publicized rising crime rate of the sixties, now attributed principally to changing demographics, was then often blamed on the police. Yet shows such as *Perry Mason* affected attitudes as well—both in and outside the courtroom. In a prescient 1958 article entitled "The Case of the Unhappy DA," *TV Guide* analyzed the problem. In one Dallas case, the district attorney had produced two eyewitnesses to a robbery, but the accused was freed by a hung jury. "Do you know what one juror told me?" the prosecutor complained. "That in every robbery case he had ever seen on a TV show, the thief had left fingerprints. So the juror decided the man must be innocent." Attorney (later Senator) Frank Moss complained that:

A good number of jurors have become convinced, through watching television, that the prosecutor is some sort of trick artist who pulls a rabbit out of his hat in the last reel. . . . [I]f he doesn't resort to theatrics, as the TV prosecutors do, they are inclined to bring in an innocent verdict.

In 1962, Brooklyn D.A. Edward Silver complained that Mason had undermined respect for all law enforcement. "[E]ven today," Howard Rosenberg wrote in the *Los Angeles Times* in 1993, "potential jurors are sometimes cautioned in court not to expect trials that feature dramatic confessions à la Perry."

By the late 1960s, with the swing back to conservatism, audiences began to tire of lawyers—even idealistic ones on shows such as *Storefront Lawyers* and *The Young Lawyers*. "[A]ll these shows had protagonists who were social-worker types," programming executive Grant Tinker once complained. "They were *anti* heroes. They were *cheek-turners*. I can't remember a cheek-turner who has ever made it on TV." Thus, television's temporarily cynical attitude toward law enforcement began to disappear, as shows such as *The Mod Squad* combined a hip style with a more favorable attitude toward the police.

Consequently, Perry Mason's glamorization of criminal-defense lawyers, foils of the police, faded as well—even if the rulings of the Warren Court lasted a good deal longer. Though TV lawyers would occasionally be portrayed positively in firms (*L.A. Law*), or as judges (*The People's Court*), Perry Mason would be the last criminal lawyer to be a real television hero. After Mason left prime time, he would serve in reruns as a reminder that there are few scenes more dramatic or timeless than a courtroom confrontation. Then Court TV got the message, and the O. J. Simpson case followed—though none of the lawyers there would be as noble and popular as their fictional counterpart. The rest, as Perry might explain to Della at the end of an episode, is history, as courtrooms became the new home of reality programming in the nineties.

19

The Dick Van Dyke Show
and the Rise of Upscale Television
(CBS: 1961–66)

Like *I Love Lucy*, *The Dick Van Dyke Show* is one of those series on virtually everyone's list of the greatest television shows of all time. And with good reason: Popular in its own day, winning more than a dozen Emmys, it has been one of the medium's most consistent and honored hits in syndication for three decades, due largely to its strong ensemble cast and incisive writing.

Yet—more than that—*The Dick Van Dyke Show* was also a series ahead of its time, which is the reason why other shows didn't begin to imitate its formulas until years, often decades, later. As a sitcom focusing on the workplace as well as the family, it paved the way for such shows as *Taxi* in the next decade, and then *Murphy Brown*. It dealt in a humorous way with realistic and unusual topics, such as marriage counseling and bar mitzvahs, doing so through the use of dream sequences and flashbacks.

Van Dyke's character, Rob Petrie, worked as a television writer—meaning that the show was about the medium. As such, it proved a self-referential product which would became a forerunner of shows like *Seinfeld*. Additionally, given its preoccupation with the adults in the family, in contrast to their interaction with the children, this series presaged such "yuppie," childless nineties sitcoms as *Mad About You* and *Friends*.

With its focus on adult concerns, comfortable surroundings, and the search for material and career success, this was upscale television before anyone had ever thought of the term—yet it sold to the masses then, and does now. Its effect was the opposite of traditional British TV comedies, which help exaggerate England's love-hate relationship with her snootier classes, and often castigate the upwardly mobile. In this country, everyone wants to be wealthy, and, times of economic crisis excepted, there is usually little resentment of those who want more—a fact that "soak the rich" Democrats often forget. One is reminded of an old joke: An Englishman and an American are standing at a bus stop when a man cruises by in his Cadillac. The American says, "Someday, I'll be driving that car, just like him." The Englishman shrugs and says, "One day, that driver will be standing here, just like me."

All this focus on work and the striving middle class was new at the time. And it was mostly planned that way by Carl Reiner, who approached the task of creating this sitcom more seriously than most would have—if only because it started out as an autobiographical project. Reiner had been a writer and occasional performer on Sid Caesar's string of shows in the 1950s, and correctly foresaw that the sitcom was replacing variety shows on television. In an effort to combine the two, Reiner came up with an idea for a show, starring himself, about a TV writer like himself, who worked in the city and lived in the suburbs with his family—again, like himself. He wanted reality, he said, in the form of "the first situation comedy where you saw where the man worked *before* he walked in and said, 'Hi, honey, I'm home! '"

To develop the idea completely, Reiner took the unprecedented step of writing 13 episodes of his show. A friend sent the scripts to Peter Lawford, who got patriarch Joseph Kennedy to finance the project. As part of an anthology series, CBS ran one pilot in the summer of 1960. It was received favorably, but the network passed on the idea. Reiner's agent then got him together with Sheldon Leonard, the producer of a number of TV shows, such as Danny Thomas's *Make Room for Daddy*.

Leonard converted Reiner's show into a "three-camera" exercise to be filmed with an audience, like *I Love Lucy,* to take advantage of the writer's quick jokes. The tendency with a three-camera show, after all, is for the writers and actors to play to the audience, and so to create more laughs, rather than the sweet "parables" seen often on a single-camera show like *Father Knows Best.* As tactfully as possible, Leonard also told Reiner that he had a wonderful idea, but was the wrong person for the lead. In his book *Comic Visions,* television historian David Marc has suggested that Milton Berle and Sid Caesar had proven "too Jewish" for the growing white-bread TV audience, and it was feared that the same fate might befall Reiner. So the show was recast with a "Middle-American" to be placed in the lead; Reiner would remain in the cast as a minor character. As a television executive would advise decades later in another context, "Write Yiddish—Cast British."

Ironically, this allowed the show to dramatize, albeit subtly, the contrasts between Gentile (Rob and Laura) and Jew (Buddy, Alan Brady, and Mel Cooley)—in much the same way that Reiner was trying to merge the Jewish comedic tradition of Berle and Sid Caesar with the waspier sitcom settings of popular fifties series like *Ozzie and Harriet*. For the lead, Leonard was torn between Johnny Carson, a popular daytime game-show host, and Dick Van Dyke, Broadway star of *Bye Bye Birdie* and an actor with a reputation for visual comedy. Van Dyke—who had been under contract to CBS since 1955—got the role, largely because he was less well-known than Carson and therefore would be more believable in the title role. Van Dyke also frequently collaborated with Reiner, who ended up using a number of incidents from Van Dyke's own life to round out the character. He made the show, wrote one critic, "warm" and "zany."

The rest of the cast featured 23-year-old Mary Tyler Moore as Rob's wife, Laura (her two biggest previous roles had been as the "Happy Hotpoint" elf selling ovens, and the disembodied legs of the sexy-voiced secretary on *Richard Diamond, Private Detective*); Morey Amsterdam (Buddy) and Rose Marie (Sally) as Petrie's co-workers on their fictional TV show; Larry Matthews as Rob and Laura's son, Richie; and Reiner as Alan Brady, Rob's employer—who wasn't actually seen until the second season. Sally was notable for being TV's best-known single professional woman then; Buddy was your typical TV writer, his "Jewishness" explicit. In one episode, "Buddy Sorrell—Man and Boy," he secretly took Bar Mitzvah lessons (others thought he was having an affair) and went through the ceremony.

Laura ("Oh, Rob") became notable for being a television wife whose role went well beyond caring for junior, as she displayed unusual sex appeal for a TV character of that time. Her most celebrated and "risqué" episode may have been when she got her toe caught in the bathtub faucet, and Rob had to shoot the bathroom door handle off. True, she had given up her career as an entertainer for housewifery: In one episode she's offered a job but announces, "I don't want to be a dancer, I want to be your wife." Yet she wore her independence on her legs and feet—failing to don the typical high heels and pearls of television's other sitcom mothers, opting instead for Capri slacks and flats. Television revolutions sometimes proceed slowly.

The show premiered on Tuesday, October 3, 1961, at 8:00 P.M. The first episode was called "The Sick Boy and the Sitter," with Rob wanting to go to a work-related party, but Laura worried about their sick son. Yet the series didn't do well in its first season up against *Bachelor Father* and *Laramie*. Moved in midseason opposite Perry Como on Wednesdays at 9:30 P.M., it did even worse, leading the network to decide to cancel the show. CBS president James Aubrey was no fan: He had wanted Rob to be an insurance salesman. Yet Leonard prevailed on CBS to continue, and by its second season (still on Wednesday nights) the show had cracked the Top Ten—largely, however, because it followed *The Beverly Hillbillies,* this sitcom's antithesis, on the schedule. And there it remained until the final season of 1965-66, when it slipped to Number 16. By then, Reiner had decided to pull the plug on the series while it was still fresh, terminating it at 158 broadcast episodes. "We wanted to quit while we were still proud of it," said Van Dyke at the time.

Many episodes became classics—at least to television aficionados. There was "It May Look Like a Walnut," wherein Rob dreams that his thumbs and sense of humor alike have been stolen by aliens from the planet Timko, who live on walnuts. And there was "Coast-to-Coast Big Mouth," in which Laura reveals on national television that Alan wears a toupee. In yet another favorite, Rob became drunk, due to a hypnotic suggestion, whenever the doorbell rang. Many of the show's topics were somewhat chancy for the time: In "Draw Me a Pear," Rob's art teacher attempts to seduce him, while in "That's My Boy," an episode told in flashback, Rob becomes convinced that he and Laura have taken the wrong baby from the hospital—only to find, when he confronts the other parents, that they are black. This sort of subject treatment was groundbreaking in those days, and the payoff scene may have produced the longest studio laugh since Jack Benny's famous much-delayed "I'm thinking!" response to a robber's spoken-for-a-second-time demand, "Your money or your life!"

In the final series episode Rob reveals, with mixed emotions, that he has been working on a novel—but it has been rejected by a publisher. Surprise!: Alan wants to turn it into a television show. So every-

one leaves happy. This, too, as Marc notes in his book, echoes a familiar theme on the series dear to Reiner's heart—the notion that television, in its own way, is real art. In the end, that was true for *The Dick
Van Dyke Show,* a sitcom more defined by its strong writing than almost any other in TV history. Because of that attribute, this show, far
more than other series of that time, was able to reflect the cultural cur-
rents of its era—the flight from the city to suburbia, the growing aspirations of the new middle class during the New Frontier, and racial
and ethnic issues.

The show was also true-to-life, as it depicted a suburban couple in
much fuller fashion than TV had before—from their nights out with
friends, to their occasional disagreements, to their consumerism.
What's more, *The Dick Van Dyke Show* presented this portrait affectionately, validating for this new suburban class both their struggles
and their successes. This series told the story of America's new pioneers, and it's a story that future generations would try to emulate as
they attempted similar journeys in more unstable times. "They [the
actors] stay real amidst the plot twists," wrote one critic at the time.
"The humor comes from the juxtaposition of believable people and
absurd events. . . ."

Television is, after all, a medium whose typical shows border on the
bizarre, from police shows (where the crook is usually apprehended)
to doctor shows (where everyone in the hospital is as attractive as a
model). This show was different and believable, and its departure created "a vacuum," one critic noted, "that never really has been satisfac-
torily filled." That's the main reason why, even though it's something
of a period piece, *The Dick Van Dyke Show* continues to resonate with
audiences, via reruns, even today.

20

Space Television

(ALL 3 NETWORKS: 1961–69)

Like the presidential press conference, the space program was one long miniseries—an eight-year joy ride to the moon, hosted by Walter Cronkite, carefully scripted each year with increasingly better pictures. It spanned the decade, beginning in 1961, with Alan Shepard's 15 minutes in space, and took us through John Glenn's orbits, Scott Carpenter's missing capsule, the space walks, the Christmas mission that orbited the moon, and finally Neil Armstrong's walk on the moon itself on July 20, 1969. As a television show, it changed as events and technology changed—from Kennedy to Nixon; from black-and-white to color; from primitive simulations with models to live shots from space. On the ultimate day the *Eagle* landed and Neil Armstrong took his "one small step for man," it was estimated that 130 million Americans were tuned to the event—one of the largest audiences in the history of television. "It was as if you could have stood on the dock and waved goodbye to Columbus," Cronkite would later say.

Scholars Daniel Dayan and Elihu Katz have written how certain "live" televised events have the ability to transfix the nation, becoming high holidays of communication during which everyone is watching the same thing and participating vicariously—for example, the Kennedy funerals, the O.J. Simpson chase, and even the Clarence Thomas-Anita Hill confrontation. What made the moon landing even bigger than those other news events was that it didn't occur unexpectedly. Beyond the obvious eight-year buildup, the networks had a chance to plan and promote their moon-landing coverage for months, with the result that this one news event was made into a show far more consciously by both participants and newsmen alike. "Everything hereafter will be stage-managed for cosmic Nielsens in the interest of national or universal establishments," wrote TV critic Robert Lewis Shayon at the time. No wonder a French journalist once asked John Glenn how it felt to be as famous as Gary Cooper. "Madam," Glenn replied, "I haven't been aboard a horse in weeks."

It had all begun on a much smaller scale about a decade earlier.

When Project Mercury began in the late fifties, there was a question as to whether rocket launches would even be covered by television, since this was considered something of a military enterprise and reporters were typically restricted in their coverage of such events. What's more, television was still in its relative infancy: When the government originally wanted to ensure important favorable coverage of the astronauts, after all, it habitually turned to *Life* for its "exclusives," not the networks. Yet television gave the launches and splashdowns (which couldn't be covered live until the late sixties, because until then there were no "space" satellites to provide the signal) hundreds of hours of coverage.

Part of the reason for this extended coverage was that the network news divisions still didn't have more than a 15-minute nightly show to put out until late 1963. Like a political convention, space gave them the chance to display their wares at a time when TV news was beginning to leave the studio. In 1965, for Gemini 3, CBS sent 110 people down to Florida for the launch, with Walter Cronkite remaining on the scene for a week, putting in 14- to 16-hour days. Many of the network correspondents had also made their names in World War II and Korea; the space program—with its emphasis on Cold War competition, its strong ties to the military, and its focus on technological gadgetry—was the closest thing to their formative military experiences.

Like the space program itself, television seemed to be part of a brave new world; the newsmen and astronauts alike saw themselves as engaged in similar endeavors. Once the visuals got better, it all was a story that had to be seen, not heard or read. Finally, it was exciting, it took place in Florida (great weather!), and the whole country was caught up in the romance of space and these new heroes. Successful TV series have been built around a lot less—though this one was notable for the hundreds of hours that the networks were willing to give to just letting cameras roll in front of their anchors.

Cronkite played a key role, helping mightily to confer status and importance on the space program. Chet Huntley and David Brinkley at NBC were political junkies, so didn't cover many of the flights— leaving the anchoring largely to Frank McGee. In contrast, Cronkite (who had always been interested in aeronautics) became something of an honorary astronaut, immersing himself in the intricacies of space travel. *The New York Times* called him "a one-man phenomenon in space coverage," and over time he would become as identified with the space program as any of the astronauts. It was Cronkite, after all, who muttered "Come on, baby! Come on, baby!" as John Glenn's rocket started to leave the launching pad, and who started to break down on camera when Scott Carpenter's Aurora 7 capsule was missing after reentry: "I'm afraid . . . we may have . . . lost an astronaut," he said, his eyes welling up—though Carpenter and Aurora were soon found intact.

A typical Cronkite introduction to a mission went something like this:

> Out there on Pad 19 stands the great 90-foot Titan missile in its erector stand, and on top of that the Gemini capsule, ready to receive Gus Grissom and John Young—the astronauts who this morning have a date with destiny out there a hundred and fifty miles above the earth.

His enthusiasm increased as additional missions presented themselves. "Go, baby! Go!" he shouted as Apollo 11 took off. And when the module landed on the moon and Neil Armstrong emerged, Walter exlaimed, "There's a foot on the moon! Look at those pictures! Wow!"—followed by "Oh, boy! Hot diggity dog! Yes Sir!"

"People have the audacity to say nothing new is going on these days," Cronkite editorialized on the air during the moon mission in July 1969, a period when CBS, like NBC, was on the air for 30 hours straight. "I'd like to know what these kids are saying who pooh-poohed this. How can one turn off from a world like this?" It may have been how many Americans felt at the time, and Cronkite may have been close to setting records by being on the air for something over 17 hours straight. Still, it was unusual behavior for an anchor, conduct which revealed how this type of news coverage differed from anything else. Perhaps we might best think of it as being rather like the way that announcers present the Olympics today.

To cap things off for the moon mission, ABC commissioned Duke Ellington to write a new piece of music; NBC countered with James Earl Jones and Rod McKuen reading poetry; and CBS featured Buckminster Fuller and Buster Crabbe (star of the old movie serial *Buck Rogers*). Thus, when the *Eagle* finally landed at 4:17 P.M. on that stellar Sunday, it seemed to some almost anticlimactic. This was truly the origin of news as stage production: Politicians would take note, and learn to drench their appearances in imagery and music based on what they had seen here.

Yet what may be most notable about television's interest in space is how soon it faded. Once that first moon mission ended, the networks began turning off—a phenomenon which became one of the themes of the film *Apollo 13*. Following Apollo 11, there were seven more Apollo missions, five more moon landings, and the shuttle program, but few remember much about any of them—with one exception. By the time the *Challenger* shuttle exploded in 1986, the major networks were not even covering launches live anymore. This was why the blowup of the *Challenger* was seen by the overwhelming majority of Americans on tape, often in excruciating slow motion.

It's a truism that sequels rarely do as well in Hollywood as the original, and viewers of the space race were gradually losing interest. In retrospect, however, a lot more had changed over the years than the productions and their historical scope. In the wake of Vietnam and Watergate, TV news grew more adversarial and laced with commentary; the adulatory coverage of the space program seemed out of place in such an environment—except, of course, when things went wrong as with *Challenger*. Television news also no longer depended on special events to hype its presence. Unlike scheduled news shows, such presentations did tend to drone on, draining commercial dollars. With the very satellites that the space program had helped launch, television now could go anywhere in the world live, with the result that special-event coverage focused increasingly on events abroad, and not on—or in—space.

Moreover, space coverage had justifiably made the astronauts and their supporting technicians alike into heroes; Walter Cronkite tried hard to be merely an emcee, à la Ed Sullivan. In future decades, television would subtly insist that its newsmen assume central roles in *any* TV drama—as commentators if nothing else. That's why the real programming sequel to the space program on CBS was the popular *60 Minutes,* which covered the news so as to always glorify the news correspondent.

Thanks in large part to television, the very definition of news would also change so much that there would be little room for something like space. On the day of the first moon landing, the main headline of the *New York Times* read "Astronauts Swing Into Moon Orbit in Preparation for Today's Landing." Right below that was a smaller headline: "Woman Passenger Killed, Kennedy Escapes in Crash." That event, of course, was Chappaquiddick.

The irony is that today Chappaquiddick seems the more contemporary and thus recognizable event. In retrospect, the moon landing marked the beginning of the end—not only of the entire old era of Cold War competition, which defined us from roughly 1945 to 1990—but also the space program and television's infatuation with exploration. On the other hand, the tabloid trail from Chappaquiddick would eventually lead to Gary Hart's door, and then on to the troubles of such now-familiar names as Charles and Di, Woody and Mia, and Tonya and Nancy, not to mention the legal problems of the Bobbitts, the Menendez brothers, Michael Jackson, the Juice, and the Kennedys redux, this time in a Palm Beach courtroom before a national TV audience. Then of course came Bill Clinton—the scandal-a-week, tabloid president. Celebrities in trouble seem to have become our national obsession; once upon a time it was getting to the moon. This move may be one small economic step forward for the men who run the networks—but it's one giant cultural step backward for mankind.

21

The Beverly Hillbillies and the Rise of Populist Television
(CBS: 1962–71)

To most critics of its time and many intellectuals since, *The Beverly Hillbillies* is symptomatic of a lot that is wrong with television. "If television is America's vast wasteland, the 'Hillbillies' must be Death Valley," wrote one detractor back then. "The show aims low and hits its target," wrote yet another, while David Susskind urged his viewers to write to their congressmen and complain. Some reviewers took it personally: The show was "deliberately concocted for mass tastelessness," charged Warren Lewis in the *Saturday Evening Post.* Even a number of CBS executives originally thought the show was too stupid to be anything but a flop. Yet this ultracorny situation comedy about a hillbilly family that strikes it rich and moves to Beverly Hills may be one of the most popular television shows of all time. David Marc and Robert Thompson make a persuasive case, in their book *Prime Time, Prime Movers,* that *The Hillbillies* may be the most popular comedy of any sort in American history.

Consider the evidence. The show rose to Number 1 in the ratings only three weeks after it premiered in September 1962—a record—and remained there for two years. The list of the Top Fifty individual programs of all time is filled mostly with special, once-a-year, or one-time-only events: Super Bowls, Miss America pageants, the last episode of *M*A*S*H,* and the like. Yet seven regular episodes of *The Hillbillies* immediately following the John F. Kennedy assassination grace the list. These episodes became the most widely watched half-hour shows in TV history, as the nation turned to utter escapism to bury its grief. In its 10 years and 274 episodes on the air (168 in color), *The Hillbillies* fell out of the Top Twenty only during its last year, and the show helped inspire not simply immediate spinoffs, such as *Petticoat Junction* and *Green Acres,* but a whole slew of odd comedies, like *My Favorite Martian* and *Gilligan's Island.* Even in 1992, the show was still being syndicated in over 50 cities and on cable, with audiences estimated at 60 million a week. A year later, it also became a feature-length movie.

The show obviously hit a nerve, and to a certain extent still does. Part of the series' success was, simply, that it was funny—if cornpone humor reminiscent of Grand Ole Opry routines, combined with one of the loudest laugh tracks in TV history, is your cup of tea. As analysts have pointed out, the suddenly rich hillbilly Clampetts (patriarch Jed, Granny, young and flirtatious Elly, and strapping Jethro) may have moved to Beverly Hills, but they made the mountain come to

Muhammad, not the other way around. Jed was played by Buddy Ebsen, who had earlier struck TV gold as Fess Parker's sidekick on Disney's Davy Crockett miniseries.

The setting for the show was originally supposed to be New York, but since Beverly Hills was just around the filming corner from Hollywood, show creator Paul Henning set the series there. In retrospect, as the cultural influence of L.A. came to eclipse that of New York, that shift turned out to be a nail in the coffin of Gotham as significant as the moving of *The Tonight Show* to Burbank. The single most-watched episode in the show's history came when Granny mistook a kangaroo for a giant jackrabbit. Shows centered on such excitements as Elly Mae's adventures at a finishing school for girls, and how Jethro's hillbilly ways utterly confused a school psychiatrist. The swimming pool was the "cee-ment pond," and pets were "critters."

JED: We're gonna be shooting some wild game called golf.
GRANNY: What in tarnation is a golf?
JED: I dunno, but they must be thicker 'n crows in a corn patch around here because everybody in Beverly Hills shoots 'em.

"Do you like Kipling?" "I don't know—I ain't never kippled" was the kind of joke that made the show a phenomenon, as was "Do you know Shaw's *Pygmalion?*" followed by "I don't know Shaw—let alone his pig." Today, of course, despite all the criticism of the effects of these hillbillies on culture, few viewers would even *get* the allusion to *Pygmalion*. "You know that no one will be killed, no one will have a brain tumor," said the show's director, a former Shakespearean actor named Richard Whorf. It also didn't hurt that the show's hillbilly theme song about a "man named Jed," written by Henning, became a hit on its own, while inspiring such other TV shows as *Gilligan's Island* to use theme songs to set up the premise of their own plots.

This show was not the first on television to celebrate the decency of down-home folk, as fans of *The Andy Griffith Show* and *The Real McCoys* will attest. Yet, on television, success inspires replication—so it's no surprise that over the course of the 1960s *The Hillbillies* would spawn imitators and spinoffs. That trick began with *Petticoat Junction*, which premiered in 1963 with cousin Pearl Bodine back in Hooterville. This was followed by *Green Acres* in 1965, whose premise was the mirror image of *The Beverly Hillbillies*—rich New Yorkers move to backwoods—allowing Henning to continue spinning out stories on the clashes between city and country life. Add *The Andy Griffith Show* and *Gomer Pyle* to the Top Ten mix in the mid-sixties and it's clear that TV audiences were hungry for a certain type of entertainment.

In retrospect, what Westerns did in the fifties to create a homespun sensibility with their veneration of traditional values, shows like this did in the sixties. Moreover, in the wake of the 1963 Kennedy assassination and the escalating Vietnam War, these backwoods shows did it without the violence. However, because "hayseed TV" appealed to a lower-income audience, and thus to fewer advertisers willing to pay top rates, it doesn't exist much anymore on commercial television—which is one reason why so many viewers now think that the networks are elitist. Shows like *Designing Women* would return to the South as a setting in the 1980s, but that one was a product of Bill and Hillary Clinton's friend Linda Bloodworth-Thomason, and reflected a kind of Arkansas-meets-Yale feminist sensibility that was almost the antithesis of that of *The Beverly Hillbillies.*

In the years since, explaining the extraordinary popularity of *The Beverly Hillbillies* has become a kind of cottage industry—though Henning himself once asked, "Why go into deep analysis about it? My shows are pure fun, just escape." Some saw in the show an allegory about the struggle between heredity and environment. A British critic even compared the TV hillbilly folk to the Beatles. "Like the [real] Hillbillies, they remain unspoilt," he wrote. "Wealth has come to them, and fast. But they are still the same simple-hearted, inarticulate Liverpudlians that they always were." Others saw the Clampetts as early hippies and back-to-the-landers, doing their own thing. Well, maybe.

The show did popularize what has become a convention in sitcom storytelling—the fish-out-of-water technique. Put hillbillies in a ritzy neighborhood, a space alien in Los Angeles or Colorado (*My Favorite Martian* or *Mork and Mindy*), a conservative in a family of liberals (*Family Ties),* or an urban rapper in rich suburbs (in a direct nineties steal from the premise of *The Beverly Hillbillies* called *The Fresh Prince of Bel-Air*), and you supposedly have all the ingredients for a half-hour of laughter. Eric Barnouw, in his history of television, *Tube of Plenty,* even tied the success of *The Beverly Hillbillies* to a popular show which had premiered two years earlier, *The Flintstones,* theorizing that both offered cultural contrasts, occasional social satire, and unsophisticated humor. *The Beverly Hillbillies* wasn't a cartoon, but it could have been—related, as it was, to Al Capp's "Li'l Abner."

Certainly this show—and others like it—struggled to uphold rural, Main Street values against an onslaught of urban modernism. Audiences laughed at these hillbillies, but more often they laughed with them. American culture has often dealt with the clash of urban and rural, new values and old, and it may be true (as some speculated) that *The Beverly Hillbillies* stood up for the Jeffersonian agrarian ideal against some kind of Hamiltonian notion of progress. If so, it's no surprise that such a theme struck a chord during the sixties, when those values seemed to be under attack—not simply by a counterculture but by the rise of those Eastern sophisticates, the Kennedys. "There's Beverly Hills for you," Granny once complained, though she could have been talking for many about America's First Family. "All flashy an' show on th'outside, but nothin' inside where it counts." The early women's movement came in for some hits, too. On an episode entitled "Women's Lib," Jethro finds his women reading a copy of *Free Women* and proclaims, "I'm gonna git me one of them."

Before *The Beverly Hillbillies,* TV comedies tended to revolve around comfortable suburban families—*Leave It to Beaver, Father Knows Best,* and even *I Love Lucy.* By contrast, *Hillbillies* was a comedy about social conventions. True, its themes were hardly new, but—love it or hate it—the show broadened TV comedy to include something of the social and political, paving the way eventually for such shows as *All in the Family* and *Murphy Brown.*

In its portrayal of those conflicts, this show obviously took the side of the hillbillies. That was significant, too. Long before politicians like Richard Nixon began courting the "great silent majority," Paul Henning was doing something similar. "I was anxious to defend the 'square' virtues," Nixon would say in his autobiography years later, and this wildly popular show helped highlight, years before Nixon's successful 1968 presidential candidacy, what those "square virtues" were. There is a modern strain of cultural and political populism that began with George Wallace and continued roughly on in different ways through Nixon, Jimmy Carter, and Ronald Reagan, and finally to H. Ross Perot and even Pat Buchanan. That populism was bred on shows like *The Beverly Hillbillies*—and the horrified reaction of the Establishment to the show only added to its allure.

All this tells us something about why such TV fare as *The Beverly Hillbillies* and *The Lawrence Welk Show* have remained popular—if only in reruns. Our cities are still in turmoil; the rich continue to fiddle while the middle and lower classes burn; the coastal elites and the heartland continue to struggle over cultural norms. In the early nineties Perot—who could easily have been a character on this show—led arguably the largest populist movement of the past half-century. *The Beverly Hillbillies* was the first telltale sign on television that the cultural unity of the fifties was splintering: It's not a stretch to say that the ongoing values debate, and even the rise of the Christian Coalition, began here. If nothing else, that distinguishes this show from an awful lot of what passes for quality television.

22

Assassination Television
(ALL 3 NETWORKS: 1963)

It was a series of sounds and images which had monumental impact and will always remain in the minds of those who watched: the blood-stained dress, the child saluting to the coffin, the funeral procession to the muffled drums, the riderless horse. Over 30 years later, American culture is still obsessed by the assassination of President John F. Kennedy, and by its greater meaning. Yet, viewed purely in television terms, the impact of the four-day coverage of the Kennedy killing and funeral looms almost as large. It's not simply that most Americans were glued to their TV sets as vicarious mourners over this four-day period. Nor was it that the death of Kennedy, America's first political TV superstar, was itself turned into a television production.

Rather, as some scholars have noted, this was the event that legitimized television in the eyes of the public, which meant that after it was over, print would never again challenge TV as the public's primary source of information and authority. Moreover, by the time it was over, this tragedy had ushered in a new age in which television, by its very presence, altered the events it was covering—thus creating a kind of televisual Heisenberg Principle. That augured a culture wherein TV would thrust itself and its reporters as much into any story as the newsmakers themselves.

Yet it was the Oswald assassination, more than that of the president, that defined the impact on the evolution of television. In looking back at those four days in November 1963, the coverage and the response can really be divided into three minishows, or phases. In the first— coverage of the presidential assassination itself—television news was still too primitive to be memorable, and thus to have much impact with such a fast-breaking story. There were, after all, no immediate pictures of the actual assassination, and the technology didn't exist to get good images or witnesses on the air quickly. Indeed, according to Gerald Posner's *Case Closed,* when NBC's Robert MacNeil dashed into the building nearest him, immediately after the shooting, he bumped into a man leaving it and asked him where there was a pay phone. The building was the Texas School Depository, and the man who directed him to the phone, MacNeil later learned, was Lee Harvey Oswald.

Still, MacNeil initially had trouble getting on the air. When he tried to call his network right after the shooting, he yelled: "This is MacNeil in Dallas!" and the voice on the other end said "Just a minute"—and never came back. Thus, in the first few hours after Kennedy was shot, radio was no different from television in conveying information, and in fact reported the headlines faster. TV anchors and reporters didn't have much more access to hard information than did the public, and mostly they just sat there, numb, talking among themselves.

What's more, most Americans weren't home in the middle of that Friday, November 22, watching television. That means most heard the news from friends or radio. Still, if only because of the endless number of times it has been repeated on anniversary shows in the more than three decades since, many Americans can recognize the moment (1:40 P.M. EST, some 10 minutes after the shooting), when CBS first preempted its regular programming (*As the World Turns,* with Nancy dusting a pile of books) with only a visual, which read "CBS News Bulletin," backed by a Walter Cronkite audio:

> In Dallas, Texas, three shots were fired at President Kennedy's motorcade in downtown Dallas. The first reports say President Kennedy has been seriously wounded by this shooting.

When it was done, CBS cut to a commercial for Nescafé.

Cronkite earned his place in TV history by accident: The CBS correspondent who should have handled midday bulletins—Harry Reasoner—was out to lunch. (Reasoner ended up anchoring the CBS coverage that night.) For much of the next hour, Cronkite and his counterparts at the other two networks attempted to glean details, mostly by reading the wire-service reports or talking to reporters by phone from the Trade Mart, where Kennedy had been scheduled to speak next. Various rumors were relayed that Kennedy was dead, and CBS radio reported that fact 18 minutes before its television network did. Cronkite waited for official confirmation—which, in those days, still meant confirmation from a print or wire reporter. At 2:38 P.M., EST, he got it, and delivered the news, his voice cracking, while he aimlessly removed his glasses and then put them back on:

> From Dallas, Texas, a flash, apparently official. President Kennedy died at 1:00 P.M., Central Standard Time, two o'clock, Eastern Standard Time—some 38 minutes ago.

Though Cronkite's announcement has now become the semiofficial one, CBS officials were so shaken by Walter's unusual loss of composure on the air that they sent him home a few minutes later, and had Charles Collingwood take over. Shortly before Cronkite left the studio, he picked up a ringing phone, only to hear from an irate viewer: "I want the people at CBS to do something about that Walter Cronkite," she began. "It's a disgrace that a man who has been trying to get John Kennedy out of office should be on the air talking at a

time like this." "Madam," the normally unflappable Cronkite answered, "this *is* Walter Cronkite, and you are a God-damned idiot."

The rest of that day's coverage completed the first stage of this
miniseries. Oswald was caught and identified, but there would be little usable footage until much later that night—though CBS's young,
relatively unknown Dallas bureau chief, Dan Rather, distinguished
himself with his scoops. The one memorable TV event of that Friday
occurred when the plane bearing the president's coffin landed at Andrews Air Force Base near Washington at around 6:00 P.M. Jackie
Kennedy, in her bloodstained dress, emerged following the casket, and
then newly sworn-in President Lyndon Johnson delivered a short
statement. On the whole, however, that night's coverage was not the
stuff of television greatness: Having dispensed with commercials and
regular programming alike, the networks ran old tapes and speeches of
President Kennedy, as well as funeral music. The TV audiences at that
time were not yet immense. That trend and the slow tempo of the
telecasts continued on through Saturday, as the networks covered the
arrival of the body at the White House and the procession of digni-
taries who arrived to pay their respects.

Phase two of the coverage came on Sunday in Dallas, though pre-
monitory scenes had appeared earlier. In an apparent effort to appease
television reporters, accused and manacled assassin Oswald had been
trotted out from his cell by the Dallas police on several occasions, and
so had the alleged murder weapon. (One notable effect: For years afterwards, network executives would not allow any rifles with tele-
scopic sights to appear on television, for fear this would recall the
assassination for viewers.) Reporters were given the chance to yell out
"Why did you kill the president?" as Oswald was led away for inter-
rogation. At times, the halls of the station had over 100 reporters, and
one session was cut off, in the words of the police chief, because "the
newsmen tried to overrun him."

Thus it was no surprise that Oswald's transfer from City Prison to
the County jail on Sunday was treated as something of a media event,
despite protests from the Justice Department in Washington that the
prisoner should be transferred secretly. Bowing to media requests, the
police scheduled the transfer by van for noon on Sunday, to be covered live on NBC and then on tape by the other two networks. This

meant that the narrow basement corridor heading to the van was filled with newsmen, wires, and blinding TV camera lights. In such chaos, it was easy for a gunman to enter the basement, and Jack Ruby did.

As Oswald emerged slowly in handcuffs, five minutes late so he could change his sweater, and flanked by two policemen, CBS radio newsman Ike Pappas thrust a microphone in his face. "Do you have anything to say in your defense?" Pappas asked. Then, a second later, Ruby stepped forward from where he had been lurking behind the reporters and shot Oswald in the stomach—live on national television, another first. "He's been shot; he's been shot; Lee Oswald has been shot," NBC reporter Tom Pettit kept repeating. Few then or since have thought to note how television itself had helped make the shooting possible. One who did at the time was Jonathan Miller, in the *New Yorker*:

> [I]n being so inquisitive, television may have become an accomplice in the crime—may have actually joggled events in the direction they took. . . . One could almost feel the lens urging Ruby out of the crowd. In fact, in the pictures, it looked as if he came out of the camera itself.

Thus television changed history twice on that day—first by literally setting up Ruby with his opportunity, and then by providing America with its first dramatic, watch-it-as-it-happens national news event. From Ruby's bullet, to CNN in Baghdad, to O.J.'s Bronco chase, the news would never be the same as it sought to capture—and sometimes create—similar moments.

Still, phase three awaited. Though the networks now had the kind of footage that in the tabloid age of the nineties would have become the centerpiece of coverage, on that weekend they dropped Oswald rather quickly. That's because they were already into the last minishow of the coverage, and the one that most everyone remembers best—the beginning of the ceremonial period of national mourning, and the funeral. From Sunday's procession and ceremonies in the Capitol and on through Monday's funeral, Americans used television to experience their grief collectively, and television delivered. "When the day's history is written," wrote Jack Gould of the *New York Times,* "the record of television as a medium will constitute a badge of honor."

Though each network provided its own news team, the three combined their camera efforts (41 units in all). This meant that the visual coverage was superb for the time, although out of courtesy there was never a full-face closeup of Jackie, the children, or any immediate members of the family. All in all, it was an impressive performance—so much so that former Federal Communications Commission chairman Newton Minow, a frequent critic of the networks, said "We always hear that television is a young medium. If so, it grew up in a couple of days."

Over the decades, television would create other times when the whole country could experience an event together. This, however, was the first moment it had done so, establishing the largest domestic audiences in the history of the medium until then. Thus those days in November had consequences for the development of the medium itself. "I think we were frightened when we saw our capability," one TV executive said later. But somehow the fear soon passed—as did the concern over lost profits: By suspending all regular programming and cancelling all commercials over those three-and-a-half days, CBS and NBC had lost an estimated $4 million; ABC a bit over $2 million.

As a consequence of this event, as Barbie Zelizer noted in her wide-ranging book on media treatment of the 1963 Kennedy assassination, *Covering the Body,* television's hold on the public vis-à-vis print was never seriously challenged again—even in the eyes of those who had once distrusted the medium. "I never in my life expected to spend six hours looking at television," said Governor Albertis Harrison of Virginia over that weekend. By the following year, when delegates at the Republican convention wanted to voice their displeasure with the press, they shook their fists at the network anchor booths above. Thus the concepts of television news and of news itself had become inseparable. TV was now more than the medium of choice; it was the only medium anyone could envision capturing an event. In one weekend, America had gone from a print-and-radio nation (we read and heard the news) to a television nation (we saw the funeral).

Through its coverage, television had also made itself a part of the story, seemingly without anyone's realizing it. When people remembered that weekend years later, what they recalled were the television images—and the TV journalists who provided them. We take TV coverage for granted now—where else could you learn so quickly and easily and completely about something?—but the assassination and its immediate aftermath were a dividing line in our cultural history. For most of those four days in November 1963, the reporters had kept quiet and let the events speak for themselves. From then on, however, TV the teller would become an inextricable part of every tale.

23

Mister Ed: How Real Were TV's Escapist Comedies?
(SYNDICATION AND CBS: 1961–66)

The 1960s have been known as the era when much of television withdrew into an almost impenetrable world of fantasy. After all, in a decade when the nation was experiencing some of the most convulsive social change in its history, the situation comedy was busy retreating into a form which television historian David Marc once dubbed "the magicom."

While the nation witnessed the hosings and church bombings in Birmingham, the assassination of a president, the beginnings of the women's movement, the makings of a youthful counterculture, and the escalation of a war in Southeast Asia, sixties television often receded into a fantasy universe which, at first glance, had nothing to do with what was going on in the culture. From *Bewitched* and *I Dream of Jeannie,* to *Gilligan's Island* and *My Favorite Martian,* to *The Munsters* and *The Addams Family,* sixties sitcoms featured few black people, fewer hippies, and even fewer feminists, while remaining awash in monsters, aliens, witches, and talking cars (on the now offbeat classic, *My Mother the Car*). To some, it all seemed proof of Dave Garroway's comment that "television started off mediocre and went steadily downhill."

Yet these odd sitcoms reflected their times more than it might at first seem. By packaging troubling cultural shifts in the guise of comic fantasy, these shows made it easier for Americans to come to grips with rapid social change.

The spiritual father of all of these sixties fantasy shows was *Mister Ed*—an odd fate for a series which never hit the Top Twenty-five in its five-and-a-half years, and was intended to be a throwback to the comedies of an earlier era by appealing mostly to children. Modeled on the old movies about Francis the Talking Mule by the same producer, Arthur Lubin, the show was originally bankrolled by George Burns; the pilot was called "The Wonderful World of Wilbur Post." When the networks passed on the concept of a talking horse, Studebaker agreed to underwrite the show, and sold it to 115 local TV stations in syndication.

The show premiered in January 1961, two weeks before President Kennedy took office. The critical reaction was not kind: "Maybe a talking horse is commercial, but there has to be more than an idea to put it across," opined *Variety*. However, after a successful first-season run of 26 episodes, during which the show frequently outdrew others in its time period, CBS bought the series for its next season, to run on Sundays at 6:30 P.M.—one of the few series in history to go from being distributed to individual stations in syndication to network prime time.

Shows about animals have always enjoyed wide appeal, as anyone who has ever watched *Rin Tin Tin* or *Lassie* knows. Yet this show was far cleverer than most critics have been willing to acknowledge, then or now—one good reason why it has fared so well with adults in syndication. Part of the credit has to go to the memorable theme song written and sung by Jay Livingstone—who also wrote the theme for *Bonanza,* as well as "Mona Lisa," "Silver Bells," and "Que Será Será." Stand in a crowded elevator, it has been said, and recite "A horse is a horse," and at least one other person will respond with the words to the song.

The premise and 143 plots were hardly complicated. The foundation was laid down as follows: Wilbur Post, an architect, and his wife, Carol, have bought a country house at 17230 Valley Spring Lane that comes with a horse. In the first episode, Wilbur ("Wiiilllbuurrr") discovers that the horse talks—but only to him.

WILBUR: It's been a long time since I was a little boy.

ED: It's been a long time since I was a pony.

WILBUR: Who said that? No, that's impossible. Did you say that? No, how could you?

ED: Did you say it?

WILBUR: No, I didn't hear it. How could I? But I did! Oh, this is impossible. I don't believe it. Now, while I'm looking right at you, say something!

ED: Like what?

WILBUR: Anything. Anything!

ED: How now, brown cow?

Burns had urged that Alan Young play the role of Wilbur: "He looks like the sort of fellow a horse would talk to," he once said. There are the predictable episodes as Wilbur pays far more attention to Ed than he should—allowing the horse to sleep in his bed; covering up for him when he uses the phone and runs up a big long-distance bill; letting him play with his favorite baseball team, the Los Angeles Dodgers; and similar horsing around.

The core of the show, though, was the unusual relationship between Wilbur and Ed. There were, of course, the usual sitcom gag lines—usually delivered by the horse: "Time and Ed wait for no man," or "I don't expect you to be perfect; you're only human." Yet the closeness of the two leads—one human, one equine—forged by sharing their enormous secret, was unusual on TV at the time. In a televisual world in which parents usually kept their distance from their children, and husbands from their wives, Ed and Wilbur were the best of pals. "Hey, buddy boy!" Ed would call out to his master.

That sort of thing was intentional. "We played the horse as a teenager," Larry Rhine, a writer for the show, once said. "So consequently, [since] this was the sixties, we were able to have Mister Ed letting his mane grow long, and wanting a pad of his own, . . . doing all the things that teenagers would do." Thus, for all its fantasy, Mister Ed may have been television's earliest real attempt to address the growing generation gap, and what it felt like to be a father in that age. The fantasy concept also allowed *Mister Ed* to address other and more serious issues, such as psychiatry and adoption: On one show, Mister Ed runs away during the holidays, so he can see his real father again. As with *The Twilight Zone,* television often became more real, the further from reality it seemed to venture. Fantasy was a cover which allowed the medium to tell the truth.

And so it went with other shows of the era as well—which were often about how odd "others" seem, and how ordinary Americans can come to grips with them. *The Munsters* and *The Addams Family* each used a family of monsters to demonstrate how intolerant and weird the rest of the "normal" world actually was. *Addams* producer Nat Perrin once wrote an article saying that his TV creations made up the most idealized family on TV because they never fought with each other, and the two parents could actually be depicted as attractive to one another.

In a somewhat similar vein, *Gilligan's Island* was something of an allegory about life in a hippy haven—and how the straighter arrows in the culture can learn to cope. It was even pitched to CBS chief William Paley as "a social microcosm"—an attempt to show how a group of disparate individuals could leave technology behind (in this case, out of necessity born of shipwreck) and forge a communal relationship. This isn't to say that *Gilligan's Island* was anything other than mass entertainment, but only to stress how it reflected what was going on in the culture at large. If hippies weren't self-castaways, what were they?

Another "magicom," *My Favorite Martian,* was a show that subtly dealt with racism in ways that never would have been possible had the issue been tackled head-on. Uncle Martin may have been depicted as a Martian, but Martians were as alien to many Americans as blacks were. By making this Martian seem both real and just like us, *My Favorite Martian* provided an allegory to the civil-rights struggle then dominating the headlines.

My Favorite Martian was also an influential shift in the culture's attitude toward "aliens." In science-fiction films of the 1950s, aliens usually were portrayed as threatening—a thinly disguised version of communists. Uncle Martin started a trend toward the positive depiction of outer-space visitors that led eventually to films like *E.T.* and *Close Encounters of the Third Kind.* After all, Ray Walston (who played Martin) once rejected a line in a script with the comment, "A Martian would never say that." In the spirit of the sixties, a meeting with an alien was now often seen as the latest way to expand your horizons. As the late Timothy Leary might have said in parody of himself: "Tune in, turn on, and shake hands with an extraterrestrial."

Similarly, *I Dream of Jeannie* and *Bewitched* (the latter of which rose as high as Number Two in the ratings) dealt in a primitive way with how the culture could learn to live with empowered women—respectively disguised here as a genie and a witch. No one would call Jeannie or Samantha liberated: The implied message of many episodes on these shows was how women must "curb their power" to be accepted into conventional society. Yet the premise of females testing the boundaries—the *real* theme of both shows—was revolutionary as sixties television, and reflected the early stages of the women's movement. As Gerard Jones has pointed out in *Honey, I'm Home,* a history of sitcoms, these shows were elaborate satires of the kinds of domestic roles against which women were beginning to rebel. Thus, their logical successor was 1966's *That Girl,* starring Marlo Thomas as a single woman pursuing a career. That show, in turn, led several years later to *The Mary Tyler Moore Show.*

There may even have been more lurking beneath the surface of these fantasy programs. *Bewitched* director Bill Asher once described his show to *TV Guide* as follows: "The show portrays a mixed marriage that overcomes by love the enormous obstacles in its path. Samantha, in her new role as housewife, represents the true values in life. Material gains mean nothing to her."

If that was in fact the case, *Bewitched* was truly ahead of its time. And perhaps so were the others. After all, *Mister Ed* predated the youth movement, just as *My Favorite Martian* premiered before the signing of the Civil Rights Act, and *Bewitched* came before *Sisterhood Is Powerful.* Perhaps the Hollywood elite who created these series meant to make a statement but that "statement" went right over the heads of the audience. Or perhaps, in some subtle sense, these programs helped promote the very movements they have been accused of evading in fantasy. The bottom-line question is this: Who's to say that shows about witches, castaways, and talking horses didn't help tell us, in an age of rebellion and psychedelia, something about who we were and might yet become?

24

The Dating Game,
Game Shows, and the Rise of Tabloid TV
(ABC: 1965–73)

It's impossible to understand the significance of *The Dating Game* and other shows like it without knowing about the tradition from which they departed. Game shows, of course, have always been a staple of radio and television. From *The Price Is Right* and *Beat the Clock* to *Password* and *Let's Make a Deal,* America has been awash for over half a century with the sounds of "Good answer!" "Come on down!" "I'll go to Rose Marie to block!" and "Will the real Stanley Jones please stand up?"

Because game shows are among the easiest and cheapest programming to produce (few stars and no real scripts), there have been about 400 of them in the past 30 years. Run almost exclusively during the daytime or early evening ever since the quiz-show scandal of the 1950s, they provide the public the chance to see ordinary people like themselves competing on television. They also tend to be popular with advertisers, since the basic ethic of most game shows (winning cash or prizes) resonates with the essential message of all advertising: *I buy, therefore I am.* "People love money," a game-show producer once put it simply.

Most involve the same formula. They're extremely easy to follow, or so the conventional wisdom goes, because the daytime audience tends to be engaged in housekeeping tasks, such as cleaning, while watching. They're pitched mostly to women, who still tend to constitute a majority of the stay-at-home daytime audience. And, like soap operas, the other traditional mainstay of daytime programming, their form is rather amorphous. "There are no endings," game show creator Mark Goodson once said. "They go on and on and on."

Game shows still rarely have anyone but a white man hosting them—if not Bill Cullen, who holds the record with over 20 shows, then preferably someone who looks as if he just stepped off the floor of a Republican convention. (It's worth noting, however, that some of television's early leading personalities also hosted such shows: Walter

Cronkite on *It's News to Me;* Mike Wallace on three shows, including *Who Pays?;* Johnny Carson in *Who Do You Trust?;* and even Rod Serling in *Liar's Club.*) Women—when they aren't contestants—are there mostly for show; Vanna White, of *Wheel of Fortune,* didn't get her job because she had the highest SAT scores in Hollywood.

It's also no surprise that these traditional stereotyped shows promoting consumption and competition tend to be most popular in conservative eras, such as the 1950s and 1980s. Conversely, game shows that tend to attract a large audience in more-liberal eras frequently soften the acquisitive and cutthroat tone of a traditional, free-wheeling game show. So it went in the 1960s, with producer Chuck Barris's *The Dating Game.* In an era when it was less fashionable to be materialistic (no one was supposed to go home from Woodstock to watch *The Price Is Right*), Barris developed a series of game shows revolving around relationships and "letting it all hang out." On the heels of *The Dating Game* came Barris's *The Newlywed Game,* and later *The Gong Show,* and even *The $1.98 Beauty Contest.* "If game shows are at the center of the television desert," the *New York Times* once wrote, "the man at the epicenter . . . is Chuck Barris."

Those Barris shows ended up changing television more than one might think. On this rather puritanical medium, they became among the first shows to acknowledge openly that people have sex. In the sixties, sexual mores changed remarkably as pre- and extramarital sex, and the discussion of it, became commonplace. Perhaps TV played a subtle role in this transformation, as the "buy now" philosophy it instilled helped disintegrate the Protestant ethic that had made it a virtue to avoid self-gratification. Yet television programming itself rarely acknowledged the sea changes in sexual habits—at least until Barris.

From Barris's shows, television also learned again the appeal of spontaneity—and then, for the first time, of voyeurism. Before, game shows had been all Q & A and stunts; the Barris shows deemphasized competition in favor of letting people speak for themselves, often in risqué and self-revelatory ways. These shows also became known for consciously humiliating the people who became the contestants, meaning that they soon evolved into a form of entertainment centered not on the support provided by relationships, but on debasement. "Daytime TV does not make meaningful statements," Barris once said. "Audiences are being entertained either in awe or shock or horror or joy over someone going bananas in public." That theme of debasement has always been popular in a democratic country such as ours, where humor is often used to show that no one is better than anyone else. To be sure, others had been there before. "You tell *me*," said an executive producer of *Let's Make a Deal*, "why a doctor who makes $150,000 a year paints himself from butt to navel like the Jolly Green Giant, stands outside in that line in the cold for an hour and a half, to win *what*, that he can't afford to buy if he wants it."

"Never has the tube provided so much exhibitionist release for America's borderline crazies," wrote *Newsweek* once. "Never has it delivered a more therapeutic catharsis to the folks at home." Which meant that these shows became an early form of the tabloid talk programs, like *Jenny Jones* or *The Maury Povich Show*, which now comprise a large part of daytime programming—replacing many of the game shows themselves. Our persistent whining, and our current culture of narcissism all started, on TV at least, in 1965 with Barris.

There had been dating shows on television before. In the early 1950s, Arlene Francis hosted a radio carryover on the DuMont network, *Blind Date* (later changed to *Your Big Moment*). Yet the idea for a set of game shows based on relationships seemed to come from Barris alone. A native of Philadelphia who had kicked around the venues of pop culture—helping with the promotion of a Floyd Patterson title fight and writing Freddy "Boom Boom" Cannon's Top Forty hit, "Palisades Park"—Barris in 1965 convinced ABC to give him $7,500 to develop a show he called *The Dating Game*. The show would involve no huge prizes, celebrities, or tests of skill or knowledge. Instead, an attractive "bachelorette" would question three bachelors she couldn't see (they were on the other side of a partition), and then select one for a date. "We stay away from kooks, and girls with big breasts," Barris said then. After sitting on the show for the better part of a year, ABC set an afternoon premiere on December 20, 1965. It was while developing the show's pilots, Barris later revealed in his book *The Game Show King,* that he discovered that many of the contestants wanted to "talk dirty" even though they were supposed to be on television.

WOMAN: Bachelor Number One, what nationality are you?

BACHELOR: Well, my father is Welsh and my mother is Hungarian, which makes me Well-Hung.

WOMAN: Bachelor Number Three, make up a poem for me.

BACHELOR: Dollar for dollar and ounce for ounce, I'll give you pleasure 'cause I'm big where it counts.

Barris ended up warning all contestants that such comments were not allowed. Still, their apparent willingness to engage in exhibitionism and "double entendres" would end up becoming a key part of this and other Barris shows. No wonder this one attracted reviews like that of a Chicago paper which ran the headline "Daytime TV Hits All-Time Low."

Audiences felt otherwise. Hosted by Jim Lange, who had once been Tennessee Ernie Ford's sidekick, *The Dating Game* quickly became noteworthy for its risqué exchanges. Long after the show had left the air, viewers would also remember "And, heeere they are!" as the bachelors appeared; as well as the Herb Alpert and the Tijuana Brass "Whipped Cream" theme song (a double entendre?), played when the woman finally met her selection face-to-face, often to her utter disappointment and her selected date's embarrassment. The show also featured a slew of future celebrities striving for attention (or maybe just wanting hot dates), including Burt Reynolds and Tom Selleck.

Thus it was no surprise when, seven months later, a new Barris show that *TV Guide* would call "the worst piece of sleaze on television today" premiered—namely, *The Newlywed Game*. It made marital squabbling a spectator sport. "If I was married, and we loved and respected each other, I just know that my wife and I would never go on 'The Newlywed Game,'" Barris once said. The show featured four newlyweds who were asked questions while their spouses were offstage, with the spouses then asked to guess the answers that had been delivered in their absence. In retrospect, the only surprise about the show might have been that so many couples wanted to appear on it—given exchanges like these:

HOST: Would you say that your husband is more urban or rural?

WIFE: I don't know what it means. . . .

HOST: Well, just pick one.
WIFE: Uhh . . . (giggles) . . . I'll say urban.
HOST: Urban? How long has he been that way?
WIFE: A few years.
HOST: What's he done about it?
WIFE: Uh . . . he went to the doctor.
HOST: Did the doctor give him anything for his urban?
WIFE: He gave me something.

Or, as Barris once related it:

HOST: What will your husband say is his least favorite condiment on his wiener?
WIFE 1: Mustard.
WIFE 2: Ketchup.
WIFE 3: Ketchup.
WIFE 4: Ben-Gay.

The show had a domestic influence: According to one estimate, 40 percent of the couples' marriages eventually ended in divorce. That may be why the show plays in the background when Mrs. Robinson first tries to seduce Ben in the film *The Graduate*. "I wish Karl Marx were alive to watch this show," wrote *Life* magazine's TV critic—following with "I wish Sigmund Freud were alive to do the same thing." Barris was the first to clearly establish the propositions that:

1. Americans would do almost anything to be on television.
2. Once on TV, there was no limit to how much they would degrade themselves.
3. There was a large audience out there, willing to watch them do it.

Within a year ABC, still the third network and as always desperate for popular cheap programming, moved both shows into prime time, where they remained for three years.

By the 1970s, game shows had been given a new life on television, principally because of a 1971 Federal Communications Commission prime-time access rule which gave back to local stations the early part of prime time (7:00–8:00 P.M.), ostensibly so they could produce their own programming. The theory was that the locals would produce high-minded entertainment. Instead, they turned to cheap, syndicated products that could generate the most advertising revenue—namely, game shows. By then, Barris had packaged what he had learned about TV and the American psyche into new shows, and others followed.

Barris's *The Gong Show,* which premiered in 1976, borrowed the concept of *Ted Mack's Original Amateur Hour,* but turned it on its head by purposely booking bad acts—like belching storytellers, incompetent jugglers, and nose whistlers—who humiliated themselves while the audience and viewers laughed at home until the contestants were "gonged." On one such show, Barris (now the host) read a letter from a viewer who criticized its "tasteless and sadistic sick video humor." "You've got it!" yelled Barris, while the audience cheered.

Fitting the mood of the times was also a hallmark of a popular seventies game-show clone which Barris didn't produce, *Family Feud.* It pitted two families in competition against each other, while making personal interactions the key tension in the show. Even *The People's Court,* with Judge Wapner, was a kind of real-life game show, as two real litigants competed for a single prize—the judge's ruling. Several versions of dating games would even return in the nineties.

Chuck Barris was obviously no Pat Weaver—the man who created the *Today* and *Tonight* shows—or Carl Reiner. He does own a claim to fame, however, as the first architect of the Oprahesque talk genre, which would come to dominate television's daytime programming in the nineties. Talk shows and game shows have always been related, TV personality Merv Griffin once told an interviewer. "Game shows," he said, "are improvisational. [Jack] Paar came out of game shows; [Johnny] Carson came out of game shows. I came out of games. It was the great learning platform for people who had a clock in their head, a sense of timing."

For better and mostly for worse, Barris thus demonstrated there was a steady audience for perverse outrageousness and exhibitionism, particularly in the daytime—the one time period ignored by those critics who might otherwise intimidate the networks. That meant Barris had helped lead the way in creating our confessional and publicity-happy culture. It was, after all, *The $1.98 Beauty Contest* whereon the host could announce, concerning a fat person, "Maxie's wildest dream is to tie her shoes without falling over!" Barris proved that people don't even need the chance to win anything in order to humiliate themselves before a national audience—that merely the opportunity to appear before the cameras is sufficient. In just such a fashion would the zeitgeist of the sixties be extended into the nineties.

25

Walter Cronkite, the *CBS Evening News,* and the Rise of News on Television

(CBS: 1963–PRESENT)

He was not only "the most trusted man" in broadcasting history; he may have been the most powerful. Yet when the *CBS Evening News* with Walter Cronkite premiered as a half-hour nightly newscast on September 2, 1963, at 7:00 P.M. EDT, featuring an exclusive interview with President John F. Kennedy, it was by no means obvious that Cronkite—or even the news—would come to play such a dominant role in the history of the medium. The fact that both did owes as much to "Uncle Walter" as it does to the news events themselves.

National Monday-through-Friday newscasting had been part of television almost since its inception. NBC began airing the 15-minute *The Camel Newsreel Theatre* at 7:45 P.M. in 1948. Converted to *The Camel News Caravan* a year later, it was narrated by John Cameron Swayze, "the nightly monarch of the air." As part of the contract, a Camel cigarette had to be burning visibly on the set, in an ashtray. CBS—considered the dominant news network because of both its radio work and its celebrity reporters, such as Edward R. Murrow and William L. Shirer—had a similar show, hosted by Douglas Edwards, at 7:30 P.M. It debuted on August 15, 1948, with no sponsors because it couldn't attract any, thus implicitly demonstrating that newspapers and radio were still the news vehicles of choice for the nation. After all, TV news then consisted of little more than an anchor reading the news while easel photos or occasional newsreels were shown. Standard set props were a globe, a map, and a phone—though it was suggested to Edwards in this pre-TelePrompTer era that he learn Braille, so he could deliver the news and look at the camera at the same time.

It also didn't help that what little film existed wasn't very good. Phil Scheffler, who once worked with Edwards, remembered:

> One afternoon we opened a can of film and the caption said "Hordes of Chinese prisoners captured on the west coast of Korea." I remember saying to producer Don Hewitt, "This footage looks awfully familiar"—and Don agreed. We looked back in our files. Sure enough, a month earlier, the newsreel people had sent us the same footage, only that stuff was captioned "Hordes of Chinese prisoners captured on the east coast of Korea."

All this began to change in the mid-1950s as television grew and the charismatic anchor team of David Brinkley and Chet Huntley rose to prominence at NBC—chiefly through their coverage of the political conventions, then the main exposure of TV news to the public. In 1956 *The Huntley–Brinkley Report* replaced John Cameron Swayze's *Camel News Caravan,* and within four years this fifteen-minute newscast had passed the CBS newscast in the ratings.

Even then, however, the news was no big deal. Prime-time shows were rarely preempted for breaking news, if only because the advertisers produced the shows themselves, and a network would have had to compensate those businesses not just for lost ad time but also for the cost of the production itself, if they interrupted the telecast. When President Eisenhower went before the cameras in the late fifties to talk about military deployments on the islands of Quemoy and Matsu, off the coast of China, the networks taped him, and ran it after their prime-time features. Indeed, Richard Nixon's celebrated "Checkers" speech of 1952 was able to reach the public through a 64-station hookup only because the Republican National Committee paid for the broadcast. Local stations didn't look to the networks for news feeds, either: In 1957, when CBS interviewed Soviet leader Nikita Khrushchev, only about a third of its stations bothered to pick up the broadcast.

In the late fifties, according to Barbara Matusow's book *The Evening Stars,* the importance of news in the programming galaxy began to increase exponentially. After the quiz-show scandals of the late 1950s, the networks were under increasing pressure from the FCC to beef up their public-service broadcasting, and news fit the bill handily. Improved technology made it easier to provide better reporting and pictures for the stories. The development of videotape in 1956 meant that footage could be aired more quickly than previously because it didn't have to be developed. The use of satellites beginning in 1962 meant that live reports could now be obtained from anywhere. What's more, journalism was undergoing a transformation as the telegenic Kennedy administration rose to power: As television reached more homes, its power and access increased, and reporters—once considered part of a lowly occupation—began to be seen as glamorous, particularly if they worked on TV.

At CBS, which considered itself a kind of "*New York Times* of the airwaves," the rise of NBC was viewed ominously. As early as the mid-fifties, there had been a move afoot to replace Edwards with Cronkite—a Murrow recruit from print journalism who had been the first CBS reporter in Washington to be assigned exclusively to television. Through the fifties and into the very early sixties, Cronkite hosted special events like the political conventions; such offerings as CBS's history shows *You Are There* and *The Twentieth Century,* and CBS's failed alternative to NBC's *Today* show, whereon Cronkite was paired with a set of puppets, including Charlemane the Lion. (When Cronkite left that venture, he was replaced by Jack Paar.) Cronkite even did cigarette commercials, correcting an ad's grammar when he insisted on saying "Winston tastes good, *as* a cigarette should," rather than "*like.*" The anchoring change on the nightly news, however, had never been made—in part because of respect for Edwards, in part because some old CBSers felt that Cronkite was somehow too comfortable on television ("the epitome of the average guy," somebody once described him), and partly because CBS president James Aubrey reportedly wanted someone with more personality, like Mike Wallace.

By the early 1960s, however, Cronkite had emerged as the consensus choice, if only because some of the other would-be contenders, such as Eric Sevareid and Charles Collingwood, saw the job of just reading the daily news as drudgery. There was talk at some point of putting Cronkite on a new quiz show in order to reveal a more whimsical side of his personality—a suggestion which never came to pass, even though it was not as ridiculous as it might seem: ABC's chief newscaster, John Daly, had been hosting *What's My Line?* for years, and Cronkite had once moderated *It's News to Me.*

In April 1962, CBS reintroduced Cronkite to the nation, with the idea in mind of going to a half-hour broadcast within a year or two. Both NBC and CBS implicitly acted together in this, beginning their longer half-hour newscasts within weeks of one another: Each network knew that if the other broadcast an entertainment show against the news, the entertainment offering would destroy the news show in the ratings.

At the same time, CBS also made changes in its nightly newscast, in order to distinguish itself from the competition at NBC—though no network followed up on Cronkite's suggestion to do an 11:00 P.M. broadcast, because the local stations wouldn't cede the time. Cronkite was made managing editor of his broadcast. The network beefed up its domestic coverage. In contrast to Huntley and Brinkley, who were the unquestioned "stars" of their broadcast, CBS decided to headline a stable of prominent on-air reporters which would eventually include Dan Rather, Roger Mudd, and Charles Kuralt, with Sevareid as a commentator and Cronkite functioning as the spoke in the wheel.

Yet Cronkite remained somewhat skeptical about the value of television news. He liked to tell the story of a man who had spent a year just reading the newspaper, and another who let it slip by while just watching TV news. "At the end of that time," he said, "the guy who had been watching television would come out with a damn strange idea of what had happened in the world."

When the changes appeared at CBS News, the predictable result was a further drop in ratings, as the public took time to adjust. It would be four years before CBS would pass NBC in the ratings, and during that time, Huntley and Brinkley unquestionably ruled the news airwaves. In 1964, CBS even removed Cronkite as anchor for the

Democratic convention, after the GOP convention earlier in the summer produced ratings in which NBC got as many viewers as CBS and ABC combined.

Yet by 1966, Cronkite was on the cover of *Time,* hailed as "the single most convincing and authoritative figure in TV news." By then, most Americans were getting their news from television, not print, and Cronkite was already the stuff of TV legend. "Viewers rarely recall or relish a Cronkite statement," the TV critic for the *Providence Journal* said then. "They believe it instead." This was the era when the nightly news brought the civil-rights struggle into every home, and made Vietnam the first living-room war. And at the vortex was Cronkite, who sometimes seemed to be the only authority figure left whom Americans could still believe.

Watching today those CBS broadcasts that were viewed by over 20 million Americans each night (about double the number who tune in today) is a reminder of just how primitive TV news was then. In 1968, nearly half of all sound bites in stories lasted 40 seconds or longer; today, fewer than 1 percent do. The stories themselves were substantially longer, the pictures were far less sophisticated and "instantaneous," and the news was much more like that from a wire service than is today's commentary-laced analysis, with its constant interplay between anchor and reporter. Cronkite had been a wire-service man, and the show grew out of his experience. This was still television which revolved around words—not theater or the use of the latest technology. It was also far less cynical and adversarial.

Still, the structure of the news hasn't changed much since those days. The anchor (a term which supposedly originated with *60 Minutes* creator Don Hewitt in 1952) was the central focus, and he did more than just "anchor" the broadcast. For starters, he gave the show more freedom: As long as he talked and viewers believed him, the newscast wasn't as dependent on pictures as it might otherwise be. The anchor sat calmly alone, in a reassuring fashion, giving impartial order to a disordered world while the shadows of subordinates scurried around the set with machines buzzing.

"Everybody's security blanket," someone once described Cronkite. Like all anchors, he remained in the world of news, but not of it—a stance some critics would compare to the role of the lonely sheriff in the Western, the traditional American hero who still remained on the home screen on such shows as *Gunsmoke* and *Bonanza*. "It's not a performance," Cronkite once said, but his resistance to playing "the star" only burnished the legend, much like that of the cowboy who rides into town to clean up the mess only because he must. When Sheriff Cronkite concluded each broadcast with "And that's the way it is," that *is* the way it was—even if in fact it wasn't. "Talking to the camera as if it were an attentive stranger, Cronkite projects an air of friendly formality, of slightly distant courtliness," was the way *Time* described the style.

Like those Western-type lawmen, as critic Edwin Diamond once noted, the anchor model was a middle-aged, middle-American white man. Uncle Walter, of course, was the Laurence Olivier of anchors, but it says something about him and the prototype he represented that, more than 30 years after he assumed his anchoring duties, the image of the ideal anchor still hasn't changed much—even if ABC tried in the seventies with Barbara Walters, and CBS did bring Connie Chung aboard to join Rather in an odd failed attempt to create a Huntley and Brinkley for the culture of the nineties.

The news show's pattern also remains largely the same as it was then. The lead stories, often presented as a package, are delivered as "hot news" seemingly put together at the last minute—an impression concretized by the fact that the anchor seems to be writing something as he is introduced. The middle stories convey less excitement, and by the last third of the news broadcast, the attention has turned to something "light," or even humorous. Very little is presented live unless an anchor is talking to a reporter, and what's shown is heavily edited, even if the viewer is not aware of that fact.

Already by the end of the sixties, sociologists like Herbert Gans were comparing TV to print journalism and noticing that "each medium favors stories which it can, or thinks it can, do best." TV news looked for events which could be easily filmed, or which featured prominent drama and action. "We [eventually] went for the stories that could be illustrated, and left alone the ones that required careful examination through text," Cronkite once said in an interview, talking about his whole industry. "This distorted the whole value of television news, to my mind. And distorts it to this day."

That distortion would eventually change the focus of the whole culture, as Americans increasingly got their information not from the world of print but from a sketchy headline service heavily dependent on visuals, sound bites, simplicity, and personalities. Decades later, Richard Schickel, a cultural critic, would write of television:

> Suddenly there were no issues except those that could be personified, symbolized by famous people. And most of these issues were eventually discussed in terms of their proponents' personal psychology (and, very often, their personal travails). The trivialization of our public life, our inability to see beyond the images of the moment, has been, for me, the most astonishing development of the last four decades.

Because of its importance in delivering national audiences, getting on the network news became the focal point of much of our politics and public life, which more and more resembled a TV production—much to the consternation of the electorate. This also put an enormous amount of power in the hands of a small group of New York and Washington journalists, who became celebrities themselves. In a country which has historically wanted power dispersed, a backlash against the press inevitably developed.

With the importance of the network news and its "stars" growing, it's no surprise that as "the living-room war" in Vietnam escalated, the job fell to Cronkite to become the figure whose February 27, 1968, critique of the war (on a special broadcast, not on the evening news) would become known as the moment when public opinion irrevocably turned against President Lyndon Johnson. Broadcasting from Vietnam for a week, Cronkite—who rarely editorialized about anything because he feared that a perceived lack of objectivity might diminish his credibility—concluded one report by saying:

> To say that we are closer to victory today is to believe, in the face of the evidence, the optimists who have been wrong in the past. . . . [I]t is increasingly clear to this reporter that the only rational way out then will be to negotiate—not as victors, but as an honorable people who lived up to their pledge to defend democracy and did the best they could.

Of the 300 or so letters and calls the network received, only a few were critical. "The nation's Uncle had rendered judgment," historian Barbara Tuchman wrote later. It is said that Johnson turned to his press secretary after hearing this and said, "If I've lost Walter Cronkite, I've lost Mr. Average Citizen." A month later, Johnson announced his decision not to seek another term.

That isn't to say that Cronkite was a constant critic of the Establishment. Sometimes he helped it enormously. For example, later that same year, he was visibly angered as he anchored CBS's coverage of the Democratic convention and watched the police beating demonstrators—and a CBS cameraman—in a Chicago street. When Dan Rather was punched on the floor of the convention, Cronkite lost his cool: "I think we've got a bunch of thugs down there, Dan," he said. Yet despite all that, when Mayor Daley visited Cronkite in the booth later, the CBS anchorman was polite to the point of obeisance. "Maybe this is a kiss-and-make-up session, but it's not intended that way," he began, as he then allowed Daley to smear the demonstrators with virtually no direct challenge. "Daley took Cronkite like Grant took Richmond," a CBS executive said later. But Cronkite's greatest regret, he once admitted, was not covering Woodstock. "I missed the boat on the rock generation," he said. "I'm a Dixieland fan."

NBC's Chet Huntley retired in 1970, breaking up the NBC team that had challenged Cronkite in the ratings. Thus, in the seventies, Cronkite became the undisputed king of TV news. "You don't have to be President of the United States to make a difference in this country," Senator Edward Kennedy told him during an interview in 1976. "You don't even have to be a congressman. You make a difference, Mr. Cronkite." Indeed, so much at the center of all major news events was Cronkite that he increasingly played an instrumental role in some of them. For example, in 1978 he helped get Egypt's Anwar Sadat to meet face-to-face with Israel's Menachem Begin first by "hooking them up live" on CBS. Two years later, he virtually pulled off a similar feat by almost forcing Ronald Reagan to offer the GOP vice-presidential nomination to Gerald Ford, who had admitted to Walter on-air that he might take the job.

Explanations for Cronkite's appeal continued. "In middle age, he's becoming a father figure to a country that seems to be looking for one," explained the *New York Times'* Harrison Salisbury. "I think he's the definitive centrist American who reflects the essential decency of American society as much as you can," gushed the often-critical-of-TV David Halberstam. And so it went on for a decade, until Cronkite left the anchor's chair in March 1981.

Cronkite's decision revealed an exquisite sense of timing. The power and prestige of television news was at its peak, but was soon to fall. Serious competition from cable and CNN—as well as local newscasts—was about to begin, thus eroding both the audience for the national nightly news and its role as the nation's headline service. In reaction, these network newscasts would evolve into something far more interpretive and increasingly controversial, with the result that viewers increasingly found them skewed toward subjects and points of view associated with liberal elites. The technology was also making it easier to broadcast news "live," with better pictures.

All of this meant that an anachronistic print journalist like Cronkite, who depended on words, would be increasingly out of place—replaced in the power hierarchy by such savvy TV producers as Roone Arledge, who led ABC to news preeminence in the eighties and nineties. Cronkite was also part of an era when paternalism was still acceptable and authority figures had more authority. After the experiences of Vietnam and Watergate, which he helped present to the American people, the public grew not to trust *anyone* anymore—even this beneficent and beloved CBS figure. The new, atomized world of television would combine with a new, skeptical America to ensure that there could never again be another Walter Cronkite.

26

The Monkees and TV's Subversion of 1960s
(NBC: 1966–68)

On September 12, 1966, at 7:30 P.M., on NBC, they came. Walkin' down the street. Got the funniest looks from, everyone they'd meet.

Hey-hey, they were the Monkees.

To many, it was hardly a debut worth noting as one of television's great events or the decade's prime accomplishments. In the pantheon of 1960s notables, few would place the Monkees alongside Mario Savio, Stokely Carmichael, and Timothy Leary—not to mention Dylan, the Jefferson Airplane, and even the Grass Roots. As mass-appeal television, this wasn't *Bonanza,* or even *Green Acres.*

Yet the Monkees, the first made-for-television rock band, are worth remembering—not so much for what they did, but for what they symbolized. They were, after all, pioneers in creating our MTV-Milli Vanilli world which has blurred the line between image and song, original and facsimile. What's more, in their time, the group played a major role in adulterating the zeitgeist of the sixties so that it could be sold to the masses. In much the same way that television transformed the Beatles into the Monkees, H. Rap Brown became Linc Hayes of the Mod Squad, Gloria Steinem became Mary Tyler Moore, and the Vietnam War became *M*A*S*H.*

By now, almost everyone knows the pop lore surrounding the Monkees. Rock fans have read how the group was formed in 1966 when two producers decided to do a weekly show about a band like the Beatles, and placed an ad in *Variety* seeking four "insane boys, age 17–21." The group was named "the Monkees"—the tail-end of the word slightly misspelled—to mimic the way that other groups like the Beatles, the Byrds, and the Cyrkle had been named. Fans probably know that future rock star Stephen Stills was rejected for a part, as was Paul Petersen, formerly of *The Donna Reed Show.* And that two members of the group—Davy Jones and Mickey Dolenz, former star of *Circus Boy*—had never played in a band (though Jones had sung), while the other two—Michael Nesmith and Peter Tork—had never acted. Still, NBC bought the pilot within 24 hours, and sold it to sponsors three days later. (" 'Do they have long hair?' whined the boys at NBC first off," wrote *Look.* " 'Yep,' said producer Bert Schneider. 'That's where it's at.' ")

The public probably realizes by now that producers hired some of the industry's top musicians and songwriters to help the group behind the scenes so that 16 months later, the Monkees could boast of three Number One hits: "Last Train to Clarksville," "I'm a Believer," and "Daydream Believer." "We're not the Beatles," said Michael Nesmith.

"We're us." And the public probably is familiar also with the fact that Jimi Hendrix was once the warm-up act on a Monkees tour. "We have the potential," said Peter Tork, "but there's no time to practice." Or that five-foot-three lead singer Davy Jones became so big that a struggling London star with the same name changed his name to David Bowie. "We're advertisers," said Mickey Dolenz. "We're selling a product. We're selling Monkees. It's gotta be that way." Or that Ensign Chekhov on *Star Trek* was intended to be a Davy Jones clone who would attract young viewers to that show. Or that Monkees record producer Don Kirshner later took the concept of a "fictional band" one step further by creating a cartoon band called the Archies that had its own Number One hit, "Sugar, Sugar."

In the history of rock music, the Monkees deserve no more than a footnote. While it's true that many of their songs still sound surprisingly fresh, the music of the Monkees was closer to "My Fair Lady" than "Light My Fire." Put another way: If the Monkees were a clone of the Beatles, they were copied from cute Paul McCartney, not iconoclastic John Lennon. They were from that part of rock which saw its roots in the music hall, not the dance hall—in occasional rhythm, but never the blues.

As a television show, however, *The Monkees* was cutting-edge, and so much so that several affiliates refused to carry it. "There is a giant resistance to kids with long hair," said coproducer Bob Rafelson at the time. That, once again, speaks volumes about the differences between TV and rock, especially in the sixties. True, *Ozzie and Harriet* used Ricky Nelson's rock songs to great effect in the late fifties. And *The Monkees* was hardly known for great sophistication, given its nonsensical plots (Mickey takes a course in body-building, or the group spends the night in a haunted house), endless chase scenes, and constant dumb jokes about Davy's height.

Still, with Paul Mazursky as a writer, the show was a trendsetter and a hit with the critics. The *New York Times* called the group "the Marx Brothers in adolescence," and its reviewer actually liked the show. "Progress can turn up in the strangest places," he wrote. With its use of fast cuts (anticipating *Laugh-In*), references to itself as a TV show (anticipating *Moonlighting*), and intermingling of music and video (anticipating MTV), *The Monkees* was different from anything the masses had seen on TV. It was so different, in fact, that the show never really got off the ground, ranking 70th its initial week even though "Last Train to Clarksville" had already hit the Top Ten. The show was canceled after two seasons, 58 episodes, and two Emmy awards.

In the end, the Monkees are remembered for both their music and their marketing. They thus symbolize a moment in which make-believe took on a much broader meaning: Like Leno or Letterman's fake ad-libs, the Monkees worked because fans didn't really care that they were an invention. That was a particular irony, because rock was a musical genre which had usually appealed to youth because it actually stood for something: a set of rebellious ideas. The group's popularity thus marked a kind of dividing line in the undermining of the original premise of rock-and-roll.

In a sense, the Monkees did that to their era as well, via television. In selling the sixties to the masses, they showed others how to domesticate the counterculture, as well as that era's politics. In their hands, after all, "The Times They Are A-Changin' " became "Pleasant Valley Sunday." In the wake of the Monkees—and what they represented—long hair became a fashion statement, not a political one; and "Join the rebellion!" became a tag line designed to sell cars, not organize protests. It wasn't long before Sonny & Cher became—well—Sonny & Cher.

The Monkees thus represent the moment when the culture of the sixties was converted into a TV series. And, because television has the awesome power to rewrite our collective memory, that—sadly—is often the way we remember those influential times today.

27

Mission: Impossible
and Its Cold War Fight to Save America
(CBS: 1966–73)

Television is a mirror of American culture—though it often works the same way a fun-house mirror does. That means you have to correct for the flaws. A case in point is the programming of the 1960s, which proved again that television is a medium which often prefers the world of stylized fantasy over reality. We have already seen how, in an era of great cultural change, situation comedies retreated into a world of Martians, genies, and talking horses.

Yet something similar also happened with dramatic programming. Though it was impossible for most Americans to ignore the Vietnam War at the time, there were no TV series directly dealing with that conflict. As with sitcoms, however, a number of dramatic shows indirectly reflected the war by revealing the mind-set of suspicion, if not paranoia, which guided much of our foreign policy. By their pervasive presence in our living rooms, these shows changed the way Americans thought about espionage, international crime, and the role of government in protecting secrets against the Evil Empire. They thus helped create the zeitgeist that made the Cold War possible.

Of all those shows, the most memorable was *Mission: Impossible.* Though it never cracked the Top Ten in its seven seasons from 1966 to 1973, it was the longest-lasting and best of the more than a dozen sixties' Cold War espionage shows—many modeled on the James Bond book-and-movie series and including such programs as *The Man From U.N.C.L.E., I Spy, The Avengers,* and even *Get Smart.* The 168 *Mission: Impossible* episodes even outnumbered any of the dozen or so military sitcoms on TV during that decade, which included the popular *Gomer Pyle, U.S.M.C., F Troop,* and *Hogan's Heroes;* and the host of military dramas, such as *Combat* and *The Rat Patrol.*

Yet it wasn't just longevity, the fact that it spawned a hit mid-nineties movie starring Tom Cruise, or its subliminal messages which made *Mission: Impossible* significant. Like several of its brethren, this show featured women and minorities in far more prominent roles than they had tended to assume in dramatic series until then. It had one of television's best intro tunes, and its most memorable opening scene. It also presented its Cold War themes with far more dramatic complexity than most television shows before or since, which is why it was eventually dubbed into 15 languages and sold to more than 70 countries. This was a plot-driven show, not a character-driven one. "You have a lot less time to tell a good, full story that has relationships and action," a writer for *Star Trek* once noted about television. "You've got to have one or the other for 41 minutes. It's very difficult to have both."

Mission: Impossible was the brainchild of Bruce Geller, who in 1965 wrote a screenplay inspired by the popular film *Topkapi*—an extremely elaborate jewel-robbery picture. When told that his idea would make a better TV show, Geller decided to make it into a series, meaning he'd have to cram two hours of plot into television's traditional one hour each week. According to John Javna in *Cult TV,* Geller did this by turning to the style of commercials—television's one genre known for condensing complicated material into a limited time through the use of fast cuts and editing. "A TV commercial in one minute must get your attention, tell an involved story, give you the message, and get off," Geller said. "The message may be hooey but the technique is masterful." To complete the filming of what was essentially a feature-length movie each week, Geller shot for seven days, and usually ran about a $50,000 deficit per episode. That made the show more cinematic—a forerunner of a series like *M*A*S*H.*

Each show opened with the head of the IMF (Impossible Missions Force) receiving a taped message, plus photographs, in a hidden location. That character was first named Dan Briggs and played by Stephen Hill, and then named Jim Phelps and played by Peter Graves, brother of James Arness of *Gunsmoke.* (Graves replaced Hill after the first season because Hill, an Orthodox Jew, couldn't shoot from Friday night to Saturday night, and the show inevitably fell behind its lengthy production schedules.) Each week the tape would begin with "Good morning, Mr. . . ." (Phelps or Briggs), and then go on to relate a complicated mission or sting during which the IMF team would have to prevent the sale of nuclear weapons to an unfriendly Third World

power, stop the slave trade in a Middle Eastern locale, or fool a mur-
der-for-hire leader by making him believe in ghosts—in countries
with names such as Santales and Svardia. Street signs were often written in some odd, vaguely Slavic language resembling English so that
audiences could guess with a modicum of certainty at "No Intretien,"
"Machina Werke," or "Zona Restrik." The typical message went something like this bit from "The Spy" during the second season:

> Good morning, Mr. Phelps. A secret detailed map of NATO's
> missile defense system was recently prepared on two overlays,
> neither of which is complete without the other. They were sent
> by separate couriers to a meeting between NATO and one of
> Europe's small, uncommitted nations. Felicia Vabar, a member of
> an enemy spy apparatus, had one of the couriers intercepted, and
> the overlay he was carrying stolen. To get the other, she has re-
> cruited Captain Miklos Cherno, an internal security officer of
> the country where the conference was being held. Your mission,
> should you decide to accept it, is to prevent Miss Vabar from get-
> ting the second overlay, without which the first is useless. As al-
> ways, should you or any of your IM Force be caught or killed,
> the secretary will disavow any knowledge of your actions. This
> recording will self-destruct in five seconds. Good luck, Jim.

And then the tape would burn up. This simple trick, of course, told
the viewer the plot at the outset, and used up only 30 to 40 seconds.
It was a brilliant idea—though it was only an updated conversion of
the title cards used in silent films.

As others have noted, in the counterespionage tradition, nearly
everything the IMF did was as illegal as what they were trying to stop.
"The villains are . . . so clever," the writers for the show were told,
"that the intricate means used to defeat them are necessary." Anyone
looking for a concise description of the foreign policy mind-set during the Cold War period needed to look no further, which is why one
staff writer could say, "We'd like to think that the CIA is awake and
watching us." "Everybody loves a thief," Graves would say later. "That
is essentially what we were."

As with *Perry Mason,* another formulaic show with some degree of dramatic complexity, Geller also relied on consistent characters. "It has very little character when you analyze it," one of the show's producers, Bruce Lansbury, once said. "The characters were all functioning for the puzzle in the plot." Rollin Hand (played by Martin Landau) and then Paris (played by Leonard Nimoy) were the team's masters of disguise. Cinnamon (played by Landau's wife, Barbara Bain) was the sexy temptress for three seasons until she was replaced, along with Landau, because of a salary dispute. Peter Lupus played strongman Willie Armitage—an early version of Arnold Schwarzenegger—while Greg Morris played Barney Collier, a black electronics expert. His character was notable for never getting captured even though in most episodes, he had suspiciously infiltrated a country where he appeared to be the only black person for hundreds of miles. "Essentially, 'Mission: Impossible' is not drama but process: not about people but technique," William Kuhns once wrote about the show.

Mission: Impossible was the culmination of a long series of shows during the 1960s which dealt implicitly with Vietnam and the Cold War. "Never in the history of American broadcasting had there been so many war programs," wrote J. Fred MacDonald in his book *Television and the Red Menace.* Yet almost all the shows that glamorized war directly—including the popular *Combat,* codirected by Robert Altman—were set during World War II; some included actual war footage. At the same time, there was a wave of wacky military comedies: In the 1965-66 season, during the escalation of the Vietnam War, *Gomer Pyle,* the adventures of a hick southerner in the Marines, hit Number 2, and *Hogan's Heroes,* the zany antics of a group of Americans in a Nazi prison camp, reached Number 9. By making those prison guards lovably comic, *Hogan's Heroes* may have been television's worst excursion into bad taste—quite an accomplishment given the medium.

From *McHale's Navy* to *I Dream of Jeannie* (whose male principals were military officers), virtually all of these shows celebrated war and the military life. They rarely, if ever, depicted death and suffering, while turning the whole experience into nothing more than a barrelful of laughs. The most subversive "Cold War show" on television turned out to be none other than *Rocky and His Friends,* made between 1957 and 1963 and then running in repeats. It could savage the

Cold War and all its tensions because the message was subsumed in a cartoon—a lesson which the creator of *The Simpsons* relearned 25 years later.

Like their military counterparts, the spy series on TV hardly shook the establishment, though they were not quite as overt in their support of the armed forces as were the *Hogan's Heroes* of the world. With the Western burning out as a genre during the New Frontier, these spy shows were often nothing more than up-to-date versions of those old American melodramas—a trend illustrated by *The Wild, Wild West,* a spy show set on the American frontier and complete with the kind of technical gadgets and tricks that earmarked the more modern spy series. Though the occasional British import (*Secret Agent* and *The Avengers*) differed from the formula, most American shows featured the obligatory buddy team—Napoleon and Illya of *The Man from U.N.C.L.E.* and Scotty and Kelly of *I Spy;* the seductive women who threw themselves in their path; the initialed but obscure agencies that waged secret war (THRUSH, CIS) with similar means and identical-looking agents; and the triumph of good over evil. These shows soon became so stereotyped that they inspired a creative satire—*Get Smart,* starring Don Adams, which ended up becoming one of the sixties' more memorable comedies, affording such often-repeated phrases as "Sorry about that, Chief!" and "Would you believe . . . ?"

These shows did have some lasting effects. With their occasional use of sexy female secret agents—Cinnamon of *Mission: Impossible* and Stefanie Powers in the forgettable spin-off, *The Girl from U.N.C.L.E.*—they became among the first dramatic shows to use women as leads. This trend was followed up on crime shows during the next two decades, on series like *The Mod Squad, Police Woman,* and *Charlie's Angels.* These spy shows were notable, too, for their use of blacks in prominent roles—Bill Cosby on *I Spy,* and Morris on *Mission: Impossible*—a trend which would also continue on such shows as *The Mod Squad.* The implicit message? Blacks and women deserved equal opportunity as long as they were good-looking and did dirty work for the national-security apparatus.

The spy shows also allowed television to continue to escalate its depiction of violence. In the sixties, critics had once again begun to object to mass killing on Westerns and in dramas. Once the shooting was invoked to fight the Evil Empire, however, most objections disappeared as producers were careful to use such devices as having enemy agents shoot each other by mistake. Of course, it also didn't hurt that the real violence on TV was now coming to viewers courtesy of the nightly news from Vietnam.

By the start of the seventies with the Vietnam War beginning to deescalate, the spy series and its preoccupation with foreign enemies had virtually disappeared from television, rarely to return except in reruns or occasional made-for-TV movies. That may be the best evidence that even though it took another two decades for the Cold War to end officially, the conflict had lost its currency with the American public long before then. Moreover, a lot of the hip, intellectual crowd that followed *Mission: Impossible* was no longer willing to watch a show which supported the clandestine efforts of the United States government abroad. By its last season in 1972, in fact, the Impossible Missions Force had begun to come home, undertaking domestic surveillance. Was it a coincidence that, at about the same time, the Nixon administration decided it could break into the Watergate complex with its own IMF-type team?

Of course, the IMF squad on TV was moving against forces like organized crime, not the Democratic National Committee. Yet that move to crime was illustrative of another trend. By the early 1970s, television executives had learned that they could continue to depict all the violence they wanted, as long as they did so in pursuit of that decade's "enemy"—namely, domestic criminals—on shows like *Kojak* and *S.W.A.T.* Television, as MacDonald noted, has often been "highly politicized" drama. During the sixties and seventies, on shows like *Mission: Impossible,* the politics were never far below the surface.

28

The Smothers Brothers Comedy Hour
and the Fate of Controversy on TV
(CBS: 1967–69)

Decades after all the controversy, the real significance of *The Smothers Brothers Comedy Hour* is still being debated among television aficionados. To some, the ill-fated show, which ran from 1967 to 1969, represents the first steps that television took toward introducing more topical humor into its prime-time programming. To these fans, the Smothers Brothers—even though they ended up being cancelled by CBS largely for political reasons after two-and-a-half seasons and 71 shows—ultimately freed television to produce more realistic social humor on such seventies shows as *All in the Family* and *The Mary Tyler Moore Show.*

On the other hand it's difficult, decades later, to see what gains the Smothers Brothers secured with their "political" variety show, which featured up-to-the-minute monologues by the hosts and short sketches by the guests. Except for sporadic outbursts on shows like *Saturday Night Live* and *The Tonight Show,* or an occasional lame joke on *Murphy Brown,* politics is still virtually absent from network entertainment—though it has achieved a degree of notoriety on the fringes of very late-night and cable on shows like *Politically Incorrect.* When it comes to politics on "basic" television, things are worse today than they were back in the sixties—though the Brothers are hardly to blame.

Two years before their variety show premiered, the Smothers Brothers had tried their hand at a conventional 1960s situation comedy about an ad executive and his brother-ghost, but it bombed. Meanwhile, CBS was having no success programming anything against NBC's *Bonanza,* Sundays at 9:00 P.M. After executives produced research showing that younger viewers were growing tired of the Ponderosa, CBS decided to throw the dice and turn the hour over, on February 6, 1967, to the Smothers Brothers. These competitors to the Cartwrights were two somewhat hip, short-haired, coat-and-tie-clad brothers named Dick and Tom, who mocked traditional folk music while appearing to be the kind of comic performers even President Lyndon Johnson might admire.

The Brothers' most famous routine involved which one Mom had liked best. Tom, the "dumb" one, would frequently get words wrong: "Hang down your head, Tom Crudely," he would sing. "We want you to be controversial, but at the same time we want everyone to agree with you," Tom Smothers once remembered a studio executive telling him. "[P]rogressive in content, but their style is leisurely conservative," observed TV critic Robert Lewis Shayon.

At first, many reviewers dismissed the show as the Brothers played to expectations. Their first hour headlined George Burns and Jack Benny, and some described the hour as a younger version of Dean Martin's laid-back show. Many of the early battles with network censors tended to be over risqué sex lines.

Once on the air for several weeks, however, the Smothers Brothers surprised their corporate sponsors by ranking Number 16 in the ratings and eventually gaining enough viewers to topple *Bonanza* from the Number 1 spot. More important, the show's brand of humor quickly changed, catching CBS off guard—not to mention the lead-in audience from *The Ed Sullivan Show*. Tom Smothers, recently divorced, was sharing an apartment with Mason Williams, a writer and musician who composed the Top Forty hit "Classical Gas." This was the sixties, and the youthful, in-your-face counterculture was beginning to sweep not only across the country but into the streets. "We'd watch TV and be appalled," Williams once said. "There was nothing on for him, me, or anybody we knew to watch. There was a void as far as a certain kind of element. You could sense there was a revolution in the works, but it wasn't being reflected on TV at all."

The Smothers Brothers tried to change that. Soon the show was presenting such rock and folk artists as the Beatles (singing "Hey Jude"), the Doors (who had become too controversial for Sullivan), Pete Seeger, and the Who—smashing guitars and all. The Blackstone Rangers, a black Chicago street gang, showed up to sing a version of "Up, Up, and Away." Supporting cast members included Glen Campbell, John Hartford, and Pat Paulsen. The gaunt and seemingly serious Paulsen delivered nonsensical commentaries—a spoof on *CBS Evening News* editorialist Eric Sevareid—and in 1968 announced his candidacy for president on the show. Network executives complained that his candidacy might spark equal-time problems, requiring them to give Hubert Humphrey, Richard Nixon, and George Wallace similar opportunities to present "commentaries." But that didn't happen, and Paulsen ended up garnering around 200,000 votes. With writers such as twenty-somethings Steve Martin and Rob Reiner joining the show, the Smothers Brothers soon found themselves in an almost weekly battle with CBS over what they could broadcast.

What actually made it to the air?

DICK: We've come a long way since that first Thanksgiving dinner in Plymouth, when the Pilgrims sat down at the table with the Indians to eat turkey.

TOM: Boy, I'll say we've come a long way. Now we're in Paris, sitting down at a table with the Viet Cong, eating crow.

On another occasion, "the Smothers Brothers poll" visited a black voter and concluded that since a tenth of all Americans were black, 10 percent of all TV performers should be, too. Dick said that this might mean that one of the Smothers Brothers would have to be black. "You can forget about that," said the black voter. "We'd probably get the dumb one."

And there was this typical Pat Paulsen editorial about the space race:

Today, as many of you know, we are well on the way towards our goal of reaching the moon. We have the rockets, the know-how; and our scientists can tell you the exact spot where the first landing will be made—and where the Hilton Hotel will go. . . .

I say this is no time to give up. Down through the ages the moon has been a mystery that has fascinated everyone—from the earliest cave men to Kate Smith. I for one would like to know once and for all: How does the moon control the tides—and why does the coyote look up at it and go ahoooooog!

If only those who criticize would take the trouble to be informed. Let me quote you from this most interesting book by the

great space expert, Werner Von Verner: "Hus gesucht und tzazza-
men ver hubbun verboten nach blutehausen"—which, translated
into English, means "If the heavy would but not necessarily the
opening, then tone it near the loping field and ram the gap into
a second phase of the sterns—and where is Martin Bohramann?"

Many of the controversies surrounding the show were the result of
its confrontational flippancy. Anything dealing with Vietnam was considered troublesome: After all, the pro-military *Gomer Pyle* was still
about as close as prime-time television had gotten to "criticizing" the
war. A Mother's Day skit with the line "Please talk peace" was axed.
One corporate memo warned the Brothers that it was acceptable "to
satirize the President, as long as you do so with respect."

Fights soon erupted as the network tried to delete Pete Seeger's
singing "Waist Deep in the Big Muddy," which implictly criticized the
Vietnam War. Despite the controversy, however, organized letter-writ-
ing campaigns were not yet in vogue: According to one report,
Seeger's performance generated all of 75 letters. Then there was the
censoring of a montage of Harry Belafonte singing in front of a clip
of demonstrations at the 1968 Chicago convention; and the refusal to
permit an interview with Dr. Benjamin Spock, who had been convicted of aiding draft evaders.

In October 1968 the Smothers Brothers, apparently feeling guilty
after LBJ pulled out of the presidential race, sent a letter to the
president which said, "Please accept our apology on behalf of the
Smothers Brothers Comedy Hour for our over-reaction in some instances. . . . If the opportunity arose in the coming election to vote for
you, we would." Yet, egged on by their liberal fans and critics, they
continued the fight. After a David Steinberg skit mocking religion that
fall, CBS took the unusual step of demanding that the Smothers
Brothers deliver a tape of each show in advance so that network affiliates could watch it first. The unintended beneficiary of CBS's then-
unprecedented decision to require this advance tape was the industry
itself. Until then, TV critics had usually reviewed shows *after* they were
broadcast. It was not long before advance tapes of shows were being
sent to TV critics too, allowing them to hype the programs *before* they
were run. This change also allowed the network promotion departments to start using brief clips for promos.

Submitting those tapes to the network seemed to work for several months for this show, but, as television historian Alex McNeil relates it, that next spring the Smothers Brothers began visiting Washington, lining up support for their show among liberal congressmen and FCC Commissioner Nicholas Johnson. Meanwhile, the censorship fights continued—particularly over a Joan Baez paean to her husband, David, imprisoned for defying the draft laws. "Anybody who lays it out in front like that generally gets busted, especially if you organize, which he did," she said, in remarks that were cut.

Though declining, ratings for the Brothers were still decent. Yet on April 7, 1969, after Tom and Dick again publicly blasted CBS, the network cancelled the show, with Walter Cronkite breaking the news on his evening newscast. The network said that the Brothers had failed to deliver a tape on time. Others believed that the real reason was a script featuring another sermonette by David Steinberg—this time on Jonah, where he said, "The gentiles, as is their wont from time to time, threw the Jew overboard." (Tom, however, said the sketch had already been dropped.)

After a series of repeats, the show was replaced in June by *Hee Haw.* The Smothers Brothers returned with a variety program in prime time on three more occasions: for ABC a year later, in the summer of 1970; for NBC as a midseason replacement in 1975; and again for CBS as a midseason replacement in 1989. Yet these shows were far tamer than the original; the variety format was all but dead, and the times had changed—meaning that the topicality of the Smothers Brothers was no longer in vogue.

The Smothers Brothers had demonstrated once again that certain types of political humor were the third rail of television—a TV fact of life which continues even today. Part of the problem, at least now, is that it's hard to make satire work in a dumbed down world. For a comedian to knock Congress, the audience has to know something about what Congress is doing, and current surveys show that roughly half the country can't even name its own representative. A mid-eighties poll showed that 44 percent of all Americans couldn't identify a picture of then-Vice President George Bush. By contrast, only 7 percent couldn't recognize Mr. Clean.

Political humor, almost by definition, also tends to be confrontational because it's antiestablishment. TV, of course, eschews taking political sides—not only because it fears antagonizing the regulators who control the airwaves, but also because alienating even small portions of the mass audience can damage ratings and drive away advertisers. *Saturday Night Live* did revive political satire some six years later, but that show appeared nonpartisan as it skewered Jimmy Carter almost as badly as it did Gerald Ford. Even in the nineties, *Politically Incorrect* seemed always careful to balance its panels with equal numbers of liberals and conservatives. Like Edward R. Murrow in the previous decade, the Smothers Brothers foundered whenever they seemed to be adversarial—which was often.

Television would also continue to eschew controversy. Because TV comes into their living rooms and bedrooms, audiences have always expected the medium's performers to behave as anyone else would who comes into their homes—to be respectful and soft-spoken. As conventional as they looked, the Smothers Brothers were in reality too brash and antagonistic. There's a reason why television's social messages have often been subsumed in sitcoms: Viewers will take their medicine willingly only if it's contained in sugar. Yet the Smothers Brothers wanted the castor oil swallowed whole. While it's true that advertisers hate leaving audiences feeling uncomfortable because it leaves them in no mood to buy, there aren't many viewers who like parting from the television at 10:00 on Sunday nights feeling angry, either.

The Smothers Brothers were part of a general move in the late 1960s toward what television scholar Robert Lichter would later call "advocacy television." In that era, the networks introduced a number of series which vaguely appeared to address social issues and challenge existing values—*The Mod Squad, Room 222,* and *Judd for the Defense.* They also headlined performers like Howard Cosell, who claimed "to tell it like it is." In fact, Cosell (especially when judged on his fights with the TV and sports establishments) could have been a third Smothers Brother, or at least their "radical" uncle. This was a sportscaster hounded for defending Muhammad Ali's right to change his name from Cassius Clay, and for making outrageous though generally accurate comments, that the Super Bowl was "prolonged hype," or that college football was a game with "bought-and-paid-for players who don't even, in most cases, belong in college and who don't ever get degrees."

Yet the overall effect on television of these shows and stars was minimal. After all, *TV Guide* backed CBS to the hilt in its fight with the Smothers Brothers, editorializing:

> We are in full accord with the Columbia Broadcasting System in its wise, determined, and wholly justified insistence on meeting its responsibilities by retaining the right to preview what it will telecast over its facilities. . . . The issue is: Shall entertainers using a mass medium for *all* the people be allowed to amuse a few by satirizing religion while offending the substantial majority?

These shows also had little influence on the counterculture itself, whose pop-culture base was in music, and which still had little use for a mainstream medium like television.

Thus, folk heroes that they become notwithstanding, the Smothers Brothers and Cosell turned out to be TV aberrations—products of the impious sixties, during which conflict and turmoil were commonplace. Their fate proved again that prime-time TV would almost always be about the tame and the tempered. For its part, *The Smothers Brothers Comedy Hour* had demonstrated anew that TV requires a very high comfort level, which meant that it would endure as a moderating force of immoderate intensity. In the 1990s, political commentators would talk about how Bill Clinton had moved to the center, but the culture of television has always pushed everyone and everything to the middle—where it roughs off the edges and eliminates the downbeat.

In those same nineties there would be a reformation of sorts—as the whole talk-show movement attempted to rebel against TV's narrow constraints by making anger its calling card. Yet by then it was too late: In 1996, the Democrats and the Republicans were staging virtually identical political conventions, as they presented packaged TV "shows" which dispensed with the old political debates about leaders and platforms. Instead they turned to a wheelchair-bound Christopher Reeve talking about funding for the disabled; to AIDS patients and rape victims, and to Liddy Dole as an Oprah wannabe. Like all successful TV shows designed to appeal to the masses, these conventions were packaged to eliminate both contention and any mention of the ideologically uncomfortable.

In doing these things, however, the organizers created a kind of politics without line-drawing or principles, which therefore was no politics at all. Where once convention delegates had rallied to end slavery or the war in Vietnam (controversial items in their time), now they met to endorse the notion that a disability was a terrible but not insurmountable thing—a proposition which, of course, could pass unanimously and therefore be the subject of any number of prime-time TV shows. In the 1960s, the Smothers Brothers had demonstrated that comedians couldn't really do politics on television. Less than 30 years later, the Republican and Democratic conventions had proved that even the politicians couldn't do it anymore, either.

29

Rowan and Martin's Laugh-In
and Acceleration as a TV Style
(NBC: 1968–73)

In some ways, *Rowan and Martin's Laugh-In* was much like *The Smothers Brothers Comedy Hour,* which had premiered a year earlier. Hosted by two conventional-looking comics who introduced the show with an old-fashioned comedy routine, it was an hour-long attempt to revive the flagging variety-show format. One of its major selling points was also its hip topicality: Rowan and Martin often featured jokes every bit as cuttingly political as anything the Smothers Brothers displayed. "You know, we only went into Vietnam as advisers," Dan Rowan said one week. "Last week we dropped over 400,000 tons of advice." And then there was the sketch in which a man leaves a five-dollar bill for a prescription, and the druggist calls to him too late that the drugs really cost twenty dollars. "What the hell," the pharmacist says, picking up the five-dollar bill. "Four dollars profit isn't bad, either."

Yet the differences between the two shows—in both content and reception—reveal a lot about the nature and evolution of television. Though often political, *Laugh-In* never became a *cause célèbre:* Political references were buried among scores of jokes about fat people, marriage, and entertainment celebrities. *Laugh-In* was also an equal-opportunity satirist: After all, many said that Richard Nixon's five-second appearance in the fall of 1968, when he exclaimed "Sock it—to me?" humanized him enough to win the presidential election weeks later. (Hubert Humphrey was also invited, but declined on the advice of his aides.)

Whereas the Smothers Brothers boasted of hosting Joan Baez and Pete Seeger, Rowan and Martin's chief writer was Paul Keyes, a friend of and former speechwriter for Nixon. That helps explain why this show would become better known for featuring cameos with names like Martha Mitchell, Wilt Chamberlain, Billy Graham, William F. Buckley Jr., and John Wayne (dressed in a bunny suit). "If a show has Robert Goulet—pays him $7,500 or $10,000—they're going to want three songs out of him," Dick Martin once told a writer for the *New York Times Magazine.* "We have Robert Goulet, pay him $210, and drop him through a trap door." Within eight weeks of its premiere in 1968, *Laugh-In* had hit Number 1, where it remained for the first two of its five seasons; the Smothers Brothers never even hit the Top Ten for a single season.

Or to paraphrase the way Dan Rowan once put it: The Smothers Brothers used comedy as a platform for doctrine, while *Laugh-In* used doctrine as a platform for comedy.

If only for that reason, *Laugh-In* turned out to be the far more influential program. Many of its catch-phrases—reminiscent of advertising slogans—became cultural icons: "Sock it to me," "You bet your sweet bippy," "Here come de judge" (an old black vaudeville line), "Verrry interesting," and "Look that up in your Funk & Wagnalls"— which ended up pumping up that dictionary's sales for years. Its rapid-fire pace with no narrative structure would influence everything from *Hee Haw* and *Sesame Street* to MTV. A feature such as "Laugh-In Looks at the News" was a spoof of the ways of television more than of the news itself; indeed, this show helped move television comedy increasingly in the direction of its own ironic, repetitive, self-referential humor. *Seinfeld* and *Late Night With David Letterman* owe their success far more to this show than they do to the Smothers Brothers.

Yet this show's hipness was almost completely one of style created by video editing; many of the jokes, after all, were warmed-over vaudeville worthy of Milton Berle. "TV only wants to *look* swinging while staying safely square," complained a *Life* critic at the time. "It was about something," NBC Entertainment President Warren Littlefield would add in retrospect. But he would be wrong: *Laugh-In* was ultimately about only novelty—which, in the end, meant that the show itself couldn't last, even if the changes it inspired revolutionized television. *I Love Lucy* would be a hit for decades in syndication; this show today has about as much freshness as last week's newspaper.

It didn't seem that way, of course, when *Rowan and Martin's Laugh-In* premiered on January 22, 1968, as a midseason NBC replacement for *The Man from U.N.C.L.E.* Slotted against favorites like *Here's Lucy* and *Gunsmoke* on CBS, the show was considered a kind of sacrificial lamb. George Schlatter, the executive producer, had only managed to get the series slotted after convincing NBC that this was a rather conventional variety show—hosted by two nightclub comics who had impressed critics when they served as substitute hosts for the successful and venerable Dean Martin on Thursday nights at 10:00.

Once it was on the air, however, on Mondays at 8:00 P.M. on NBC, Schlatter changed variety's form, beginning with the first show—which featured Rowan and Martin's cartoon-humor approach, as well as Tiny Tim singing "Tiptoe Through the Tulips." A disciple of Ernie Kovacs (with whom his wife had worked), Schlatter tried to combine elements of the old Kovacs show—which had pioneered spoofs of television and quick-cut humor almost two decades earlier—with the more outrageous elements of burlesque and vaudeville then being squeezed out of network television. It was a return to the roots of variety, with a twist: The utter lack of narrative, which became the *Laugh-In* trademark, was reminiscent of something that had been on television since its inception—advertisements. Welcome to the seamless web.

Working with a regular weekly cast which included Arte Johnson, Judy Carne, Henry Gibson, Ruth Buzzi, and later Goldie Hawn and Lily Tomlin, Schlatter made them the stars; the famous guests appeared mostly in cameos. "A stock company of nuts," Dick Martin once described them, and they provided the model for the *Saturday Night Live* troupe only a few years later. The jokes came flying by the dozens, courtesy of fast-cut editing featuring over 300 segments in each show. " 'Laugh-In' is not a comedy show, but a comedy deluge," wrote Joan Barthels in the *New York Times Magazine* at the time. This variety series could succeed by offering something for everybody: If you didn't like a joke or act, there'd be a new one in 10 seconds, not 10 minutes. "Nobody has time for slow jokes anymore," Schlatter once told a reporter. He went on:

> By the time they're 18, kids today have seen every level of professional entertainment there is. . . . The pace is faster now, and the humor irreverent. . . . It's all visual. You *can listen* to other TV shows and get the drift, but you have to *watch* this.

At another point, he said, "The world has simply run out of squares."

The show was loosely tied together by a series of regular stunts and skits: The Fickle Finger of Fate Award; Goldie as the giggling dumb blonde; Lily Tomlin as Ernestine, the phone operator ("One ringy-dingy . . . two ringy-dingies"); Arte Johnson as the Dirty Old man, or the German soldier smoking and falling off his bike; and Ruth Buzzi as the purse-wielding matron with the face-altering hair net.

Each show opened with a rather conventional monologue (here a sample) by the tuxedo-wearing hosts:

> DAN: How does it feel to have a few shows under your belt?
> DICK: Something shows under my belt?
> DAN: Maybe I should try another tack.
> DICK: There's a tack under my belt?

That was later followed by a cocktail party of one-liners, and the show ended with the joke wall—a quick series of still more one-liners delivered by the cast peeking through holes in a wall.

Some critics called the show "sophomoric," and they had a point: The jokes, though topical, were somewhat heavily based on the double entendre:

> "If Shirley Temple Black had married Tyrone Power, she'd be Shirley Black Power."
> "The KKK is full of sheet."

"Boris says capitalism doesn't work. But then, neither does Boris."

"My girlfriend and I went to a wild masquerade party. She went as Goliath and I went as the Sistine Chapel. By 12 o'clock, she was stoned and I was plastered."

"George Wallace: Your sheets are ready."

"This is your slum. Keep it clean."

"Luther Burbank dug pansies."

"Forest fires prevent bears."

"You know, I think 'God Save the Queen' was written for Oscar Wilde."

"Miners get the shaft."

"Hi!" [followed by the reply] "You, too?"

And Henry Gibson would read his poems, such as "Elements":

I used to like fresh air
When it was there.
And water, I enjoyed it
Till we destroyed it.
Each day, the land's diminished.
I think I'm finished.

Sight gags were also a constant. Judy Carne asked Sammy Davis, Jr.: "What is black and white and has two eyes?" The answer: "You and Moshe Dayan." Then there was Flip Wilson doing an Al Jolson black-face imitation and complaining at the end that he couldn't wash off the makeup. Bad jokes were a constant, too—to keep the show camp, like TV's *Batman*. There was bipartisan humor: "I hear there's a new cocktail called the William F. Buckley: Three drinks and you don't know what you're talking about." This was perhaps balanced with "My boyfriend is so militant he thinks a honky-tonk is a Chinese bigot."

Though the show was notable for the number of women it featured in prominent roles, they were often portrayed in bikinis, shown stepping out of showers, parading graffiti in body paint, doused in water for saying "Sock it to Me!"—and made the butt of yet another sexual double entendre:

DAN: For your own good, you should pick up some weight.
DICK: Shoulda been with me last night. I picked up 118 pounds.
DAN: I don't want to hear about it.
DICK: It was for my own good, too.

The show featured so many jokes each week that when it won its first Emmy, ten writers appeared onstage as one of them announced, "I'm sorry we all couldn't be here tonight."

Like a lot of other popular culture phenomena of the sixties, *Laugh-In* was uniquely of its time. Yet the accelerated *Laugh-In* style is what hit immediately, made a big splash, and stuck like glue. Other TV programs were forced to change as quickly as possible, to get up to combat speed. Bob Finkel, the executive producer of shows for Jerry Lewis and Phyllis Diller, complained: "Our old form is archaic, old-fashioned." *Time* reported shorter skits, more slapstick, and racier material throughout the medium. When CBS cancelled the Smothers Brothers in 1969, the network replaced that show with *Hee Haw,* which was little more than *Green Acres* meets *Laugh-In,* down to the copied joke wall. Meanwhile, when PBS started *Sesame Street* in the fall of 1969, it aped the ensemble, quick-cut, and live-fused-with-tape format of the most popular show then on television. Rowan and Martin thus handed the baton to Big Bird, and television entered a new era.

The acceleration of pace on television brought on by *Laugh-In* had larger cultural consequences, too. Like so much else on TV, this change had begun with advertising, which was in the process in the late sixties of moving from 60-second spots to 30-second ones. Madison Avenue always wants to speed up television: If you can get two-thirds of your message across in half the time and at half the cost, you can, of course, run more ads. Less than two decades later, advertisers would push the fast-forward switch again—going to 15-second ads, which further accelerated the culture of television. Yet the faster things moved, the more images there were, and the harder it became for viewers to differentiate one pitch from another. The result was clutter.

How have presentations managed to stand out among all this clutter? Over the past three decades we've seen (beginning with *Laugh-In*) closer close-ups, quicker cuts, brighter colors, and the diminished use of language and plot become ever more characteristic of an emerging style of programming designed to snap viewers out of their trances and break through the jumble. The point no longer was to force the TV audience to think, but rather to have it pay attention. One critic would call the result "sensation television."

The results were inevitable. For instance, within two decades the average sound bite for a presidential candidate on the network news had shrunk from some 45 seconds to less than 10. Television would increasingly generate a style which discouraged reflection, reduced tolerance for delay, and produced viewers increasingly concerned with feeling rather than logic. This sort of television also tended to exacerbate the conditions that spawned it. Accelerated commercials led to accelerated programming. Accelerated programming led to more clutter. More clutter led to more sensation television, which led to less audience reflection. And that led to even more accelerated programming and even more clutter.

Laugh-In was thus the catalyst in a process that leads to a kind of video oblivion. The faster the entertainment unfolds, the more we behold. Until, one day, we discover we can longer see at all.

Part IV

THE SEVENTIES

Sesame Street • **The Super Bowl** • *The Brady Bunch*
All in the Family • *The Mary Tyler Moore Show*
Masterpiece Theatre • **The Local News**
The Tonight Show • *60 Minutes* • *Saturday Night Live*
Roots • *All My Children* • *M★A★S★H*

With its genres firmly in place at last, this was the decade when television redefined them. Shows like *All in the Family*, *M★A★S★H*, and *The Mary Tyler Moore Show* revolutionized the sitcom; *60 Minutes* and the rise of local reportage changed the presentation of news; *Roots* helped redefine the structure of dramatic programming; and *All My Children* helped redesign the soap opera. The growth of public television also brought a new force into programming. Technologically, it was early in this decade (1972) that sales of color sets passed sales of black-and-white ones for the first time. As with the fifties and sixties, CBS has more shows in this section than any other network, but its preeminence is slipping: Only in news and comedies does it continue to emblematize the best of television.

30

Sesame Street: The Last Remnant of the Counterculture
(PBS: 1969–PRESENT)

Sesame Street, in many ways the most celebrated show in the history of television, is also one of its more anachronistic. That may explain why the critics love it as much as, if not more than, the preschoolers at whom it is aimed. After all, it is something of a live musical variety show—a genre which has long since disappeared from television. It is an urban show, coming from a New York setting reminiscent of television's early days in the 1940s and early fifties. Its use of puppets, rather than cartoon characters, owes far more to *Howdy Doody* than to Walt Disney, ostensibly the biggest influence on children's entertainment in the culture.

Most importantly, *Sesame Street* is at heart a child of the 1960s—perhaps the most culturally vibrant vestige of the flower-power era left. That's the real reason why the show so irks conservatives who want to defund the Public Broadcasting Service (PBS). It goes well beyond the much-lampooned *Sesame Street* political correctness: Surrounded on the dial by children's shows that wear their violence (or at least their blatant commercialism) on their sleeves, *Sesame Street* is notable for its constant emphasis on the amiable, nonmaterialistic values of sharing, inclusiveness, and environmentalism which characterized the sixties' counterculture. One halfway expects the episodes on the letter "H" to mention Hermann Hesse, or for Bob Dylan and Joan Baez to stroll through at any moment. Even the show's implicit and somewhat quixotic philosophy that TV and technology together can still be a force for education and good in the culture seems straight out of another age. To answer the question in the theme song, turn left at Haight-Ashbury and you're sure to get to Sesame Street.

It's thus no surprise that the idea for this program came straight out of the social consciousness of the 1960s, largely through the funding of the Carnegie Corporation and the perseverance of one woman: Joan Ganz Cooney. Cooney was a New York public-TV producer who had won an Emmy for a documentary called *Poverty, Anti-Poverty and the Poor.* "The 'War on Poverty' and Head Start had an immense impact," Cooney once told a reporter. "[I]t never occurred to us that we couldn't change the world." According to James Day's history of public television, *The Vanishing Vision,* Cooney wanted to develop a TV series for preschoolers, especially those from underprivileged backgrounds, which would help prepare them for school, while also being consistently entertaining.

Her project ended up among the most extensively researched and planned shows in television history. Backed by Carnegie, Cooney produced a 1967 report which recommended the development of an hour-long daily magazine show, broadcast twice a day, which—unlike much of the programming on PBS or elsewhere for children—would feature the latest in production techniques. She even recommended incorporating the zeitgeist of advertising. "If we accept the premise that commercials are effective teachers," she wrote, "it is important to be aware of their characteristics, the most obvious being frequent repetition, clever visual presentation, brevity and clarity." Thus came the plan to "advertise" letters and numbers: "Today's show was brought to you by the letter 'M' and the number '2'."

The show would also end up borrowing from the quick-cut style of the nation's hottest programs of the time by using some 25 segments per show. "We looked at what kids seemed to like," Paul Connell, the executive producer, once remarked. " 'Laugh-In' [and] 'Get Smart.'" By making the show so televisually fluent, Cooney was ensuring that baby-boom parents would want to watch, too—a key ingredient if the show was to be successful. Over time, that philosophy would lead *Sesame Street* to feature celebrities from Hillary Rodham Clinton to Robin Williams; to parrot rock songs like Smokey Robinson's "*U* Really Got a Hold on Me" to teach that letter, and to satirize TV shows with names like "Miami Mice" and "Squeal of Fortune" (with ubiquitous puppet host Guy Smiley).

"What the show really is about is comedy," Martin Stiles, a writer for the program, once said—but no one thought to question what introducing three-year-olds to all this comedy would do to their world views. In fact, some critics found the "postmodern" irony that pervaded these satires to be one of the chief cultural consequences of the show, as children learned that the truest form of expression was to make fun of something else on television: What *Sesame Street* began for these young viewers, *Saturday Night Live* continued.

The Carnegie report soon led to the development of the Children's Television Workshop, with Cooney as director. As Day relates it, Cooney then recruited a number of producers, some from *Captain Kangaroo*—whose own show, a morning mainstay on CBS for almost two decades, thus indirectly imparted its sweet sensibility to *Sesame Street*. This was ironic, given that *Sesame Street* would eventually drive the Captain from television by making his far-less-sophisticated show seem tame by comparison.

With help from extensive empirical research on what drew children to television in the first place, the show took form. It would be set on an inner-city street so that those children could, at long last, recognize something of their lives on television. "Most of the children in this country live in cities, but all the shows are set in the country, or the suburbs, or never-never land," Cooney once said. The program would feature skits, with very little straight lecturing. There would also be cartoon-like inserts focusing on such educational material as letters of the alphabet, and original songs—such as the unforgettable theme sung as the show opened:

> Sunny day, keeping the clouds away—
> On my way to where the air is sweet.
> Can you tell me how to get,
> How to get to Sesame Street?★

All of this and more would eventually lead the show away from the once traditional gambits of reading stories or using animals, though trial-and-error provided the producers with at least some guidance. For example, Professor Hastings—a humorous first-year character who frequently fell asleep—apparently had a soporific effect on wee viewers too, and soon was allowed to drift right off the show.

The program would feature a racially diverse, regular ensemble cast

---

★"Sesame Street Theme": Hart/Stone/Raposo © Sesame Street, Inc. (ASCAP). Used by permission of Children's Television Workshop.

of almost exclusively adults, with no stars or hosts except for an unusually lifelike group of puppets called the Muppets with whom they would frequently intermingle. These mobile stuffed marvels were provided by a bearded wizard named Jim Henson, and operated somehow by himself and a bunch of similarly bemused overgrown kids. Henson had caught the producers' attention after successful appearances on *The Ed Sullivan Show* and elsewhere, though he had been more or less kicking around television for over ten years on shows like Jimmy Dean's—using figures like Kermit the Frog, which he'd created out of his mother's green coat.

After a few trials, Henson concocted two characters especially for *Sesame Street*. There was Oscar the Grouch—developed, according to Day, to let children know it was all right to feel grumpy sometimes. And there was the soon-to-be-famous Big Bird (not a puppet at all), there to let children know that it was OK to stumble through tasks as long as one did it good-naturedly. "Big Bird is like the bumbling, younger son in so many folktales," Carroll Spinney, who plays Big Bird, once said. "People don't think much of his talents and often overlook him, but he does all right in the end and surprises everybody."

By the time the show premiered on November 10, 1969, Cooney and her cohorts had also gone around the country to make sure that local PBS affiliates ran the segments at the hour that the Workshop thought would have the maximum impact—9:00 A.M., when about 20 percent of all preschoolers are watching TV anyway. They also heavily promoted the show (staffers even hit the streets of Harlem with bullhorns), ending with an NBC special two nights before the premiere. Still, the program was not telecast initially in Mississippi because of its racially diverse cast.

The result was that *Sesame Street* took off at its inception, and what with an initial $8 million budget, has never really looked back. Within a year, the show was being watched by over half of the nation's 12 million children between the ages of 3 and 5. Today, it is seen in over 11 million households daily, on over 300 PBS stations. *Sesame Street* has won more Emmys than any other show in TV history. And its range has constantly expanded: The "curriculum" today is said to cover more than 200 subjects (the original had a half-dozen), and the show's features are almost as likely to be set in Japan or Alaska as New York City. The diverse cast of characters has gradually been expanded to include Hispanics and the disabled.

Yet what's striking is how little the whole zeitgeist of the show has changed in its 25 years plus—including the cast of characters, which encompasses now, as then: Gordon, Oscar, Bert, Ernie, Kermit, Grover, the Cookie Monster ("C is for Cookie"), and—of course—Big Bird. The same consistency holds true of debates about the show which now, as then, focus on whether a TV show can really teach children how to learn, or merely how to watch more television. In fact, this one probably did *both*. Standardized test scores over the years would show that the bottom quarter of students have improved their performance—perhaps a tribute to this show's influence. Unfortunately, this seems to have been accomplished at the expense of the scores in the other three quarters, which in the same period have all gone down.

Over the years, the show had its share of memorable moments— most notably when Luis and Maria got married in 1988, and when Will Lee, the actor who played Mr. Hooper, died and the show decided to try to explain to children what had happened. After much promotion, the latter show was broadcast over the Thanksgiving holidays in order to increase the likelihood that children would view it with their parents—and it was never repeated. "When people die, they don't come back—*ever*?" asked Big Bird. Kermit's song "It's Not Easy Being Green" would become something of a national children's hit, while "Me Want Cookie" eventually wound up in *Bartlett's Quotations*.

On the twentieth anniversary of *Sesame Street* it was honored with a special exhibit at the Smithsonian. By 1990, 79 countries were either broadcasting the original show or staging their own version of it. By about that time also, the *Sesame Street* puppet characters had become so popular that about two-thirds of the show's budget was covered by licensing and royalty fees for roughly 5,000 different play figures, videos, and books—even though the show itself never promoted the products directly. One estimate had around $750 million worth of merchandise related to the show selling each year, prompting critics to wonder why more of that money didn't go back into the show's production budget, thus obviating the need for any public or charitable funding.

The show has also had its share of controversy. Even as early as 1971 it was being criticized, by educators like John Holt, for preparing children for the routine of school rather than for learning itself. Holt also wondered why the street had to be imaginary, and why more real people weren't included. "An actor in the program plays the part of a grocer," he wrote. "Has New York City run out of real grocers?" "Maybe we ought to include more scenes of family life," Carroll Spinney once mused. "Big Bird doesn't have a family. He is only six years old. I wonder why he doesn't live with his parents. Kids don't seem to mind, though."

Then there was the politics. "The show is definitely male-oriented," Cooney once said. "This was done in order to upgrade the black male." Yet, in its first year, women's groups complained that Susan didn't have a job so she became a public-health nurse. In 1971, the BBC decided not to run the program because of the way it threatened "indoctrination" of its views. "I am particularly worried," the BBC's children's-program director said, "by the program's authoritarian aims. Right answers are demanded and praised." Throughout the show's history *Sesame Street* has also drawn the ire of conservatives for its "politically correct" philosophy. Even in the early days it was known for featuring such guests as Jesse Jackson, who sat on a stoop on Sesame Street and proclaimed, "I am somebody. I may be four, but I am somebody. I am black. I am brown. I am somebody."

What makes any television show memorable, however, are not its unusual or controversial moments, but a kind of relentless quality. That's a standard that *Sesame Street* has always achieved as it has blended its dozens of hours of new segments each year seamlessly with the old. For a boomer generation that many say never grew up, it's only fitting that the most enduring TV product of its adulthood was the most successful children's show in the history of television.

Still, the show's effects on television as a whole have been far harder to see, if only because the high costs and extensive planning that led to its launch and success are unlikely to be replicated. In the beginning, producer Jon Stone had said "[W]hat we've proved with this show is that . . . kids will watch quality shows and will choose them over sleazy competition." *Sesame Street* was so successful, however, that it had the ironic effect of allowing the major networks to cede virtually all the responsibility for producing good children's programming to PBS—at least, that is, until the mid-nineties, when the networks had to begin producing three hours of educational programming a week. (*Captain Kangaroo,* the last previous daily kids' show on the major networks, had left the air in 1982.)

Sesame Street's effects on the whole culture were equally mixed. Some three decades after the show's premiere, do we have a nation of intellectually curious young adults and children instilled with a love of learning? Or do we have a generation with short attention spans, demanding to be entertained, and convinced that there always are simple solutions to complex problems?

And of course there was always the politics: Even in the nineties, *Sesame Street* would reflect the moods, modes, and styles of the "peace and love" era which spawned it. Yet given a choice among the violence of cartoons, the commercialism of Nickelodeon, and the gentle but earnest boomer preachiness of the folks on *Sesame Street*, it remained clear what a lot of today's parents would pick. Whether their children will do the same with their kids is another question, but no matter: In a culture which has long since left recollections of the sixties to Oliver Stone and oldies' stations, *Sesame Street* remains a warm daily reminder to many of the way things once were—but would never be again.

31
TV's Biggest Show: The Super Bowl
(ABC, NBC, Fox, and CBS: 1967–Present)

The Super Bowl has been called a "mythic spectacle," a "symbolic ritual," even a "prototype of American values." Perhaps it's all of these. But what it's really all about is television.

It is often said that we have become a nation obsessed with watching sports. But we don't really watch sports as much as we watch television—lots of it. NFL football may turn us on, but so do *ER, Seinfeld,* and *Murphy Brown.* "It's relaxation, escapism," producer Michael Weisman once said—but that hardly distinguishes sports from anything else on the medium. In the world of television a program is a program, whether it takes place on the playing field of the Rose Bowl or in the halls of the Hill Street precinct.

But let's not defame the Super Bowl. In the gallery of network programming, football holds an honored place. And the Super Bowl, which began in 1967 but really became America's premiere TV sporting event in the decade of the seventies, holds the most honored place of all. Consider these facts:

More than 100 million people in this country, and close to a billion worldwide, watch each Super Bowl, making it—almost always—the largest audience for a TV show each year.

Super Bowls constitute around half the Top Twenty rated TV shows of all time—and, as of 1996, the 14 highest-rated sports shows of all time.

Advertising for the game goes for more than $1 million a minute—the highest rates on the medium.

Critics often say that without television, not only wouldn't there be any pro football, but sports *en masse* would hardly have achieved their monumental influence in what William F. Buckley, Jr., once called "the United States of Sports." And they're right—contrary to the original predictions that TV might wipe out sports because no one would want to attend the events any longer. It goes without saying that television has transformed the sports landscape—changing everything from the salaries, number of teams, and color of uniforms, to the way that fans conceive of sports and athletes alike. This was the medium which once had players fake injuries in a soccer game so commercials could be fit in, and had the second-half kickoff to Super Bowl I done over because NBC had gone to a commercial during the first one. "There have been comparable times in history when sports has been at the center of a culture and seemed to dominate the landscape," ABC News President Roone Arledge once told a reporter. "But everything is magnified by television."

Yet even if television has inflated sports beyond earlier recognition, TV hasn't done badly by the arrangement, either. Ask a typical American male to recall the medium's magic moments and he's likely to remember Al Michaels at the end of the 1980 USSR-USA Olympic hockey game, screaming "Do you believe in miracles? Yes!"; or Jim McKay on *ABC's Wide World of Sports,* leading in with a rich "Spanning the globe to bring you the constant variety of sport"; or Howard Cosell and his irrepressible and irritating intonations all during *N.F.L. Monday Night Football;* or the 1968 *Heidi* game, when NBC interrupted the final crucial moments of a close Oakland Raiders-New York Jets football game to start showing a child's film. That fatal break in the action triggered thousands more irate calls than the Smothers Brothers ever attracted, as New York's emergency numbers were tied up for hours. Even large numbers of women have occasionally been hooked on TV sports, especially when they have been able to see members of their sex represented. That's what happened with the Summer Olympics in 1996, Olympic figure skating with Tonya Harding and Nancy Kerrigan in 1994, and the Billie Jean King-Bobby Riggs tennis match (which attracted strong ratings and saw King win) in 1973.

Yet it all comes back to football and the Super Bowl, a story whose origins date back to the early days of the medium. Sure, football made it to the top of the heap because of some smart entrepreneurs like NFL Commissioner Pete Rozelle, and its share of lucky breaks. Yet it is where it is today because it met three major needs of television: drama, technical proficiency, and profitability.

Take drama, which is supposed to be at the core of all television programming. It's what keeps viewers in their living-room seats. Yet most prime-time TV series are surprisingly unexciting; the plots on a *Home Improvement* or even *The X-Files* may vary, but only within strict limits. That's intentional; the networks prefer filmed series precisely because their predictability makes them easier to market to advertisers. And reruns provide additional returns.

By contrast, live programs, and especially sports, remain among the few shows on television whose endings aren't predictable. The rise of pro football, beginning with the thrilling overtime title-game victory by the Baltimore Colts over the New York Giants in 1958, coincided with the decline of the era of live TV. The Game of the Week replaced

The $64,000 Question. Howard Cosell became the second coming of Ed Sullivan.

"People like to watch people in dramatic situations; they like the unpredictable, the unknown," wrote Arledge, the former head of ABC Sports in a 1966 *Sports Illustrated* article that is among the most perceptive ever written about television. "They want to watch something that has the quality of an event. If television goes to more and more Academy Awards, Miss Americas, live pickups, it will satisfy some of the viewer's need for sports."

Violence is also a traditional calling card of prime-time television because it attracts attention, forcing the viewer to stop turning channels and watch. Football, of course, does the same. "There is . . . a kind of excitement generated when people are dressed to avoid injury," wrote Arledge in his article. "The uniforms themselves are a premonition of danger; in a sport where the participants wear crash helmets, you are constantly reminded of the presence of death."

Yet drama is only one element in football's popularity. Another is technical proficiency. Though TV sports broadcasting began with Bill Stern describing the 1939 Princeton-Columbia baseball game to those 400 New Yorkers who had TV sets, even in the 1950s television didn't take to football because the game was too spread out for adequate coverage with a single camera—just about the only technique then available. By contrast, boxing and wrestling—sports that take place in a small ring—initially did well. Thus figures like Antonio (Argentino) Rocca, "Nature Boy" Buddy Rodgers, and Bruno Sammartino become household names, setting the stage for the World Wrestling Federation to follow decades later. Boxing, by contrast, gradually faded on television (too much blood in the home!); the Friday Night Fights were cancelled in 1964.

In late 1963, however, in the days following President Kennedy's assassination, the primitive technology that had favored these relatively stationary sports began to grow more sophisticated. According to television historian Eric Barnouw, one singularly important innovation grew out of network coverage of the shooting of Lee Harvey Oswald. "Only NBC was covering Oswald's transfer live that Sunday," Barnouw once recalled in an interview. "The other two networks were covering the events from Washington. The minute the shooting occurred, the other two networks showed it on tape. And then they showed replays of the shooting for hours, again and again."

Within a few weeks, "instant replay" had made its appearance at an Army-Navy football game. (Announcer Lindsay Nelson's reaction was: "You're going to do *what*?") Soon after, thanks to a few more technical advances (multiple cameras, isolated cameras, slow motion), football on television became a different game. For starters, once the Fall fad became easier to cover, its technical advantages over other sports became apparent. Compare it to baseball—a game played on an open-ended field without a clock, and thus a programmer's nightmare; a game at which spectators can see more in the park than they can at home, no matter how the Fox network tries to jazz up its coverage. Baseball's definition of a "big" technical innovation was to post a centerfield camera for the 1957 World Series—proving, if nothing else, that this game could no longer truly be the national pastime as soon as TV hit the scene.

Football is different; it's so much better on television that many newer stadiums now have giant screens, to show replays. Again, listen to Arledge: "The shape of the field corresponds to that of the screen. The action, although spread out, starts with a predictable portion of the field. . . . The flow is natural and continuous, not like in baseball, where there is a play at third, then you cut to second, then cut to home plate."

Yet there is more to it than that. A football team plays only once a week, giving the TV publicity machine time to crank up between games. The NFL's honchos were also more savvy than the leaders in other sports—marketing their games nationally, not locally, and thus conforming to the homogenous national programming of the networks themselves. In the 1950s, pro football teams had made their own TV deals with local stations, as in baseball. Once football began to catch on in the late fifties, however, CBS (which already had the rights to the telecasts of games involving three-quarters of the teams) asked for a league-wide national package—and the team owners gave it to the network.

Equally important: With its new technology, TV explained how football really works, enhancing viewers' understanding of the sport in ways we now take for granted. In a typical scene shown during practically every game, the camera catches a receiver waiting for a punt. The camera focuses on his eyes, which first look up at the ball, then downfield at the oncoming tacklers, then up at the ball again. Before TV, few could see that sequence well enough to appreciate its going on during a kick.

All the same, the bottom line in television is money. But here, too, football enjoys a bucketful of advantages. Part of the reason is demographics. Pro football attracts Madison Avenue's most coveted audience, middle- and upper-class males—the car-, computer-, and wine- (more than beer) buyers of America who are usually outnumbered by women during normal prime-time programming. (On the other hand, college football tends to attract an audience more tilted to the South, whose viewers often are poorer and somewhat less well-educated.)

Another reason for football's advantageous standing is that the games are broadcast mainly on Sunday afternoons. "Before football, those time periods were filled with religious programs and round-table talk shows," Barnouw recalled in that interview. "Those time periods were a 'cultural ghetto' that was unsalable. Football and sports narrowed that unsalable period down to Sunday morning."

In other words, football was a bonanza to the networks—a true case of converting dust into gold. Yet move the gold out of its time slot, and it loses its luster. Even on its celebrated Monday Night Football telecasts, now more than 25 years on the air and counting, football doesn't dominate the ratings the way it does on Sunday—a time period which *New York Times* columnist Robert Lipsyte once described as our "socially acceptable way" for men to tune out women on Sunday afternoons.

Eventually that "tune-out" time period would spread. TV football would gradually expand to cover Thanksgiving and New Year's, and thus would the old activities of walking or group outings on holidays be replaced by gatherings of men around the set, while the women occasionally tried to get in a word edgewise. Television had always interfered with family intimacy anyway, by making the group concentrate on the screen, not on each other. Football, however, managed to do so at formerly sacred times when that intimacy was supposed to be celebrated—and it did it in such a way as to drive the genders apart.

Not only that: While it was often claimed that fathers and sons forged new links through TV sports, the communication that came at such moments usually concerned ads or plays—if it occurred at all. Sports TV, like all TV, was fragmenting old bonds and alliances, and replacing them with allegiance to itself.

By the 1990s, it was clear that football telecasts had become influential in other ways as well. It's hardly a novel thought that sports and war are closely linked: The Duke of Wellington could say a battle was won on the playing fields of Eton without ever having set foot in Giants Stadium. Football, too, would borrow liberally from war, with the Lombardis replacing the Pattons as male heroes and a corresponding vocabulary of blitzes, bombs, and blowouts.

Yet by the time of the Gulf War in 1991, it had become clear that the military had learned something from football, too—or, better yet, football on television. That brief but spectacular war was obviously billed as news and presented by reporters, but that didn't necessarily make coverage of the event a news show. Instead, it was packaged and presented to TV viewers primarily in the format of football programming—and in particular the pre- and post-game shows.

After all, in both sports and war-news shows, there is always a lead anchor. With the Gulf War, as in football, there was endless speculation before the fact about what might happen, from a group of technical experts who looked and sounded like coaches. Then there was the postgame analysis by the same group of obsequious technical experts, often with slow-motion instant replay of "the bombs." Because all these experts used to be generals (or coaches), they also had a stake in telling us how great the game and its participants were. How many times do you hear a coach criticize a fellow coach, or an officer a fellow officer?

As with athletes, the participants in a military exercise were usually asked fawning, trivial questions along the lines of "How did it feel out there?" In truth, even sports coverage is infinitely more revealing than this sort of "war journalism," if only because, with sports, the networks at least show us the actual game. In the Gulf War, because of censorship, we got the pre- and post-game show, but the contest itself was usually blacked out. Did Phil Simms really hit Mark Bavarro over Baghdad? Who knew unless General Schwarzkopf told us?

Thus the wide world of sports became the wide world of war, and developed into a new kind of journalism. Rooting for the home team was encouraged, which led to self-censorship. Accuracy tended to get lost—not so much because reporters lied but rather because they were encouraged to get caught up in the emotions of the moment. The model for a celebrated incident during the Gulf War, when NBC newsman Arthur Kent started yelling to his cameraman during an air raid, was not really Walter Cronkite but John Madden.

Yet it was all readily and thankfully accepted, thanks to the legacy of football and television. And it's a legacy we celebrate on Super Sunday—a holiday in the truest sense, a day when the crime rate drops and traffic vanishes and people remain at home. The day now has its own icons: Namath, Montana, and Bradshaw. Are people really honoring the two teams, or a game? Neither, really. Holidays commemorate our most important values and pastimes, and in the affluent society few things are as important as the way we spend our leisure time. Super Sunday thus celebrates the true cynosure of the American way of life. It is a tribute to eternities spent in secluded living rooms, watching beams of light flickering from a cathode-ray tube.

32

The Brady Bunch: As Television Icon
(ABC: 1969–74)

In a sign to many that even the worst parts of popular culture will always be recycled, *The Brady Bunch* keeps coming back—in reruns, books, plays, and feature-length movies no less. As Marcia Brady might say, "Groovy!" Yet even the show's detractors—and they are legion— have to admit that this rather clichéd series about a widower with three boys, who marries a widow with three girls, has become one of the phenomenons of modern American culture.

After all, in its five seasons on the air on ABC on Friday nights, the show never even cracked the annual Top Twenty—unlike the saga of a similar clan, *The Partridge Family,* which was a hit at the same time but never did that well in its afterlife. When the Bradys premiered in 1969, Cleveland Amory, in *TV Guide,* called the series a "mish-mash." Yet, over the years, a cult around the Bradys has developed—so much so that a recent MTV survey of 21- to 25-year-olds found the show to be their all-time favorite program, and a survey of fifth-graders found the same. Still on in close to 100 markets in the early nineties, the show is one of the top hits ever in syndication. Much of Generation X can recite the plots to all 117 episodes, and college professors have described how their new students exchange "Brady trivia" as a way of forging common bonds. "We can make fun of it, laugh at it, but all of us who grew up with it (which means nearly everyone born since it went on the air) are affected by it," related writer Bill McKibben in his book *The Age of Missing Information.*

It's not worth boring any reader with a lot of Brady trivia, such as who said "Oh No! Tomorrow's graduation and I've got orange hair!" (It was Greg, and lead actor Robert Reed considered the episode so dumb that he originally refused to appear in it.) Or what the show was originally supposed to be called *(The Brady Brood).* Or who were the stand-ins on the set for the Brady kids (a midget couple). Or who Sherwood Schwartz, the show's creator, wanted to play the role of Mike Brady before he settled on Robert Reed (Gene Hackman, who was rejected because he wasn't well-enough known). Reed, however, disliked the show intensely: "It was just as inconsequential as can be," he once said. "I do not want it on my tombstone." The names of the kids are also a matter of public record (Greg, Peter, Bobby, Marcia, Jan, and Cindy). Yet, at times that's information worth knowing: A few years ago, a Massachusetts prisoner escaped to the roof of a building, and threatened to jump unless authorities could come up with that list.

It's not worth reciting the plots of all the episodes, either, even if there is interest in how Bobby became the hall monitor, Marcia got braces, Cindy dealt with her lisp, or the celebrated trip to King's Island came off. Further, despite rumors to the contrary, Mike and Carol were not the first TV couple to share a bed who were not married in real life: The Munsters, for one, had already done that.

The Brady Bunch premiered in 1969 with Mike and Carol getting married, and the cat making a mess out of the wedding. At that time, television was trying both to accommodate the hipness of the sixties and to appeal to the growing youth market—which is why the show featured occasional guest stars like Joe Namath, and Davy Jones of the Monkees. Schwartz, the creator of *Gilligan's Island,* had read in 1966 that almost 30 percent of all marriages included children from previous marriages. That led him to create the Bradys—which is a lot like the premise of Gilligan, only with children: Take a group of disparate people and throw them together to see what happens.

Schwartz, however, was unable to interest the networks in the concept until the popularity of a Lucille Ball/Henry Fonda movie with a similar premise, *Yours, Mine, and Ours.* In 1969 he forged ahead, creating a synthetic, utterly predictable series about a widow with three daughters, who marries a widower with wild hair(!) and three sons, throwing in the obligatory Hazel-like housekeeper and enough bell-bottoms and bubble-gum rock to make the show seem at least somewhat hip. (Carol was actually supposed to be divorced, but that wasn't yet allowed in TV land.) As Barry Williams (who played Greg) once put it, "It was a bit like being Gary Puckett at the heyday of the Doors."

Adults never bought into it, however—which is one very good reason why the show never really made it in prime time. Yet the Bradys lived long and prospered, at least in television terms. One reason why is that, despite its surface attempts at early-seventies hipness, this was one of those rare shows told from the viewpoint of the kids, and aimed at an audience slightly younger than the cast—meaning 6-to-12-year-olds.

Unlike most other shows, this one also appealed to both sexes. The real genius of the premise was that, for kids, there was almost always a Brady of the same age and sex with whom to identify. "This was not a show for adults or their problems," Schwartz once said. "It's a show primarily for kids and their problems. A lot of those problems were relevant 100 years before the show, and I'm sure that those same problems will be relevant 100 years after the show." Thus there were episodes in which Greg fell in love with his teacher; Peter hit Marcia in the nose with a football; Jan lost a locket which a friend had given her; and the boys built a clubhouse which the girls tried to take over. It's no surprise that the success in syndication of the Bradys paralleled that of *Leave It to Beaver*—another show told from the kids' standpoint which also didn't do well in its original form. Both caught on culturally only when they were syndicated and run in the afternoons, after school, which traditionally is when kids make up a high proportion of the audience.

In an odd way, *The Brady Bunch*—with its family of boys meeting a family of girls—also dealt with perhaps the greatest social issue of our time: In the post-feminist age, how are men and women to get along? Remember that this show's heyday in prime time came when the women's movement was first beginning to gain headlines and Bobby Riggs played tennis against Billie Jean King. This series played out similar issues in more compelling fashion—at least for 10-year-olds— as Peter tried to join the Sunflower girls and Marcia the Frontier Scouts, and Marcia's slumber party got crashed.

What's more, in its idealized view of how two single-parent families can merge, this show anticipated the subsequent breakup of the traditional family and the search for alternatives—a theme which remains contemporary. "I have my students write a journal on 'My Relationship With TV'," Bowling Green University popular-culture professor Crystal Kyle once told an interviewer. "A lot of the Brady Bunch kids tell me a lot about their parents' divorce, coming home when they were eight or nine to an empty house, sitting down and watching *The Brady Bunch*." Though he may not have intended it at the time, Schwartz would later agree: "There are so many damn dysfunctional families in America that I think it's a longing for a more innocent, pleasant life, for that family that was very functional," he said.

This isn't to say that this product of the seventies either was or is fraught with great social significance. Still, the series had its moments, which continue to resonate with viewers. "Find out what you do best and then do your best with it" was the articulated message of one episode. On another, Mom and Dad Brady said: "Money and fame are very important things, but sometimes there are other things that are more important—like people!" Now, ask yourself: Could Shakespeare have put it any better?

33

All in the Family and the Sitcom "Revolution"
(CBS: 1971–83)

The celebrated *All in the Family* was the beginning of "reality" programming. That realism enabled this show to capture the frustrations and aspirations of the downscale lower-middle classes—10 years after *The Dick Van Dyke Show* had done somewhat the same for the cheerfully striving upper-middle classes. Yet *All in the Family* was not only a critical success: In its 12 years on the air in its various permutations on CBS from 1971 to 1983, this series won the season's ratings race five times in a row (1971-76)—more than any other show in TV history. With its use of previously forbidden language ("hebe," "spade"), and exploration of similarly off-limits topics (racism, abortion, rape, impotence), the show altered the conventions of television comedy. Because sitcoms could now tackle a broader range of issues and concerns, they again became the dominant form in prime time.

The show began on Tuesday, January 12, 1971, with an introduction that this series would "throw a humorous spotlight on our frailties, prejudices, and concerns. By making them a source of laughter, we hope to show—in a mature fashion—just how absurd they are." At the time, CBS was so wary of putting such a controversial comedy on the air that it booked dozens of switchboard operators to answer the irate calls. The first episode opened to the sound of a toilet flushing, and featured this typical exchange:

> ARCHIE: If your spics and spades want their rightful share of the American dream, let them get out there and hustle for it like I done. I didn't have no people marchin' and protestin' to get me my job.
>
> EDITH: No, his uncle got it for him.

By the third show, audiences were treated to a story line about how Archie hoped to get a larger settlement in a traffic case because he had hired a Jewish lawyer. The following week, the show focused on how Archie was afraid to give blood because his fluids might get mixed up with those from another race. Yet few calls came in, and of those that did, most were favorable—a point which fans of the show would later invoke to show that Americans were far ahead of the timid networks. Maybe so—though perhaps viewers were flocking to the show for reasons that had nothing to do with its supposed subversive message and style.

Although the program was the brainchild of Norman Lear, its spiritual founding father was Bob Wood, president of CBS. When Wood took over as CBS honcho in 1969, he found himself running a network known for such shows as *The Beverly Hillbillies, Green Acres,* and *Hee Haw*—and with a corresponding hold on rural and older audiences, not the more-desirable urban or younger ones. With advertisers increasingly concerned about demographics (the income of those who watched the shows, not just numbers), Wood resolved to turn around his network's programming with topicality, and he eventually cancelled some of CBS's more notable shows and sitcoms, 13 in all, including *Lassie, Mayberry RFD,* and those *Hillbillies.* In the fall of 1970, Wood put *The Mary Tyler Moore Show* on the schedule, and four months later he followed that up with *All in the Family* as a midseason replacement.

The idea for the show had actually been kicking around for several years at other networks. Norman Lear had been a television writer in the fifties, working for Jerry Lewis, George Gobel, and Carol Channing. Convinced that TV comedy would not allow him room for realism or experimentation, Lear left for film work in the late fifties, when he cowrote and coproduced mostly forgettable films—*Divorce American Style* and *The Night They Raided Minsky's* among them.

In 1968, however, Lear came up with the idea of doing a somewhat autobiographical American version of the British sitcom *Till Death Do Us Part,* a show about the generational conflicts between a bigoted middle-aged man and his son-in-law who lives with him. Lear moved the family to working-class Queens at 704 Houser Street, and added wives for the men in the cast—as well as the full panoply of American generational conflicts currently flooding the news as the counterculture and protests against the Vietnam War continued to dominate national attention. Lear then produced two pilots for ABC starring Carroll O'Connor, a Broadway actor who reportedly gained the role when Mickey Rooney turned it down. ABC eventually passed on the idea, in part because of the network's bad experience in doing another topical show (*Turn-On,* the failed copy of *Laugh-In*), and in part because *All in the Family* still seemed too offensive—particularly because it didn't test well with sample audiences.

At CBS, Wood reacted differently, even though a somewhat related CBS show, *Arnie,* about a blue-collar worker who becomes an executive, was floundering in the ratings. Part of the reason, TV analyst Les Brown would speculate, was that between the time *All in the Family* was first tested at ABC, and then later at CBS in the early days of the new Nixon administration, the nation's generational and cultural split seemed to be widening; the country appeared to be on the verge of disintegration, so audiences needed a comedic safety valve. It also didn't hurt that Wood tested his pilots in front of New York audiences, rather than those in Los Angeles, where the reaction to such an urban, loud show would undoubtedly be better. ("I don't experience it as yelling but as passion," Lear once said of his decibel-bursting efforts.)

Despite its topicality, in many ways *All in the Family* was a throwback to the television comedy of the 1950s—set in a city like New York, and not a suburb like southern California; working-class like *The Honeymooners,* and not solidly middle-class like *Father Knows Best* or *My Three Sons;* it was also taped before a live audience, and thus genuinely funny like fifties vaudeville-influenced shows—not a sweet morality play like most sixties sitcoms.

The show premiered on that January night at 9:30, after a fight between Lear and Wood over how graphic its language could be. O'Connor played Archie Bunker, the loading-dock foreman with the foul mouth: "Listen, we didn't come from no monkeys, you atheistic, pinko, meathead," he would say. He was joined by Jean Stapleton as his faithful wife, Edith. She often spoke the truth, and was therefore rewarded with the appellation "the dingbat" by her husband—though Lear later dropped the line, and O'Connor's character did mellow a bit over the years. "You think it's fun living with a saint?" Archie would yell. "You ain't human." When Edith would protest, Archie would come back with "Prove it: Do something rotten." Then came the two live-in relatives who always fought with Archie about politics and cultural mores: long-haired son-in-law Mike (played by Rob Reiner) and his wife Gloria (played by Sally Struthers).

In the beginning the show stalled, and the ratings remained mediocre throughout that first half-season. Moreover, many critics found the show offensive, with far too much conflict. ("That's my constant observation about life," Lear said.) One critic called the show "a welcome breath of stale air"; *Daily Variety* declared it a "plotless wonder" and "an insult"; and the *New York Post* dubbed it "a flop"— while John Leonard in *Life,* saw it to be "a wretched program," agreeing with a *New York Times* essay (one of three, as the *Times* typically managed to take all sides) which had asked "Are Racism and Bigotry Funny?" and concluded they weren't, and couldn't be.

On the other hand, the show had its defenders, including *TV Guide,* which touted *All in the Family* as the "best show on commercial television," and weekly *Variety,* which labeled the series "the best TV comedy since the original 'The Honeymooners.'" Ironically, the debate among intellectuals—which expanded into the pages of the *New Yorker* and *Saturday Review* ("Love That Hate" the latter captioned)—generated a fair amount of publicity for a show floundering in the ratings. As a result, over the summer of 1971 during rerun season, more people sampled the show. When *All in the Family* premiered the next fall, in a new time slot—Saturdays at 8:00 P.M., when the audience tends to be older, poorer, and more conservative—an appreciable viewing audience was primed to see what all the fuss was about.

Evidently they liked what they saw. The show opened that Saturday at Number 12, and by the next week was in first place in the ratings, where it remained for half the decade. Over the years, viewers would be treated to scores of celebrated "serious" shows on topical issues: Archie courts an affair, or finds a swastika on his front door and is offered protection by a militant Jewish group; Edith discovers a lump in her breast, or confronts a would-be rapist; Gloria decides to become more sexually aggressive, or Mike brings a draft-evader home to Christmas dinner. Yet, for all its topicality, what held the show together were many of the things that had worked for sitcoms in the fifties but had been abandoned in the decade since: strong vaudeville humor without children present, delivered by a group of realistic characters who seemed, like the audience, actually to evolve as some tumultuous years went by. A touch of softness allowed *All in the Family* to be confrontational yet acceptably so, unlike *The Smothers Brothers Comedy Hour* several years before—though it also helped that this show's politics were rather more ambiguous. Some of the scenes, such as when Archie comes home from work to find that Gloria has suffered a miscarriage, were gems. In that particular scene, Archie visits her in her room and keeps mumbling inanities, until she states what might rather be asked: "You love me." He nods, unable to answer. "I love you too, Dad," she says.

This was also a series which focused on language far more than had sitcoms in the past. There were, of course, all the well-publicized epithets ("meathead" and "spic"), but the show also thrived on word-play and argument. *All in the Family* had fewer of the sight gags that funny TV comedies like *I Love Lucy* and *The Dick Van Dyke Show* had used, and many of the scenes took place as Archie just sat in his chair arguing with everybody.

That form of discourse and focus on language was unusual for television then, but this show's "argument for argument's sake" would become a popular mode of communication in the decades to come on talk television and talk radio, and eventually in politics and much of our social life. In a way, Archie changed the way we thought about speech: The sophistry of Pat Buchanan and Michael Kinsley on CNN's *Crossfire* was only an upper-class version of the Bunker style. It's even possible to imagine Mike and Gloria, learning from their elders, flinging insults on *The McLaughlin Group* in the nineties.

By emphasizing serious issues, rather than the exaggerated "situations" that were the bread and butter of most TV comedy, *All in the Family* also extended the definition of the sitcom. Nowadays no one is surprised if *Mad About You* or *Home Improvement* does a serious show with little or no laughter, yet that was unheard of before *All in the Family*. The show's primary appeal, as Lear himself once said, lay in its ability to portray "real people dealing with real issues." Even by filming on videotape before a live audience, usually at 5:30 P.M. and then again at 8:00 P.M. so the directors could pick the best cut, the series changed the way that sitcoms are presented, making them appear more true-to-life. When a reporter interviewed the patriarch of a real family like the Bunkers to see how it viewed the show, he replied,

"The difference between us and the Bunkers is we scream more." This was television's first imperfect stab at "reality" programming—the seventies' version of the talk TV of Sally Jessy Raphael and even of such downscale "news" shows as *Inside Edition* and *America's Most Wanted*. And it clicked, particularly in an era when so much else on the medium was still so unreal.

Yet, for all the talk among intellectuals about how *All in the Family* lampooned bigotry, thus helping to make it unacceptable, several studies done in the 1970s found that a majority of viewers liked Archie because they agreed with much of what he had to say. It says something about Lear's talent that he created a television character whose persona 25 years later still defines a character type—but it also says something about America that it so took this man to heart. Because the Bunkers were people trapped in the city and the East, there was always a bleak, wintry, almost angry edge to the show, which opened up a darker window on the national psyche. In its own way, this wildly popular show may have helped to create a political mood that still haunts America: The national malaise that Jimmy Carter would describe at the end of the decade began here. In the 1950s and sixties, Archie could never have been an icon; then, the nation's future looked too bright for this portrait in pathos to be a national symbol.

Thus *All in the Family* may have been designed to satirize Archie's angry bigotry, but in many ways it unknowingly ended up legitimizing the anger, if not the prejudice. It was no accident that one survey found that 95 percent of this show's audience was white—a disproportionate figure indeed. Critic Dorothy Rabinowitz wrote, at the time:

> Its appeal is rooted not in the show's endorsement of liberal values, but, on the contrary, in its vivid, usual demonstration of the abiding attractiveness of the familiar, as opposed to the strange, the old virtues as opposed to the new nonsense.

Say goodbye to the sixties: No wonder President Nixon let it be known that he felt sorry for America's most famous lead character, after an episode in which Archie found out that an ex-football-star friend was gay. "That was awful," said Nixon. "It made a fool out of a good man." Soon, political strategists were talking about "the Bunker vote," which was really an early description of "the Reagan Democrats." In 1972, Archie even got one vote for vice-president at the Democratic convention in Miami.

Lear himself would exclaim, "This is a whole movement, opening up the mass media." He ended up spinning off a number of characters and similar situations into other popular shows—*Maude, Good Times, The Jeffersons,* and *Sanford and Son*—the latter two among the first series about blacks to appeal to whites. In 1975, Lear had three of the Top Four shows on television with *All in the Family, Sanford,* and *The Jeffersons;* his satirical soap opera, *Mary Hartman, Mary Hartman,* sold in syndication, was the critical rage of the 1975-76 season. As for *All in the Family,* it ended up becoming transmogrified into so many casts, permutations, and titles (concluding with *Archie Bunker's Place* without any of the other three leads) that it lasted until 1983, well beyond the conflicted times that spawned it.

Yet for all the controversy, what made *All in the Family* memorable was the way its newfound freedom allowed the show to capture character, which then allowed it to plumb the social landscape. If *Sanford and Son* worked, it was because its portrait of father and son transcended the issue of race. *"All in the Family,"* Rob Reiner once said, showed that "people can be ignorant and still have loving, human qualities." Norman Lear blazed a new path for television by discovering that the contentious could be made appealing, as long as it was built around the familiar.

34

The Mary Tyler Moore Show
and America's Newest "Families"
(CBS: 1970–77)

More, perhaps, than any other sitcom, *The Mary Tyler Moore Show* (*MTM*) changed television comedy in ways still noticeable today. Though it never cracked the annual Top Five in its seven-year run from 1970 to 1977 (making it far less popular and notorious then than its CBS Saturday night partner, *All in the Family*), this show is important to television history for a multitude of reasons that go beyond both its quality and its continued success via reruns in the two decades since it left the air in 1977, after 168 episodes.

This was the show that really popularized the notion of "the workplace comedy"—an idea which would influence shows from *Taxi* to *Murphy Brown* in the years that followed. It took place in Minneapolis (in an apartment in a house, no less)—not, as one might have come to expect, in New York, Los Angeles, or any of the indistinguishable California suburbs that have harbored most television shows. Thus it cleverly utilized a symbolic transfer of locale that reflected the atomization of power from the old urban centers on both coasts to newer ones. The series focused on the travails of a growing segment of society which television, until then, had ignored—namely single adults, and particularly women. Given its saga of their "struggles" in the city, it would of course be copied constantly over the years, most recently on shows like *Friends* and *Caroline in the City*.

Most importantly, *The Mary Tyler Moore Show* presented a genuinely different type of comedy on television, one revolving far more around characters than the traditional implausible situations that had driven everything from *I Love Lucy* to *Gilligan's Island*. In the end, this meant that this series often sacrificed laughs for what one writer would call "epiphanies"—the rarest of trade-offs on television. The show was often moving and insightful, but consistently funny it wasn't. "Perhaps perkiness will save the world," grumbled TV critic John Leonard.

At the outset, few would have predicted that the program would become such a pathbreaker—particularly given the notoriety of *All in the Family,* which premiered four months later and eventually moved into a time slot in the same Saturday-night lineup. Having *All in the Family* overshadow this "kinder and gentler" show, however, allowed *MTM* to evolve in ways it might never have otherwise. As analyst Richard Corliss once pointed out, in many ways *The Mary Tyler Moore Show* and *All in the Family* were mirrors of each other: repression vs. aggression, character lines vs. punch lines, getting along vs. confrontation.

CBS had been interested in the series as a showcase for Mary Tyler Moore, who had starred as Rob Petrie's wife, Laura, on *The Dick Van Dyke Show* a decade earlier. Yet when the concept for the show (developed primarily by James Brooks) was presented to studio executives, they were skeptical. For starters, though the characters seemed well-crafted—the dumb and self-absorbed anchorman, the gruff-but-sweet news director, the fellow single woman from New York who lived upstairs—no one in the ensemble cast for this sitcom about a local news station was really considered a comedian. And that was a real liability for a show meant to be filmed before a live audience.

More important, however, was the fact that Brooks wanted Moore to play a recent divorcee, and executives were adamant that audiences would never stand for that. Producer Allan Burns was later fond of recalling how he was told that certain topics and attributes were forbidden on television—among them divorce and mustaches. According to one story, a CBS official said that if Mary were to be presented as formerly married, viewers would think she had divorced Dick Van Dyke, and "nobody divorces Dick Van Dyke." So Moore's character was altered: She became the single Mary Richards whose engagement had recently been broken off. And, in the entire run of the series, she was never really paired with a man. The show's creators said that the audience never found one acceptable for Mary—an interesting commentary on how viewers viewed her sexuality, if not also men themselves. Yet even that caught on: "The important thing," Nora Ephron once wrote, "was that Mary Richards didn't even seem to care."

Ironically, the change made the show more appealing and marketable by making it more conventional, like the sixties' sitcom *That Girl* with Marlo Thomas, and even the fifties' *Our Miss Brooks.* "A series is like a dinner guest," Gary David Goldberg, who created *Family Ties* and *Spin City,* once said. "If you're scintillating but you open a wound, you won't get invited back. You must be nonthreatening." As a number of television historians, such as David Marc, have subsequently noted, the shift also made Mary a figure with whom many viewers could truly identify, since demographically this was an age in which millions of single baby-boom women—much like Mary Richards—were heading out for the first time and trying to make it on their own. "Woodstock Nation," Marc wrote, "had become Planet of the Singles." In 1970, however, television had virtually no programming which reflected the lives of the unpaired.

Yet perhaps because it represented a new concept, the show seemed to stumble out of the starting gate at the beginning of the fall of 1970. *Time* wrote:

> "The Mary Tyler Moore Show," on opening night at least, was a disaster for the old co-star of "The Dick Van Dyke Show." She plays an inadvertent career girl, jilted by the rounder she put through medical school, and working as a "gofer" at a Minneapolis TV station. Her bosses, a drunken clown of a news director and a narcissistic nincompoop of an anchorman, do an injustice to even the worst of local TV news.

Jack Gould of the *New York Times* wrote: "Mary Tyler Moore is caught in a preposterous item about life as an 'associate producer' in a TV newsroom." The show didn't crack the Top Twenty in its first season on the air at 9:30 P.M. Saturday, even though it began its Emmy run as two of its supporting principals won acting awards—Ed Asner for Lou Grant, and Valerie Harper for Rhoda, in an episode in which Mary fixes Rhoda up with an old boyfriend, who then shows up with his wife.

Yet, by the second season, something had changed with the audience. The *New York Times* reported a growing number of what would be known a decade later as "yuppies" flocking to the program. "Mary is so IN, actually," Daniel Menaker would write, "that it has become especially fashionable to drift into the den at a party—or even go home at nine on a Saturday because you simply must not miss the program." A West Coast sociology professor was quoted as saying, "[I]f I'm stoned, it's the only show that doesn't make me feel like committing suicide."

The attraction was a combination of forces, beyond the obvious fact that *The Mary Tyler Moore Show* remains one of television's best-written and -acted shows. For starters, there were no children, no traditional families, and not much in the way of notable plots, either (Mary and Rhoda sign up for a club for divorcées, so they can get a group rate to Paris; Mary dates the man who is auditing her tax return). Its appeal was in its characters. One wag even dubbed it a "warmedy"—one of the reasons why CBS executives were so thrown by its concept in the beginning. "Even when they had a poor story," Carl Reiner once said, "the characters always worked." Writers for this show would argue that Mary was able to tackle issues like birth control even more easily than Archie Bunker and company because the emphasis on people made the topicality seem less threatening.

Perhaps the creators of this show made a virtue of necessity, because Mary Tyler Moore wasn't as much of a comic performer as was (for example) Lucille Ball or Dick Van Dyke. Her strength was in the repartee and the reaction: Recall her most famous line from *The Dick Van Dyke Show* had been "Oh—*Rob!*" On the other hand, *The Mary Tyler Moore Show* did provide one of television's classic comic episodes—the "Chuckles the Clown" show, during which a clown dressed as a peanut is killed in a circus parade by an elephant. Ted solemnly announces a tribute: "A little song—a little dance—a little seltzer down your pants." When Mary begins giggling during the funeral, she is told:

> Laugh out loud. Don't you see, nothing would have made Chuckles happier? He lived to make people laugh. Tears were offensive to him, deeply offensive. He hated to see people cry. So go ahead, dear—laugh for Chuckles.

At which point, Mary breaks into sobs.

Still, this show needed a strong ensemble cast so they could all play off of Mary. Critic Ella Taylor has described *The Mary Tyler Moore Show* as a comedy of "embarrassment"—though, in Mary's case, the humiliation arises not because she has gotten herself into trouble à la Lucy, but because the social interactions between men and women had changed so much in such a short time that often neither sex knew what to do in any given situation anymore. Unlike most sitcom worlds, which are stable to the core, this show was built on subtle instability—which is one very big reason it struck its audience as so realistic. (It may also have had special appeal to women because all the men, in their own ways, were losers.) "Really the only issue that I care about," James Brooks once said, "is that we don't recreate the old Ozzie and Harriet myth of an ideal family and an ideal world." "Jim finds *everything* painful," someone once said. Listen to the audience laughter on this show and you will notice that the wild guffaws of other sitcoms are usually missing: The giggling is empathetic, if not bittersweet. The show, after all, had a theme song which proclaimed, somewhat tentatively, "You're gonna make it after all," and eventually did deal with divorce—if not Mary's, then boss Lou Grant's. Not unexpectedly, then, over the years, MTM Productions—founded by Moore and her then-husband, Grant Tinker, in a kind of 1970s counterpart to Lucy and Desi's Desilu Productions—would become known for producing both comedies that had drama *(Lou Grant)* and dramas that could be comedic *(Hill Street Blues)*.

Part of the show's appeal also grew out of its status as the first major ensemble workplace comedy—though, again, *The Dick Van Dyke Show* had explored some of the terrain a decade earlier. All TV sitcoms revolve around families—did then, and do now. But until then, the family had usually been a nuclear one, and the venue was never so focused around a workplace. This show changed that forever, at just the time the status of the nuclear family was collapsing in America. This was, in one critic's words, "All in the Work-Family." That's why Mary's last words, on the last episode, when everyone has been fired except the incompetent Ted, are "I thought about something last night. What is a family? And I think I know. A family is people who make you feel less alone and really loved. Thank you for being my family."

By the mid-1990s, of course, when clones like *Caroline in the City* were all over TV, the pendulum had swung the other way: Seemingly the only path no longer open for single women on TV now was to settle down, get married, and raise a traditional family. With Mary as an icon, an entire generation of women put their independence and career ahead of having that family. In 1960, 44 percent of single women worked, but post-Mary, 20 years later, with far more women remaining single or divorced, the figure was 67 percent. Yet the most extraordinary demographic change concerning women and work, this show never profiled. By the mid-nineties, around 60 percent of women with very young children worked—and no sitcom has yet to really come to terms with how anyone can deal with that.

So Mary's life choice raised an important social question for women: Could the workplace really replace the traditional family as the focus of one's life? The answer that many women would give today, even those who call themselves feminists, is a resounding "No!" Still, perhaps Mary was saying something more subtle as she talked to us as viewers. Perhaps her real point was that the vast television audience was the new family unit in America, wiping out the old one in the way it changed how we spend time with each other. In the mid-nineties, long after this show had stopped production, Robert Putnam, a Harvard professor, would argue that television had been a major factor in the nation's declining level of social trust and group participation: People stopped doing everything else so they could watch more TV. *The Mary Tyler Moore Show,* however, pointed in the opposite direction: This series created, if nothing else, a community of people who watched and shared its values. Leave it to a television show to suggest that only television could provide us with a sense of community any longer. The sad thing is that it may have been right.

35

Masterpiece Theatre and the Failure of PBS
(PBS: 1971–PRESENT)

One of the great failures of American television has been the inability of its public version either to attract large audiences or to develop a consistent vision. There's no doubt about the low ratings: In prime time, even on good nights, the Public Broadcasting Service (PBS) usually attracts audiences about one-sixth of any of the commercial networks. With a few notable exceptions (Ken Burns's *Civil War* series in the fall of 1990), it's rare for even the most acclaimed PBS show to beat anything running on the three major networks. Until recently, among the most-watched shows in prime time on PBS in many markets were repeats of *The Lawrence Welk Show*, an ABC Saturday-night mainstay over 30 years ago.

Yet the fact that some public stations can run Welk repeats is indicative of a larger problem: Public television has never figured out what it's supposed to offer the public. There is a strong argument afloat that with public TV, ratings shouldn't count: The point, some say, isn't to be popular, but rather to offer a consistent alternative to commercial TV, even if few tune in. Yet public television hasn't endorsed that approach, either—a state of affairs illustrated by the way stations often manage to churn out old VH-1-style rock concerts for baby boomers whenever there's a pledge drive. Faced with the ever-present problem of inadequate funding, public television has chosen to make itself a network which primarily serves the tastes of its corporate benefactors and aging, Establishment, upper-crust clientele. The result has been those rock reunions with faded stars from the sixties, along with Louis Rukeyser, old movies, Julia Child, John Tesh concerts, and *The Newshour With Jim Lehrer*. And, of course, *Masterpiece Theatre*.

Therein lies the contradiction. In its more than 25 years on the air, *Masterpiece Theatre* has provided its viewers with some of television's finest moments—from *Upstairs Downstairs* and *I, Claudius* to *Jewel in the Crown* and *House of Cards*. The series has won close to 30 Emmy Awards, and has often attracted some 4-5 million viewers per episode. Yet it's worth asking just why American public television's crown jewel turned out to be a forum for such rampant anglophilia—devoted as it is to televising almost exclusively British productions and British period pieces. In its infancy, American commercial television had been devoted to producing American dramas written by such fine young playwrights as Paddy Chayefsky, author of *Marty*, and Rod Serling, author of *Requiem for a Heavyweight*. Yet *Masterpiece Theatre*, through its underwriter Mobil, has rarely been inclined to replace those efforts, choosing instead to become a conduit for the BBC and other British production companies. Not to sound like H. Ross Perot, but what's wrong with American productions?

In 1969, a little more than two years after President Lyndon Johnson signed the first Public Broadcasting Act, PBS was launched to provide an alternative to the commercial fare then offered by the three mainstream networks. It's striking that many of the mainstays of PBS's programming more than 25 years later are still shows established in those first few years, if not before. *Washington Week in Review* was launched in 1967 on NET (National Educational Television), the predecessor to PBS, as was *Mister Rogers' Neighborhood. Sesame Street* premiered in 1969. *Wall Street Week* began in 1970, *NOVA* started in 1974, and *The MacNeil-Lehrer Report* in 1976.

Masterpiece Theatre premiered in the winter of 1971 in the wake of the first real ratings success on public television—a 1969-70, 26-week, Sunday-night production of *The Forsyte Saga,* a black-and-white BBC adaptation of the sweeping John Galsworthy novels about several wealthy English families. With some 120 characters, the series had captivated the United Kingdom the year before. NET had planned to follow up the Forsytes with the documentary series *Civilization,* but some producers at Boston's public station WGBH came up with the idea of trying to launch a series of British classics, much like *The Forsyte Saga,* to fill the time slot.

There were public-television series at that time presenting American drama, including *N.E.T. Playhouse* and *Hollywood Television Theatre.* Like most Boston Brahmin institutions, however, WGBH—as did Henry James in the century before—tended to look across the Atlantic for its culture, rather than to its own country. The show is "a living repository of our culture," the producer of *Masterpiece Theatre* once said, but "our culture" in upper-crust Boston has always meant something different than it does in the rest of America. To introduce the show each week, the series signed up the urbane Alistair Cooke, a Brit-turned-American who had been filing dispatches on the United States for the BBC and British papers for decades.

This was something of a reprise for Cooke: He had played a similar role in the early fifties for CBS's *Omnibus*—the no-commercials, 90-minute cultural series sponsored by the Ford Foundation, whose first show featured a preview of PBS things to come with a production of *The Trial of Anne Boleyn*. For *Masterpiece Theatre,* Cooke gave his introductions while sitting in an imaginary English country house—a practice which lasted more than 20 years until he retired and a suitably home-grown American, Russell Baker, finally made the grade and replaced him.

The show made its debut on January 10, 1971, with theme music by Mouret (even if he wasn't British) and a BBC production of *The First Churchills.* That series was selected, even though it wasn't thought to be very good, because one of its leads had starred in *The Forsyte Saga* and the series had "Churchills" in the title. (It was assumed that most Americans could at least recognize the name.) The money was supplied by Mobil, as in "*Masterpiece Theatre* is made possible by a grant from the Mobil Corporation," delivered at the beginning of each show in the clipped British accent of the show's first executive producer, Christopher Sarson. One twist: In the midst of a seventies energy crisis which caused the public's view of oil companies to sink to new lows, this show enabled Mobil to improve its image. In 1996, PBS even changed the name of the show to *Mobil Masterpiece Theatre* to honor its sole underwriter.

More significant was a second twist: Although WGBH originally promised to present a fair number of American works or productions, it rarely did. "The huge disappointment to me," even Sarson would later say, "is that it didn't turn to American serial drama." After 25 years there was Dickens (six times, no less!), but no Twain; Paul Scott, but no Updike; portraits of Disraeli and Churchill (who was a character in three separate productions), but not Jefferson or Jackson. OK, so there was *The Last of the Mohicans* in that first season, and Edith Wharton's *The Buccaneers* in the 25th. Yet A. J. Cronin got two more of his novels adapted than did Ernest Hemingway, and there were even three series that dealt with British mining in some way—*Sons & Lovers,* set in Nottingham; *Poldark,* situated in Cornwall; and *How Green Was My Valley,* set in South Wales. Americans would learn a lot more about British-Indian racial conflicts through this series than they would about their own. The reason for all this, a series producer once explained, was that it's cheaper to import productions which the BBC or other British companies have already done. Besides, she said, "we need to train our script writers and give our actors a chance to perform with continuity. After all, the British have been doing this since the 1940s."

The productions were first-class, though the miniseries that put *Masterpiece Theatre* on the map in 1974—*Upstairs, Downstairs*—was rejected at first by WGBH because it was original and considered too risqué, too soap-operatic, and not a "masterpiece." As Anthony Burgess would write, good books often transferred to the small screen better than great ones. "It," he wrote of the first Galsworthy saga, "has been waiting all these years to slide into its true medium—the leisurely, middlebrow television serial."

Over the years, the series presented a veritable catalogue of both good and great novels, done for TV, which featured memorable performances by many of Britain's finest actors and actresses—Derek Jacobi in *I, Claudius,* Glenda Jackson in *Elizabeth R,* Alan Bates in *The Mayor of Casterbridge,* and John Hurt in *Crime and Punishment.* With the success of this format, public television encouraged the commercial networks to launch similar ventures: The first network miniseries, *Rich Man, Poor Man,* appeared in 1976 on ABC and was something like *Upstairs Downstairs* down to even the title. *Roots* was our own version of the sweeping historical drama, as were *Lonesome Dove* and *The Winds of War.* Still, the American miniseries would always end up borrowing more from Danielle Steel than Daniel Defoe.

There were other crossover effects. The fact that British television featured so many of its finest talents helped persuade American entertainers that TV didn't necessarily have to be a second-class enclave to the movies, improving the quality of television generally. And, in an odd way, the anglophobia that gripped upper-crust America in the wake of *Masterpiece Theatre* helped pave the way for Charles and Di to become cross-Atlantic media stars—which probably made it easier for glossy American periodicals to turn to British editors and writers, as they did in the eighties and nineties at *Vogue, Vanity Fair,* the *New Republic,* and that formerly American institution, the *New Yorker.*

"Have you hugged a Brit today?" once asked the *Washington Post,* in noting the increasing cultural currency in this country of marmalade, fruitcake, and the phrase "on holiday." Perhaps Americans were driven to seek out British culture because, in an age of increasing diversity and confusion, they couldn't quite figure out what or where their own roots were. In any event, where *Masterpiece Theatre* led Jane Austen and even Hugh Grant one day followed, as did the notoriously British preoccupation with the sexual peccadillos of politicians.

Certainly the success of this series influenced PBS, which went on to import British mysteries for *Mystery,* and such "comedies" as *Benny Hill* and *Fawlty Towers,* whose boisterous bawdy British humor was lost on all but a few Americans. "We are all anglophiles," said PBS's president in 1994, but 15 years earlier, the chairman of the Carnegie Commission on Public Broadcasting had noted that public TV "is a national treasure; the problem is that the sublime moments do not come sufficiently often [and] many of them have British accents." In 1992, one prominent critic estimated that up to 60 percent of American public television was produced in the United Kingdom, including shows such as *Nature.* (Are even their animals better than ours?)

A similar kind of criticism could be made of other elements in the public television lineup. Admittedly, the government here never funded PBS nearly as well as other countries subsidized their public-broadcasting ventures. In the mid-1990s, despite all the debate in Washington about federal funding for PBS, only about one-sixth of the PBS budget came from that source; the rest was a mixture of corporate underwriting, along with state-government, viewer, and business contributions. The result was that stations here constantly had to pander for funds, leading some to wonder whether the acronym PBS in fact stood for Perpetual Begging System. Public television thus became heavily dependent on programming which appealed either to corporations that could put up money, or to the older, richer, and generally more staid audiences willing to contribute during pledge drives. Thus, in many markets, a show such as *The McLaughlin Group* became a feature of *public* television simply because GE paid for it!

PBS was additionally crippled by the fact that the public TV system here was exceedingly decentralized, with each local public station exerting far more control over its on-air product than local commercial stations could their own. "Most of the marvels cited by [PBS's] angry devotees are wonders of uncontroversial blandness," complained even *New York Times* columnist Russell Baker before he went on to take

Cooke's place as host of *Masterpiece Theatre.* "Another airing of Pavarotti; more great animal films, this time from the African veldt; a really neat piece on science—all very valuable, to be sure, very high-minded, but spiceless and dull."

Even when cable television changed the programming mix on the tube, influencing the "free" networks to experiment more, public television hardly changed its programming in order to offer more diversity. Thus *Washington Week in Review*—a show virtually identical to a dozen others now like it on television—continued to roll merrily along. So did a movie-review show, even though Siskel and Ebert had long since demonstrated that there was a ready market for an identical show on commercial television. Other PBS stations have been known to run *Star Trek,* or yet more home shopping services.

It is more than a little interesting to note that even the highly acclaimed *Baseball* series by Ken Burns (in 1994) was the kind of project that likely could have been produced elsewhere but appeared on PBS because it appealed to the "right" kind of people—most notably, perhaps, vocal public-television critic George Will, who, through no fault of his own, managed to pop up throughout as the sport's *eminence grise.* "You can be sure that if baseball were truly important, timid, white-bread PBS would not give it 18 hours nor would shrewd, greedy General Motors give it a cap-less payroll," wrote *New York Times* columnist Robert Lipsyte at the time. "Can Ken Burns, as good as he is at production and promotion, get that package for guns, dope, health care?"

The answer was that he could not, and *Masterpiece Theatre* was at least part of the reason. If PBS had truly been committed to a mission of offering news, educational, and cultural programming that Americans couldn't get elsewhere (no matter what the ratings), it still would have been able to present almost all of its children's programming, not to mention opera in prime time, the first-rate documentaries of *Frontline* and *The American Experience,* and even that other Brahmin favorite—the Boston Pops.

Once, however, PBS made itself into a reflection of the upper-class patrons who populated its fundraisers, and of the TV production lines in Boston, New York, Washington, and San Francisco, it lost its way. In one sense, PBS traded in the sponsor-driven system of network television for just another form of corporate sponsorship, this time with some pledge-drive donations thrown in. The result was a public-television network with no ads, but no consistent alternative vision, either—which is why we often ended up celebrating the warmed-over artifacts of another culture. *Masterpiece Theatre* has always been one of the best shows on television. Whether it should have been the leading prime-time success story of this country's system of public television, however, is another matter entirely.

36

Television's Biggest Scandal: The Local News
(ALL MAJOR AFFILIATES: 1970–PRESENT)

Turn on the television set at 5 P.M. or 6 P.M. in any part of America, or do the same at 10 o'clock or 11 o'clock, and you are likely to encounter one of the oddest, if not most pernicious, phenomenons on television: the local newscast. What makes these programs so strange is that they are so eerily alike from Maine to Mississippi, no matter the network affiliation. There are always the breathless promos ("Nude man found in mall: Film at 11!"). There are always the two amiable chatting anchors, usually a middle-aged man and a somewhat younger woman. There are the younger roving reporters, featured live at various points around the community or nation, where they chat up the anchors. ("Do we know why the man was wearing no clothes, Jim?" "We're waiting on that, Susan.") There's the joking weatherman, the jock sportscaster, and more recently, the health editor and the lifestyle reporter. In a nation of enormous diversity, there's something both comforting and appalling in knowing that no matter where you are, the local news—like the local McDonalds—is always the same.

What makes most of these newscasts pernicious is that they are at the same time so influential and so awful—at least in journalistic terms. In recent years, the local newscast has replaced the network evening news and the newspaper alike as the average American's main source of news: A study by the Pew Research Center for the People and the Press in 1996 found that 65 percent of all adults said they regularly watched the local TV news; only 42 percent reported that they did the same with a network newscast. In about two-thirds of all markets, according to another study, the early-evening local news shows attracted better ratings than the network newscasts that followed them—and the local news is on for a longer time. Though local newscasts have been studied far less systematically than the national news, nearly everyone who has examined their content has come away with the same conclusion. For example:

A 1995 study of the local TV news in 50 major markets by the Rocky Mountain Media Watch found that crime and disaster news make up about 53 percent of the news on local newscasts— the grislier the crime, the better. ("Son shoots mother five times with bow and arrow.") Fluff—defined by the study as "soft news, anchor chatter, teases, and celebrity items"—takes up about 31 percent of the whole newscast, on average (items such as "Girl reunited with dog" or "How to tango").

An informal 1993 survey by the *Washington Post* of local newscasts on stations in five big cities found the percentage of stories involving crime, sex, disasters, accidents, or public fears running at anywhere from 46 to 74. In its survey, the *Post* found local newscasts obsessed with murders, serial killers, snakebites, spider bites, tornadoes, floods, mudslides, explosions, and satanic activity.

A 1990 study published by the *Columbia Journalism Review* found that 18 of the 32 stories analyzed on local newscasts were inaccurate or misleading, and the station usually made no attempt to correct the mistakes. A report published the same year in the *L.A. Reader,* following examination of a week's worth of stories in that market, found stations routinely airing PR footage provided by companies with no acknowledgment that this was what was going on.

In a 1991 book examining the local news, *Making Local News,* Phyllis Kaniss found, among other things, that local TV news reporters are more likely to accept their sources' viewpoints than are print reporters.

A Chicago reporter looking at "sweeps week" on Los Angeles television found heavily promoted news stories on lesbian nuns, Geraldo Rivera's love life, and sex after 60.

As a critic once put it: The worst scandal the local news could ever uncover is itself.

Local news didn't start out this way. Until about 1970, local news—with its mix of local stories, weather, and sports delivered in a low-key broadcast—was an insignificant part of the television day. In the late sixties and early seventies, however, stations began to recognize the economic values of these newscasts. A news program is often less expensive than a dramatic show to produce, and, unlike national programming, the local station can retain the profits. Once they commenced in earnest, these newscasts began generating about one-third to half of the profits of local stations. Thus, in many markets, the local newscast started to expand—to a half-hour before the evening network news, then an hour, and in many markets to 90 minutes in the early evening and several other times throughout the day.

National network news had grown from radio, along with a concomitant duty recognized by the networks to deliver information responsibly to their viewers. Run by journalists, it was assumed these broadcasts would be loss leaders. By contrast, the local news arose because there was money to be made; the notion of what could possibly fill these hours came later, and in many cases the shows were run by television people with no use for traditional, pavement-pounding journalism.

Like the tabloid press at the turn of the century—faced with a similar dilemma about how to bring a larger audience to news—the locals frequently turned to such sensationalistic topics as crime. They also turned to the same small group of media consultants, who in turn tended to give them the same instructions whether they were in Laredo or Los Angeles. That explains the subsequent uniformity. In fact, anyone watching prime-time television knew how the medium worked in the seventies, and could have guessed the advice: Crime shows like *Kojak* attract the largest audience. Viewers respond to likable characters. All sitcoms revolve around families. It was the "genius" of these marketers to take the principles of prime-time fictional television and bring them to every local newscast in the nation, where they still remain in force. As one consultant's report put it:

> It is not surprising . . . that research indicates ratings rise when the broadcast is successful in exposing the listener to what he wants to hear, in the very personal way he wants to hear it. In terms of news, this means ratings are improved not when listeners are told what they should know, but what they want to hear.

In other words, news would become a form of entertainment.

The whole style had begun, of all places, on public television in the late 1960s, when KQED in San Francisco had experimented with a daily newscast for nine weeks during a local newspaper strike. For this newscast the reporters gathered at a long table, where they discussed the stories they presented in depth with an anchor. The first commercial stations to adopt the practice—beginning with the local San Francisco ABC affiliate—borrowed KQED's style, not its substance. Thus "happy talk" became an early feature of the local newscast, not to highlight the news but rather the news*casters.*

According to Ron Powers, who chronicled the rise of local news in his book *The Newscasters,* this style then became the signature of many ABC-owned stations around the country, and others soon followed. One station had a typical ad campaign which went: "So good news or bad, laugh a little with your News-4 favorites: You'll feel better." The industry trotted forth the usual analysts to explain its decision. "Audiences," said one, "have diametrically opposed needs: The desire to know, and a tremendous fear of finding out what happened. The communicator has to be someone they like if he is to put the whole frightening world together for them." By 1971, *Time* was already complaining. "What counts is not how the banana men relate the news," it wrote, "but how they relate to each other."

The main competitor to happy news on the local newscircuit was the closely related concept of "action news," dubbed in many places "Eyewitness News." Also developed by consulting firms, its signature was a high story count, an increasing number of striking visuals, and exciting upbeat music. Typical consultant recommendations called for "simplifying and limiting treatment of complex news, and elimination of 'upper-class English.'" Key to all this was the presence of a personable male anchor—although if things went wrong in the ratings, he was usually the guy blamed. That may explain why New York's WNBC in this formative period for local news went through a half-dozen or so anchormen—including Jim Hartz, Gabe Pressman, John Palmer, and Frank McGee—in a search for the holy ratings grail. It wasn't long, of course, before the two styles merged, so that virtually every station was using "happy talk" along with the impressionistic, tabloid approach of "action news." "You must have action in the first 12 seconds," Don Hewitt, the producer of *60 Minutes*, would say one day. "It doesn't matter what the action is."

Over the years, these approaches have continued to dominate the style of local TV news, though improvements in technology have affected the mix. The use of satellites allowed stations to send more reporters "live" into the field, with the result that most newscasts eventually featured the daily obligatory story or two of reporters wandering around a crime scene with little to report but their own presence.

By the 1980s, the technology had also improved enough that many local stations could send reporters to both national and international events, to report back live. They usually managed to do that even before the network news had come on the air. In the past, the networks had restricted to their own national shows both the national and international footage they obtained—if not to preserve the quality of the reporting, then to maintain their exclusive franchise and keep ratings high. At the same time that local stations began traveling around, however, CNN broke the networks' monopoly on world and national footage by offering such feeds to the locals.

The result was that local stations began to become the average viewer's window on the whole world, rather than just the local area. The same sketchy, tabloid coverage that had characterized local events now became the trademark of national and international coverage.

"Can you imagine how the civil-rights movement would have been affected if only local stations handled it?" former CBS News President Richard Salant once asked a reporter. Actually, the question might have been *if* they had covered it at all, since local stations always seemed to prefer stories like plane crashes or hurricanes, which allowed them to fly their reporters somewhere, put them on a beach in rain gear, and encourage them to babble and act fearful.

Ironically, national feeds of all sorts became so easy for local stations to pick up that they stopped doing some of the harder work of local reporting. "Why have a reporter hang around City Hall when he or she can sit in your tape room in Des Moines or wherever, monitor an incoming feed on, say, Michael Jackson leaving a New York hospital, and then report 'live from the newsroom' on the story?" a former network news executive questioningly complained to former *New York Times* editor and current magazine columnist Max Frankel.

A similar inclination to laziness and self-promotion increasingly led the locals to use "news stories" to promote entertainment shows on their own network. "Meet *The Beast* at 9, then meet the man who created it at 11!" screamed one NBC promo in New York in the nineties (*The Beast* was a made-for-TV movie.) In Washington, D.C., it was "The author of *The Beast* tells you what to fear right here in D.C.!" "You saw *Law and Order*," asked another, "but can it really happen?"

The effect of all this was to change the content of the national network newscasts themselves—which saw their ratings beginning to tumble as they faced this local threat. "After you have watched an hour of local news," Tom Bettag, an executive producer of the *CBS Evening News* asked in 1990, "why would you watch another half-hour of network?" So national anchors like Dan Rather hit the road, and the networks began becoming more tabloid themselves in an attempt to win back the audience they had lost to the locals.

By the nineties, the tail was wagging the dog: Now, local news was setting the journalistic standard for the networks. The result was that tabloid-like stories about Michael Jackson or Tonya Harding and Nancy Kerrigan also became the province of national newscasts—as did the perennial local obsession with crime. Even excluding the O.J. Simpson case, the three network newscasts spent four times as many hours covering murder cases in 1994 as they had only four years earlier. In 1995, the three network newscasts broadcast 2,574 crime stories—nearly one out of every five stories ran. That was four times the number of crime stories they had run as late as 1991, even though crime had actually declined in this later period.

With local stations providing an alternative to national broadcasts, newsmakers also had the option of going to them to make their case. During his presidency, George Bush often used local media to get his message across, knowing that local anchors—awed by the presidency and their own lack of national experience—would ask less-threatening questions than the network reporters. The practice continued in earnest throughout the 1992 campaign, when Bill Clinton did the same thing—beginning in the New Hampshire primary, as he circumvented national reporters who seemed to want to talk only about Gennifer Flowers.

On the one hand, these local stations do provide a venue for national figures to talk about issues when the national press tends to get bogged down talking about "insider" strategy rather than substance. On the other hand, such reports often provide virtually no critical analysis; many congressmen have been known to get their canned "news feeds" directly on the air, particularly in smaller markets. Communication it is, but journalism it isn't.

Improved technology also gave greater prominence on the local newscast to the weather—for very practical reasons often the heart of the show. Weather is only a small part of newspaper journalism, but it has been an integral part of local TV news since its inception in the 1950s. After all, the introduction of weather news permitted another commercial between segments—and, with news in those primitive days consisting entirely of a sober anchor reading a script at a desk, it allowed local news shows to introduce their first non-hard-news personalities. Joining the early ranks were New York's Tex Antoine with Uncle Wethbee and Washington's Willard Scott, who occasionally would dress up as Robin Hood, George Washington, or whomever, and once said "A trained gorilla could do what I do." In the 1950s some stations even turned to attractive "weather girls," one of whom once said "The temperature in New York is 46—and me, I'm 36-26-36."

With the development of weather satellites in the seventies and eighties, however, the visuals improved greatly—allowing viewers to observe the process of weather formation in ways they couldn't before. In fact, with the hiring of meteorologists as weather forecasters, weather reporting became so good on TV that once the cable industry was up and running, one of its more successful stations proved to be the Weather Channel. In late summer, Americans would begin tracking every tropical storm, hour by hour, and in the winter they did the same with snow. "The news media, particularly if there are no other big events, tend to overhype the storms compared to what storms actually do," Bill Gray, a professor of atmospheric science at Colorado State University once told a reporter. "You have a lot of these beautiful satellite pictures that create a lot of interest. And people have a natural interest in damage and other people's problems. It makes your own problems seem a little less."

Yet on the local news, weather would always take a back seat to crime. And studies showed that an overload of crime news tends to make viewers ever more fearful, and increasingly likely to support ever more radical measures designed to curb disorder. "What I object to is the lack of context," a local TV news reporter once said. "It all goes hurtling by, and the world is a frightening and inexplicable place."

Moreover, what gets ignored gets forgotten. "[C]overage of the environment, education, the economy, science, the arts, children, civil rights, parenting, conflict resolution, and homelessness didn't make the news today on most stations," stated the aforementioned Rocky Mountain Media Watch study, reporting on the results of its survey of a day in the life of local news. "And if it's not in the news, it's not on our public agenda."

In his book *The Newscasters,* Ron Powers suggested 20 years ago that local TV news had an obligation to sacrifice some of its profits to give its community better-informed newscasts. Yet, better-informed citizens now know to avoid local TV news for much of anything but weather and sports. In an atomized market, where wealthier viewers can turn to computers or cable (including around-the-clock local cable news in many areas), local TV news is increasingly left with a downscale audience which doesn't think that "journalism" as practiced in the *National Enquirer* or the tabloids is all that terrible. The producers of these newscasts are right when they proclaim that local TV news gives viewers what they want. It just doesn't give them what they need.

37

The Tonight Show and Its Hold on America
(NBC: 1954–PRESENT)

It's hard to imagine going to bed with anything other than *The Tonight Show*. At least until recently, this was one of television's most profitable shows, dominating the ratings in its time slot after the local news for 40 years. *The Tonight Show* also defined just about the only type of successful programming the networks can run after prime-time, with *Nightline* the notable exception. There is a long list of people, including Merv Griffin, Joey Bishop, Arsenio Hall, Dick Cavett, Joan Rivers, Les Crane, Bill Dana, Chevy Chase, and Joe Pyne, who have tried—and mostly failed—to challenge the hegemony of *The Tonight Show*.

What makes the dominance all the more striking is that *The Tonight Show* has never really been one smoothly evolving show, but four different ones—each sharply reflecting its host. In the hands of Steve Allen, beginning in September 1954, *The Tonight Show* was something of a comedy and musical cabaret. Though the show had guests, the focus was always on Allen and his cast of regulars, which included Gene Rayburn and orchestra leader Skitch Henderson. Instead of an outright comedy show, it would be a "service show with comedy," creator Pat Weaver once wrote.

In the hands of Jack Paar, who hosted the show from July 29, 1957 to March 30, 1962, *The Tonight Show* became more of a talk program—featuring serious guests, such as the presidential candidates of 1960. "He is one of a whole new class of TV-age entertainers—the just-talkers," wrote *Time* in 1958; and his trademark line, "I kid you not," became common parlance. Yet even though intellectuals considered the literate Paar a kind of late-night Edward R. Murrow or Adlai Stevenson, it was his mercurialness that became his trademark. The temperamental Paar was known to burst into tears on a moment's notice, and his on-air feuds with critical columnists Walter Winchell (who he said wore "too-tight underwear") and Dorothy Kilgallen (who he charged "must use Novocain lipstick") became legendary. On February 10, 1960, Paar even walked off his own broadcast (after NBC had on the night before censored a joke which used the initials W.C.), leaving surprised sidekick Hugh Downs to take over. Paar returned a month later, beginning his monologue with "As I was saying before I was interrupted...."

It was during Johnny Carson's tenure from 1962 to 1992, however, that *The Tonight Show* became a television institution. And it was in the 1970s that Carson really established himself. Other than Walter Cronkite, no TV personality persevered for as long, with as much audience respect. In fact, the comparisons with Cronkite go further. Like the nation's leading anchorman, Carson delivered his version of the news each day through his celebrated monologue. The two bracketed the night's entertainment: The Cronkite version came right before prime time—announcing, in effect, the beginning of entertainment; Carson's came after. Like Cronkite, Carson rarely appeared in prime time, where it might have been discovered that his appeal was really to the elites who follow news or stay up late. And, like an anchorman (or a president), Carson was one of the few performers whom TV etiquette allowed to address the camera directly—the culture's ultimate sign of respect and authority.

Carson was always a step behind most trends, but that gave this product of Nebraska his hold on his audience. If Carson began poking endless fun at Jimmy Carter or Richard Nixon, it was a sign that the end was near. The show itself was rather conventional. As TV scholar Brian Rose has noted, thanks in large part to Carson, all late-night talk shows now tend to look the same. They open with a host (almost always a male comedian) emerging onstage to an orchestra blast. What follows is a monologue before a live audience—often marked by banter between the host and the orchestra leader or sidekick. After a short skit or comic break a few guests are welcomed; they usually just joke and exchange small talk with the host.

Yet the format hardly accounts for Carson's astonishing renown, or the way that this embodiment of the conventional defied the conventional wisdom by remaining topical on TV for so long. He went beyond popular: Carson was viewed more frequently than almost anyone else in history. For more than 5,000 nights we watched the same imaginary golf swings, the same references to his alimony, the same pets from the San Diego Zoo, and the same jokes about Ed McMahon's drinking and Doc Severinsen's clothes. And we kept on watching, to the tune of 8 million a night.

Yet despite constant exposure on a medium thought to reveal the deepest intimacies of character, Carson always remained remarkably impenetrable. "It's his elusivity that keeps him fresh," Jimmie Reeves, a television scholar, once said. "We can put ourselves into him. He's familiar enough to be recognizable, yet unique enough to be interesting. There's more to Johnny Carson than meets the eye."

Reeves was on to something. After all, in far less time than Carson's 30 years, we became familiar with Jack Paar's temper, Howard Cosell's assertiveness, and Joan Rivers' abrasiveness. If we have imagined inviting Barbara Walters, Tim Allen, or even Bill Clinton into our homes, television has already disclosed how they might act and what they might say. But Carson? Aside from a few chosen facts—the long vacations, the frequent divorces, the love of tennis, the Nebraska boyhood—audiences had little sense of the man. In the world of the utterly known, Carson managed to remain unknowable.

It was a facet of his persona that others noted frequently. Carson was rarely photographed, and even less often sat for interviews. He never overexposed himself—taking plenty of vacation time, and even reducing the length of the broadcast twice over his 30-year span. Once he took over *The Tonight Show* he had no other major media roles, no movie roles, no Broadway shows, and he wrote no books. The few reporters who got through usually came away frustrated. A *Playboy* magazine interviewer described him in 1967 as "paradoxical"; *Rolling Stone* 12 years later found him "elusive." "Nobody really knows Johnny," an associate was once quoted as saying. "He's sealed as tight as an egg. And the shell is unbreakable."

Even his show defied easy description. It was a talk show without much meaningful talk, a variety show without variety, a "live" show taped earlier in the day. Opening every night with an excited "Heeere's Johnny," a musical blast, and a host who appeared from behind a curtain, *The Tonight Show* promised the old-time glitz of show business. Yet its major attraction lay in its relentlessly upbeat regularity. Looking back over 30 years of Carson, in fact, it's hard to recall many extraordinary moments. Ed Ames throwing a tomahawk at a target in 1965 and hitting it in the crotch? Tiny Tim's wedding in 1969? Alex Haley's 1977 presentation of Carson's genealogical chart? Another appearance by Carl Sagan? Carson invoked the familiar so repeatedly that his prime-time anniversary shows often were reduced to showing bloopers: When something went awry on *The Tonight Show, that* was news. The show, like its host, was unique in popular culture—memorable, yet incapable of being remembered.

Part of the mystery of Carson's appeal derived from his many roles. He was an outstanding stand-up comedian, an improviser, and a host who let others talk while he politely listened. He also played himself—a somewhat unusual role for a regular television entertainer, though one explored earlier on the medium by George Burns and Jack Benny. (Carson had the same producer, Fred de Cordova). After all, when Don Johnson played Sonny Crockett or Bill Cosby portrayed Dr. Cliff Huxtable, it was easy to separate the performer from the role—a fictional composite of the efforts of writers, directors, and camera personnel, not to mention the actor. But when the 100-member staff of *The Tonight Show* pushed Carson forward every night into one of TV's last bastions of nonfictional entertainment, who was he? "Himself," de Cordova once said. "George Burns and Jack Benny assumed a facade. Johnny Carson is not a character named Johnny Carson."

Yet Carson read many of his lines, just like other actors. And it was frequently difficult to judge where reality stopped and facade took over. Did Johnny actually pay all that alimony? Did Ed really drink that much? As David Marc, author of *Comic Visions,* once pointed out, the stand-up comic traditionally creates a persona, making no distinction between stage and world, teller and tale. Carson, the one-time host of the quiz show *Who Do You Trust?,* seemed to profess: "I'm telling you the truth; I am who I am." Was it possible, ever, to believe him?

The hour at which Carson was on TV also added to his mystery. He rarely appeared outside that late-night time slot, a time when we drift between wakefulness and sleep. "Television extends the dream world," anthropologist Edmund Carpenter once said. "Its content is the stuff of dreams and its format is pure dream." Ordinary yet dislocated, relevant yet forgettable, Carson's show served as a bridge between our tangible world and the world of our dreams. And at its center stood the ambiguous Carson—Carnac the Magnificent—refusing to disclose himself.

After all, Johnny started out in show business as a magician, performing sleights of hand. He ultimately became a late-night magician of persona, performing sleights of mind. Yet Carson's inscrutability was what enabled him to survive and prosper over three decades. By defying the TV reductionism that renders all things knowable and ultimately trivial, Carson made himself into one of the medium's only characters worth watching, night after night. After 30 years, we knew Johnny Carson like we knew ourselves. Which is to say we hardly knew him at all.

Following up this act in 1992, of course, would have been difficult for anybody. Yet the press made it harder, initially, for Jay Leno, NBC's chosen successor, than it should have been. Following enormous controversy and speculation about who would succeed Johnny, Leno stepped in on May 25, 1992. From that point on, the press constantly focused on the battle between Leno's version of *The Tonight Show* and the *Late Show With David Letterman*—which premiered on CBS on August 30, 1993, amid extravagant predictions that Letterman, the proclaimed "king of irony," would drown Leno in the ratings.

Letterman, who most critics thought should have inherited Carson's chair, had made a name for himself by following *The Tonight Show* at 12:30 A.M. on NBC for ten years with *Late Night With David Letterman*. Borrowing heavily from the TV antics of Ernie Kovacs, Letterman created a show with particular appeal to the 18-to-34-year-old crowd, as he attempted to stretch the boundaries of the conventional talk show with frequent stunts both outside the studio (interviewing New York City taxi drivers) and within (throwing himself up against, and sticking to, a special wall while dressed in clothes made of Velcro).

After an initial surge in the ratings, however, the predicted ambush of Leno by Letterman never came off. Indeed, by the mid-1990s Leno was regularly beating Letterman in the ratings. Yet what was more striking than Leno's victory was the enormous attention the press and public paid to it. Bill Carter of the *New York Times* even wrote a whole book about the subject, *Late Shift,* which spawned a made-for-TV movie. Why all the ads, magazine covers, and commotion over what was, after all, only an hour of TV running when more than half of all America has gone to bed? Sure, there were network profits and prestige at stake, but there was rather more to it than that: The Letterman-Leno battle became the latest volley in an age-old war between New York (home of the Letterman show) and California (adopted home of Leno)—if not of the whole East and West—as to who better represented the country and had the superior way of life.

It is a struggle, after all, that has defined America: East vs. West, city vs. frontier, sophistication vs. brawn. "Millions are to be grabbed out here and your only competition is idiots," Herman J. Mankiewicz wired Ben Hecht from Hollywood in the 1930s, a theme Woody Allen milked in *Annie Hall.* Not to be outdone, Hollywood has often depicted New York the way it did in the movie *Ghost*—as a place populated by scheming yuppies and terrorizing thugs.

As any census expert or politician will tell you, this is a battle of images and demography which the West won decades ago—precisely why Leno was bound to prevail. After all, Ronald Reagan became president, not Nelson Rockefeller or Mario Cuomo; and Hollywood—not New York—has for decades controlled the propaganda machine that is the entertainment industry. Too, a majority of Americans now live in suburbs after the southern California model, not in cities. Still, reality has a way of getting discarded when the New York-based press, the New York advertising industry, and a New York-centered network are promoting yet another contender to reclaim for that city the right to call itself a national symbol—as they did with Letterman.

Playing host to the late-night king is an important role to New Yorkers, who like to think they inhabit the only "city that never sleeps." Remember that *The Tonight Show* had been designed by Weaver as a *New Yorker*esque, video "Talk of the Town." Its late-night predecessor was in fact called *Broadway Open House*. By the time Weaver had turned that show into *The Tonight Show* in the mid-fifties, it had become the supposed venue for scintillating late-night New York sophistication—a gathering point for such comedians as Lenny Bruce and Mort Sahl, then considered too hot for Hollywood, and thus for prime time.

Remember, too, that with Jack Paar at the helm for almost five years, the show had, if anything, enhanced that urbane reputation. Given that prime-time TV—now firmly in the grasp of Hollywood— was then on its way to becoming Newton Minow's "vast wasteland," many intellectuals saw Paar as the medium's salvation. His was, after all, a "serious" talk show that not only featured the Zsa Zsa Gabors, but Eleanor Roosevelt, Albert Schweitzer, and John F. Kennedy—the last president from the East. In 1961, Paar even took a crew to West Berlin, right after the Wall went up.

That's something that Carson never would have done. Losing TV and movie production was one thing, bidding farewell to the Dodgers was another, and having California surpass New York in population was yet a third slight to Gotham. But having Carson take *The Tonight Show* in 1972 to—of all places—Burbank may well have proved the unkindest cut of all. Yet that's one key reason why, as the nation's soul moved to the West both spiritually and demographically, *The Tonight Show*'s audience more than doubled, despite efforts to reestablish many New York alternatives. In the years since Carson moved to the West Coast, New York's only real claim to TV fame has been that it hosted *Sesame Street,* a few sitcoms, the news, and *Saturday Night Live.*

Then in 1992 came Leno, taped in California, and Letterman, taped in New York: The battle was joined. Fittingly, Letterman operated out of the Ed Sullivan Theater—home of TV's last great New York hit. The Letterman show even opened with New York night scenes, with a fake skyscraper montage behind Letterman's desk. By contrast, there has never been much of a sense of place on the California show that Leno inherited from Carson: It stands for the proposition that a TV studio is a TV studio because, once the lights go out, there's no there there.

Letterman's humor was also more quintessentially New York—

more pointed, insulting, and almost always more ironic than Leno's. If Letterman was far more cynical than a Carson or a Leno, it's because world-weary New Yorkers aren't the optimists that Westerners are. If they were, they would have gotten into a wagon (station *or* covered) long ago, and left for greener pastures, too. New York jokes have an edgy undertone of "Aren't we sophisticated!" with Letterman's foil often being Middle Americans—the kind of people who enjoyed playing Carson's old routine, "Stump the Band."

Letterman's show also appeared more spontaneous—in the tradition of New York vaudeville. By contrast, southern California late-night jokes are more like prime-time TV humor: If the laughter isn't canned, at least the jokes sure seem like they are. A Reagan, a Carson, and a Leno tell stories as much as they tell jokes. Their comedic tradition owes less to the Borscht Belt and more to the Western "tall tale." What's more, in the Paar tradition, Letterman was always the witty star, even if he was talking to a guest. In contrast, Leno didn't star—he hosted. *The Tonight Show* was thus more like a Hollywood studio production, as it depended on many players. Even in Carson's heyday, after all, the public referred to the program as *The Tonight Show*—the system and the industry are always bigger than the star. Letterman's show, however, is still almost always referred to as *Letterman,* and he makes his biggest laughs by bashing the medium, if not also his employer. If he lived in the company town, he might see things differently.

One can, of course, read too much into the Leno–Letterman struggle. There will always be a place and a constituency for New York. What's more, this ratings struggle was hardly going to change American history. Americans would continue moving westward, as they always had, no matter who prevailed late at night, and by early 1997, in fact, there were rumors that Letterman himself might someday move his show to California. These symbolic regional struggles are almost always staged after the fact: The cultural battles between the North and South reached their peak only when it became obvious that the South had lost its national influence. Sure, New York may be a nice place to revisit at night occasionally. But, in the end, few Americans really want to live there anymore—either today or *Tonight.*

38

60 Minutes and the
Evolution of News to Entertainment
(CBS: 1968–PRESENT)

On Tuesday, September 24, 1968, at 10:00 P.M., CBS aired a news show with a different concept. The idea, according to producer Don Hewitt, former studio producer of Edward R. Murrow's *See It Now,* was to offer an alternative to the usual television presentation of news—which until then had meant a sober, single-issue documentary or traditional account in a straitlaced newscast. "Instead of dealing with issues, we [will] tell stories," Hewitt said. "If we package reality as well as Hollywood packages fiction, I'll bet we could double the rating."

That first show offered the prototype, with several video "articles" presented somewhat as in such popular print magazines of the day as *Look* or *Life.* "This is *60 Minutes,*" said cohost Harry Reasoner, in introducing that first broadcast. "It's a kind of magazine for television, which means it has the flexibility and diversity of a magazine adapted to broadcast journalism." The cameras then took the viewer inside the Nixon and Humphrey presidential campaigns; headlined a tense interview between Mike Wallace and then-Attorney General Ramsey Clark about conflicts between the police and citizens; took a lighthearted look at a recent animated film; and featured a short essay by humor columnist Art Buchwald. The early critical reaction was mixed: While the *New York Times* described the show as "[s]omething television has long needed," *Variety* said, "If it had been a newspaper, it would not have sold many copies. The stories were dated and the magazine format, lifted from print, pretentious."

The public seemed to agree with *Variety*'s assessment—not just then, but for six years. During that time, *60 Minutes* was moved around from time slot to time slot, and languished in the ratings; it never even ran two weeks in succession until 15 months after its premiere. It was thus no surprise that the show never moved into the Top Fifty for a season, and frequently ranked at the bottom (in its third season it was

101st out of 103 shows). Yet even in the show's early days, *Time* was already noting that *60 Minutes* seemed to draw most of its story lines from "the world of pop sociology"—skiing, Janis Joplin, even the topic of ugliness. And the approach? Already critics were complaining that in a story featuring French student leader Daniel Cohn-Bendit, "Mike Wallace seemed more intent on discrediting Cohn-Bendit's radical ideas than on hearing out his position."

Over the next three decades, the program's philosophy and organization never deviated much from that first episode's, but the critical and audience reaction certainly did. Almost 30 years later, the *60 Minutes* stopwatch is still ticking, making the show the longest-running prime-time series in television history to run under the same name. The other broadcasting records it holds are legion: *60 Minutes* is the only show to hit Number 1 for a season in three separate decades (1979-80, 1982-83, and 1992-93). It is the highest-rated public-affairs program in TV history, with ratings that never fell out of the annual Top Ten from 1977 through 1997. What Hewitt and his gang accomplished was what Edward R. Murrow tried to do but failed—to find a place for news in prime time. "That which is important is often dull; they [the producers of *60 Minutes*] don't have any tolerance for that," Fred Friendly, Murrow's collaborator, once said. "But what they have done is interest the blue-collar worker, the non-serious news-reader, in a way that not Murrow or Cronkite or I have done."

With its success, *60 Minutes* changed the face of programming and journalism. Muckrakers had been notorious since Lincoln Steffens, but—more than even Bob Woodward and Carl Bernstein—*60 Minutes* made journalists into national icons. Moreover, because news shows are cheaper for the networks to produce than fictional prime-time programming, *60 Minutes* became the most profitable prime-time show that television ever developed. Richard Campbell, author of a perceptive history of the show, *60 Minutes and the News,* once calculated that the program has made more than $1 billion for CBS. *60 Minutes* made the TV world safe for the news-magazine format— which soon proliferated all over the dial.

There was an underside, however, to that success. News had once been a loss leader for the networks, which presented such programs during television's first two-and-a-half decades as something of a public service to their viewers. Once the networks saw that these shows could be gold mines, the approach changed, with TV executives demanding that news make a profit just like other programming. That, in turn, altered the way in which news was presented to the public. No wonder Hewitt was quoted several years ago as saying that *60 Minutes* had "singlehandedly ruined television." "No one can report news today without making money," Hewitt complained.

Through it all, this program never wandered far from the basic formula and story mix with which it began that first episode. Dan Rather once divided *60 Minutes* stories into four classifications: the exposé, the profile, the travel story, and the unpredictable. In his book and subsequent articles, Campbell has chronicled how *60 Minutes* closely resembles a fictional prime-time series, with its ensemble of reporters cast as the heroes. These reporters often function as detectives, and the plots are not very different from the story lines on prime-time television's favorite dramatic genre—the crime show. "I think people watch *60 Minutes,*" Hewitt once said, "because they're interested in seeing Morley, Dan, and Mike pursue a story, just as they like to see Kojak" (the TV detective popular at the same time that *60 Minutes* finally caught on). If the trench-coated Mike Wallace is the modern version of Joe Friday from *Dragnet,* some of his compatriots oddly resemble the fictional Jessica Fletcher, an aging detective on *Murder, She Wrote*— a show that successfully followed *60 Minutes* on Sunday nights for years.

Because of its success, *60 Minutes* has probably been written about more than any other show in television history. It's been both satirized on *Saturday Night Live* and the subject of David Letterman's Top Ten list. ("Things the *60 Minutes* staff doesn't want you to know: Stopwatch is five minutes fast. . . . Nobody actually watches, but the Nielsen Company knows what to do to avoid an investigation.") Anyone who has read those accounts—from Hewitt's own *Minute by Minute,* to Campbell's more academic study, and on to Axel Madsden's *60 Minutes: The Power and the Politics of America's Most Popular TV News Show*—knows that making the news world a source of endless profit and entertainment hadn't been the goal of Hewitt, though drawing larger audiences clearly was. "[S]ometime in 1967 it dawned on me that if we split those public-affairs hours into three parts to deal with the viewers' short attention span—not to mention my own—and came up with personal journalism . . . in which a reporter takes the viewer along with him on the story, I was willing to bet that we could take informational programming out of the ratings cellar," Hewitt wrote in his book.

In its early, unknown years, the network either ran *60 Minutes* biweekly, or moved it opposite the most popular series on television, *Marcus Welby, M.D.*, and therefore relatively few saw the hosts, Wallace and Reasoner (who was replaced by Morley Safer in 1970), do the following: profile Eldridge Cleaver, Jack Anderson, and Billie Jean King; investigate the South Vietnamese army and the Gulf of Tonkin incident; and interview Clifford Irving about the incredible Howard Hughes hoax. Those first shows also introduced a regular feature highlighting a brief exchange of opinion between conservative pundit James J. Kilpatrick and liberal Nicholas von Hoffman, in an early version of CNN's *Crossfire*.

In 1970, the network moved the show to the 6:00 P.M. Sunday time slot—but on so early in the evening, and often up against football, the series continued to languish in the ratings. Still, the network, perhaps sensing something, stuck by the show—albeit continually moving it around the schedule. The result of this blurring of its time slot was that viewers could never quite figure out where it was going to pop up next.

Then, in the 1975-76 season, *60 Minutes* finally began to catch on, even though it still ended up ranking only 52nd for that season. Campbell writes that the Watergate scandal and the subsequent downfall of President Nixon had created an almost insatiable thirst for news coverage. Having Dan Rather, CBS's best-known reporter and former White House correspondent, join the show as a third reporter undoubtedly helped the ratings, too. CBS also moved the program to Sunday at 7:00 P.M.—putting *60 Minutes* up against what had traditionally been solely a "children's hour" on television: While *The Wonderful World of Disney* had dominated the slot for over a decade, adults finally had something to watch, too! Following NFL football on the CBS schedule also allowed this show to inherit a large male audience—and, since the games often ran late, inveterate CBS viewers were frequently stuck with *60 Minutes,* since programming on the other two networks had already started.

It also didn't hurt that, over the years preceding these changes, *60 Minutes* had also altered its focus—gradually doing fewer lighter features and taking on more of the exposé investigative pieces, à la Woodward and Bernstein, that would make the show famous. "He can ask somebody, 'Where did you go to college?' and make it seem like an indictment," the *New Yorker's* E. J. Kahn once wrote of Mike Wallace, who made Barbra Streisand weep, and told the Ayatollah Khomeini that Anwar Sadat thought he was a "lunatic." And it wasn't just Wallace: Diane Sawyer revealed that one in three chickens sold in American groceries had salmonella; Rather led an exposé of an insecticide that led to several indictments; and Safer took up the cause of a black man wrongly convicted of robbing a Texas restaurant. In his book, Madsden calculated that a full 20 percent of the stories on *60 Minutes* deal with one kind of scam or another—from fraud in Medicaid billing to the sale of Romanian babies. "A crook doesn't believe he's made it as a crook until he's been on *60 Minutes,*" Safer once said.

Over the years, the audience grew. By April 1977 at just about the time Barbara Walters was creating another new approach to "news" with her celebrity, prime-time specials, *60 Minutes* was finally posting a profit. Harry Reasoner returned in 1978, and a new feature, "A Few Minutes With Andy Rooney," was added starring Reasoner's old writer. Ed Bradley joined the show in 1981, replacing Rather (who took over Cronkite's anchor chair), and in 1984 Sawyer became the first female in the ensemble.

In more recent times, Meredith Vieira has come and gone, and Steve Kroft has joined the "repertory company" (Hewitt's words), as has Lesley Stahl—who replaced Sawyer when she left for ABC in 1989. With Safer and Wallace remaining, the show's core has stayed remarkably intact—and, because of that, *60 Minutes* now features a cast almost as old as that of *The Golden Girls:* Wallace is in his late seventies, Rooney his early seventies, and Safer his mid-sixties. This may be why at least half the audience for *60 Minutes* each week is usually over 50—and the show ranked only 34th in 1994-95 among adults of ages 18 to 49.

During its tenure, *60 Minutes* has produced any number of memorable pieces, from Bill Clinton's virtual confession of adultery in 1992 in the wake of the Gennifer Flowers episode, to Dan Rather's dressing up as an Afghan rebel to cover the war there in 1980. The show helped make Supreme Court libel law through a suit filed by Col. Anthony Herbert, who maintained that the show defamed him in a report. (After a decade of litigation, the case was eventually thrown out.) The show created its own controversy when it suspended Rooney briefly in 1990 for supposedly derogatory remarks he made against homosexuals on another show. (The suspension was supposed to run for three months, but was ended after three weeks when the ratings of *60 Minutes* began to fall.) The program has profiled everyone from Jesse Jackson and Helen Hayes to Hyman Rickover and Don Imus. It has also spawned a whole group of consultants who advise businessmen how to act in front of the cameras if *60 Minutes* (or one of its clones) comes calling, knocking on the door or car window and demanding information.

60 Minutes has also become infamous for its methods: On a few occasions, the show paid for interviews. One critic has complained about the show's 10:1 film-to-on-air ratio, charging that it has improperly edited stories. And the show has also gained a certain amount of notoriety for the stories it has supposedly tried to duck. In 1981, it was revealed that Wallace had dissuaded Safer from doing a story in Haiti because Wallace's wife had relatives there who feared trouble. (To its credit, after the revelation, *60 Minutes* went ahead and did the story anyway, with another correspondent.) Then, in 1995, CBS lawyers killed a Wallace interview with Jeffrey Wigand, the highest-ranking tobacco executive to turn against the industry—though (once again, after an uproar) the interview later appeared on the show.

It is also no secret that, like all similarly successful television shows, *60 Minutes* venerates its stars, and its stars are reporters: Campbell once calculated that the reporters are often featured more frequently in *60 Minutes* stories than are the subjects of the stories themselves. "Television is more a business of personalities than it is about ideas," Hewitt once said. Only TV journalism, for example, could make such a big deal about subjects who decline interviews, following them from their cars and into their homes. If a print journalist inserted into a story that he had tried to interview a source and had been refused, he'd be considered a joke—or a least a lousy journalist. But on a show where the journalist is the hero, standards change.

Yet the success of *60 Minutes* inevitably spawned imitators that were not as good or as principled in walking the fine line between entertainment and news. *20/20,* a solid show once it reunited the old *Today* team of Hugh Downs and Barbara Walters, was the first such show to appear in 1978, and more inevitably followed. It was in the nineties, however, that the networks really turned to magazine shows (11 in 1993 alone), primarily because—in an era of cutbacks—they cost less than half of a regular drama show's tab to put on. As Hewitt told a reporter: "No one believes that ABC and NBC woke up one morning and said to themselves, 'You know, we're not doing enough to inform the public.' What they woke up one morning and said was, 'Holy cow, can you believe how much money *60 Minutes* makes?'"

Yet, as news shows replaced entertainment shows in the prime-time constellation, the news on these series inevitably became more "entertaining" and took on a tabloid tone. *Dateline* helped fake a truck explosion to make a point and CBS's Connie Chung seemed joined at the hip to a skating figure named Tonya Harding. In contrast to *60 Minutes,* television's other newsmagazines were as likely to feature a closeup on Charles Manson and his followers as a story about nuclear radiation. As these magazine series became preoccupied with celebrities, they also increasingly became obsessed with promoting their own journalistic celebrities like Stone Phillips or Diane Sawyer, whose quest for big scoops and big contracts after she left CBS frequently became stories in themselves in other venues.

60 Minutes may also have sparked another trend. By the mid-1980s, legal analysts had begun noting a sharp rise in the number, if not the notoriety of, libel and tort suits against the media. Though there were a number of reasons behind the increase, one was that, in the age of television, the viewing public no longer thought of the press as the press viewed itself—as a group of well-meaning independent crusaders acting in society's best interest. Instead, it began to think of Mike Wallace and all of those cameras as intruders, as the muckraking distrust of big business that *60 Minutes* had helped breed for decades migrated to the media itself. To the public, television networks were now among our most powerful and visible institutions, making them prime targets for the same type of malpractice suits as those brought against the powerful in other professions.

By the mid-1990s, some of the *60 Minutes* clones began to disappear as their ratings dropped—victims of both duplication and a growing distrust of the very kind of tabloid journalism these shows had tried to popularize. Faced with a drop in its own ratings in the mid-nineties, in no small part because CBS lost its valuable NFL football lead-in to the Fox network, *60 Minutes* retooled—covering more breaking stories, and eventually hiring CNN international reporter Christiane Amanpour. Yet by then the damage had been done, and it seemed difficult to believe that *60 Minutes* would ever again be the cultural force it once had been.

"Competition in mass media doesn't weed out the bad," Walter Goodman, TV critic of the *New York Times* once said; "it weeds out the good." The irony, then, is that *60 Minutes*—a show which had helped create the concept in the seventies that journalists were heroes—helped set in motion a process which would ultimately discredit the reporting profession.

39
TV's Most Self-Congratulatory Hit:
Saturday Night Live
(NBC: 1975–PRESENT)

Critics have often hailed *Saturday Night Live (SNL)* as "the show that changed television." *New York* magazine included the show's debut in a special issue on 25 key events in the life of the city over the past 25 years, and Richard Zoglin of *Time* has hardly been alone in describing it as the show that "seemed to break new ground almost weekly." It pushed "the boundaries of permissible language and subject matter, rejuvenating political satire, breaking the 'fourth wall' to make fun of the TV medium itself," he wrote. ABC's Jeff Greenfield has gone even further: "[I]t is impossible to think about what our popular culture would look like without 'Saturday Night Live,'" he wrote.

Actually, it wouldn't look terribly different. Despite the enormous publicity the show has always received, the *Saturday Night* revolution affected only the margins of television, and specifically late-night entertainment for which the audiences tend to be younger, smaller in number, and closer in sensibility than otherwise to the prominent television critics and executives who huddle on both coasts. Prime-time sitcoms and dramas—the mainstays of broadcast entertainment—aren't much different from what they were before the fall of 1975, when *SNL* premiered; and what differences there are can hardly be attributed to this show. *Saturday Night Live* lampooned presidents and other political figures freely, but impersonators had been doing the same on *The Ed Sullivan Show* for years. *Saturday Night Live* may have made the world safer for David Letterman and Garry Shandling, but it's difficult to argue that a medium which had already accommodated Ernie Kovacs and the Smothers Brothers in prime time, if only briefly, would never have found a role for other offbeat comics.

True, the show was occasionally innovative: *SNL* displayed its own urban style, resurrecting the prominence of New York as a center for TV production, though in many ways it was only a baby boom version of the early fifties' Saturday night fixture, *Your Show of Shows,* with Sid Caesar and Imogene Coca. *SNL* did change the look of television, at least at its late hour. "A lot of the [original performers] wouldn't have gotten past a network casting session for prime time," writer Jim Downey once said. It popularized what *Newsweek* would call "college humor"—a "behavioral humor of outrage," as movie director John Landis once described it—a style that culminated in the movie classic, *Animal House.* And, the show did, as Greenfield and others have noted, add a bunch of catch phrases to the pop-culture lexicon: "But no-o-o-o!" and "You look mahvelous!" and "Yeah. That's the ticket" and "Well, isn't that special?"

Yet a lot of its supposed antiestablishment humor was actually directed at the 1960s, which often made the show oddly conservative. "The '60s were being demythologized," creator Lorne Michaels once said. "Comedy became part of that process." "The counterculture wasn't a superior culture," *SNL* comedian John Belushi once said. "We were for drugs and ended up getting bashed or OD'd. . . . We were for peace and ended up in violent street activities."

As a writer for the show once observed, Michaels "wasn't in the business of producing shows but in the business of making stars." Thus, what *Saturday Night Live* did for pop culture, more than anything else, was launch movie careers for its patented names—beginning with Chevy Chase (who lasted only a season on *SNL*) and continuing through John Belushi, Dan Aykroyd, Billy Crystal, Eddie Murphy, Dana Carvey, Mike Myers, and the remainder of a list that includes over 50 cast members. Yet except for Phil Hartman, Dennis Miller, and two women never considered funny enough to be stars on the show (Jane Curtin and Julia Louis-Dreyfuss, who went on to star, respectively, on *Kate & Allie* and *Seinfeld*), *Saturday Night Live* launched few successful television careers: Its headliners went for the big screen, where, with a few notable exceptions like *Wayne's World* and the wondrous works of Bill Murray, they made utterly undistinguished and forgettable films.

Moreover, in contrast to most other TV shows, *Saturday Night Live* seemed designed to propel only its male writers and stars to greater cultural prominence: Except for Gilda Radner, one of *SNL's* original performers, this was a boys' club, and the whole style of the show reflected it—from the farting jokes and the guys dressing up as girls, to the teams of male performers the show made famous like the Blues Brothers, Wayne's World, and the Wild and Crazy Guys. Belushi once locked himself in a dressing room because a piece in which he was supposed to appear had been *written* by a woman.

It's true that *Saturday Night Live* was probably the closest that network television ever came to building on the spirit of the sixties' youth culture, if only because, in retrospect, it helped to be stoned to enjoy it. Designed as yet another of the medium's efforts to tap the elusive youth market in the 1970s, *Saturday Night Live* was different—and more successful—because NBC gave the show unusual independence from the network's normal practices and procedures. The network mistakenly viewed the production as just a forum from which performers and ideas could be spun off: The show was slotted for 11:30 P.M. on Saturday, an hour when NBC usually ran Johnny Carson reruns.

As conceived by Michaels, a former junior writer at *Laugh-In, Saturday Night Live* would be a bold, baby-boom reaction to staid, traditional television: John Belushi arrived for his audition yelling "TV sucks!"—and at the show's first meeting of cast and writers, Michaels made it clear that the current variety-show style then on TV, perhaps best exemplified by Carol Burnett (another woman), encompassed everything that this show hoped to avoid. "I wanted to get away from that," Michaels once said, "by coming to New York instead of L.A., by going on live, by taking chances, and by keeping it as much like theatre as possible. The feeling of outlaw here is strong—and I think that's what the audiences respond to." Though billed as a variety show with weekly musical guests, Michaels hoped to place particular emphasis on his regular troupe of young, improvisational comedians modeled on the actors in the successful British comedy show *Monty Python's Flying Circus,* yet another all-male bastion on television.

The first show, which ran on October 11, 1975, had George Carlin as host, with musical guests Janis Ian and Billy Preston. "Live from New York—it's Saturday Night!" was announced at the beginning of the show, as it would be for all the rest to come. Critical reaction was mixed: *The Washington Post* described the show as a "live, lovely, raucously disdainful view of a world that television largely shaped," while the *New York Times* complained that "quality [was] an ingredient conspicuously absent from the dreadfully uneven comedy efforts of the new series." Within weeks, however, the "Not Ready for Prime Time Players" had assumed the central role, and the show had developed its trademarks—even amid the chaotic unevenness that would always characterize this series and give it both its energy and its absence of professionalism.

"Any good humor is sophomoric," writer Michael O'Donoghue once opined. "Sophomoric is the liberal word for funny." And *SNL* was sophomoric in spades. There were Chevy Chase's overdone pratfalls in imitation of Gerald Ford, and absurdly perverted weekend news updates. Belushi had his Samurai Warrior, Aykroyd his Jimmy Carter imitation, and Radner her elderly Emily Litella. (Emily's hook was always that she'd misunderstood the words of a TV news story— she wondered, for instance, why there was so much fuss over Soviet "jewelry"—and would inevitably feel she had to apologize, by saying "Never mind.") In the beginning there were also Jim Henson and the Muppets, who soon disappeared—as did a regular film segment with

Albert Brooks, described charitably by one critic as "ten minutes of boredom."

Over time, there were the Coneheads, the Blues Brothers, the Killer Bees (who appeared on eight of the first 10 shows), and the Wild and Crazy Guys. And, there were always the musical groups, as well as the takeoffs on well-known commercials and such pop-culture phenomena as *Jaws, Star Trek,* and Tom Snyder. "It is an attempt, finally, to provide entertainment on television," wrote the *New Yorker's* Michael Arlen, "that tries to deal with the morass of media-induced show-business culture that increasingly pervades American life."

The program continued to retain its odd anti-1960s gloss. "Suddenly things I once felt so strongly about, I didn't feel strongly about at all," Michaels once said. "It was hard for me to believe I actually once grew my hair long to stop the war. We had to learn to laugh at ourselves—at our follies." The first show thus featured a mock ad with Jerry Rubin selling graffiti wallpaper, a noted contrast to, say, the attitude of the Smothers Brothers only seven years before. Like *Laugh-In, SNL* was always careful to be a bipartisan satirist.

Yet the key thing to the network was that the show was a hit in its time slot, particularly among younger viewers. Seventy-five percent of those who watched were between the ages of 18 and 49, the highest percentage in TV ratings, and one estimate had up to 25 million viewers eventually watching when groups like the Rolling Stones appeared. "Getting together with friends to watch it became a social ceremony in itself," cultural analyst Susan Orlean once wrote. Since "youth" was a demographic group whom television had traditionally had trouble reaching, NBC late-night programming vice-president Dick Ebersol described the program as "the most attractive show to advertisers in 25 years." It was also important that this was *Saturday* Night Live, not Monday or Wednesday. The ritual of turning on the show after an evening of partying with friends added immensely to its allure.

According to Frank Serpas, an aficionado who has written about the show on the World Wide Web, *Saturday Night Live* has gone through several cycles. In the first (1975-79), the original cast of Aykroyd, Belushi, Chase, Curtin, Radner, Laraine Newman, and Garrett Morris—with Murray joining soon thereafter—created the essential concept of the program. In fact, the show's ratings peaked in the third year, and never approached that height again. During 1980–83, the show (with an entirely new cast) went through a fallow period, though Eddie Murphy and Joe Piscopo did provide some stellar moments. In 1984, Billy Crystal and Martin Short joined *SNL;* and when Michaels returned to produce the show from 1985 through 1989, it enjoyed yet another strong period, with Jon Lovitz and Dennis Miller as stars, further joined by Carvey in 1986 and Myers in 1989. Yet, in the nineties, the show gradually seemed to lose steam, and even a virtual housecleaning failed to reverse the tide for the 1995–96 season. Through the end of 1995, Steve Martin held the record for hosting the show the most (13 times), and Kevin Nealon had stayed the longest (nine seasons). Michaels's friend Paul Simon copped the musical-guest record with nine appearances.

The show had a mix of odd and venerable moments. Charlton Heston, Desi Arnaz, and Billy Martin (sometime manager of the New York Yankees) all hosted. Sinead O'Connor generated over 5,000 calls when she on-camera tore up a picture of the Pope in 1992. The only noncelebrity to host was a certain Mikel Spillman, who won an "Anyone Can Host" contest in 1977. Among the many jokes which didn't make it past the censors were Al Franken's "If Helen Keller were alone in the forest and fell down, would she make a sound?" and a sketch, "Jesus of Nashville," featuring Dan Aykroyd on a cross while wearing a cowboy shirt.

Still, what's striking about *SNL*'s 20-plus years—even as the show oscillated widely in both quality and popularity—is how little the formulas changed after the originality of the first few years. "We're in the information age," performer Mike Myers once said. "We're also in the retro age and we're in the age of synthesis. There doesn't seem to be new stuff." Instead of Bill Murray's lounge singer, there was Adam Sandler's inane warbling. Instead of the patented Ford and Carter imitations, there was one of George Bush by Dana Carvey—and the Church Lady, played also by Carvey, became the new Litella. The opening monologue remained, as did Weekend Update. And always there were the guys dressing up as girls (a trend Milton Berle had first popularized on TV decades earlier)—Carvey as the Church Lady,

Mike Myers as the coffee-klatsch woman, Martin Short as Martina Navratilova, and Joe Piscopo as Barbra Streisand.

It's certainly true that, even after its initial creative rush, the show had many moments of innovative brilliance, particularly in the hands of Murray, Murphy, and Carvey. By and large, however, the show survived by taking a few stock characters and routines—Master Thespian, Stuart Smalley, dweeb Ed Grimley, Rob Schneider by the Xerox machine—and redoing them again and again, as the audience roared its approval. Did it make for some entertaining television? Sure. But bottom line, wasn't formula comedy precisely the kind of thing that *Saturday Night Live* was supposed to be rebelling against in the first place?

This was not the worst show in the history of television by a long shot. However, it may well have been the most self-congratulatory and self-absorbed—yet another example of baby boomers believing they had invented the wheel just because they had a show that reflected their sensibilities. This egotistical generational trait would be a characteristic of boomer culture long after *Saturday Night Live* was influencing anybody. "In their behavior and comedy," Frank Rich once wrote of the show, "one sees not so much the keeping of the Woodstock flame as the dawning of the age of narcissism."

The fact is that, at 11:30 P.M. on Saturday, not that many people watched it, in comparison to the number who watched TV in prime time. It didn't do that much that other shows hadn't tried before, or that other shows didn't do better later on (or even in the same era, as fans of *SCTV* knew). For a show that lasted over 20 years, not many people attempted to copy it. Lorne Michaels didn't become another Pat Weaver or Norman Lear, and few of its stars went on to do better work. These seeming negatives add up in a very real way to a tribute to the fact that, like the rock-music genre it emulated, the *SNL* team produced a show that was occasionally even more than the sum of its parts—a display of the sixties' communal sensibility it supposedly mocked.

Yet the celebrated "politics" of *Saturday Night Live* soon ended up tamer than Johnny Carson's, and its innovations less notable than those seen on just the kind of shows it purported to mock. Sarcastic to a fault, *Saturday Night Live* also made everything into a joke, which ultimately meant that the show itself could never really be taken seriously as a cultural force. In the end, the nihilistic sensibility of *SNL* devoured everything, from its stars to its influence. Sure, they still scream "Live from New York—it's Saturday Night!" every week. But even if this show was a terrifically big deal once, it isn't anymore—and hasn't been for a long, long time.

40

The Miniseries as History: Did *Roots* Change America?
(ABC: 1977)

If ratings guaranteed lasting impact, *Roots* would have changed our racial relations forever. For eight consecutive nights over 12 hours, beginning on January 23, 1977, the audiences for Alex Haley's narrative about his African ancestors and their struggles in slavery over four generations steadily grew. This was much to the surprise of ABC, which was so nervous about how the series would do that it scheduled *Roots* to run two weeks before the ratings "sweeps" period began, and sold ads at bargain rates. After all, even *Time* had previewed the series by dismissing it as a "middle-of-the-road *Mandingo*." By the time *Roots* had ended, however, all eight telecasts ranked among the 13 highest-rated individual programs of all time, and the final segment was the highest-rated regular show until that moment—only to be surpassed in later years by the final episode of *M*A*S*H* and the "Who Shot J.R.?" episode of *Dallas*. When it was all over, it was estimated that over half the country had watched some portion of *Roots,* with seven of every ten TV sets tuned to the series at some point.

In the aftermath, the success of *Roots* was hailed by many as the dawn of a new era in race relations in America. *Roots,* however, changed the medium more than it changed us. Twenty years later, it's hard to pinpoint *Roots* as any kind of turning point in the nation's troubled racial history, as the show's sensitive treatment of racial issues from a black perspective ended up as the exception on television. Instead, the show's principal cultural contribution was to encourage television executives to embrace the whole concept of the mini-series—with the result that programming changed dramatically at the networks. The real progeny of *Roots* were not *The Cosby Show* or *Eyes on the Prize* but miniseries like *The Thorn Birds* and even those now weekly "topical" television movies on subjects like Amy Fisher (the "Long Island Lolita") or David Koresh of Waco fame.

Roots was not the first made-for-TV movie. The genre dated back to 1964; *Brian's Song*—the highly acclaimed movie about the friendship between black football star Gale Sayers and a dying white teammate, Brian Piccolo—had become the talk of the 1971 season. What tended to make TV movies different from their counterparts on the big screen was that TV concentrated on "the more intense personal drama," producer Quinn Martin once said, "while the theatrical film is big, external entertainment." Over the years, his analysis would be proven correct as made-for-TV movies eschewed comedy to give the nation some of its most memorable portraits of such issues as spousal abuse *(The Burning Bed),* the domestic impact of the war in Vietnam *(Friendly Fire),* and incest *(Something About Amelia).*

Roots was also not the first television miniseries. The Brits had been doing such productions for years—and so therefore had PBS's *Masterpiece Theatre. Rich Man, Poor Man,* a 12-hour weekly adaptation of the Irwin Shaw novel, ran on ABC a year before *Roots,* to terrific ratings. Prior to *Roots,* however, no one had ever come up with the idea of running such shows back-to-back over several consecutive nights.

The planning for *Roots* actually began years before it appeared, when actors Ossie Davis and Ruby Dee told producer David Wolper of a book which a friend of theirs was writing about his black ancestors. For a reported $250,000, Wolper bought the necessary permissions from Alex Haley—who still had a way to go to finish the manuscript and was selling the rights in order to raise money to do so. Wolper went to ABC with the idea, after convincing Haley that a two-hour theatrical film would cut too much of his plot. And the initial reaction? "Here's 12 hours of a story where the whites are the villains and the blacks are the heroes in a country that is 85 percent white," ABC's Fred Silverman was quoted as saying later. "It doesn't sound like a good idea at first blush."

On the other hand, *Roots* producer Stan Margulies remembered asking and telling ABC at that time: "What have you got to lose? You're Number 3. If *Roots* fails, you'll still be Number 3." Moreover, the dramatic story of the descendants of Kunta Kinte, the African hunter sold into slavery, sold itself—particularly as the plot expanded to include such grim and graphic scenes as the raping and beating of slaves, the selling-off of children to new owners, and the hacking of Kinte's foot at the ankle by his owner. With a $6 million budget and a star-studded cast that included LeVar Burton, Cicely Tyson, Ed Asner, Leslie Uggams, and—yes—O. J. Simpson (and with the publicity that Haley's now-published book had garnered), ABC thought it just might have a hit on its hands. The whole thing was still too new and different for the network to be fully confident, however—particularly since the series had eight different writers and directors.

That's when Silverman made his unprecedented decision to schedule the show over eight consecutive nights, much in the same fashion as ABC had presented the recent Summer Olympics. Though Silverman could hardly have realized it at the time, this programming decision allowed the show to dominate the nation's consciousness and conversation in a way which might have eluded it otherwise. " 'Roots' Remakes TV World in Eight Nights!" went the subsequent headline in *Variety*.

Once the show had received its unprecedented reaction, analysts—not to mention TV executives—spent the next several months trying to figure out why *Roots* had touched such a popular nerve. The cynical concluded that a record-breaking January cold-weather snap had kept audiences indoors, whereas others theorized that what with its eight-part drama and focus on family life, *Roots* was a compressed, glamorized, black version of the soap operas that had done so well on radio and TV before. After all, *Triumph of an American Family* was the show's subtitle, and *Newsweek*'s Harry Waters had previewed the series by saying "At times, the series comes perilously close to melodrama, a sort of 'Rich White, Poor Slave.' " "There was the threat of violence, the appeal of sex, all building up to a wonderful climax—all the things that make for good television," noted one historian.

Others would later point out that the show premiered during the week in which Jimmy Carter was inaugurated. This was the man, after all, whose election had seemed to promise a reunion of South with North, black with white, and who had convinced Dr. Martin Luther King Sr. to join him at the podium after his convention acceptance speech to sing "We Shall Overcome."

At the time, many analysts hailed *Roots* as just such a moment of national reconciliation. William Greider of the *Washington Post* called the series "a stunning passage in the mass culture of America." "[I]t allows white Americans," he wrote, "to watch that terrible racial history and instead of consuming guilt, they are encouraged to say to themselves—hey—that's my story too." Others, notably some black critics, were more wary, and in retrospect more accurate. Clyde Taylor, writing in *The Black Scholar* later that year, titled his piece on the series "A Modern Minstrel Show," while Chuck Stone, writing in the same journal, concluded that *Roots* was "an electronic orgy in white guilt." Analysts, both then and later, would also point out that the series came during a wave of cultural interest in history and genealogy. The U.S. Bicentennial celebration had occurred only six months before; novels such as John Jakes's *Kent Family Chronicles* were enormously popular then; and even TV commercials of the mid-seventies often referenced the nation's preoccupation with the search for family roots and oral history.

At that time, it looked like the success of *Roots* would trigger a wave of television programming by and about blacks, if not other groups as well. *Holocaust,* a *Roots*-like retelling of the genocidal slaughter of Jews during World War II, drew strong ratings and plaudits a year later. Yet a three-part NBC miniseries about Martin Luther King Jr. in that same season turned into a ratings disaster, and even though the 1979 sequel *Roots: The Next Generations* (which took the story from the Civil War to the present day) did well in the ratings, the networks concluded that there wasn't much of a future in this type of programming. "It's a white country," a TV executive once told cultural analyst Todd Gitlin, "and a commercial business."

Television did go on, however, to embrace the concept of the night-to-night miniseries that Silverman had developed. "Part of *Roots'* brilliance was in the programming," said an admiring CBS executive at the time. "ABC caused an explosion by compressing the presentation." Over the next two decades, those miniseries that had gone from concept to realized project—*Lonesome Dove, The Thorn Birds, War and Remembrance,* and even *North and South*—provided television with some of its more memorable programming. Like *Roots* but unlike much of regular television, these miniseries were able to attract some of the best actors and actresses in the business, tell a continuing story in more than two hours, and begin to approach the epic scale that had previously characterized only the movies.

David Wolper—who produced not only *Roots* but *North and South* and *The Thorn Birds*—would later conclude that, for a miniseries to be successful, it either had to condense a well-known novel, have "sociological significance," or be a family saga. (Preferably all three.) Wolper had begun his own career in documentaries, and so retained a strong interest in history. It's thus no coincidence that many of these miniseries, like *Roots*, had sweeping historical themes—becoming, in a sense, TV's bastardized versions of the historical plays that Shakespeare had written centuries before.

Television, however, didn't only do historical docudramas after *Roots*. It also accelerated its production of what one writer would call "headline docudramas"—shorter, two-hour movies produced with a quick turnaround time which theatrical releases couldn't match. These were occasionally based on such news events as the mass cult suicides at Jonestown and the Israeli raid on the Entebbe airport, though more often on lurid crimes—like the Charles Stuart murder case in Boston, and the Amy Fisher case (which inspired docudramas on all three major networks).

None of these minimovies, however, could ever replicate the national experience of *Roots*—if only because the rise of cable programming a few years later guaranteed an atomization of the audience which prevented so many viewers from sharing the same experience. Yet there was a paradox in that wide viewership. By creating an accessible and emotional tale of slavery, *Roots* had allowed many white viewers to feel the injustice of racism viscerally. By making this powerful story into a television "show," however, with simple characters, an optimistic ending, and commercials scattered throughout, the series inevitably trivialized slavery—much as television itself trivializes almost anything serious or tragic that's assigned to it.

"If you ever see a real fistfight in a restaurant, it's shattering," Larry

Gelbart, the coproducer of *M*A*S*H,* once told an interviewer. "You shake for half an hour—it's so violent, so ugly." Yet television violence is stylized violence, and the horror it presents is packaged in such a way that viewers almost always shut off their TV sets feeling better about things. And so it went here: There was an implicit, self-congratulatory message in *Roots.* Our racial problems may have been horrible then, it seemed to imply—but since we're not that bad today, look at the progress we've made!

Yet even though the nation's politics changed not at all as a result of the show, it was still a singular achievement for American television—and indeed the nation—to give *Roots* the commitment it did. "From now on, I will see black through different eyes," said one white viewer at the time, in a typical comment. It says something about the medium and the country which produced *Roots* that, 20 years later, it's hard to imagine that anything like it could ever happen here again.

41

All My Children, Soaps, and
the Feminization of America
(ABC: 1970–Present)

Recently, critics have taken to describing shows like *Law and Order* and *ER* as part of a second Golden Age of Television, the current incarnation of the writing of Charles Dickens and the American realism of Theodore Dreiser. Yet it says more about the pretensions of TV writers and critics that only rarely does anyone mention that the major influence for these new prime-time dramas is not really Dickens, but a woman named Irna Phillips.

More than anyone else, Phillips created the daytime soap opera—one of radio and television's oldest and most enduring genres, and usually its most ridiculed. Confined primarily to the afternoons (when most critics and intellectuals don't watch television), and with creators and a following still composed primarily of women, soap operas have rarely received the plaudits they deserve. Yet these shows have been enormously successful and influential—not only by creating a form which now dominates prime-time drama, but by developing narrative themes which permeate all TV genres. Even today, when programmers want to attract a large audience of women, as they did for the 1996 Summer Olympics and the political conventions later that summer, they still turn to the the soap opera for guidance. Thus, its precepts have become an important means of structuring experience culture-wide, which is why our national life so often appears to be one big soap opera.

In terms of TV history, these were among the first dramatic shows to deal consistently with controversial topics such as sex and abortion that puritanical prime time usually avoided. Moreover, no other TV genre has generated such a consistent following as the soap opera. Whereas most TV shows tend to last a few seasons at best, *The Guiding Light* has chugged along, first on radio and then on TV, for over half a century. Of the 10 current network soaps, seven are at least 25 years old. Soaps still account for around 50 hours of daytime programming a week, appealing to roughly the same audience they always have: women—particularly in nonmetropolitan areas, and especially in the South.

The popular *All My Children* (*AMC*) is not the longest-running soap opera made specifically for television: That honor goes to *As the World Turns,* which premiered on CBS on April 2, 1956, almost 14 years before this show. Nor has *All My Children* been the most popular. While it was TV's top-rated soap opera in 1978–79, and the first such show not on CBS to achieve that rating, the titular honor of most popular in modern times goes—it's a tossup—either to CBS's *The Young and the Restless* or to *General Hospital* (whose wedding of Luke and Laura in November 1981 attracted the largest TV audience ever for a daytime drama). *AMC,* however, is clearly among the best soap operas, with more Emmy nominations than any other such program in TV history. Its 15-to-20-million fans are among the most devoted, and the show still ranks as the Number 1 soap among 18-to-49-year-olds. What's more, as the principal success of creator

Agnes Nixon, a student of Phillips and the mother of the contemporary "hip" soap opera, *All My Children* provides a means for examining why soap operas evolved the way they did, and how they've changed both television and the culture at large.

The histories of broadcasting and soap opera are intertwined. Daytime soaps—so-called because they usually were sponsored in the early days by such firms as Procter & Gamble, who used them to sell soap and detergents to housewives—made their debut on Chicago radio in the first years of the Great Depression. In 1930, Irna Phillips developed a daytime serial called *Painted Dreams* (she also starred in it), whose claim to fame was that it offered listeners "true to life" family situations worked out under a penumbra of romantic fantasy. "[R]elationships don't have to be sordid to be interesting," Phillips told *Broadcasting* magazine in the early 1970s, and it was this emphasis on relationships, often within families, which provided the backbone of this type of entertainment.

Throughout the thirties and forties, the genre grew on radio, affording such titles as *The Romance of Helen Trent* and *Young Dr. Malone.* Because of the audience's close involvement with the characters, and the prodigious fan mail, the soap—then only 15 minutes long—became a forerunner of interactive culture. Yet it didn't transfer instantly to television, because it was far more expensive and elaborate to stage a soap on TV than on radio. Moreover, as related by TV historian J. Fred MacDonald, NBC programming executive Pat Weaver, the innovative creator of the *Today* and *Tonight* shows, didn't want soap operas on his network, preferring instead to develop original and magazine-type drama shows specifically geared to television.

It is a tribute to Weaver's continuing influence that even when he made a mistake it lasted: NBC has never had a Number 1 rated soap yet. Thus, with ABC still a weak third among the networks, it fell to CBS to begin importing soaps from radio to the afternoon schedule, as it did with Phillips' *The Guiding Light,* the first radio soap to cross over successfully. In the spring of 1956, the TV soap went to a half-hour with two Phillips creations—*The Edge of Night* and *As the World Turns.*

On television, producers used the camera to close in on the faces (and as it were the emotions) of characters. More important, by changing the pace of the story as they went to a half-hour (and eventually an hour), they effectively changed the whole genre. Presented five times a week, soaps have always been able to approximate real time more closely than other narrative forms in the culture, and for some time now even celebrations of holidays on the shows have been able to occur on the holidays themselves. What's more, given five hours of programming time per week, writers can regularly deal with more issues in greater depth than can the average TV show.

With their grounding in relationships and time realism, soap operas are thus far less dependent on the constant action that traditionally drives prime-time TV drama. The purpose of a soap opera, critic Dennis Porter once noted, "is to never end, and its beginnings are always lost sight of." "Make them laugh, make them cry, make them wait," was the way Agnes Nixon once summed up her philosophy.

In fact, plot is so unimportant in the grand soap-opera scheme of things that it is often dealt with superficially and melodramatically. Any fan knows the litany of soap conventions: Women who want to get pregnant never can, but those who don't want to usually end up with a child, even after a presumably safe one-night dalliance. Amnesia is almost as frequent as the common cold. No one accused of murder is ever the guilty party. The parents of characters often are not the "real" parents.

Other odd conventions of soap plotting grow out of its narrative and casting requirements. People get killed in accidents, only to have long-lost twins somehow mysteriously show up months later, when the actor or actress playing the characters returns to the soap from another engagement. Children rarely appear on air between the time they're born and the time they're teenagers and old enough to have a romance. Characters seldom talk on the telephone (that makes for bad television), preferring instead to drop in on people, even if they have to drive a long distance. What's more, to keep attractive young people in town and on the set, many dignified soap-opera towns boast a major university, like Pine Valley University.

As part of this narrative structure, soaps also don't make as much use of the visuals so important to other forms of television programming. The scenes are almost always set indoors, in a rather simple room which resembles the stage set that indeed it is. To the extent that we know Pine Valley, Port Charles, and Oakdale, we know them primarily from the inside—which, of course, is where most of the people who watch soaps have to spend their days, too.

What soaps offer as a substitute for the action and exciting settings of most other TV genres is a lot of talk, plus a focus on character and feelings. Again, soaps may be making a virtue of necessity, but the popular settings in these dramas tend to be places where people can converse—such as at work stations in hospitals, or (most notably today) in bedrooms. In a study of conversation on soap operas, scholar Marlene Fine found that soap-opera characters talk to one another more than people do in real life. That's a startling shift from the norm on most TV dramas (or at least it was until the voluble nineties) and from traditional pop-culture heroes like strong, silent cowboys or private detectives.

One doesn't have to be a disciple of scholars Carol Gilligan or Deborah Tannen to recognize the ways in which soap operas—like romance novels—thus structure experience from a feminine, rather than the usually predominant masculine, point of view. The matter was put cogently (if somewhat academically) by Martha Nochimson in her book, *No End to Her: Soap Opera and the Female Subject*:

> As the Hollywood film tends toward a masculine narrative because its syntax is dictated by the aesthetics of closure, soap opera tends toward a feminine story because its syntax is dictated by the resistance to closure. . . . Truth in the Hollywood film is the truth of linearity, the truth of mastery and control. . . . In soap opera, truth is the multiple-perspective reality of the unclosed line, of mutuality and intimacy. . . . Beauty in soap opera is the beauty of dialogue, mutuality, and connection.

From this modus flows most of the "values" that critics and creators have found inherent in the soaps. Community is so important that when Agnes Nixon created *All My Children,* she wanted the town of Pine Valley, modeled on a suburb of Philadelphia, to be "almost as important in our story as the characters themselves." In other words, it takes a village. Walter Karp once found the soaps' obsession with interior lives and domestic grief uplifting because they stressed the preeminence of matters of the heart over the culture's usual fascination with money or evil. Characters on soaps "must suffer the consequences," Agnes Nixon once said. "Audiences are bound, not by the chains of hero worship, but by the easily recognized bonds of human frailty and human valor."

Yet *All My Children* took these notions and stretched them further. It premiered at a time when soaps were slumping because they were too old-fashioned, both in their support of "traditional values" and in their frequent emphasis on staid, older characters. With "realism" in vogue on prime time in 1970—as new shows like *All in the Family* and *The Mary Tyler Moore Show* redefined the sitcom—Agnes Nixon tried to do something similar here when her show debuted on January 5, 1970, in black and white—going to color in 1971. For example, she focused on younger lovers, lavish sets, and glamorous clothes—attributes which prime-time soaps like *Dallas* and *Dynasty* would borrow a decade later. Over the years, Nixon's show would feature a number of prominent guest stars, including Elizabeth Taylor, Stevie Wonder, and Carol Burnett. (Before she was famous, Julia Roberts once auditioned for a full-time role.) In due time, *All My Children* would also deal with major social and personal issues—war protests, infertility, interracial romance, date rape, homosexuality, and even Vietnam MIA's. With her previous soap opera, *One Life to Live,* Nixon had vowed "to take soap operas out of WASP Valley," and she certainly succeeded here.

Like other soap operas, *All My Children* has had more than its share of weird moments and plot twists over its more than 25 years. This is, after all, a program which has had at least two major books devoted to its history, and has every episode divided, in the writers' minds, into six acts totaling over 80 pages. To take but one example: In the course of one season-and-a-half in 1991–92, Natalie was forced to spend weeks at the bottom of a well, thanks to the actions of her deranged, long-lost look-alike sister who stole her fiancé, married him, and then had his baby. Natalie then became engaged to the man who rescued her, only to find that he was secretly married to a woman in a coma. Upon returning to her original fiancé, Natalie was blinded by a house fire, only to regain her sight miraculously on Christmas Eve as carolers sang "Hark! The Herald Angels Sing."

Yet what has made *All My Children* tick over time is what always makes the best soap operas notable—good writing, and memorable characters, in this case built around two core families, the Tylers and the Martins. Mary Fickett, who played Ruth Martin, once said:

> There has to be some core around which other people disinte-grate and come together again. If the place were in chaos all the time, you wouldn't have some place to bounce off of. They've had problems—Ruth was raped and she had an affair—but view-ers want to believe there is a core.

The show has featured the usual love triangles (Travis, Erica, and Jackson; and Tad, Hillary, and Dottie), and at least a dozen prominent weddings, from Joe and Ruth in 1972 to Cliff and Nina—married to each other four times over a decade while being divorced in between. *All My Children* has also specialized in the usual male troublemakers, like Ray Gardner, Langley Wallingford, Billy Clyde Tuggle, and Dr. Damon Lazarre, leader of a religious cult. In 1996, four characters still remained from the original show: Dr. Joe Martin, Ruth Martin, Phoebe Tyler, and Erica Kane—played by Susan Lucci ever since the character was a 14-year-old high-school student. As of 1996, Erica has been married to eight men, including Tom Cudahy, Adam Chandler, Travis Montgomery, and Dimitri Marick. "He is just a man, and I am Erica Kane. Need I say more?" she once huffed. Through the years, Erica would survive a kidnapping, a plane crash, an abortion, drug ad-diction, and a confrontation with a grizzly bear.

Over time, the serial presentation of soaps and their focus on a mul-titude of characters alike became the model for almost all successful prime-time drama—from *Dallas* and *Masterpiece Theatre* in the 1970s through *Hill Street Blues* and *L.A. Law* in the 1980s and on to *Picket Fences* and *ER* in the 1990s. That adaptation enabled prime-time drama to do things it hadn't done before: show the evolution of char-acters, depict their vulnerabilities, and capture them in less extraordi-nary situations. Contrast *Perry Mason* with Arnie Becker, or Marcus Welby with Doug Ross, and you get a perspective on the seeds that the soaps planted in prime time. While situation comedies have always joined soap operas in their focus on families, even they have seen their content swayed over time by the soaps' pioneering focus on dysfunction within those families. Where *All My Children* would tread, *The Simpsons* one day would follow.

Certainly the rise of talk television shows like *Sally Jessy Raphael* owes a lot to the soaps, because these talk shows deal with many of the same steamy topics that used to be the sole province of daytime drama. The irony, of course, is that because talk shows cost far less to produce, and take less time to build an audience, soaps have gradually begun to lose their place in the culture to this new form of programming. By 1990, ABC executives had begun to complain that the gross revenues for soaps were now less than what their profits used to be, and by the mid-nineties there were twice as many daytime talk shows as soaps.

The women's movement has also had an impact: With women increasingly working outside the home, there are now half the number of soaps there were 25 years ago when *All My Children* debuted, and the networks have launched only one successful soap—*The Bold and the Beautiful*—in the last 10 years. As women have increasingly become integrated into society—and society has become "feminized" as a result—it's been no surprise that soap operas have gradually lost some of their traditional audience, even while prime-time programming has become more like the soaps. And there may be a real loss in this. There is something appealing—even comforting—in the leisurely pace of the soaps: Relationships develop over months, not minutes; and nuances can be played out in a way uncommon in an MTV age. Further, plots which can devote six weeks instead of 60 seconds to subjects like infertility or substance abuse serve a dual educational and support function for viewers.

Yet the cultural ramifications are even more striking. The genre that gave women their first real voice in broadcasting is now pervasive, and its sentiment of sentimentality has become universal. Discussions of public policy now had to revolve around individual anecdotes of successful "welfare moms" and testaments of crime victims. Network coverage of the Olympics focuses on "up close and personal" portraits of the athletes and their struggles against hardship, virtually to the exclusion of the events themselves. Events like plane crashes and hurricanes dominate the news, allowing the networks to give us, without casting or other costs, never-ending melodrama featuring a cavalcade of real victims. Even our political rhetoric is now bathed in personal disclosure and bathos. We live in Soap Nation: We are the children of *All My Children*.

42

The Oddly Winning Dark Sensibility of *M*A*S*H*
(CBS: 1972–83)

On the night of February 28, 1983, America virtually stopped for two-and-a-half hours. In San Francisco 82 percent of the television viewing audience was watching CBS, and in New York and Chicago the figure was 72 percent. All in all, 125 million viewers nationally tuned in to the swan song of *M*A*S*H*—the largest audience for a regular show in TV history. The subject matter of that final episode tells you something about this show's dissimilarities from other programming: The lead character on this "comedy," an army doctor, spends the first half of the series in a psychiatric ward after suffering a breakdown from seeing a Korean woman kill her baby so that its cries wouldn't attract enemy soldiers. Commercials went for almost a million dollars a minute (unheard of then), and the New York City Department of Environmental Protection soon reported that three minutes after the show was over, the city's water flow had increased by 300 million gallons as thousands finally went to the bathroom after sitting transfixed in front of their TV sets.

The episode that marked the end of *M*A*S*H* (official title: "Goodbye, Farewell, and Amen") concluded one of the stranger phenomenons in television history. When this show premiered in 1972, it was billed in one magazine as "Young doctors in an Army mobile hospital in Korea alternate saving lives with hours of some notable high jinks." Yet it was much more than that—and full of contradictions. This was a comedy that wasn't funny; a male army show that appealed to women; and a secular show that was often preachier than anything even Pat Robertson could envision. Despite its record-setting finale and a critically acclaimed run of 11 years, 14 Emmys, and 251 episodes, this was a series that never hit either Number 1 or Number 2 for a season, and wasn't really popular at all in its first years on the air.

Moreover, on a medium where any sniff of success brings replication, this was a show whose themes and innovations were never copied successfully by anyone else: Television never had a popular wartime show again. The stars of M*A*S*H—most notably Alan Alda and Mike Farrell—never had another TV hit. Even the show's lengthy and lusty attempt to create a new television genre—a synthesis of comedy and drama later called "dramedy"—failed utterly. Bottom line: M*A*S*H may well go down in history as TV's greatest one-night stand. Yet, in retrospect, it's somewhat difficult to understand why, on a medium wedded to the upbeat, the wrapup of this exercise in downbeat comedy touched such a nerve on that February evening.

Certainly no one had such extravagant expectations for the show when it premiered in the fall of 1972, as George McGovern's presidential campaign, built on similar antiwar sentiments, crumbled beneath the landslide for Richard Nixon. M*A*S*H was envisioned as a thinly disguised antiwar allegory on the then-still-raging Vietnam War. It was based on a popular Robert Altman movie of the same name about the Korean War, starring Donald Sutherland and Elliott Gould, which had been a modest success several years earlier.

Series creators Larry Gelbart and Gene Reynolds, however, took what had essentially been a high-energy, somewhat slapstick movie and turned it into a larger, albeit darker, ensemble series. "We all felt very keenly that inasmuch as an actual war was going on," Gelbart later told a reporter, "we owed it to the sensibilities and the sensitivities of an audience to take cognizance of the fact that Americans were really being killed every week."

That acknowledgment was apparent from the opening credits on that first Sunday night in September 1972, when the theme tune, "Suicide Is Painless," played as army helicopters brought in the wounded to the M*A*S*H (Mobile Army Surgical Hospital) unit. From the beginning, the show had a political point of view, which it wore on its sleeve. "I don't know why they're shooting at us," Hawkeye once said, in one of the show's more notable soliloquies:

All we want to do is bring them democracy and white bread, to transplant the American dream: freedom, achievement, hyper-acidity, affluence, flatulence, technology, tension, the inalienable right to a coronary at your desk while plotting to stab your boss in the back.

M*A*S*H thinly disguised its anti-Vietnam War message in the ear-lier Korean conflict—America's "forgotten war," at least until this show. That had the odd effect of making the Korean conflict seem as pointless and ignoble as the one in Vietnam—which, of course, was unfair.

Shot like a theatrical film with no audience (not at all like the then-popular *All in the Family*), the show's principal character was Hawk-eye—a multifaceted, Captain-level doctor played by Alan Alda, a little-known actor at the time. He was surrounded by a supporting cast which originally included the womanizing Capt. Trapper John (another complex physician), chaplain Father Mulcahy, Lt. Col. Henry Blake (Hawkeye's laid-back superior), Cpl. Radar O'Reilly (the fre-netic company clerk), and Margaret "Hot Lips" Houlihan (the base head of nursing and originally a Captain), who not so secretly was having a fling with Maj. Frank Burns, the authoritarian officer. Then there was Cpl. Maxwell Klinger, the drag queen who kept trying to get out of the army on a Section-8 "psycho" discharge.

Episodes during that first year focused at times on such wartime goings-on as how Trapper entered a boxing tournament in order to keep a nurse from being transferred, and how Hawkeye and Trapper created an imaginary officer so they could donate his salary to an or-phanage. Still using a traditional sitcom laugh track—except for scenes in the operating room, which CBS hadn't wanted to feature at all— *M*A*S*H* tried to become something of a synthesis of the best of *Hogan's Heroes* (with its take on military hijinks and red tape), *Combat* (with its portrayal of war), *Marcus Welby, M.D.* (with its focus on doc-tors), and *The Mary Tyler Moore Show* (with its deeper character devel-opment). In theory, such a formula could appeal to both men, what with the war and the show's predominantly male cast, and women, given the overall preoccupation with relationships.

Somewhat predictably, the writers had difficulty pulling it all off.

The show languished in the ratings, finishing 46th after that first season. Worse, with its uneven tone, the show wasn't much of a critical success, either. It was only when *M*A*S*H* was moved for its second season in 1973 into the coveted Saturday-night slot between *All in the Family* and *The Mary Tyler Moore Show*—and the nation's mood darkened considerably in the wake of Watergate—that the show began to find both its voice and its audience. "We could have repaired flat tires in that time slot and gotten a good rating," Gelbart once admitted.

Yet *M*A*S*H* did much more than just be in the right place at the right time, as it moved beyond the typical military-comedy themes of men chasing women, and discord between officers and "the men." One analyst would later see in the *M*A*S*H* cast a "microcosm of American society itself"—the liberal, the member of the upper crust, the religious figure, the feminist woman, and the dissenter—all serving together in a collage that could reassure the anxious audience that melting-pot America still worked, even during the stress of an unpopular war. As *Newsweek* would write:

> The joke—which wasn't a joke to begin with, anyway, but a manifest irony: doctors sent to war to save lives, subversives in fatigues—has steadily gone deeper. . . . "M*A*S*H" is the most moral entertainment on commercial television. It proposes craft against butchery, humor against despair, wit as a defense mechanism against the senseless enormity of the situation.

In their constant attempts to keep the show realistic, Gelbart and Reynolds even made a field trip to Korea. "We've spoken to almost every doctor who was in Korea," Burt Metcalfe, a *M*A*S*H* producer once claimed. "At least 60 percent of the plots dealing with medical or military incidents were taken from real life." Thus, when Father Mulcahy graphically described in an episode how cutting open a patient in the operating room helps keep the doctors warm (the steam rises from the body), he was merely repeating what a Korean War doctor had once told Gelbart.

Over the years, *M*A*S*H* became known for trying what other shows would never attempt, much less do successfully. Its politics were frequently as transparent as those of the Smothers Brothers. The writers had two main characters, Hot Lips and Hawkeye, sleep together in a one-foxhole stand. One sixth-season show, titled "Our Finest Hour," was shot as a one-hour, black-and-white documentary featuring "unscripted" interviews with each of the cast's major characters. "Do you see anything good coming out of this war?" a correspondent asked Hawkeye. "Yeah, me alive," said Hawkeye. "That would be nice." Another episode, "Point of View," was shot through the eyes of a soldier brought into the hospital. And when McLean Stevenson (Lt. Col. Blake) wanted to leave the show, the writers decided to kill him off in a plane crash: What gave the scene extra power was that the writers didn't tell the cast what would happen until right before filming.

Yet all this darkness fit a post-Watergate, disillusioned nation that was on its way to experiencing gas lines, rising inflation, Three Mile Island, Jonestown, and the humiliation of the takeover of our embassy in Tehran by Iranian radicals. President Jimmy Carter would urge Americans "to have faith in our country—not only in the government, but in our own ability to solve great problems." Yet, every week, *M*A*S*H* was bittersweetly asking, in effect, "Why bother?" Looking back, one can detect a distinct sense that people expected to be depressed in the 1970s—and that *M*A*S*H* did not disappoint them.

M*A*S*H also managed to survive a changeover of half its cast during its run, in fact using the losses to the show's advantage by allowing it to add more deeply sketched figures, like surgeon B. J. Hunnicutt (played by Mike Farrell), the upper-class Maj. Charles Winchester (played by David Ogden Stiers), and Col. Sherman Potter (played by Harry Morgan) as Blake's replacement. Morgan became known, in his role at the hospital, for his paintings and also his "Potterisms"—such as "horse hockey!", "cow cookies!", and "What in the name of Great Caesar's salad?" Over time, somewhat understandably, the characters also became more like the actors playing them, particularly when Alda began writing and directing shows, and made his character as volubly empathetic and didactic as he was.

When the series was moved in 1978 to a new time slot on Mondays at 9:00 P.M. (and Gelbart had left), *M*A*S*H* became yet another successful example of counterprogramming, as it left the audience of men to ABC's *N.F.L. Monday Night Football* and concentrated on its appeal to women. That meant, of course, that *M*A*S*H* now veered even farther in the direction of antiwar sentiment and softer characterization, as Alan Alda became the poster boy for the new, less-macho ideal of masculinity, and "Hot Lips" moved from her former caricature to a sympathetic, more-rounded character now known as Margaret. In retrospect, given its complexity and changing tone, the wonder of M*A*S*H may be not that it never hit Number 1 for a season, but that the masses watched it at all.

Certainly they rarely watched the shows that tried to imitate it. After M*A*S*H left the air in 1983 (with a final scene in its last episode showing Hawkeye gazing down at the hospital from his helicopter and seeing a giant "goodbye" etched in the dust, courtesy of Hunnicutt), TV soon was full of similar shows attempting to fuse drama and comedy: *Hooperman, Frank's Place, The "Slap" Maxwell Story, The Wonder Years,* and *The Days and Nights of Molly Dodd.* These programs attempted to go beyond M*A*S*H by dispensing with laugh tracks altogether—those arrays of chuckles, grunts, and belly laughs traditionally punctuating sitcoms at the rate of one per six seconds. The track was originally used to make viewers feel part of a community. "Television is a medium whereby millions of people can listen to the same joke and still remain lonesome," T. S. Eliot had once complained, and apparently he'd been heard. The track was also "a carry-over from radio," Gelbart once recalled, "where all shows had a live audience and listeners got used to the idea of people laughing at the other end."

Radio comedy—as opposed to film comedy—had been essentially vaudeville humor, and its heavy use of exaggeration, quick entrances and exits, physical stunts (even on the radio), and rapid-fire one-liners still remains the defining characteristic of most sitcoms. By contrast, M*A*S*H—and then these other shows—tried to move TV comedy off the stage and onto film. With less reliance on jokes and physical comedy, "these shows became character comedies, as opposed to the traditional event or 'situation comedy,' " University of Texas professor Horace Newcomb once said. Shows like *Hooperman* even tried to explore issues like AIDS and teen suicide.

Yet—except for *The Wonder Years,* which had more in common with *Leave It to Beaver* than anything else running in the 1980s—these "laughterless" comedies went nowhere. "I just don't get it," NBC entertainment president Brandon Tartikoff once said, after watching *Frank's Place,* and millions agreed with him. Traditional sitcoms, after all, have been the foundation of television because they are such an ideal form for a medium whose audiences don't pay that much attention, and watch primarily at the end of the day as a form of escape from their troubles. Matt Williams, a creator of the sitcom *Home Improvement,* once had this to say about his genre:

> I used to have grand designs. The truth is, it's 22 minutes, you're constantly interrupted by commercials, the phone's going to ring, and the dog's going to pee on the carpet. . . . If you want to delve deep into the human condition, go write a novel, or a film script no one will make.

Credit *M*A*S*H* for this: Virtually alone on television, it managed to swim against the tide.

What undoubtedly helped *M*A*S*H* to pull this off was the way it exploited, if not shaped, that unique post-Watergate mood of the mid-1970s, in much the same way that once-in-a-lifetime political phenomenon Jimmy Carter did. In fact Alda, Carter, and Phil Donahue—another cultural figure who emerged during this period—shared a certain naive, pious humorlessness which made them endearing to some but utterly unpalatable to others.

Yet both friends and foes alike of Alda must have watched that record-setting last show in 1983, which benefited from nostalgia for two completely distinct periods. On the one hand, Reagan-era nostalgia for the 1950s was beginning to run rampant: The *M*A*S*H* finale's reminders of the Korean War did indeed hit a nerve. On the other hand, Americans were now so obsessed with the very recent past that they could take events which had happened only a few years earlier and start getting wistful about them. Remember, for example, that *American Graffiti,* the movie that lamented the death of innocence in 1962, came out only 11 years after the demise of the long-lost age it lamented.

In much the same way, the final episode of *M*A*S*H* revived memories of the earnest, early-1970s antiwar and feminist eras that had launched the show only a decade earlier. This all came together, of course, at a moment right before the mass television audience was about to be atomized by the rise of cable programming. The final episode of M*A*S*H thus became the last time that virtually the entire country would be transfixed by an entertainment show. By the early 1980s, we could already start to sense a loss of both community and a higher national purpose as the unusual cohesion that network TV had helped bring us collapsed. So, with a growing sense of bereavement, we either saluted or waved goodbye to M*A*S*H and the seventies, and embraced the Reagan era.

Part V

THE EIGHTIES

The Hostage Crisis • *Dallas*
The Ronald Reagan Show • CNN • *Hill Street Blues*
MTV • Bob Newhart • *Entertainment Tonight*
The Cosby Show • *Star Trek* • *Roseanne*

This decade saw the decline of the hegemony of the three major networks. Before 1980, cable networks really didn't exist as any kind of programming force. By 1990, about 60 percent of all households had basic cable, there were better than two dozen viable cable networks, and the combined share of the prime-time audience for CBS, NBC, and ABC had declined from over 90 percent to around 70 percent. Improved technology also made it easier for local stations to receive syndicated shows or news feeds, which further diminished network control. In programming, the order of the day was increased competition and diversity: This decade marked the rise of influential cable networks devoted to one subject—like news, sports, or rock videos. With less of a "mass audience" available, network shows experimented more as they tried to carve out a niche among wealthy viewers. In prime-time popularity, soaps like *Dallas* dominated the first half of the decade; sitcoms ruled the second half.

43
The Hostage Crisis as Metaphor
(ALL MAJOR NETWORKS: 1979–80, 1985)

Hostage crises were an important defining element in the history of television news during the late 1970s and well into the 1980s, from the takeover of the American embassy in Tehran in 1979 and 1980 to the TWA hijacking in Beirut in 1985. After the initial seizure of captives, television initiated an around-the-clock crisis mode—interviewing family members, breaking in with breathless bulletins which often offered little real news, and giving a frequent open microphone to either the terrorists or their allies. In 1980, Walter Cronkite began signing off every edition of the *CBS Evening News* by updating the number of days that the hostages had been held in Iran—and the count went to over 400 before they were released. That Iranian hostage crisis may have destroyed Jimmy Carter, but it made Ted Koppel and his *Nightline,* which grew out of a late-night ABC news program called *The Iran Crisis: America Held Hostage,* first appearing four days after the embassy takeover.

With each crisis, discussions about the role of television itself also became a staple of coverage. In the Iranian crisis, television took its share of criticism: We were told that the small screen aided the terrorists by making them seem less despicable, thwarted American foreign policy by focusing obsessively on the hostages' safe return, and converted anchormen into surrogate cabinet officers.

Fair enough. Television has always been an example of what ABC commentator Jeff Greenfield once described as a kind of Heisenberg principle: By observing, television changes what is being observed. Yet it does this in unexpected ways. For example, television molds public opinion not so much by its pictures *per se,* but by the way it converts events into its own soap-opera-like narratives—complete with good guys and bad guys, cliff-hanging suspense, and the pathos of real people. Life can imitate art, even pop art.

Though it's now the conventional wisdom that TV coverage of the

Vietnam War hastened its end, several opinion researchers concluded that this isn't true. Certainly pictures are worth a thousand words, and seeing any war up-close, through photographs or TV images, adds impact. Yet in the case of Vietnam—when TV news was still in its early days, and too much like print journalism to make the conflict into a miniseries—TV coverage had no more qualitative impact than did print coverage. The only difference between the two was that a major network could command a far greater audience than could any single newspaper or magazine.

Within only a short time, however, TV coverage had become significantly different from print coverage. Contrast the TV treatment of Vietnam, for example, with the Gulf War two decades later—with the latter's sophisticated graphics and logos, "up-close and personal" looks at heroic newsmen and generals (but not "grunt" soldiers, thanks to censorship), ongoing around-the-clock drama, and strict military control of the coverage—and you begin to appreciate how much television changed in a short time. Not surprisingly, that changed the medium's impact, too.

In that transformation, these hostage crises were significant—yet another dividing line in the way television no longer just covered the news but also helped create it. After all, were it not for the small screen, and the worldwide access it now provided to anyone who could afford a bomb and a pair of sunglasses, these incidents might have unfolded in far different ways—if they had occurred at all. During Vietnam we seldom, if ever, heard live from the leaders of North Vietnam, but during the Iranian hostage crisis (when 50 Americans were held captive in the American embassy in Tehran for over a year) Tehran's Bani Sadr became an American TV personality as ubiquitous as J. R. Ewing. Access to TV and worldwide fame alters events—especially ones in which the actors feed on publicity. Governments may establish policies not to talk with terrorists or dictators, but the networks will almost always give the troublemakers a microphone.

Why did television become obsessed with these particular stories? The answer is not as simple as it seems. After all, the visuals were usually terrible: How many times could one watch a picture of an embassy, or a map of a city? There were always scores of studio interviews, but "talking heads" are what TV directors put before the cameras when they can't find anything else.

Nevertheless, it worked. Obviously, one way to attract an audience is through live theater—and the technology was now making it easier than ever to seek out and stage those live theatrics everywhere around the globe. Communications theorist Ernest Bormann once wrote that "television news coverage is, in many respects, an exercise in creative dramatics in which a cast of familiar characters assembles . . . and imposes a drama according to a stock scenario." Of course, this is nothing new for a medium whose function has always been to attract the largest possible audience for the sponsors who pay its bills. No scriptwriter could have come up with anything approaching the happenings in Tehran: If you liked this miniseries, you loved *The Winds of War.*

Yet the cameras weren't there just because of the drama. Television, Marshall McLuhan often reminded us, is grounded in the perception of process. What it does best is reveal and unfold, like the weatherman's map that illustrates the development of tomorrow's climate, or the slow-motion instant replay that tells us what really happened on third and 10. A hostage crisis is that process raised to allegory. Every day there are the periodic bulletins, *Nightlines,* and television announcers proclaiming: "The latest in the hostage crisis. Details at six." Yet what are the details? No one knows. After all, not much has happened.

But that, too, is part of the process. In the world of television crisis reporting, no news is good news: As long as the story continues, TV still has its extravaganza. That's why CNN and the networks, applying the hostage-crisis lessons of the seventies and eighties, would remain on the scenes of the TWA crash off Long Island and the Oklahoma City bombing for weeks in the nineties, even though investigators were producing next-to-nothing informative. The same approach would inform storm coverage on the local news. Like the soap operas on which news events were now often modeled, all of these slow-moving spectacles were presented as "up-close and personal" narratives without any clear endings. In fact, if the story was compelling enough, TV viewers would continue to demand "news" long after the pageant had seemingly ended. In perhaps the most striking example of this phenomenon, Geraldo Rivera managed to keep his nightly, one-hour, CNBC review of the O.J. Simpson case going for more than a year after the criminal trial had ended, the civil trial had yet to begin, and the "news" had seemingly stopped.

Over time, TV's addiction to a certain kind of narrative would become the imperative that would frequently govern our public lives. In the early 1990s, after the bombing of a marketplace in Sarajevo, it was widely predicted that these moving television images would incite Americans to action. Yet they had little impact because the pictures were never framed as part of larger, more compelling drama that could run for weeks, and feature heroic Americans, families at home, and identifiable villains like Saddam Hussein and Muammar Kadaffi—who often seemed like they had just stepped off the set of *Miami Vice*. It also didn't help that many of the principals in Sarajevo couldn't speak English, one reason why, say, Israel (or even the Philippines) still often gets more coverage than Mexico.

Just as television had once changed sports, education, and politics, it was inevitable that it would also change foreign policy, war, and the nature of terrorism. Over the years, analysts would wring their hands over TV's distortion of events—but it was too late to talk about having it any other way. In the media age, there really is no business like show business. And, as we all know, the show must go on.

44

Dallas and the Rise of Republican Mythology
(CBS: 1978–91)

By taking the themes and settings of the traditional Western and thoroughly reweaving them into the fabric of contemporary America, *Dallas* launched the zeitgeist of the 1980s on prime-time television. In so doing, it ended up as one of the top-rated dramatic shows of all time, hitting Number 1 for three seasons, and Number 2 for two others. The show was also a monster hit abroad, becoming one of the first mass exports in an industry beginning to discover in the eighties that there's more to making money than how well you do domestically the first time around. Not for nothing in 1983 did a French Minister for Culture call *Dallas*—with its Western themes, opulent settings, and sheer infatuation with materialism—"the symbol of American cultural imperialism." "[I]t has become the perfect hate symbol, the cultural poverty . . . against which one struggles," wrote another disillusioned European writer.

For 13 years and 356 episodes, the series made good despite violating several shibboleths about what makes a successful TV show. In a world of sitcoms, it still remains one of the few dramatic shows in the past 30 years to win a season's ratings race. (The others are the *Dallas* clone *Dynasty, ER,* and *Marcus Welby, M.D.*) It is television gospel that all series must revolve around sympathetic characters with whom audiences can identify. Yet *Dallas* made the villainous J. R. Ewing, played by Larry Hagman, the focus of its drama about the struggles between two extremely wealthy Texas oil families—the Ewings and the Barneses—now linked by the marriage of Bobby Ewing and Pam Barnes in a remake of the premise of Romeo and Juliet. This focus surprised even the show's creators, who began by making the show revolve around Pamela and Bobby (J.R.'s younger brother), only to find that J.R. kept dominating the episodes, and audiences kept responding.

Dallas also radically changed prime time by popularizing the serial format of soap-opera daytime TV, which until then had rarely been used in the evening. By the 1984–85 season, the Top Ten had four serials about wealthy families—*Dallas, Dynasty, Falcon Crest,* and *Knots Landing,* the Dallas spinoff. Yet where *Dallas* led, such shows as *Hill Street Blues, Northern Exposure,* and *Homicide* also ventured, with the result that prime-time television, freed from the one-hour time limit on storytelling, began to develop complex plotting and characterization for virtually the first time. The show's reliance on the melodramatic conventions of soap opera also allowed it to introduce a new wrinkle to dramatic television: the season-ending cliff-hanger that kept people talking about a show all summer during rerun season, until the plot picked up again in the fall.

The show premiered as a late-season replacement on April 2, 1978, and *Variety* promptly panned it. "Prime time soap operas about the rich and powerful haven't worked all that well in the last few seasons," it wrote. "'Dallas' is just as dull and contrived as two recent Nielsen failures . . . so there's no reason to expect that its five episodes will fare any better this spring." As David Marc and Robert Thompson pointed out in their book *Prime Time, Prime Movers, Dallas* was in many ways the brainchild of executive producer Lee Rich, who had helped create *The Waltons* and *Eight Is Enough*—shows which oddly foreshadowed *Dallas* in their emphasis on a large family living in the same house, and enduring their share of crises in multiple plots.

On *Dallas,* Rich and his minions took the concept several steps further. By the end of the second season, the show had already introduced close to 40 principal characters—a number which grew to almost 100 by the time the show ended—who endured the usual soap-opera panoply of affairs, double-dealing, diseases, kidnappings, car crashes, fires, shootings, oil spills, and even a rattlesnake biting or two. "'Dallas' may be trash," wrote Harry Waters in *Newsweek,* "but it is splendidly crafted trash"—though no more splendid, really, than what daytime viewers had been watching on soaps like *General Hospital* for years.

Here, however, the soap-opera genre, with its roots in feminine forms of discourse tailored to the daytime audience, had been "masculinized." In an era when traditional Westerns, geared to men, had all but disappeared from American culture, this was TV's version of Suburban Cowboy: The outsider vs. the community, the clash of modernity and tradition, and the urge to plunder the land yet leave it untouched for the next generation were all themes prevalent in *Dallas.* Equally important, the traditional male villain of daytime soap opera, a supporting character there, became the lead here. At the center of *Dallas* was television's ultimate scoundrel, J. R. Ewing—a man *Time* once described as "that human oil slick." "Once you give up on integrity," he explained to someone he was blackmailing, "the rest is a piece of cake."

As had been the case with most other soap operas, the same things seemed to keep happening over and over, and the series became known (like most daytime drama) for its unbelievable plot twists, often presented at the ends or beginnings of seasons. It all started in the spring of 1979, when the producers decided to have Sue Ellen, J.R.'s pregnant wife, drive into a telephone pole in the last episode of the season, leaving the audience hanging about her fate over the summer. At the end of the next season, when the show staged a similar ploy with the shooting of J.R., assailant unknown, the network built up the suspense for months, letting followers know that four different endings had been filmed so that even the principals didn't know what would finally happen.

When the next episode finally aired on November 21, 1980, two months late because of an actors' strike, more than 80 million domestic viewers tuned in to learn "Who Shot J.R.?" (For the record, it was Kristin—J.R.'s scorned sister-in-law.) That episode is still the second-highest-rated regular show in television history, eclipsed only by the last episode of *M*A*S*H* in 1983. Then there was the scene opening up the 1986 season wherein Bobby, who was supposed to have been dead for a year, emerged in a shower. The reason? Pam had dreamed his death, meaning that all the previous year's episodes were out the window. Some critics say the show never recovered from that *deus ex machina,* though the final regular show of all in 1991 ended with J.R. offscreen, a gunshot, and a character screaming, "Oh, no!"

There were as many theories advanced to explain *Dallas*'s popularity as there were subplots on the show. Some critics thought that many viewers tuned in to see how the rich, despite their wealth, could be even more miserable than the average viewer. Some saw the depiction of J.R. as typical of television's distrust of businessmen. On the other hand, others wrote that viewers identified with the melodramatic evil of J.R. and his immoral cohorts, and that this identification reflected a greater social breakdown that reflected the go-go avarice of the Reagan years. Where J.R. led, one imagines, Ivan Boesky followed.

These attitudes extended beyond our borders. As Tamar Liebes and Elihu Katz detailed in their book, *The Export of Meaning, Dallas* was a hit in over 90 countries, though different audiences tended to like the show for different reasons. More-traditional audiences (like Arabs and Moroccan Jews) took the program more seriously, even though they were often repelled by the message; westernized audiences viewed *Dallas* more "playfully." The one major country where the show never caught on was Japan, where audiences seemed frustrated, according to

Liebes and Katz, over the plot inconsistencies and the show's darkness. "We don't want to live with unhappiness until next week," was the way the authors described the Japanese reaction. *Dallas* never did particularly well in domestic syndication, however: Viewers either already knew the plots, or didn't enjoy the suspense as much when the episodes were presented on the usual syndication schedule of nightly, rather than weekly, showings.

The success of *Dallas* is a reminder of the not-too-distant, precable days when a television show could still become a national sensation, talked about endlessly around the proverbial water cooler. Once cable arrived and atomized the audience, that kind of unifying experience was rarely possible for a dramatic show—televised on only one network—to achieve. (Such actual events as the O. J. Simpson chase, covered by several networks, were another story.) As more than one critic has theorized, *Dallas* is also a reminder that drama shows often wear their conservatism on their sleeves, as they frequently end up sanctifying police work—or, in this case, the pursuit of the almighty dollar. By contrast, sitcoms, at least since 1960, have often carried liberal messages, perhaps because that's the only way to convey such a statement without the audience's complaining. From *The Dick Van Dyke Show* and *All in the Family* to *The Mary Tyler Moore Show, M*A*S*H,* and even *Seinfeld,* sitcoms have often been associated with either liberal ideas or an appeal to a more upscale, socially liberal audience.

With its love of money and glorification of business and conspicuous consumption, *Dallas* did become the televisual embodiment of a Reagan era which featured the Donald Trumps and Michael Milkens as icons. Yet it is faint praise to say that *Dallas* mirrored its times: Anybody, after all, can write the news into a show. What set *Dallas* apart was the way it not only reflected its times but also helped define them. Remember that *Dallas* premiered in 1978, when Jimmy Carter was still president and the values of the old Democratic era still seemed to be riding high. The series thus served as an embodiment of the Reagan era before we even knew there would be a Reagan era—one reason why the show floundered initially. In its celebration of opulence, its glorification of the Sunbelt, and its portrayal of a new American entrepreneurial class, *Dallas* helped shape a mood that changed America. No Democrat could lead a nation, or indeed a world, that saw itself in *Dallas*—as Jimmy Carter would learn several seasons after the show premiered.

After all, the popular shows of the previous era—*The Mary Tyler Moore Show, All in the Family,* and even *The Waltons*—were programs that glorified locales closer to the old Democratic Party mainstream. The mythic worlds of *Dallas,* by contrast, were GOP territory—the board room and suburban ranch—and it is hardly happenstance that Reagan would surround himself with the imagery and inhabitants of both places.

It is no coincidence either that the GOP convention that renominated Reagan for president in 1984 was held in Dallas, where delegates were treated to tours of Southfork, J.R.'s mythical home. Nor is it simply fortuitous that his successor George Bush, once from Connecticut and Maine, chose to reinvent himself in roughly the same profession, and in that part of the country from which the Ewings and Barneses sprang. To a 1960s liberal, and in the old mythology of television, Dallas had been the city of the Texas School Book Depository, Love Field, and Parkman Hospital. After this show, Dallas was the new symbol of Ronald Reagan's America. When critic Richard Corliss paid tribute to the show in 1990 in the *Los Angeles Times,* his piece was headlined "The 'Dallas' Shot That Was Heard Around the World." So it was that J.R.'s shooting helped wipe out the memory of another Dallas shooting, and thus changed the image of both the city and the region.

Yet even the memories of J.R.'s shooting have faded as *Dallas* has receded in the nineties. Like the Western whose themes it incorporated, Dallas was an exercise in nostalgia. If a J.R.'s work is never done, it is because a cowboy ultimately never wins. Eventually civilization and all that it connotes does arrive: Tombstone becomes Tucson; someday Dallas will be another Detroit. "The world I know is disappearin' real fast," J.R. was heard to lament in the show's final season. In many ways, *Dallas* embodied that sentiment—and when it left the air in 1991, nothing in the culture replaced it. Not surprisingly, a Democrat would win the next presidential election.

45

Debating Our Politics: The Ronald Reagan Show

(ALL MAJOR NETWORKS: 1967–89)

He was without doubt the greatest television act in American political history. Yet in the very early days of the small screen, Ronald Reagan, a.k.a. "the Great Communicator," had avoided the medium. "[M]ost television series expired after two or three years," he once wrote, "and from then on, audiences and producers tended to think of you only as the character you'd played on the TV series." Thus Reagan made his regular debut on TV in 1954 playing himself—becoming for eight years and around 300 episodes the first and only future president to host a hit television series. *General Electric Theater,* a CBS half-hour dramatic anthology show, would eventually rise as high as Number 3 in the 1956–57 season, behind only *I Love Lucy* and *The Ed Sullivan Show.* Despite his reluctance to act on the small screen, Reagan even performed in several episodes, including "A Turkey for the President," wherein (joined by his wife Nancy) he played an American Indian.

That connection to GE would prove to be a crucial facet of Reagan's career. His relationship with the company wasn't limited just to hosting the show. Reagan toured their plants, and met with their executives—and, through these and related experiences, became a staunch convert to the ideals and grievances of corporate America. This was a side of the country with which Reagan had been largely unfamiliar before, and it was the combination of his acting background and his absorption of a big-business mentality that shaped him as a political creature.

Yet there was one character type other than host that Reagan always yearned to play in Hollywood: the traditional Western hero. As president, he was frequently shown riding at his ranch. His best-known campaign photo looked remarkably similar to an earlier television commercial featuring the well-known "Marlboro man." It had been one of the great disappointments of Reagan's film career that he had never gotten a chance to star in a first-rate Western—though, when he first ran for governor of California in 1966, many Americans still knew him from his one year of hosting another TV show, the syndicated *Death Valley Days.* Of Reagan's 53 movies, only a handful were Westerns, and even the most noteworthy (*Tennessee Partner* and *Cattle Queen of Montana,* with Barbara Stanwyck) weren't enthusiastically received. "They didn't want them good," Reagan once explained. "They wanted them Thursday." Reagan also seemed to lack the presence of a Gary Cooper or a John Wayne, a trait that prompted one movie executive to comment, when Reagan first ran for governor, "No—Jimmy Stewart for governor. Reagan for best friend."

Once on the political scene, however, Reagan seemed to grow into the roles he never had a chance to play in Hollywood. His national speech on behalf of Barry Goldwater in 1964 was a classic, launching his successful candidacy for governor of California two years later. And throughout his presidency, whether in oval-office addresses, press conferences, or impromptu remarks, he was always a master of the medium. For starters, his advisers knew that his every appearance should be conceived of and packaged as a television appearance. They also knew that TV reporters and crews, being basically lazy, want things done for them. Thus, it was mutually beneficial if Reagan's handlers had already lit the stage, selected the backdrop, and found a suitable place to position the camera. Over time, as analysts would demonstrate, political reporters began writing less about policy and more about stagecraft—grading candidates and presidents more on their television skills than on anything else.

Nowhere did Reagan demonstrate his talents better than in his appearances in televised debates, those somewhat unscripted performances that made and capped his political career. Looking back at those debates over two decades—against opponents as disparate as Robert Kennedy, William F. Buckley, Jr., George Bush, and Jimmy Carter—what is striking is how Reagan turned virtually every debate into a virtuoso TV performance. "No producer should ever mess with that guy," Stuart Spencer, one of his political advisers, once said.

But why not? What was Reagan's secret? Some would say that it all began with his 1930s experience in recreating baseball games on the radio. "Reagan's use of his voice has been his most valuable professional skill," Garry Wills wrote in his biography of Reagan. "It gave dignity to his movie appearances even when his body was still, or unconvincing." Reagan's vocal style was reminiscent of another radio personality who also made it big on television during the 1950s: Arthur Godfrey. Columnist Ben Gross once tried to analyze Godfrey's appeal with descriptions that could apply to Reagan: "Godfrey is handsome in a rugged athletic manner," he wrote. "[T]he women tell me he has sex appeal; his voice, resonant and tinted with warm tones, conveys an inherent magnetism."

Others would say that Reagan's secret was that he knew how to "use television." There was the commanding presence, the humor, the use of throwaway lines, the calm and measured approach. "It begins with eye contact," Edwin Diamond, the noted media analyst, once said. "He doesn't exactly make love to the camera, but he's warm and friendly." He has the quality, another critic once wrote, of "déjà vu personified."

Part of it was also Reagan's personality. "He's a competitor. He enjoys it," Lou Cannon, the *Washington Post*'s veteran Reagan-watcher once said. "It's why he loved football." Certainly it's difficult to find another political figure who practiced as much as Reagan did: There's said to be an underground videotape of President Reagan repeating again and again his coin flip within the Oval Office, by way of preparing to open the 1985 Super Bowl. "It is heads," he pronounces. Then "It is tails."

Part of it all was also Reagan's political talent at work on the screen. "People still don't realize that President Reagan has a sense of the essence of issues," David Gergen, Reagan's former communications director, said over a decade ago. "He doesn't play the great jargon game—he talks in terms people can relate to."

Whatever the reasons for Reagan's success in debates, a reexamination of those televised confrontations reveals that his approach never wavered much over two decades. The rhetorical questions, the homespun tales, the distorted facts, and the "aw shucks" approach were always staples of Reagan's career. Looking back, it all seems so recognizable. Yet, in the beginning, it was unique.

It was in the spring of 1967 that CBS decided to test a new communications satellite via an internationally televised, prime-time, split-screen debate between Reagan—then the new governor of

California—in Sacramento, and New York's Senator Robert F. Kennedy in Washington. "They were going to have students from around the world asking questions," Kennedy press secretary Frank Mankiewicz recalled, "and it seemed like the kind of thing we should do. We figured this third-rate governor would be easy prey." Another Kennedy staffer recalled that "Bobby prepared for the thing by skiing in Switzerland." What gave Kennedy and his advisers particular confidence was that the two men had appeared jointly at a Gridiron Club dinner in Washington two months earlier, and Kennedy had outshone Reagan, who left saying "I blew it."

Two months later came this debate, and Reagan had done his homework. "The show lasted an hour but it seemed like it took a week," Mankiewicz reported. "It was a shambles. First, Kennedy answered the questions, and he looked at the narrator, rather than the camera. So what the viewers saw was this distracted fellow looking at something they couldn't see. And you have to remember that Robert Kennedy was not that eloquent in this sort of setting. He was a hot participant in a cool medium."

But not Reagan. "I learned a marvelous lesson that night," Mankiewicz said. "Never underestimate Ronald Reagan. He looked right at the camera and continually said things like, 'This is a great country,' and 'We'll try again next year.'"

Consider this first exchange over the war in Vietnam:

RFK: I have some reservations as I've stated them before about some aspects of the war, but think that the United States is making every effort to make it possible for the people of South Vietnam to determine their own destiny. . . . I think that we're all agreed in the United States that if the war can be settled and the people of South Vietnam can determine their own destiny and determine their own future, that we want to leave Vietnam.

REAGAN: I think we're very much in agreement on this, that this country of ours has a long history of nonaggression but also a willingness to befriend and go to the aid of those who want to be free and determine their own destiny. Now I think all of us are agreed that war is probably man's greatest stupidity, and

I think peace is the dream that lies in the hearts of everyone, wherever he may be in this world. But unfortunately, unlike a family quarrel, it doesn't take two to make a war. It only takes one.

Later, when asked about his opposition to civil-rights legislation, Reagan responded, in part:

I happen to bridge a time span in which I was a radio sports announcer for major-league sports in our country, in athletics, many years ago. At that time, the great American game of baseball had a rulebook whose opening line was, "Baseball is a game for Caucasian gentlemen." And up until that time, up until World War II, there'd never been a Negro player in organized baseball in America. And one man defied that rule—a man named Branch Rickey, of one of the major-league teams. And today, baseball is far better off, and our country is far better off, because he destroyed that by handpicking one man and putting him on his baseball team, and the rule disappeared.

It all sounds so familiar today—the household analogy, the appeal to patriotism, the cute but inapposite story about a "rulebook." But back then, no one had heard this kind of rhetoric in politics. And it worked: Kennedy and his staff knew they had been beaten, and badly. Mankiewicz would say later: "From that day on until the day he died, Bobby would often interrupt me when I said something in a meeting. And he would say, 'Don't listen to him; he's the guy who told me to debate Ronald Reagan.' "

Almost 11 years later, on January 13, 1978, Reagan again appeared in a nationally televised debate—this time on William F. Buckley's *Firing Line*. The subject was the Panama Canal Treaties, which Reagan opposed, and he was up against both Buckley and George Will, no slouches in the debate department. The face-off came at a crucial time in Reagan's career, for the press had begun to write stories suggesting that the 67-year-old governor—in between campaigns for president—was too old to run anymore. "Reagan will be placing his political future on the line this week as he debates . . . another prominent conservative, William F. Buckley, on national television," said one pre-debate editorial.

Anyone who saw the debate stopped writing such stories, for Reagan more than held his own. Yet his style was different from what it had been in the Kennedy confrontation of a decade earlier. Putting his photographic memory to work, Reagan overwhelmed Buckley with facts and statistics. Said one viewer, "He [Reagan] was eloquent and gave the appearance of great in-depth study of the question. The appearance of a learned man was he!" By contrast, the viewer said, Buckley appeared to flounder as he kept "looking hopelessly for audience approval."

Here is part of Reagan's introduction discussing the history of the canal:

> Our own Senate took three months fighting over it, and then the vote was 66 to 14. The United States paid Panama $10 million in gold. Later in 1922, we paid Colombia $25 million because the land was actually theirs. We also gave Panama $250,000 a year that was a railroad royalty which had previously gone to Colombia. We've since raised that to about two million—three.

Never mind that the facts might be a bit off; Reagan sounded great. And, as would become apparent in later presidential tête-à-têtes, Reagan knew how to both disarm an opponent and use rhetorical questions to his advantage.

MODERATOR: The chair will recognize Governor Reagan and give him the privilege of questioning William Buckley for seven minutes.

REAGAN: Seven minutes? [laughter]

MODERATOR: Seven minutes.

REAGAN: Well, Bill, my first question is why haven't you already rushed across the room to tell me that you've seen the light? [laughter and applause]

"He'll give you that sweet little smile," Lou Cannon once said, "and then he'll cut your heart out."

It was at the February 23, 1980, debate with George Bush in Nashua, New Hampshire—during which Reagan shouted angrily, "I paid for this microphone, Mr. Green"—that many first noted Reagan's "star" TV quality. In the wake of Bush's emergence as Reagan's principal challenger for the GOP presidential nomination on the strength of an upset victory in the Iowa caucuses, Reagan and Bush had apparently agreed to a face-to-face debate in New Hampshire. But in the hours before the debate, Reagan's campaign chief, John Sears, decided to throw Bush a curve, and invited such other candidates as Bob Dole and Howard Baker to participate. "One of the things you look for in campaigns," Sears told one writer later, "is an opportunity for your opponent to have to make decisions in public . . . on his feet, on the spot." Knowing how well Reagan handled such opportunities, Sears arranged for the other candidates to show up on the podium as the debate began.

As the additional candidates arrived onstage, Bush sat frozen while Reagan grabbed the microphone and began to explain why the others should participate. Jon Breen, executive editor of the *Nashua Telegraph,* however, saw Reagan as changing the rules at the last minute. "Turn off Mr. Reagan's microphone," he ordered. Reagan exploded, yelling "I paid for this microphone, Mr. Green [sic]." Coincidence or not, it was a statement quite similar to the line that presidential candidate Spencer Tracy had delivered in the 1948 film *State of the Union.* (Halted in the middle of a radio broadcast, Tracy cries, "I'm paying for this broadcast!")

No matter that Bush had been set up; he came off as the heavy. And the media and home viewers, ignoring the substantive part of the debate, acclaimed Reagan the master improviser. "Reagan looked 20 years younger," gushed columnist Mary McGrory. *The Boston Globe,* which had run only one article about a debate involving all the candidates three nights earlier in Manchester, ran six on Nashua, including an article that exclaimed, "Eugene Ionesco or Harold Pinter could not have scripted a livelier prelude to the debates." Peter Teely, Bush's pollster, told his candidate, "The bad news is that the media is playing up the confrontation. The good news is that they're ignoring the debate, and you lost that, too." Three days later, in the New Hampshire primary, Reagan trounced Bush, 50 percent-23 percent, and the Republican race was as good as over.

That year, however, Reagan still had two debates to go. The fall campaign began with incumbent President Jimmy Carter's refusal to debate both independent candidate John Anderson and Reagan, and Reagan's refusal to appear unless Anderson was included. So the first presidential debate on September 21 featured just Reagan and Anderson. "We prepared two briefing books for him," Gergen remembered later. "And we brought him in four or five days before the debate for a series of practices. We went out to Wexford, a farmhouse, where we set up a mock debate studio with two debate podiums, exactly as it would be on television. And David Stockman, who had worked for Anderson, played Anderson in the mock debate."

Gergen and the other Reagan advisers then videotaped Reagan and Stockman, and reviewed the tapes with Reagan. "On the first run-through, to be honest, Stockman knocked him out of the ring," Gergen recalled. "But by the third run-through, he cleaned up Stockman. We didn't try to pack Reagan with information—lecturing at him isn't effective. What he needed was to think his answers through so they fit the debate's time format."

The preparations paid off. "The main thing that struck me during the debate," Gergen remembered, "was how much better Stockman was at playing Anderson than Anderson was himself. And I don't think anything came up in that debate that we hadn't been through before." Reagan himself later remarked, "After Stockman, both Anderson and Carter were easy."

The Wall Street Journal called the Anderson–Reagan debate a "surprisingly good show." And it was vintage Reagan. Besides expressing himself on a number of issues, including the MX missile, abortion ("I've noticed that everybody who is for abortion has already been born"), and taxes, Reagan resorted to his old debate ploys. When Anderson accurately accused Reagan of raising spending as governor of California, Reagan responded: "Well, some people look up figures and some people make up figures. And John has just made up some very interesting figures." And, in arguing for lower taxes, Reagan said, "If you've got a kid that's extravagant, you can lecture him all you want to about his extravagance, or you can cut his allowance."

Finally there was this Reagan summation:

> For 200 years, we've lived in the future, believing that tomorrow would be better than today, and today would be better than yesterday. I still believe that. I'm not running for the presidency because I believe that I can solve the problems we've discussed tonight. I believe the people of this country can. And together, we can begin the world over again. We can meet our destiny. And that destiny—to build a land here that will be for all mankind a shining city on a hill. I think we ought to get at it.

Because of his performance against Anderson, Reagan became convinced he should debate Carter, despite the advice of some aides that it was too great a risk. Reagan again prepared at Wexford by debating Stockman (this time playing Carter), with George Will and Jeane Kirkpatrick playing the roles of the news panel.

What political junkies remember about that Carter-Reagan debate during the last week of the 1980 campaign are three moments. First, there was Carter's ill-fated reference to arms-control conversations with his daughter Amy: "I had a discussion with my daughter Amy the other day before I came here to ask her what the most important issue was. She said she thought nuclear weaponry and the control of nuclear arms." As Reagan aide Michael Deaver said later, "People may not understand the intricacies of arms control, but they know you don't ask your 12-year-old for the solution." What Carter undoubtedly was trying to do was match Reagan, who moments before had said:

> I have seen four wars in my lifetime. I am a father of sons; I have a grandson. I don't ever want to see another generation of young Americans bleed their lives into sandy beachheads in the Pacific or rice paddies and jungles of Asia or the muddy battlefields of Europe.

Carter tried to—but couldn't—match the folksy eloquence without making a gaffe.

Then there was the "There you go again" remark of Reagan, a response to a Carter charge that Reagan had once campaigned against Medicare. In fact, the charge was true—but no one either cared about or later remembered that. And, as Reagan biographer Cannon pointed out long after, the response which seemed so casual and off-the-cuff in the debate had actually been rehearsed during the preparations. Reagan, who loved one-liners, had reserved practice time at Wexford simply to review some of his best lines. After one of the rehearsals, Reagan's aides told him they didn't like his response to a Stockman-Carter charge that he was weak on arms control. Reagan told them: "I was about ready to say "There you go again.' I may save it for the debate."

Finally, there was Reagan's closing, with its famous line, "Are you better off today than you were four years ago?" In fact, Reagan asked five rhetorical questions in a row:

> Are you better off today than you were four years ago? Is it easier for you to go and buy things in the stores than it was four years ago? Is there more or less unemployment in the country than there was four years ago? Is America as respected throughout the world as it was? Do you feel our security is as safe, that we're as strong, as we were four years ago?

"We planned that," remembered Gergen later. "Very few people can handle rhetorical questions well, but Reagan can." Less than a week after that debate, an election that had looked close had turned into a landslide.

Reagan's last two debate performances—at the age of 74 against Walter Mondale in October 1984—were clearly not his best. His advisers had opposed his debating at all, if not because of his age then because he had nothing to gain by debating an opponent who trailed him by around 20 points in the polls. It also didn't help that Stockman was so good at playing a disdainful Mondale in the rehearsals that he broke Reagan's confidence. "You better send me some flowers," Reagan said to Stockman after a practice session, "because you've been nasty to me."

The result was that Reagan overcompensated by cramming his an-

swers with so much detail in that first debate with Mondale that both
the viewer *and* Reagan got lost. At one point, Reagan confused Washington with Hollywood and began rambling about defense spending
for "food and wardrobe." At another, when asked about an increase in
poverty during his presidency, Reagan said: "Yes, there has been an increase in poverty, but it is a lower rate of increase than it was in the
preceding years before we got here. It has begun to decline, but it is
still going up." The low point for Reagan came when he tried to re-
cycle his old quip from the 1980 debate, "There you go again," on a
question about taxes. Mondale had prepared an answer. He turned to
Reagan:

> Now, Mr. President, you said: "There you go again." Right. Re-
> member the last time you said that?

Reagan nodded feebly.

> You said it when President Carter said that you were going to
> cut Medicare. And you said: "Oh, no, there you go again, Mr.
> President." And what did you do right after the election? You
> went out and tried to cut $20 billion out of Medicare. And so
> when you say, "There you go again," people remember this, you
> know.

For the next debate, Reagan's advisers were careful to get him
properly motivated, bringing in political adviser Roger Ailes for a pre-
debate pep talk. "Chuckle again and have fun out there," Jim Baker
suggested to Reagan as he went onstage—and, for the most part, Reagan did. His best moments actually came with two canned jokes: "I
am not going to make age an issue in this campaign," Reagan said at
one point. "I am not going to exploit for political purposes my opponent's youth and inexperience." At another, Reagan attacked a Mondale ad in which the Democratic candidate was talking from the deck
of the *Nimitz*. If Mondale had been president, Reagan said, "he would
have been deep in the water out there, because when the *Nimitz* was
built, he was against it."

On the whole, however, Reagan was a shadow of his former debating self—a survivor only because Mondale chose on this night to mail in an even worse performance. At one point, Reagan veered off into a casual discussion of Armageddon and biblical destruction. And in his closing, after 90 minutes of standing in front of a podium, Reagan stumbled badly. First, he became confused and seemed to forget he was running against Mondale, not Carter. Then he tried to conclude with a story he had told many times about a time capsule, and what he would put in a letter to tell future generations about nuclear weapons. But Reagan never got around to saying what he would put in the letter, or really what was the point of the story. When moderator Edwin Newman finally cut the President off, he was praising vice-president Bush and reminiscing about what a "wonderful experience" campaigning was. "We have met your sons and daughters," Reagan was saying, when Newman stopped him, much like a boxing referee trained to stop a fight before a pugilist suffers serious damage.

Oh, well. Reagan later said that he had intended to finish with a story about how the current generation must remember the next. But his troubled conclusion still couldn't diminish a lifetime of virtuoso television performances. And it was hardly happenstance that, just one generation after television had penetrated the American psyche, we elected this actor President. This was the logical culmination of a process which had started with John Kennedy and demanded that a successful candidate and officeholder understand television, become a master of it, and—as Reagan's advisers demonstrated—be able to control it. An actor has natural advantages for the presidency: He has experience wearing makeup, reciting lines effectively, using his voice and body with purpose, and taking direction from professionals. In the end, Reagan's triumph was also a triumph of the medium itself—and no politician could ever escape it.

46

CNN and the Changing Definition of News

(1980–PRESENT)

"The news continues, from now on and forever" pledged (or better yet, threatened) anchor Lois Hart on opening night, June 1, 1980. So far, her words have been prophetic. It has been estimated that about 15 million Americans watch the Cable News Network, or CNN, at least once a day, and millions more abroad tune in, too. Other all-news cable networks have now joined the fray, from MSNBC and the Fox News Channel to more than a dozen local cable outlets like New York One.

CNN's domestic ratings are still way below those of the newscasts on the three major networks. Yet its influence goes well beyond numbers, or even its intensive coverage of such specific events as the Gulf War. By altering both the dissemination and the very definition of news, CNN was an instrumental part of a process which transformed the news media and ultimately the culture.

Like its cable cousin MTV, CNN was also one of a handful of cable stations in the eighties and nineties whose style and economic success ended up changing the whole television industry. Though it did feature shows—*Larry King Live* or *Early Prime*—CNN itself was really the show, as viewers tuned in to get the news, identifying with the network rather than a particular program. And an economically successful "show" it was: By 1996, CNN was more profitable than the three major network news divisions combined, which undoubtedly made its new owner, Time Warner, very happy.

Yet, for all the praise CNN has received for creating the new "global village" with its extensive international coverage, whenever there's been a trend which cheapens TV journalism, CNN has usually been in the middle of that too. From its constant, unedited "live" coverage to its celebrity worship via Larry King, and from *Crossfire* with its superficial treatment of public issues to its hyping of the O. J. Simpson criminal trial, CNN has often ended up setting the declining standard for all TV news.

It hardly appeared that way at first for what detractors deemed the

"*Chicken Noodle Network*" because it seemed so shoestring and unlikely to succeed. Founder Ted Turner, an Atlanta entrepreneur, owned the local baseball team and WTBS, the first cable superstation—a local, independent station which was made available by satellite to cable systems all over the country, thus enabling the station to raise its ad rates and attract national advertising. Turner was hardly a man identified with a commitment to news. "I hate the news. News is evil," he had once said, and he was known throughout the industry as the man whose Atlanta superstation had one day featured a newscast coanchored by a dog.

Turner was convinced, however, that in the age of cable, an all-news network—run from out of Georgia, a right-to-work state where labor costs were cheaper—could make money. "There are only four things that television does," an associate once remembered Turner telling him. "It does movies and HBO has beaten me to that. It does sports and now ESPN's got that. There's the regular series kinda stuff, and all three networks have beaten me to that. All that's left is news!" As the plans left the drawing board, Turner concentrated on the business aspects and the technological problems, leaving the actual details of what the station would put on the air to others. When one of his associates suggested hiring a big name such as Dan Rather, Turner's response was typical: "Who's Dan Rather?" he reportedly asked.

When the station went on the air in 1980, it was hardly a match for the news resources of the networks. What CNN offered that the others didn't was continuous coverage and immediacy: With correspondents and feeders eventually scattered throughout the globe, CNN would cut to any event, anywhere, at any time. Over the years, those attributes would remain the hallmark of the network—in both its approach to news and the reaction of the public. With its technological reach and commitment solely to news, CNN frequently matched or beat the major networks in the early hours of many stories. No other network covered the blowup of the *Challenger* space shuttle live on January 28, 1986 (the networks had long since stopped televising space launches live), and CNN was well ahead of the Big Three in the early hours of Tiananmen Square and the aborted coup in the Soviet Union. Its most celebrated moments came during the early days of the Gulf War in January 1991, when the network's decision to ignore a recommendation to evacuate Baghdad, and CNN's securing of a dedicated phone line, allowed the organization to cover the bombing barrage far better than the competition.

The problem for CNN always was that once the major networks caught up and decided to cover an event in-depth, CNN's audience evaporated and its coverage paled. On the night the Gulf War began, CNN's ratings were 20 times normal: around 11 million homes. Within weeks, however, things were back to the norm—around 400,000 homes at any one time, a pattern that was repeated five years later when viewers flocked to the more than 500 hours of CNN's gavel-to-gavel O. J. coverage (the major networks covered only key events in the trial), and left CNN again once the trial ended.

This trend always provided a subtle impetus for CNN to stress live or—better yet—live continuing events that the major networks might avoid because their news value was questionable. CNN would become known for being the network that covered *ad nauseam* any major tabloid trial (Claus Von Bulow, William Kennedy Smith, and even John Wayne Bobbitt), or any passing of a major public figure from the deathbed to the cemetery (Richard Nixon and Jackie Kennedy). It also tended to stay on the scene of a major news event long after the cameras of the other major networks had gone elsewhere—and for good reason. What with time to fill, "You're going to get stuff," former NBC News head Reuven Frank once said on CNN during a political convention. "But don't call it news."

As media critic Tom Rosenstiel once pointed out in an astute critique of the network for *The New Republic,* for all its renown, CNN never offered much in the way of innovative news coverage. Its news segments were seldom much longer than those shown on the network, and the reports were formatted like those on the local and national news: a couple of anchors, with correspondents in the field. The network's entertainment, sports, and business shows were virtual clones of the competition. Though a few of its foreign reporters, such as Peter Arnett and Christiane Amanpour have distinguished themselves, there isn't a single CNN domestic reporter who in more than 15 years has become anything close to either a household name or a journalistic icon.

Turner would always make a point that his newscasts—headquartered in Atlanta, not the usual news capitals of New York or Washington—didn't share the bias of the competition: When he was unsuccessfully attempting to take over CBS, Turner vowed to take *60 Minutes* and "try and increase the objectivity of it," complaining that Mike Wallace had been impolite in an interview with former president Jimmy Carter, a fellow Georgian. "In the race for ratings," Turner once charged in another early speech, "their newscasts dig up the most sordid things human beings do, or the biggest disasters, and try to make them seem as exciting as possible." This from the head of a network which would later feature special theme music and logos for the Gulf War, the Oklahoma City bombing, and the 1996 TWA explosion off the coast of Long Island.

Those CNN programs that weren't clones of existing TV newscasts were often borrowed from radio—which was the medium, after all, that already had experience in how to fill up long 24-hour days with news. *Crossfire* and *Larry King Live* were actual crossovers from radio. When talk radio became popular in the 1990s, CNN inevitably aped the approach—adding a call-in, audience participation show, as well as call-ins to some newscasts. In 1990, the network even put up a 1-900 number so viewers could call in to vote on whether they favored the invasion of Panama (and pay for the privilege of casting an electronic ballot).

CNN thus found itself in the middle of a number of questionable media trends in the eighties and nineties. One of CNN's most obvious effects was on the networks themselves. In part because the networks figured that anyone could now get the headlines at any time from cable television (CNN had started a companion network, Headline News, in 1982) the producers of those network newscasts reexamined their role, much as newspaper editors had done a generation before when TV had usurped print's position as the initial disperser of news.

The result was a refocusing of network coverage on what the networks could do better or more easily than CNN. Network nightly news became more like a magazine, particularly in the way it offered interpretive stories, and news divisions started to experiment further with prime-time formats which merged news and entertainment on shows like *48 Hours* and *Prime Time Live*. As Rosenstiel and others have pointed out, the irony is that while the networks refocused their coverage based on the assumption that viewers were getting the headlines from CNN, relatively few viewers were actually watching the cable network. CNN has always had a far stronger following among Washington reporters and in newsrooms than among the general public.

CNN didn't only change the networks, however. It was a key part of a process which helped redefine the public's concept of "news." Unlike the news habit of the past, when there was a need for it only several times a day (to fill an edition or an evening newscast), there was now a 24-hour demand for news, even though not that much of importance might be going on. The result was a considerable broadening of what was considered reportable news and analysis, particularly on television. For example, we now have fields of news that didn't even exist before—like entertainment "reporting." (There have always been traffickers in gossip, but until *Entertainment Tonight* hit it big in the cable era, they tended not to get their own shows, complete with a reporting staff.) News from the tabloids is now considered fair game. That's one reason why the national television news has increasingly been drawn to the kind of salacious stories it once would have ignored, focusing on the personal lives of celebrities and politicians from Michael Jackson to Bill Clinton. CNN broadcast live, for example, Gennifer Flowers' 1992 press conference detailing her affair with Clinton.

Call-in TV shows also put forth any "expert" they can drum up, even as they encourage callers to speculate and gossip. Television commentary—once the province of the Moyerses and Sevareids—has been expanded to include the combative, always high-decibel *Capital Gang* and *Crossfire*. These shows are to traditional journalism what pro wrestling is to sports. Yet because of their presence, the television pundit has come to assume a greater role in our civic life, usurping the role once held by journalists like Walter Lippmann, or even conventional politicians. After all, it was CNN's Pat Buchanan, host of *Crossfire*, who blazed a new path to national politics by using his notoriety on this network to launch two presidential campaigns—slipping back into his TV role, courtesy of CNN, between them. "For ratings," A. M. Rosenthal of the *New York Times* would complain, "news executives

transformed Buchanan the politician into Buchanan the journalist."
When Buchanan announced for president in 1991, he even bragged,
"No other American has spent as many hundreds of hours debating
the great questions of our day on national television."

In the news culture that CNN helped create, information was also
presented to the public more quickly. In the rush to meet the demand,
the inevitable result was a thinner line between fact and rumor—one
reason why, say, false reports about Dan Quayle's past or Michael
Dukakis's mental health were disseminated so widely during the 1988
campaign. News was digested faster, too, with the odd result that some
events, such as election results, were now frequently analyzed *before*
they took place. The effects of Clinton's bombing of Iraq in the late
summer of 1996 were being scrutinized before a weapon had even
been fired. Sometimes such haste got news outlets into trouble: Broadcast reports seemed to indicate in the summer of 1996 that Richard
Jewell faced imminent arrest for the Olympic bombing, but the warrant never followed (both NBC and CNN eventually made an out-
of-court settlement with Jewell). Exit polls in 1992 indicated that Pat
Buchanan would run neck and neck with George Bush in the New
Hampshire primary, and most of the media analysis for the rest of the
evening proceeded from that assumption. When the final vote was tal-
lied, however, Bush had won a double-digit victory.

Over 30 years ago, historian Daniel Boorstin created the term
"pseudo-event" to describe the nonspontaneous, often planted happenings that were increasingly driving journalism—anniversaries,
public relations events, and polls which become important only because the poll-taker claims they're important. So it went at CNN:
During the 1996 fall campaign, for example, CNN took to the air one
Saturday to announce that Clinton's lead over Bob Dole had shrunk
to nine points in its daily tracking poll, only to announce two uneventful days later that the lead was now at 25 points. Faced with the
problem of how to fill up air time 24 hours a day, seven days a week,
CNN thus often made itself into a kind of pseudo-event network—
at least in the periods between major stories.

Perhaps the best illustration of the changes that CNN helped ce-
ment in the culture is the preeminence it helped bring Larry King,
the host of CNN's most popular show. With his six-night-a-week call-

in and interview show, broadcast around the world at 9:00 P.M. eastern time and featuring political and entertainment-world celebrities, King is—far and away—CNN's top draw. (With a little over a million domestic households viewing each night, his ratings are still far below those of the major network competition, however.) In a 1993 article in the *Washingtonian* examining the Washington press corps, King's platform was rated the vehicle a politician would seek out first—before David Broder's *Washington Post* column, a piece by a correspondent for the major networks, or *Nightline* (a show with much higher ratings). King's show was widely credited with giving H. Ross Perot the credibility he needed in 1992 to mount the second most successful third-party candidacy of this century, and then ruining Perot's attempts to defeat NAFTA when it staged a debate on the issue between the Texan and Vice-President Al Gore in the fall of 1993. Bill Clinton once bragged that he can stiff the traditional press corps because Larry King had "liberated" him to speak to the American people directly; Clinton took the proffered opportunity four times in the first three years of his presidency.

Still, even though CNN bills itself as a news network, King is no journalist—nor would he claim to be. His interview list is as likely to include a Sharon Stone as a Newt Gingrich; a journalist profiling King once called him the "mutant blob of celebrity." During the first Simpson trial, King turned his show over to the subject of the trial virtually for months, dissecting each day's events in minute detail. To be sure, there is a tradition in television news of merging entertainment with news, this dating back to Edward R. Murrow and the *Today* show. The difference between King and a Barbara Walters, however, lies in King's attitude toward his guests, which could politely be called obsequiously reverential. When the Iraqi delegate to the United Nations showed up on King's show around the time of the Gulf War, he had to handle this softball: "I mean, personally, is it hard?"

Those who appear on King's show say he gives them a vehicle to appeal to the public without the negative filter of contemporary journalism, but Kathleen Hall Jamieson, dean of the Annenberg School at the University of Pennsylvania, has perhaps better described an interview with King as a "free ride"—which is the reason why guests seek him out in the first place. "If you come off Larry King looking bad," Pat Buchanan has said, "it's your own fault." "He's not confrontational like some of these talk-show hosts," Turner once said. "The guests like him." Even O. J. Simpson found it safe to call in to the King show the night he was acquitted.

There is, of course, room for a Larry King in the entertainment galaxy. The question is why he has become the star attraction on what bills itself as a *news* network. With the rise of King—and news shows elsewhere which are similarly personality-driven, subjective, and thus less informed by fact (King brags that he seldom reads the books he helps authors to promote on the air)—it is no surprise that the public has drawn the conclusion that journalism itself is as subjective as he is. After all, if listeners on call-in shows can replace journalists as questioners, what does that say about journalism itself?

To be fair, CNN didn't invent our current news culture. (I should know: For a short time, I was a maladroit monthly commentator on the network's successful *Showbiz Today*.) The lines between entertainment, politics, and journalism have been blurred for a long time. Before King, there was Walter Winchell. Woodrow Wilson had D. W. Griffith's *The Birth of a Nation* screened at the White House in 1915; John Kennedy's presidency was a press agent's dream, and Ronald Reagan treated the presidency as the role of a lifetime.

Yet this network's notoriety was a harbinger of a new age which saw, in Daniel Boorstin's words, information replacing knowledge. In the old days before radio and television, when news wasn't instantly available, people had comparatively endless time to ponder the meaning of any new particulars. That was a culture with a deficiency of data but a surplus of ways to interpret that data. What was well-developed in the culture, therefore, were the belief systems that could provide meaning in the absence of information—religion, regional identity, or political ideology.

Now the situation has reversed. Thanks in part to CNN and the cultural changes it helped trigger, we can get facts or news almost instantaneously. Yet we're overloaded: We don't know what all that information means or what we should do with it. The cultural deficit today is not in Joe Friday's "facts." It's in the old institutions whose tenets of belief made it easier for us to organize the world and give it meaning—and which have been greatly eroded by television itself. "News," even for 24 hours a day courtesy of CNN, is hardly a substitute.

47
Hill Street Blues and TV's New Elite Style
(NBC: 1981–87)

"'Hill Street Blues' has been the TV show of the 1980s," wrote *Los Angeles Times* TV critic Howard Rosenberg when the show left the air in the spring of 1987. After its six-and-a-half seasons and 147 episodes on NBC, many agreed with him—and still do. Along with its odd twin, *Dallas* (another show which borrowed heavily from soap operas), *Hill Street* brought new complexity to storytelling in prime time, with its multiple open-ended plots and large cast of characters. Yet, unlike *Dallas,* which tended to appeal to a different audience, *Hill Street* had a gritty, darkish, and even "messy" look and sound: Its shooting and editing utilized hand-held cameras and overlapping dialogue, respectively. The show also featured far-more-developed and less-stereotypical characters than most other TV dramas—from the quiet intensity of Frank Furillo to the self-doubt of Lucy Bates. *Hill Street* was not a typical police show in which the cops always got their man, and its depiction of sex, for example, was franker than anything previously seen on prime-time television.

Hill Street was also a show which appealed to the right audiences— wealthy professionals, or the kind of people who before this series would never have considered themselves regular viewers of TV drama, even though they had been hard-core fans of such sitcoms as *The Mary Tyler Moore Show.* (MTM Productions, incidentally, also produced *Hill Street.*) "*Hill Street* is a gold mine for us," Gerald Joffe, NBC's vice-president for research projects, once told a reporter. "It gets a dynamite audience."

Attracting that upscale audience not only allowed *Hill Street,* developed by Steven Bochco and Michael Kozoll, to survive and eventually prosper; it also paved the way for TV's "second golden age"—a slew of similar drama shows pitched to elite audiences like *St. Elsewhere, L.A. Law, Moonlighting, thirtysomething,* and eventually the 1990s' wave of *NYPD Blue, Homicide,* and *Picket Fences.* To get that upscale audience, *Hill Street* created a style that changed the way people—or, better yet, wealthy and better-educated people—watched television.

For them, prime-time TV would no longer be a matter of escape, but instead a means of engagement. This meant that for some ten years after the premiere of *Hill Street,* TV would be the battlefield for a kind of class warfare through the airwaves over who preferred what type of programming. All of that oddly mirrored a larger political debate, during the Reagan-Bush years, about the direction of the country.

It all began in the early 1980s and came, like many other innovations in television, when the network in question was mired in last place in the ratings and willing to try almost anything. NBC head Fred Silverman—the man who had been so instrumental in the production of *Roots* on ABC—wanted to do an hour-long police show combining the sitcom humor of *Barney Miller* with the social realism of a forthcoming movie, *Fort Apache, the Bronx,* all while focusing on the private lives of the characters. At the time, Bochco and Kozoll had been toying with the notion of doing a show based on Arthur Hailey's book *Hotel* (which did make it to the tube in 1983, in other hands). This would allow them to tell several stories at once, following in the shoes of both *Dallas* and *The Love Boat.*

The three came together to produce *Hill Street Blues*—set in an urban police station with 13 highly developed regular characters of all genders and races, average age 35 (a bit higher than the TV norm). After one look at the series, the Broadcast Standards evaluators at the network had seen enough: They pronounced the show "too violent, too sexy, too grim."

Shot in the *cinema verité* style that *Hill Street* would make famous, the pilot—shown on January 15, 1981, at 10:00 P.M.—threw all of these elements at an unsuspecting audience. It began with the traditional morning call to order, with Sergeant Esterhaus's soon-to-be-famous weekly admonition "Let's be careful out there." "It is not entirely like anything," wrote the *Washington Post's* savvy Tom Shales after that first episode, which featured an undercover policeman who once bit a suspect's nose off; an ex-wife storming into the office to seek child support from the captain; and a police sergeant who left his wife so he could date a high-school senior—combined with a hostage standoff, a SWAT team, and the shooting of two cops. The female public defender called Captain Furillo a Fascist, yet at the end of the episode the audience found her in bed with her lover, the same captain. "Less is more" was the line producer's motto, brandishing what analyst Todd Gitlin would call a "kinetic technique" which featured dimmer lighting, continuous dialogue, and scenes shot in shadows.

As many critics grew to love this character-driven show, the series developed the kind of elite audience following that only an occasional *Masterpiece Theatre* had produced so far. Yet many wouldn't make such a viewing commitment. "They run the risk," wrote critic William Henry of Bochco and company, "of confusing the audience, of letting the plot disintegrate, of replacing hero worship of one or two stars with a loose attachment to an ambience and a milieu." At the end of that first half-season, *Hill Street* ranked 83rd out of 97 shows in prime time. Still, NBC stuck by the show (which went on to win eight Emmys that fall, a single-season record), extracting from the producers a promise to complete at least one story line each week, and thus give the episodes *some* closure.

Hill Street refined its "improvisational" approach over the next few years, experimenting more than the average show since it wasn't doing that well in the ratings. With the help of talented writers, the series probed the ethical dilemmas of police work—taking many topics straight from the newspapers, hardly a revolutionary approach anywhere but on dramatic television which had traditionally substituted allegory and action for realism. The show also dealt frequently with what it meant to be a male cop in an age defined by feminism, an approach which allowed *Hill Street* to appeal to younger men while retaining a following among women.

By the fall of 1982, in fact, *Hill Street* had become prime time's top show among men aged 18 to 34. While that small audience never would have been enough to save the show in a prior era (men in that age group watch less TV than their elders), the advent of competition from cable stations and VCRs in the eighties meant that the major networks' share of the programming audience was beginning to diminish—particularly among desirable, affluent young viewers living in cities like the one portrayed on *Hill Street*. If this show could bring these viewers to NBC, the theory went, the network would have a foothold among television's best audience for advertisers. Thus *Hill Street* became the first show of the new cable era to make it on the strength of its demographics rather than the size of its audience. In fact, the programming strategy behind it resulted in the fall 1982 premiere of *St. Elsewhere*—another MTM production on NBC which was essentially *Hill Street* set in a hospital, and which produced similar initial ratings (86th in the ratings out of 98 shows in its first season).

There was a brooding, Victorian quality to these dramas, much like that in the old Sherlock Holmes stories that illustrate the contrast between a violent underclass and a group of professionals trying to manage the damage. "It was about despair and about the way men and women tried to keep that despair at arm's length," Bochco once said of *Hill Street*—which explained why his show, even more than *M*A*S*H*, eschewed television's typical reliance on happy endings. "We don't solve problems, by and large," Bochco said.

What appealed to audiences, however, wasn't only higher-quality drama, acting, and writing. Many of the viewers who gravitated to these shows were single or divorced professionals, and in the eighties, the workplace—not the family—was the main focus of their lives. By focusing on personal conflicts in that workplace, these shows presented dramatically what *The Mary Tyler Moore Show* had portrayed humorously. These hour-long dramas affirmed the power of community—displaying a 1960s collectivist theme (a work commune) notable because it came during an era when the individualistic politics of the country were moving very much in the opposite direction. It was ironic that at the same time that the affirmation of the workplace community was becoming a trend in TV drama, the stockholder-driven politics of the era was beginning to produce quite a different workplace environment as the IBMs and AT&Ts of the world began to restructure. (That was a trend forecast in the final episode of *Mary Tyler Moore* when the station is sold, and almost everyone is laid off.) For all their supposed realism, *Hill Street* and its progeny were yet another televisual shading of the truth, as they presented a romanticized image of the workplace.

Throughout the Reagan years, *Hill Street* kept churning out quality drama. Bochco's favorite episode was said to be "Trial by Fury"—the Emmy-winning episode that opened the third season with Mick Belker getting advice for his father from a male prostitute; Captain Furillo going up against defense lawyer Joyce Davenport, his lover and future wife, as he tried to convict the attackers of a nun; and Lieutenant Catellano undergoing an IRS audit. The show withstood the real-life death of actor Michael Conrad (who played Sergeant Esterhaus) in late 1983, the screen death of Sgt. Coffey (played by former football star Ed Marinaro), and even the departure of Bochco himself, who was dismissed after five seasons—supposedly for cost overruns. (With its large cast, the show cost about $1.5 million an episode to produce.)

By the time the show left the air in 1987, devoted fans knew which cop had his pants burned off while on duty (Joe Coffey), which lost a fortune in the soybean market (Jesus Martinez), and which always went to the bathroom after morning roll call (Andy Renko). Yet, in its later years, *Hill Street* and its characters became quirky to the point of distraction—another attribute of many of Bochco's shows—as plot lines grew to include cannibalism, cops in drag, mooning, transvestites, and an orangutan. In the last episode the station house burned down, and Lt. Norman Buntz was dismissed for punching the police chief.

What followed in the wake of the critical and demographic success of *Hill Street* and *St. Elsewhere* was a wave of similar shows in the eighties—from Bochco's own *L.A. Law* (the *Hill Street* precinct house as a law firm) to *thirtysomething* and even *Moonlighting.* If the non-Bochco shows didn't imitate his gritty style, they did attempt to capture the demographic appeal and psychological realism in other ways.

Yet none proved as memorable as *Hill Street Blues* and most wore their elitism on their sleeves. *thirtysomething,* the first adult show named for its demographics, ran from 1987 to 1991 on ABC to critical (but not particular ratings) success. It was in many ways *The Big Chill* made into a weekly, soap-opera-like series. The uncapitalized and unhyphenated *thirtysomething* featured an ensemble cast, similar to that of *Hill Street,* with a focus on the self-absorbed tribulations of baby boomers trying to combine family and career while remaining true to the zeitgeist of the sixties—whatever that was. As Hope said to husband Michael, in the show's first episode:

[W]e expect too much. Because we've always gotten too much. I think that our parents got together in 1946 and said "Let's all have lots of kids and give them everything they want so they can grow up and be totally messed up and unable to cope with real life."

By contrast, *Moonlighting,* which ran on ABC from 1985 to 1989 starring Cybil Shepherd and Bruce Willis as two private detectives, attempted to appeal to the same elite as *Hill Street* by combining writing reminiscent of the screwball comedies of the 1930s with an ironic sensibility and use of "postmodern" television ploys, such as facing the camera and acknowledging the audience. As the 1980s turned into the 1990s, there were shows such as Bochco's *Cop Rock* (police try to sing their way through their day) and *Civil Wars* (a two-person divorce firm has eccentric associates and clients, like the woman who wants to divorce her husband because he thinks he's Elvis). Most of these shows were admired by the critics but disdained by mass audiences, and eventually by smaller ones too. Except for *Moonlighting* and *Northern Exposure,* none ever hit the Top Ten for a season (and those two only did it for a season each)—something of a problem on a mass medium, no matter how wealthy the audience.

The most outrageous of these elite dramas was *Twin Peaks,* developed by movie director David Lynch. It premiered on ABC in the spring of 1990. Because the show defied some TV conventions and mocked others, it was the darling of critics and people who prefer movies to television—the kind of elite viewers who tend to live in places like Cambridge and Manhattan. Initially built around the mystery of who killed Laura Palmer, a high-school student in an odd northwestern town, *Twin Peaks* seemed to break every rule about what makes successful television: On a medium celebrated for escapism, this show offered viewers the rare chance to flee to a place worse than home. With its depiction of incest and reincarnation, *Twin Peaks* was hiply eerie and dark, to the point of absurdity. After its first episode, the series offered little in the way of action as it self-consciously celebrated style over substance with an array of odd shots and dream sequences featuring a dancing dwarf. While a few of its stars were truly memorable (especially FBI agent Dale Cooper, played by Kyle MacLachlan), there were so many quirky characters that it was impossible to tell them apart at times. "It started out as a wonderful show," Meredith Berlin, an editor at *Soap Opera Digest,* once told a reporter, "but they lost sight of two things: story and character."

If nothing else, the cancellation of *Twin Peaks* after little more than a year underlined the point that, despite the success of *Hill Street,* television's conventions exist for a reason. Most TV series feature pre-

dictable plots and a small number of lead characters because few people want to watch the small screen with the same intensity that they
view a staged play or a big-screen movie.

The failure of *Twin Peaks*—and other shows like it—also proved
that a network television series can't succeed *simply* by appealing to
elites, no matter how much money those viewers have. Because
wealthy baby boomers are the target audience for many advertisers,
their interests and needs have always received attention far disproportionate to their importance and numbers. Love of gourmet restau-
rants, suspenders, and *thirtysomething* were never mass phenomena in
the eighties, though one might have thought so from reading
newsweeklies of the era.

At bottom, network television is almost always "democratic": Like
any other political movement or cause, it needs to avoid alienating the
masses to survive. *Hill Street Blues* managed to walk the fine line between appealing to elites and snotty self-parody, yet others were not
nearly so skillful in achieving that balance—whether they were making *Twin Peaks* or managing the 1980s Democratic Party, which embraced a kind of cultural liberalism in that decade which turned off
voters in a similar fashion. Take the 1988 presidential campaign of
Massachusetts Governor Michael Dukakis, which tried to make a
virtue of his ACLU membership, his veto of a state bill requiring
teachers to lead the Pledge of Allegiance in classrooms, or his furlough
of convicted murderer Willie Horton. These positions may have
played well in *thirtysomething* country, but not elsewhere.

By comparison, the popular prime-time dramas of the Reagan
era—*Dallas, Dynasty,* and *Magnum, P.I.*—were middle-American and
Sunbelt contrasts to the coastal social liberalism embodied in the rise
of the elite drama. The lesson of shows like *Twin Peaks* and *thirtysomething* was that producers and political figures alike often have a choice
when they want to reach Americans: They can appeal to a small elite
and receive rave notices from coastal critics, or they can fashion something broader that will speak to the rest of the people, too. *Hill Street*
notwithstanding, the makers of a lot of these rarefied shows of the
eighties and early nineties apparently chose the former—which, in the
end, provided both America and the Democratic Party of that era
with something of a political lesson as well.

48
What MTV Hath Wrought
(1981–Present)

There were extravagant predictions made about how MTV—short for Music Television—would change the music industry when it debuted in 1981. It was said by some that by putting the emphasis on visuals, rather than on sound, MTV would change the type of rock artists who would succeed. Others noted that MTV would diminish the importance of live performances, help take political rebellion out of the music, and blur the distinction between programming and commercials—since rock videos were little more than sophisticated advertisements for the record companies and artists producing them. And it was all true.

By the end of the eighties, in fact, many assumed that MTV had been "the most influential single cultural product of the [past] decade," as one writer put it—the source of everything from that decade's ironic style to the rise of television programming geared not to the masses but to a specific demographic group (sometimes called "narrowcasting"). Less than two years later, *Newsweek* was saying that "MTV has changed the way we talk, dress, dance, make and consume music, and how we process information." *Billboard* went further: "[N]o other single force on television has had such a strong and startling impact on our culture since the advent of TV itself." If anything, the accolades have multiplied in the years since. Today, MTV has become virtually synonymous with American culture.

In retrospect, it's no surprise that MTV proved a force in the recording and musical industries dominated by young consumers, as its continuous televising of short music videos drew a small but steady audience. Nor is there any issue about MTV's innovativeness or profitability, given its low overhead.

Instead, the question is why this small cable network changed a mass medium like television at all, which, in turn, enabled it to influence the whole culture. After all, MTV's videos—often infused with a surrealistic style that recalled experimental movies—have never been popular with the vast majority of people who watch TV. A 1991 survey found that, in a typical moment, MTV was watched by less than one home out of 160 with cable, and one in 300 overall. By contrast, the major networks routinely post ratings some 50 times better than MTV—which tends to attract only about 350,000 households at any one time. At best, MTV is an acquired taste even for most of its young target audience, who watch for an average of 18 minutes at a time. Yet taste it we all have, whether we like it or not, and most of us fuddy-duddies do not.

To be fair: MTV was never designed to reach the masses. "The plan to create a hipness for MTV was to position it as the very opposite of the three networks—a sort of 'stick-it-in-your-eye' approach," former MTV president Bob Pittman once wrote. Meticulously organized from demographic research in the early days of cable in 1980 and 1981, the network was designed to appeal to the notoriously hard-to-reach 18-to-29-year-old age group—sought after by advertisers because it has so much discretionary income, but ignored by the major networks because this group's preferred programming doesn't tend to appeal to the masses.

To reach these young viewers, a group of young executives decided to develop a channel merging rock and television by telecasting continuous music videos—a form that had been kicking around for some 40 years and shown sporadically in rock and dance clubs. Though some videos cost millions to make and were in every way striking, many were surprisingly amateurish—almost like five-minute home movies. Sometimes they had some narrative roughly parallel to the song, but more often they consisted merely of the band (or singer) clowning in front of the camera while a wave of scantily-clad women or surrealistic images unconnected to the music danced by.

Equally important to MTV's success, founder Bob Pittman decided he had to build not only a channel but a sensibility. With that in mind, the network tried to create an "environment"—a "channel with no programs, no beginning, no middle, no end." "We understood that music videos were program elements, not complete programs by themselves," Pittman once wrote. "MTV was the program." A similar approach would come to distinguish other cable networks owned by the parent company—sister VH-1, which played videos for older viewers, and Nickelodeon, which replayed old TV series for baby boomers in prime time, and original programming for their kids during the day. "In every case," one MTV chairman said, "we try to make the audience associate with the network first, the shows second." To the extent that this notion succeeded, it would be said that the first generation of TV viewers watched individual programs, while the second generation watched networks or just television.

MTV debuted on August 1, 1981, with the voice-over announcement "Ladies and gentlemen—rock and roll!" followed by a prophetic video by the Buggles, "Video Killed the Radio Star." Within just three years the network was profitable—the good fortune helped considerably by record companies which supplied the videos for free because of the way they boosted sales. Thanks, in part, to the Dire Straits song "Money for Nothing," the saying "I want my MTV" became an international battle cry. By 1984, MTV had become the highest-rated basic cable network, with a 1.1 rating—though this was still in the early days of cable, when only about one in five homes was wired for the service. And that translated into little more than 160,000 homes at any one time.

As critic John Leland once wrote, perhaps MTV offered the first type of TV programming that hadn't been adapted from radio, the stage, or the movies—though playing a series of songs every hour was a format straight out of the radio playbook. Yet, within months, MTV was rescuing a moribund recording industry, even while rearranging the elements that had traditionally led to pop stardom. In the new universe of visual sensation, such rock acts as Duran Duran and Madonna flourished—as did others who were photogenic or produced flashy themes that could be illustrated easily. Meanwhile, critics charged that MTV both regularly shortchanged black artists and often displayed videos notorious for their violence and misogyny.

By 1983, MTV was already influencing movie-making: Much of the popular *Flashdance* was little more than a dance video at greater length. Still, even though MTV had an immediate effect on both rock and movies, its influence on television programming was subtler. Those initially drawn to its style were advertisers—no surprise, perhaps, since MTV was a network devoted solely to running a form of 24-hour-a-day commercials. *Washington Post* critic Tom Shales was not alone in noticing how, as a purely *commercial* network, the MTV zeitgeist celebrated "conspicuous consumption nonstop." "Words and phrases like 'commercialize,' 'selling out' and 'the establishment' seem irrelevant in the context of an MTV culture," he wrote in 1985.

The videos' use of rock music, quick cuts, hand-held cameras, art-film techniques, and outrageous visuals also appealed to advertisers. By harnessing the rock culture visually, these techniques gave products a youthful patina and sensibility—equally sought-after attributes in a culture that worships adolescence. If advertising could become indistinguishable from programming (as it often did on MTV), it could also help eliminate the new problem of "zapping"—viewer manipulation of remote-control devices which allowed those viewers to switch away from commercials and over to other networks.

The style of MTV also elevated feeling and sensation over thought—one reason why rock critic Greil Marcus would label the process "semiotic pornography." "The art of montage has changed both the way we look at things and the way we hear things," MTV host Kurt Loder once told a reporter. "You can deliver pure sensation and dispense with narrative." In that world of "pure sensation," advertisers wield more-than-average persuasive power, since if consumers actually think about whether they need another product, the game is lost. It recalls what Pittman once told a writer about his channel. "The strongest appeal you make is emotional," he said. "MTV fits in with all of this because music deals with mood, not continuity or plot."

By 1984, political observers were already noting how commercials for Ronald Reagan's reelection were "short on story and substantive message and long on quick bursts of sight and sound stimulation." "They don't call on the viewers to think deeply, just to rock along with their images," wrote Ferrel Guillory. That sensibility, political scientist Benjamin Barber would later argue, is "not good for the kind of deliberative consensus-building and the arbitration of differences that democracy is about." To which a popular video of the time might reply, "Beat It."

In commercial television, ads are often the tail that wags the programming dog, if only so those ads won't clash with the shows. So the MTV style came to network television too, whether the masses liked it or not. In the same autumn that those Reagan ads appeared, a new show premiered on NBC: *Miami Vice*. Described as "MTV Cops" be-

fore the show actually had a name, *Miami Vice* took the traditional police show and turned it into a kind of weekly hour-long rock video
replete with musical sound track, jagged narrative, emphasis on stylized violence, and sharp visuals. "No earth tones," said creator Michael
Mann, when asked what made his show distinctive. Leads Don Johnson and Phillip Michael Thomas even exchanged the old police uniform for expensive Italian designer outfits: unstructured jackets worn
over T-shirts and pleated pants. "[W]here did they get the clothes—
and the boat and the Ferrari—on cop pay?" asked the literal critic
John Leonard. Within months the style was being imitated on everything from other cop shows like *Hollywood Beat* to a new CBS news
show, *West 57th,* which tried to merge the sensibilities of *60 Minutes*
and *Miami Vice* in a hip news show for younger viewers that one network wag labeled "yup to the minute."

As ads had followed MTV in becoming more experimental, visually
appealing, and accelerated, so too did TV programming. Shows like
Moonlighting tried out (and wore out) rapid-fire dialogue impossible to
catch on a first viewing, and also shot several segments in black and
white. From *Peewee's Playhouse,* a kids' show that used special effects, to
Late Night With David Letterman and its camera tricks, television now
seemed infused with the MTV sensibility. Longer shows with one continuous plot seemed to lose popularity too, in favor of dramas like *L.A.
Law*—which stayed with one plot for only a few minutes before
switching to another. (Compare *L.A. Law* to its predecessor, the detail-
oriented *Perry Mason.*) Even a show like *thirtysomething* exhibited the
trend to diminution of plot (try to describe in more than one sentence
what happened on any single episode), relying instead on flashbacks
and character development to create a feeling.

By increasing the viewer's craving for visual stimulation, MTV was
also part of a process which helped create tabloid television. *Hard
Copy* and *Inside Edition*—with their emphases on emotion, celebrities,
and blood-and-guts reporting—were the logical culmination of an
MTV-inspired approach to news. MTV also helped blur the line between programming and advertising, which led eventually to the popularity of the Home Shopping Network and "infomercials," if not to
a much stronger ethic of consumption across the nation.

Because this was an age in which image would become as impor-

tant as song in marketing records, MTV's emergence would also mark
the triumph of simulation over reality, though that transformation had
been inevitable ever since television hit the scene—as any student of
the quiz scandals or the rise of the Monkees knows. It is no coincidence that our first MTV-era president, Ronald Reagan, was fond of
telling audiences stories of how he had helped liberate concentration
camps at the end of World War II, when his only experience with a
Dachau or Treblinka was sitting in a darkened room watching movies
of those events. "You believed in it because you wanted to believe it,"
Reagan once told a reporter who thought he had seen Reagan on the
set of a movie which didn't feature him at all. "There's nothing wrong
with that. I do it all the time."

Yet the problem would eventually go well beyond the entertainment industry and Reagan himself. Take the matter of "ghosting."
Everyone now casually accepts the fact that most politicians and business leaders don't write their speeches, many judges don't write their
opinions, and many professors have students write their research
tomes. Half the books on the best-seller nonfiction list are ghostwrit-
ten. Yet few people ask: Are these works *real*? If her "music" cannot be
reproduced on stage, who is Madonna? If his lines are mostly written
by joke writers, who is Letterman? Was Ronald Reagan president, or
only playing the role? In an environment in which no one knows
what to believe, *anything* is believable, just as long as you believe
strongly enough.

The irony, of course, is that the MTV style was never particularly
popular: This was one change in the teleculture that was not democratic. Most of the shows that aped MTV— *Miami Vice, West 57th,* and even
Letterman's—were far more popular with the avant-garde critics in
New York than they were with the masses. By the early 1990s, the real
story at MTV was how the network was becoming more like the rest of
television, not the other way around. The parade of videos had become,
in one critic's words, "the most electrifying bore on television."

In fact, by the nineties even the seamless, programless format had
been scrapped on MTV to make way for news broadcasts with Tabitha
Soren, shopping shows, *Beavis and Butt-Head,* game shows, and soap
operas. By 1995, two-thirds of MTV's prime-time programming no
longer even directly concerned music, and its highest-rated shows

were *Road Rules,* a soap, and *Singled Out,* a dating show. What's more, the hour-long drama show, declared dead five years earlier by all the critics who said audiences would no longer sit still because of the changes MTV had inspired, suddenly underwent a renaissance, as shows such as *ER* and *NYPD Blue* soared in the ratings. TV is tougher to change than it looks to be.

Nevertheless, as cable television grew in influence, and channel grazing became a way of life, the quick cuts and other attributes of the MTV style remained—if not as much in programming, then in the hands of viewers themselves. "What is cable TV for," *New York Times* columnist Russell Baker had once asked, "if you don't keep changing the channels?" The remote-control device had existed since 1955, but before there were all these choices in cable America, it didn't have a true function. As a scholar would point out, channel surfing in the nineties became "a way of making up your own mosaic of images"— a kind of nightly, self-made MTV video. "In America," Huey Long had once said, "every man a king." Now, in the post-MTV era, it's every man an auteur.

49

Bob Newhart as the Embodiment of TV Culture
(CBS: 1972–78; 1982–90; 1992–93)

In our culture, the hyped and sensational get special attention: Witness the O. J. Simpson case. Because they watch so much television, critics tend to be attracted to the unusual—the appearance of *Twin Peaks* and the near-breakup of Paul and Jamie on *Mad About You*. On television, however, the leads who reappear year after year without anyone's even noticing are frequently the most revealing and significant—people like Michael Landon, Andy Griffith, Bill Cosby, and James Garner. At the top of that list is Bob Newhart.

True, Newhart has received a few favorable notices over the years.

By and large, however, he has been ignored. His shows never make anyone's "Top Ten." Anthologies of television scarcely mention him. Even when he was on, few people ever came into work and asked, "Hey, did you see Bob Newhart last night?"

Everyone seemed to watch him, however, and almost everyone liked him. In a culture in which no one seems to last much longer than Andy Warhol's now proverbial 15 minutes, this high priest of blandness survived for over 30 years. From his comedy routines previously recorded on "The Button-Down Mind of Bob Newhart" and an unsuccessful stint as a TV variety host in the 1960s; to MTM's *The Bob Newhart Show,* which followed *The Mary Tyler Moore Show* on the Saturday night schedule in the 1970s; to simply *Newhart* in the 1980s; to his less-successful and even more simply titled *Bob* in the 1990s, Newhart mostly endured and prospered. Sure, he was cast as a psychologist from 1972 to 1978, an innkeeper from 1982 to 1990, and a cartoonist in 1992 and 1993. What he really just kept portraying, however, was the same bemused, ironic, and somewhat boring embodiment of conventionality he played so well for so long.

What was Newhart's secret, and what does it tell us about America? A lot of his appeal obviously lay in his grayness. Because television comes into our homes, the personalities who tend to last on the medium are those who keep it extremely understated. An evening with Dennis Miller or any character from *The X-Files* might be OK for most Americans occasionally. But every week for a year? A decade? Like Garry Moore, Hugh Downs, and Lawrence Welk, Newhart lasted because he was so moderate that he was reassuring over inordinately long periods of time.

There was more to Newhart's popularity than simple blandness, however; otherwise, everyone's accountant would be a television star. As critic Michael Pollan once noted, Newhart's character also told us how to react to outrageousness. The persona he perfected over three decades—the straight man good-humoredly putting up with the crazies in an asylum called the world—played to his comedic strength, which was the slow reaction. His style was peculiarly suited to television because of the subtle facial expressions which could be caught by a camera. Contrast Newhart's manner, for example, with his antithesis, Milton Berle: understated vs. outrageous, laconic vs. voluble, suburban vs. urban.

Critics such as Harry Castleman and Walter Podrazik have also written how the roles of a psychologist and an innkeeper fit Newhart's persona perfectly because they put him in a position where he had to listen—and respond—to weirdness. Both shows featured strong supporting casts: Newhart's neurotic patients of the first show became the nutty townspeople (like the two Darryls and the compulsive liar who owns a nearby cafe) of the second. In fact, most of us see ourselves to be a lot like Newhart—getting by in an increasingly complex culture in which our co-workers, relatives, and elected representatives often seem to have lost their minds. Newhart responded to all that disorder in ways in which most of us would like to see ourselves reacting. Like all great popular art, Newhart provided a window into his audience—or at least into its aspirations.

Newhart's daily TV existence was also one with which most Americans could identify. What little did happen on these shows often seemed oddly interchangeable: The Minuteman Cafe got sold, Michael and Stephanie continued their self-centered courtship, Howard dropped by from the apartment next door. In fact, the two shows were so similar that in the classic final episode of his second sitcom in 1990, Newhart revealed he was still the psychologist from the first show and had simply dreamt up this second series about an innkeeper. Yet that focus on the mundane was realistic: Not much extraordinary happens in the daily lives of most viewers, either.

Newhart also told us something, believe it or not, about our leaders. Because politics is presented to the public almost exclusively over television, it conforms to TV's entertainment dictates. In today's world, we all know that summits are presented as miniseries, and the presidency as a television drama lasting four years. It's true that ideology still counts more than personality, and it's also true that our leaders don't have to be TV stars like Ronald Reagan. Yet they can't clash with the culture of television either, if only because TV *is* America.

Simply put, if you take most of the recent Republican presidents—Dwight Eisenhower, Gerald Ford, Reagan, even the George Bush of 1988—and put them in Newhart's backyard for a barbecue, you can imagine everyone's hitting it off and having a pretty good time. But take a similar group of Democrats—Mike Dukakis, Walter Mondale, Jimmy Carter, even Mario Cuomo—and, well, you get the idea. The "button-down" Jack Kennedy was the last Democratic nominee who understood Bob Newhart before Bill Clinton came along.

There's a lesson in all this. Commentators may deplore our political and cultural preferences, but the American electorate has almost always wanted its leaders to be situated comfortably within the center of American culture. Leaders must embody, as media critic Mark Crispin Miller once put it, "that perfect averageness which is American."

From 1968 to 1992, national Republicans did a better job than their Democratic counterparts in understanding this truth. We always liked Newhart. Which, in many ways, is why we so often end up with the leaders we do.

50

Entertainment Tonight and the Expansion of the Tabloid, Celebrity Culture

(SYNDICATION: 1981–PRESENT)

On September 14, 1981, at the dawn of the Reagan era, a new syndicated news show which critics called "the $22 million gamble" hit the airwaves. The first story covered was the Emmy Awards. That was followed by interviews with Burt Reynolds, Lana Turner, and Richard Chamberlain. "It's sad to lose, but afterwards it doesn't really matter anymore," Chamberlain said.

A success had been launched, at least in commercial terms. Over the years, *Entertainment Tonight,* or *ET* as it's affectionately called, has nightly plumbed the heights of celebrity and show-business gossip, covering an average of 12 Hollywood Walk of Fame ceremonies, 17 awards ceremonies, and 27 celebrity obituaries a year. At last count, Arnold Schwarzenegger had been interviewed over 200 times, and Shirley MacLaine more than 150.

This is the show that made the world safe for anchors Mary Hart and John Tesh—who left in 1996 to pursue his New Age music career. Never have so many (a staff of almost 200) talked so much (at last count to 179 stations covering 95 percent of this nation, and 17 foreign countries) about so little. *ET,* wrote the *Los Angeles Times'* Howard Rosenberg, "excels at the say-nothing interview," and "seems never to have met a film it didn't like or a story it couldn't transform into a flesh market." This was a "news" show on Prozac: Everything was repackaged as something relentlessly upbeat.

ET didn't create the culture that blurred the distinctions between politics and show business, or gossip and news, as anyone who ever listened to Walter Winchell more than 50 years ago knows. As early as 1952, *Today* was pioneering television's attempts to merge the worlds of news and entertainment, and *People* magazine did the same on the print side later. *ET* helped accelerate these changes, however—and, if nothing else, made the world safe for celebrity birthdays. (The show has almost 4,000 on file!) Indeed the practice of reporting box-office gross and ratings winners—now done even by the *New York Times*—was popularized by this show.

ET was the ultimate in the triumph of TV style over substance: The show did all this while presenting itself as if it were the *CBS Evening News,* complete with anchors and reports from the field which sounded and looked like news. Yet it wasn't—at least until the *CBS Evening News* began to imitate *ET* and the other tabloid shows that were this show's mirror image, with its own reports about celebrity scandals and the like. *ET* also helped change the look of news on the networks with its high-tech graphics of split screens, spin frames, animation, charts, and inserts. Bill Moyers once complained of his stint with CBS: "In meeting after meeting, *Entertainment Tonight* was touted as the model—breezy, entertaining, undemanding. . . . Instead of . . . gathering, weighing, sorting and explaining the flux of events and issues, we began to be influenced by the desire first to please the audience." The theorist Neil Postman once wrote:

> Whereas television taught the magazines that news is nothing but entertainment, the magazines have taught television that nothing but entertainment is news. Television programs, such as

"Entertainment Tonight," turn information about entertainers and celebrities into "serious" cultural content, so that the circle begins to close: Both the form and content of news becomes entertainment.

The relentlessly upbeat style of *Entertainment Tonight* also became the model for much of television news, especially on local stations. "I'm not saying that *Entertainment Tonight* is directly responsible for this," cultural analyst Mark Crispin Miller once told a reporter. "But I will say that people are so habituated to a certain level of hysterical cheer, so habituated to a constant stream of happy endings, that it has become harder and harder than ever for them to tolerate any downbeat or discouraging reports or images." After *ET* became popular, with nightly ratings that virtually equaled any of the network newscasts, it became *de rigueur* for local news stations to hire their own entertainment "reporters," whose job was to deliver similar flattering celebrity profiles and puffball reviews.

The inevitable string of clones followed: Fox's *Entertainment Daily Journal,* eventually an entire network, E!, devoted just to entertainment hype. (E!, a writer once said, is like "a science-fiction movie in which a Hollywood publicist takes over your brain.") Once *ET* showed how "news" could be repackaged as a salable syndicatable commodity, more tabloid shows, such as *A Current Affair* and *Inside Edition,* rushed in to help broaden (and often pollute) the definition of news throughout the medium.

An *ET* reporter was once quoted as saying that, in the beginning, *Entertainment Tonight* was supposed to be more like a traditional news broadcast. "But then," the source said, "the research showed that if you want more people to watch, you've got to program what they want, and research revealed that viewers were more interested in celebrity coverage than in hard news." Over the years, that puffy celebrity coverage has been the *ET* claim to fame—or black mark, given your opinion of a program which has been defined as a press agent's dream. "[T]he show has dropped almost all pretense of being anything but an arm of the Hollywood publicity machine," Richard Zoglin wrote in *Time* in 1994. The show seems to feature an odd emphasis on health matters—perhaps because, in the kingdom of Hollywood, no one is supposed to grow old. The *Entertainment Tonight* segments that are said to have attracted the most mail are Elizabeth Taylor's hip surgery, Michael Landon's announcement that he had pancreatic cancer, Jim Nabors' need for a liver donor, and the word that Bill Bixby had prostate cancer.

The line between celebrity-reporter and celebrity-subject on this show is so exceedingly gray that *ET* once did a piece on coanchor Mary Hart's new album of lullabies. (Hart's other claim to fame is that the *New England Journal of Medicine* once reported that the sound of her voice was triggering epileptic seizures in a viewer.) Of course, there is more to such an obsequious attitude toward celebrity than just pleasing the audience, as the research demands: *Entertainment Tonight* is owned by Paramount, which is in the entertainment business that this show endlessly promotes.

ET wouldn't have been possible until the 1980s, when satellite technology made it possible for local stations easily to receive quick feeds of syndicated shows sold to stations independently by huge production companies. Like *Wheel of Fortune* and *Jeopardy!* (two other eighties success stories), the show was also aided by FCC rules which effectively prevented the networks from beginning their prime-time broadcasts until 8:00 P.M. The thought was that this would eventually encourage local stations to produce their own shows.

Instead, beginning in the eighties, many local stations turned to this show, as well as to tabloid news shows earlier in the afternoon, like *A Current Affair* (premiering in 1987), *Inside Edition* (premiering in 1988), and *Hard Copy* (premiering in 1989). All three of these other "news" shows offered a smattering of the same celebrity gossip as *Entertainment Tonight,* but focused instead on the seamier side of fame— particularly if it involved sex—and sensational crime stories reminiscent of the New York tabloids and the *National Enquirer.* "It's the evening news without all those boring stories from foreign countries," wrote *Entertainment Weekly*'s Bruce Fretts about *Hard Copy,* which assigned 30 staffers to cover the O. J. Simpson murder case.

The ratings of these syndicated "Tabloid Three" would soon rival the traditional newscasts for the three networks, which then took the predictable step of beginning to ape the tabloids to win over their audience. *Inside Edition* did a special interview with Tonya Harding, and

CBS's Connie Chung followed just days later. *Hard Copy* got a scoop on alleged molestation charges against Michael Jackson, and the reporter then appeared on the *CBS Morning News*. In 1993, for the first time, news about the entertainment industry and its stars became among the Top Ten most heavily reported subjects on the evening newscasts of all of the three major networks.

If *ET* was overly saccharine, then *A Current Affair, Hard Copy,* and *Inside Edition* frequently offered up a nightly dose of acid—which is why TV analyst Ron Powers once called these shows and *ET* "two halves of the same whole." "We are a fearful, angry nation," he once said. "So [on tabloid shows] we demonize a culture we have allowed to spring up, while at the same time, I think the country takes refuge in celebrity worship. It's withdrawal into two complementary, mutually reinforcing forms of fantasy." These scrappy news shows, which wore their tabloid populism on their sleeves and appealed to a working-class audience, came to do so well in the ratings that *Entertainment Tonight* eventually hired away Linda Bell Blue of *Hard Copy* to produce its show—a move soon reflected in innovations like the upbeat *ET* viewer poll on whether South Carolina child-murderer Susan Smith should be executed. The characterization of news on *Entertainment Tonight* was merging with the downbeat ethos of the tabloids to offer a truly alternative vision of national "journalism"—a sharp, raffish contrast to the way in which Walter Cronkite and his cohorts had once defined it.

All of these syndicated "news" shows were the outgrowth of a renewed emphasis on gossip and scandal throughout the news which began to flourish in the 1980s when a former Hollywood actor became president. After a while, it became hard to tell where the entertainment news about Hugh Grant stopped and the political news about Bill Clinton and Paula Jones or Gennifer Flowers began. Part of the reason for the focus on sexual scandal was—for lack of a better term—the pornographication of American culture. Frankness is one thing, but beginning in the eighties, Americans could now routinely find in their VCR stores the kind of sexual exhibitionism they had to travel to Times Square to view in earlier decades. Throughout the culture, standards for public discourse—and news—thus widened considerably.

Part of the increased exposure to gossip was also due, oddly, to the transformation of a slogan from the sixties: "The personal is political." In the 1960s, that credo was intended to mean, broadly, that how people choose to live and work is a political statement. In the years following, however, the motto came to stand for the privacy-eroding proposition that the public had a right to know even the most private details of both a politician's and an entertainer's life.

The feminization of American culture—through the women's movement—also had the unintended effect of broadening the acceptability of gossip news. In her bestselling *You Just Don't Understand*, linguist Deborah Tannen wrote that what has traditionally been labeled as gossip by men is often a positive way in which women discuss the world in order to understand and build relationships. As women have gained power, this private phenomenon has become a more accepted public form, though it is far more destructive in the hands of journalists (caustic cynics by professional nature) than in those of two people talking over coffee.

Before he died, Republican strategist Lee Atwater also offered another theory as to why crime and scandal news could now infatuate the public more than ever. "Bull permeates everything," he said. "In other words, my theory is that the American people think politics and politicians are full of baloney. They think the media and journalists are full of baloney. They think big business is full of baloney." In this atmosphere, crime and gossip news are appealing because they purport to show viewers something authentic and spontaneous. If voters think that all candidates are packaged by consultants, and stars by publicists, stories about drug use or sexual liaisons reveal those shielded celebrities in unrehearsed moments. In an age of hype and fabrication, the tabloid shows purported to offer reality.

As Alexis de Tocqueville noted long ago, Americans have always been drawn to gossip—the better to demonstrate why the famous are no better than anyone else. If "No man is a hero to his valet," it is not surprising that, in an egalitarian country which glorifies the common man and woman, everyone becomes a kind of valet. The flip side of that sentiment, however, is that a culture needs leaders to set standards and build aspirations. Gossip—even the positive kind about Hollywood celebrities—ultimately erodes trust in figures we once admired.

"The celebrity media cater to a double impulse—to admire and to envy the famous," USC professor Leo Braudy once said. Thus what these shows built up, they soon destroyed, as *Entertainment Tonight* produced the admiration, and the *Hard Copy* types supplied the envy. And, in each case, they obscured the definition of real achievement. Daniel Boorstin got it right: Once upon a time, American society had heroes. Now, it just has celebrities.

51

The Forgotten Promise of *The Cosby Show*
(NBC: 1984–92)

It's always seemed a bit odd that *The Cosby Show* was *the* sitcom of the conservative 1980s. For four of its eight seasons on the air, it was rated Number 1—placing it with *Gunsmoke* and *All in the Family* as one of the most popular shows of all time. In the ratings, it swept every demographic, age, and racial group, and it appealed to audiences in foreign locales as unlikely as pre-Mandela South Africa.

Bill Cosby was not the first black performer to hit it big in popular culture. It's true the 1950s and early 1960s were a time of notorious racism on the small screen: *The Amos and Andy Show,* the old stereotyped radio carryover, was a hit, and Nat "King" Cole had his variety show cancelled by NBC after a year because it couldn't attract a sponsor. Yet, while TV has hardly been an equal playing field, since the mid-1960s likable and heroic black stars were appearing regularly on the small screen, appealing to largely white audiences on everything from *Julia, The Mod Squad,* and *Star Trek* to *The Jeffersons, Sanford and Son,* and *Roots.*

Cosby, however, was in a different universe altogether. In some key ways, he was similar to Lucille Ball. Like Lucy 30 years earlier, Cosby tried to remake the situation comedy so it could reflect his unique-to-television comic persona. In her case, the uniqueness flowed partly from gender; in his, from race. Like Lucy, Cosby was phenomenally successful in selling that vision to the masses. Once he left the air, Cosby also found—like Lucy—that, despite comedian Fred Allen's observation that "imitation is the sincerest form of television," the road was soon closed to others like him to repeat his success.

However, an important difference between the experiences of Lucy and Cosby began to emerge in the years after *The Cosby Show* left prime time in 1992 for syndication. Whereas *I Love Lucy* became a television icon virtually from the moment it stopped production (and remains one today), *The Cosby Show* has done a slow fade in influence from the pop-culture scene. The major reason? Beginning with the Clarence Thomas-Anita Hill confrontation in 1991, the 1992 L.A. riots that struck on the night of the last episode of *The Cosby Show,* and on through the O. J. Simpson trials, a very different set of TV images conspired to obliterate the ones that Cosby had cultivated—rendering his obsolete, at least in the eyes of the white viewing audience.

Before this show premiered in the fall of 1984, Cosby had already been a television semiregular for two decades. Yet, throughout his earlier career, Cosby had displayed little evidence that he would eventually produce one of the more celebrated shows in television history. Cosby had started out in show business as a stand-up comedian in the 1960s, which is when his steadfast refusal to do explicitly racial humor drew fire from his more liberal critics—as it successively would. Cosby was known for his long, humorous stories that usually centered on childhood—though his most celebrated routine concerned a conversation that Noah allegedly had with God, about building an ark. (When God approaches him, Noah asks, "Am I on *Candid Camera?*") In 1965, Cosby was paired with Robert Culp on the espionage series *I Spy*—a mostly forgettable show except for Cosby, the first black to have a regular starring role on television. He went on to win three consecutive Emmy Awards for his portrayal of a wisecracking Rhodes scholar spy, masquerading as a tennis pro.

After that role, along with regular stints on *The Tonight Show* and a few specials, Cosby starred in *The Bill Cosby Show,* a 1969-71 Sunday-night NBC series which went up against Ed Sullivan. On this show, Cosby played a middle-class high-school gym teacher, and the critical reaction thereto was mixed—as some again charged Cosby with a responsibility to do shows with more explicit racial themes. He's "easy-going, likable, and at times too farcical to be true," wrote one critic in the *New York Times.* "He's everybody's friend, usually all the time."

Though Cosby did develop one interesting Saturday-morning cartoon in the seventies (*Fat Albert and the Cosby Kids*), his television and cinematic forays in that decade were forgettable. At the movies, there were films like *Hickey and Boggs* and *Mother, Jugs and Speed*—neither one on anyone's list of the top 10,000 of all time. On television, *The New Bill Cosby Show* (1972-73) and *Cos* (1976), both comedy-variety shows, bombed. Cosby then approached the networks with an idea for a detective show "without violence," and the networks politely took a pass. Only in the realm of pitchman was Cosby anything like a national icon, as his commercials for products like Jell-O, Coca-Cola, and Ford caught on. Cosby himself would one day say, "I think my popularity came from doing solid 30-second commercials. They can cause people to love you and see more of you than in a full 30-minute show.

In the early 1980s, when Cosby came up with the idea of *The Cosby Show,* a sitcom about a professional black family living in New York, many in the television industry were in no mood to listen. ABC turned the project down cold. The problem wasn't either Cosby's string of nonhits, or his race: After all, *Roots* had hit it big in the seventies, as had a variety series like *The Flip Wilson Show.* It's that sitcoms themselves were out of favor. In 1983, the year before *The Cosby Show* premiered, only one of the Top 13 shows, *Kate & Allie,* was a comedy.

Television sitcoms had seemingly hit a dead end. First, the "comedies" that tended to be in vogue then were the so-called "laughterless" sitcoms, following *M*A*S*H,* which weren't really comedies in the traditional sense. Second, the "relevant" sitcoms of the 1970s, like *All in the Family* and *The Mary Tyler Moore Show,* were hardly a model any longer because they presented either too much conflict or liberal content for a country now rushing headlong into the conservative nostalgia of the Reagan years. Finally, the Beaveresque "family" sitcom had fallen on hard times years earlier, because the traditional family on which it was based was splintering—with divorce rates rising and women growing more independent. That's one reason why sitcoms after the early sixties often took refuge in the workplace, on a desert island, or in the odd convention that one parent—usually a father, as in *My Three Sons* or *Diff'rent Strokes*—raised the children himself. That, of course, was hardly the way it was in the real world, where nearly six times as many single households were headed by women as men, and things weren't nearly as hunky-dory as they might have appeared in the Douglas household.

Part of Cosby's genius was to capitalize on America's yearning for the recent past by designing a sitcom set in the present that felt like a 1950s show because it dared to present a traditional family with traditional values. Yet Cosby, this show's star and creator, put together something far more innovative than just a revival of old formulas from the fifties. This series concerned the family life of a working couple (Cliff Huxtable was a doctor, and his wife was a lawyer), meaning that it was one of the first shows on television to approximate—albeit in an idealized way—the lives of much of the viewing audience. What *The Mary Tyler Moore Show* did for single women, this show did for professional couples, at least ones with very high incomes.

This was also a series presented from the parents' viewpoint—a notable shift from the zeitgeist of the fifties, but one more in keeping with the attitudes of the huge baby-boom audience that was now raising kids and suddenly thought better of adult supremacy. On the first episode, Cliff's son Theo says he doesn't want a career. "Dad," he asks, "can't you just accept me and love me 'cause I'm your son?" "That's the dumbest thing I've ever heard!" Cliff answers.

As critics would notice almost immediately, Cosby's character took a somewhat jaundiced view of the joys of parenting. "Why did we have four children?" Mrs. Huxtable asks Cliff as he returns home from work one day. "Because we did not want to have five," he answers. (Ironically, a fifth child joined the show later that season.) "The Cosby Show has amazingly little feel for—or even much interest in—the concerns of children," wrote Richard Zoglin in *Time* in 1985. Yet the show still took a loving view of family life, in contrast to shows like *Married . . . With Children,* which would follow.

The Cosby Show was also innovative in its focus on what critic Harry Waters would call "small moments," replicating the old 1950s formula of designing a sitcom where laughs took a distinct back seat to a "moral." Forsaking the easy slapstick laughs of most sitcoms, the focus on character of *The Mary Tyler Moore Show,* and the social comedy of *The Beverly Hillbillies, The Cosby Show* dealt with the kind of everyday incidents that really make up people's lives—a child being frightened by a scary movie, singing songs in the living room, and so on. Like the creators of *Leave It to Beaver,* Cosby was known for taking incidents with his own children—how to deal with a dead goldfish, practicing the clarinet—and weaving them into the show. John Markus and Matt Williams, two writers for the show, said Cosby had two rules which struck them as odd at first: No conflict, and no jokes. "Make it real," Markus would later say. "Then make it funny." If the show frequently wasn't memorable, it was because it often didn't give viewers much to remember. By taking sitcoms in the direction of everydayness, however, Cosby pointed the way for a show like *Seinfeld*—which took the art of portraying "nothing" to new heights.

Even though *The Cosby Show* wasn't particularly hilarious, however, it did help revive the situation comedy on television. Within three years of its premiere, seven of the Top Ten shows on TV were sitcoms—a remarkable turnaround. That turned out to be a key transformation in the entertainment life of the nation. Sitcoms revolve around likable characters surrounded by lovable families—whether those families are traditional nuclear units or a group of patrons in a bar. By contrast, drama shows, though usually conservative in tone, often revolve around law enforcement, and thus reinforce positive attitudes about a public entity. In the eighties' swing to "family values" and privatization, *The Cosby Show* was an unwitting catalyst.

Most sitcoms are also funny. In a country where comedy was becoming one of the predominant forms of political dialogue and cultural introspection—an eighties trend displayed in everything from the growth of comedy clubs and cable comedy channels to the importance placed on the Top Ten list of Letterman or the monologue of *The Tonight Show*— *The Cosby Show* was, again, something of an unintentional stimulus.

Obviously, race was also a key ingredient in this program's appeal and importance. One has only to picture what the same series would look like with a white family—and what the tepid reaction would have been—to realize that the show's blackness is what gave the whole thing its cutting edge, its impact, and ultimately its audience. Yet the show's ostensible themes were generally about other things with admittedly broader appeal.

That bothered a lot of people. Critics often attacked *The Cosby Show* for portraying blacks as too much like whites. *The Cosby Show* was Boyz II Men, not 2 Live Crew; Colin Powell, not Jesse Jackson. By weaving a social reality that was relentlessly upbeat and relatively apolitical, this show did become something of a complement to the Reagan-Bush years. Cosby once told a reporter:

> It would have been wonderful if I had been able to bring on children in the family who had drug problems and make that funny, or had a daughter get pregnant out of wedlock and make that funny, or have had Dr. Huxtable having two or three nurses on the side and make adultery funny. But I just could not deal with the humor in those situations.

Yet by doing his show and making it so successful, Cosby was a kind of racial trailblazer. What *The Cosby Show* gave blacks was the freedom to be apolitical, just like most Americans. By implication, the series also told viewers that you don't have to be white to be upper-middle class and acquisitive, and to have a stable family. Those may seem like truisms today, hence the show's occasionally dated quality—but even in the mid-eighties, rest assured that they were not. From 1955 to 1986, for example, the Center for Media and Public Affairs found, in a random survey of TV programming, that 94 percent of the white characters were educated professionals; 50 percent of the blacks on TV were high-school dropouts.

Thus, as this show approached its 198th and penultimate episode in May 1992, the general feeling was that racial attitudes in the culture were maturing—and that Cosby had played a role in that evolution. "This is the 'Cosby' decade. America loves black people," one character says to another in the movie *Soul Man*. Maybe it was a myth, but it was a myth that people believed—and myths can move mountains.

Then came the L.A. riots on the night of Cosby's last show. L.A. Mayor Tom Bradley plaintively pleaded with his constituents to "observe the curfew and watch the Cosby Show." Two years later, there was the O. J. Simpson arrest and trial, which drove blacks and whites more apart, and further shattered interest in a sitcom highlighting their commonality. While the networks—especially the new UPN and WB challengers—would introduce a number of series by and about blacks in the wake of the success of *The Cosby Show,* it soon became apparent that not enough whites would watch to make them successful.

In fact, by the mid-1990s, demographers would note that the list of weekly Top Ten TV shows for black viewers was often completely different from the list for whites. Not even a new sitcom starring Cosby himself, premiering in the fall of 1996 on CBS, could change the pattern, as that show fell out of the Top Ten several weeks after its premiere. To paraphrase the 1968 Kerner Commission: Two nations—two viewing patterns. Thus *The Cosby Show,* a healing, inclusive program which had appealed to everyone, became an increasing anachronism, as societal events, including the tragic murder of Cosby's own son Ennis, overwhelmed its gentle optimism. *I Love Lucy* had turned out to be something of a harbinger of things to come. Sadly, no one believes that now about *The Cosby Show.*

52

The *Star Trek* Galaxy and Its Glimpse of TV's Future
(NBC: 1966–69; SYNDICATION: 1987–94; SYNDICATION: 1993–PRESENT; UPN: 1995–PRESENT)

In a popular culture where little seems to glimmer longer than a few seasons at best, *Star Trek* has lived long and prospered. The lexicon and sayings of the show are now part of the language, as in "Beam me up, Scottie," and "He's dead, Jim." The opening of the original *Star Trek* is among television's most quoted:

> Space, the final frontier
> These are the voyages of the Starship *Enterprise*
> Its five-year mission

To explore strange new worlds
To seek out new life and civilization   ,
To boldly go where no man has gone before!

Captain Kirk, Mr. Spock, and Dr. McCoy have long since become household names—not to mention Picard, Crusher, Riker, and Data. A 30-year-plus engagement as an international hit puts this show in the rarefied company of James Bond and Donald Duck as an icon with almost immutable appeal.

Even though the show flopped in its first go-around on NBC in the late 1960s, lasting only three years and 79 shows, by the mid-nineties one could add to those numbers 178 episodes of the syndicated sequel—*Star Trek: The Next Generation,* two other TV sequels (*Deep Space Nine* and *Star Trek: Voyager*), a cartoon series, eight movies grossing over $500 million, the most popular current paperback series in publishing, an estimated $2 billion in merchandise, and countless *Star Trek* conventions. Exploring television worlds its predecessor never dreamed of, *The Next Generation*—which lasted from 1987 to 1994, when it was retired to push a movie with the same crew—even became the highest-rated syndicated drama in the history of television, and one of the most popular shows of the early 1990s for men aged 18 to 49.

You don't have to be a Trekkie to know that the original series premiered on September 8, 1966, and was promptly panned by *Variety* as an "incredible and dreary mess." Or that the series, which originally ran Thursdays at 8:30 P.M., never placed higher than 52nd in the annual ratings because it was watched primarily by teenagers and children (especially boys). Or that the network originally wanted Spock's character off the show because they thought he looked so weird. (The response? "No ears, no pilot.") Or that Nichelle Nichols (Uhura) was planning to leave the series but was persuaded to remain by Martin Luther King, Jr. so she could be a role model to aspiring black actresses. Or that in the 30 years since the show premiered, *Star Trek* has been translated into almost 50 languages, televised in 40 countries, and is still shown more than 200 times a day nationally in syndication. It even prompted a United States space shuttle to be renamed the *Enterprise.*

By television standards, *Star Trek* was almost always quality drama, which helps explain why it is still one of the few TV series that appeal to people who also read. It was planned that way from the beginning, as creator Gene Roddenberry once recalled:

> [W]e had a concept meeting for every show. We sat down and said, "This is the kind of planet we're on; this is the history of the people; this is their level of technology. . . . How would the people act with the temperature and weather conditions of the planet—what would they wear?" We would get deeply into these things, and outsiders would come in and say, "What the hell are you people doing? You're supposed to be making a television show."

Under the tutelage of Rodenberry, a former Los Angeles policeman who had sold scripts to a number of TV shows over the years, including *Dragnet,* the series was notable—at least in its first two versions—for its strong ensemble cast, philosophical messages, and creative plots. After all, where else on TV could you watch a show about what to do with a spaceshipful of supermen in suspended animation?

Like most good science fiction, the show used the future as a metaphor to talk about the present. There was, for example, the episode in the original series wherein the crew confronted a race of aliens who were black on the right half of their bodies and white on the left, and hated those who were their mirror images. Or the episode "The City on the Edge of Forever," in which the crew went back in time to prevent McCoy from saving a woman (played by Joan Collins) with whom he had fallen in love, because interfering with history would allow the Nazis to win World War II. If these seem tame, remember that this all came during a period when television entertainment tended to *Gomer Pyle, U.S.M.C.* and *Hogan's Heroes*—shows hardly known for directly referencing reality, much less issues of the era such as the civil-rights movement and the Vietnam War.

The 1980s sequel had many of the same strong attributes as the original, down to the allegorical plots. Indeed, its very premiere had a deity-like figure named "Q" putting humanity on trial for its crimes. Yet this *Trek* featured an entirely new cast, and was allowed to change with the times. The crew explored space 78 years after the original crew did. The *Enterprise* got bigger. Picard was less authoritarian than Kirk. The show's original sixtyish New Frontier themes—fraught with earthly manifest destiny—were replaced by an eighties and nineties caution about the use of power. "If winning is not important," Worf once questioned, "then, Commander, why keep score?" Shows dealt with themes like environmentalism and the importance of family. Even the promise to boldly go where no *man* had gone before became where *no one* had gone before. One bit of tradition the Next Generation could have done without, however: The crew continued to look like it was wearing pajamas, indicating that there just might not be any good clothes designers in the future.

What accounts for the *Star Trek* phenomenon of initial mass indifference followed by decades of cult notoriety, which really heated up in the eighties? For starters, that pattern has been the fate of several similar TV series, such as *The Prisoner* and even *The Twilight Zone*. Science fiction tends to have a small but devoted following, centered particularly among upscale teenage boys and young men. That formula hardly guarantees enough viewers to ensure a hit on a medium like network television, which needs a mass audience to survive, and often turns out lowest-common-denominator programming as a result. That's why, until the nineties, network television never went in for science fiction in a big way, despite the cult popularity of *The Outer Limits* and even Boris Karloff's *Thriller* of the early 1960s.

The sci-fi formula, however, can lift a vehicle to triumph in a universe where intensity of following is almost as important as numbers—cable television, syndication, and the movies. If there are only 15 million Trekkies in America but they're all willing to watch the show at any hour on any station (and later to shell out $7 to see the cast at a local theater, and another $7 to buy the paperback), you've got a monster hit in TV syndication, a strong movie, a profitable book—but a network TV failure.

With the diminution of the networks in the face of cable competition, the narrow but intense appeal of *Star Trek* in the sixties thus turned out to be two decades ahead of its time. In the new, atomized age of multichannel cable and syndication, most programmers want "to seek out new life and civilization" of any sort, even if that audience is relatively small. Therefore, by the mid-1990s, the descendants of *Star Trek* would include a number of shows on the new Fox network—which made a decision to program for audiences younger than those attracted to the three established networks. Thus came new shows like *The X-Files*—a kind of tabloid, New Age version of the traditional sci-fi show; *The Simpsons;* and even such series as *Beverly Hills 90210,* which attempted to appeal to younger Star Trek-like fans and their female counterparts through something other than their brains. But, no matter: In the new postcable galaxy of television, there is now a place for diversity, for a few aliens, for shows about almost anything. In more ways than one, the *Star Trek* saga was a harbinger of things to come.

The series also had a cultural impact. With its progressive social themes and perfectly balanced multiracial cast (which led to television's first real interracial kiss between Kirk and Uhuru), *Star Trek* was politically correct even before anyone had invented the concept. Yet, as writers like *TV Guide's* Michael Logan would point out, *Star Trek* packaged these sentiments in a larger, typically American quest to conquer a frontier. The dilemmas and challenges that faced the crews were similar to the ones that had confronted our own pioneer forebears a century before. *Star Trek* was a kind of liberal, New Age Western: While its success may not have led Americans to continue their exploration of space, it did help sell the show's "PC vision" to the masses. Moreover, though it was usually unspoken on these shows, space exploration is a mission of collaborative world government (make that Big World Government), a double *bête noire* of the Right. In its own inimitable fashion, the permanence of *Star Trek* was a conservative's worst nightmare.

53
How *Roseanne* Made Trash TV Respectable
(ABC: 1988–97)

In the fall of 1988, prime-time TV was in an era of drift. Television drama no longer seemed capable of attracting mass audiences, and prominent critics were predicting it would never return in force to the tube. Yet it wasn't only that. The Number 1 rated series, *The Cosby Show*, was beginning to run out of gas, and most of the shows that followed it in the ratings—*A Different World*, *The Golden Girls*, *Who's the Boss?*, and *ALF* would never be confused with products from television's golden age.

In the midst of that drift (and of a television writers' strike which ended the 1987-88 season prematurely, and delayed the following season's opening until December), Mort Downey, Jr. and Geraldo Rivera helped fill the pop-culture vacuum. Their shows became known as the leaders of "trash TV"—a collection of cheaply produced daytime "video vérité" shows which attracted an audience primarily through the shock value of insulting guests and staging minibrawls. Rivera taped a show at a topless donut shop in Colorado; Downey once wrapped an American flag over his bottom and told an Iranian to kiss it. "Call us confrotainment," said one of Downey's associates.

It was in that context that *Roseanne* created such a sensation, going from Number 2 in its first season to the top slot a year later, where it drew an estimated 36 million viewers a week. Developed originally by the same team that assembled *The Cosby Show*, TV's biggest hit of the 1980s, the show superficially shared certain similarities with the sitcom it replaced at the top of the charts. Like *The Cosby Show*, *Roseanne* was a comedy about a family. And it starred a professional comedian who gave the show its name and focus.

There, however, the similarities ended: *Roseanne* was about a woman, not a man—TV's most celebrated Number 1 show about a woman since *I Love Lucy*. Whereas *The Cosby Show* was relentlessly upscale, *Roseanne* was about a working-class couple: Roseanne was a wisecracking married and harried mother, working first in a plastics factory, and later, successively as a waitress, a barmaid, and a beautician.

The show was also rather unrefined—based as it was on Roseanne Barr's nightclub routines which had focused on "the housewife from Hell." "She's got a personality as big as life" read the early PR copy for the show, "big mouth, big ideas, big, biting sense of humor, and big body to go with it all."

These attributes immediately led critics to call *Roseanne* the harbinger of a promising new shift in television. "Earthy, raw, and honest," is the way one typical reviewer described the show. "Her feminism has the grand vision, the expansive moral force of humanism," wrote another. In 1989, according to *Advertising Age,* Barr appeared on more magazine covers in one year than anyone else in history ever had; the *Wall Street Journal* called her "the human tabloid." Some scholars even found precursors of Roseanne in literary history, as the archetype of "the unruly woman." Years later, the tributes had hardly stopped. "Roseanne has redefined for female comedy the phallic aggression which is traditionally associated with male humor, whose totem, the Fool's sceptre, is actually the penis," wrote John Lahr in an idolizing 1995 *New Yorker* profile.

Television has changed so much, and Roseanne altered the show and herself so often over the years, that it is sometimes difficult to remember what made the series popular at first. For her part, Roseanne underwent more lifestyle and cosmetic changes than anyone else in pop culture (save Michael Jackson) as, in the most public of fashions imaginable, she married, divorced, remarried, fired writers, made confessions, grabbed her crotch while singing the National Anthem at a baseball game, guest-edited the *New Yorker,* got pregnant via *in vitro* treatments, disclosed her past of abuse, and lost weight. Her TV character even won the lottery during the show's final season, as art imitated life.

It is true that on a medium then overrun by the Ewings, Carringtons, Arnie Beckers, and Michael Steadmans (the season's premiere of *thirtysomething* in the year that Roseanne first appeared concerned the angst surrounding a home radon test), there was something refreshing about a loud, studiously sloppy comedy whose lead was a woman 50 pounds overweight. On this blue-collar series, the plots revolved around bowling, and the characters perambulated in their undershirts—insulting each other and belching. "We're not yuppies," said

Dan when Roseanne's pregnancy test once turned out positive. "We're supposed to have babies when we're young and stupid."

There was also a great deal of verisimilitude on the show, including normal-looking characters, two parents who had to work, a messy and therefore realistic set, and typical kids: What other series ever dealt with teen sex, and had a morose adolescent who didn't want to spend time with her folks but instead hung out in her own bedroom most of the time? The show was also funny in the belly-laugh sense, and its leads—Barr and John Goodman (who played husband Dan)—were talented. Barr would eventually end up in charge of virtually the whole production, which is why some would put her in a category with Woody Allen and Charlie Chaplin as one of the few American comics who had ever been in control of the product.

Yet, for all its surface nonconformity and wear-it-on-your-sleeve feminism, *Roseanne* didn't do that much more than recirculate formulas popularized a generation before by *The Honeymooners* and even *The Flintstones.* Instead, the show's real significance lay in the way it helped bring the values of "trash TV" into popular, prime-time circulation. If *Geraldo* and the travails of its screaming studio audience had been made into a sitcom, it would have borne more than a hint of resemblance to *Roseanne.*

It's true TV has traditionally ignored anyone who can't afford to buy a five-bedroom home next to the Andersons and Petries. From *Leave It to Beaver* and *Perry Mason* to *Friends* and *ER,* television has been grounded in upper-middle-class experience. On TV, even the cops live in homes or co-ops which would make an investment banker envious. After all, most Hollywood writers and producers tend to create characters like themselves. Moreover, the middle class is the group that can be used most easily to dramatize the ethic of consumption, which from an advertiser's point of view is the key purpose of the programming for which it pays dearly. After all, the rich don't need more possessions, and the poor can't afford them. One look at the Huxtables' wardrobe on *The Cosby Show,* however, and viewers are bound to find something they wish they had, but don't.

Of course, once every decade or so, the television industry congratulates itself for rediscovering the working class. And whether it's

The Life of Riley or *All in the Family,* these "revolutionary" shows are almost always alike. Like *Roseanne,* they tend to be comedies, so the harsh edges can be blunted. The lovable leads are overweight: On television, the fatter the character, the lower the income. Their houses are a mess. Unlike white-collar workers like the Keatons or Jim Anderson, the Archie Bunkers and Roseanne Conners don't like their jobs, and often make fun of them. Yet they rarely berate those on the ladder above them, except in general terms. Archie Bunker hated "liberals," and Roseanne—at least in her early days—made fun of yuppie waiters or teachers. This is life on the rung below as seen by those on the rung above, though *Roseanne* was better than most in remaining true to the people it depicted. After all, Roseanne Barr was herself that rare thing in TV, a former working-class person who had once lived in a trailer park. When she got her own show, she became infamous in Hollywood for fighting to keep her vision of it intact, even bragging at one point that she kept the nominal executive producers off the set. To some, it was a sign of class consciousness: After all, hadn't Barr called the show an attempt to create "a comic vocabulary of material resentment"?

However, if *Roseanne* was hailed as radically different from its predecessors, it was primarily because a woman had taken the lead role once assumed by a man. Dan was the "daddy of dysfunction," said one critic, "hiding from family conflicts by working on his bike in the garage, or behind the sports supplement." Queen of the house like most other television wives, Roseanne also had the more successful career: Her contractor-husband, at least in the early days, was always having trouble finding work, and in the 1992 season his motorcycle shop went broke. Moreover, Roseanne consciously stressed her sisterhood—giving co-workers advice about how awful men were in relationships, and deriding the fact that her husband hadn't helped with the housework in decades. "The world is run by women, contrary to what you believe," she was known to tell her writers—"especially the family, especially the working-class family."

Still, the male-bashing heard on *Roseanne*—comparing men to chocolate donuts which had to be molded—wasn't really new to television either. For starters, it was all over daytime talk shows of the late 1980s, on which a standard week of topics could include such subjects as "Men Who Work Too Hard," "Men Who Are Obnoxious," and "Men Who Won't Pay Their Child Support."

But even prime time had been intimating similar ideas for years. Was there any doubt, 35 years before, who was really the buffoon in the Ricardo household? The Kramden? Or the Bunker? Whether it's *The Flintstones* or *Family Ties*, sitcom dads almost always tend to come off looking like idiots, while the moms, with a wink and a smile, are really the ones in tune with kids and audience alike. *Roseanne* only made explicit what had been implicit.

Where *Roseanne* really stood alone in sitcom history—at least in the early years when the show made its major impact—was in her willingness to dump on her children. Though Archie Bunker was far more verbally abusive to his kids than any upper-class TV parent would dream of being, *Roseanne* raised verbal child-bashing to an art form: The kids are a pain, the kids are selfish, the kids are lazy. "Why are you so mean?" one of her children asks. "Because I hate kids and I'm not your real Mom," she answers to audience laughter. "They've left for school. Quick—change the locks!" was the cry on another episode; while on yet another, she jokingly offers to trade one of her offspring for a dishwasher. Instead of venerating children, like virtually all other domestic sitcoms, *Roseanne* good-humoredly violated the once-inviolate—one reason why the show was less popular in the rural South, where traditional motherhood is more revered. Even Barr herself eventually seemed to notice: For her last season in 1996-97, she told *TV Guide,* she planned a new and upbeat approach to family, in order to "correct . . . a kind of negative" portrait of family life.

That child-bashing attitude was the one thing about *Roseanne* that really was revolutionary. When the baby boomers and TV were young, television celebrated childhood, even creating an occasional series from the vantage point of a character like the Beaver; adults were occasionally the butts of jokes. Now, however, that the baby boomers were the same age as the elder Andersons and Cleavers had been, shows seemingly as different as *L.A. Law, thirtysomething,* and *Roseanne* gave us the reverse: children through the eyes of self-absorbed parents. The abuse that the boomers once aimed at their parents was now pointed in the opposite direction—at the younger generation. Yet many were unable to see it. "Those who despise Roseanne—her TV character or her public persona—often seem to hate her for not being a 1950s sit-com wife," wrote novelist Alice Hoffman, who didn't seem to realize that the real problem with Roseanne for some was that they thought she could be a better mother—or at least a less angry one.

It was thus no accident that a culture initially titillated by *Roseanne* was also mesmerized during the same era by news events, such as the Steinberg child-abuse trial, featuring Hedda Nussbaum, in New York. After all, those abusers only did what Roseanne claimed every week she'd like to do herself, ha-ha. It was also no accident that this show thrived in an era when there were few lovable children, along the lines of the Beaver or Shirley Temple, as pop-culture role models. *Roseanne* was the television counterpart of a wider social trend which saw funding for everything from schools to libraries cut, while the number of latch-key children dramatically increased, as children spent an average of 40 percent less time with their parents than 25 years before.

It was also no accident that *Roseanne* thrived at the same time as the Downeys, the Geraldos, and tabloid news shows like *Hard Copy* and *A Current Affair.* The controlled threats of violence in *Roseanne,* plus its high volume, its insults, its burps, its unattractive personas, and even the sheer size of its star, all were characteristic of "trash TV." "I do offensive things," she once said. "That's who I am. That's my act." "It's like this," she told John Lahr of the *New Yorker:*

> I gave birth to ya and I can take ya out, too. I think that's what makes me a bit different from other women. Because I'll beat the shit out of them, and not just verbally. I'm not opposed to violence. In fact, I think it's great. I think women should be more violent—kill more of their husbands.

In the escalating bombardment of images in the new, multichannel universe—where often the most important thing for a show to do was just attract attention—*Roseanne* thus became a hit, and its star an icon. Moreover, in a culture so hungry for real experience that it would watch daytime shows on which people yell at each other for hours, *Roseanne* offered many viewers a respectable nighttime alternative. Sure, the show changed a lot in its nine seasons on the air. But when it counted *Roseanne* wasn't a hit because it was revolutionary. It was a hit because it was revolting.

Part VI
THE NINETIES

America's Funniest Home Videos
The Hill-Thomas Hearings • *The Oprah Winfrey Show*
A Tale of Two Sitcoms: *Home Improvement* **and** *Seinfeld*
QVC • *ER* • *Wheel of Fortune* **Abroad**

With cable continuing to cause the atomization of the mass audience, and with viewers empowered by VCRs and hand-held remotes to create their own schedules and viewing patterns, the nineties have been marked by the growing democratization of television. New genres like home shopping, "reality television," "talk television," and even "camcorder television" all share in common an ethos which celebrates ordinary people, in contrast to the "stars" who dominated programming before.

54

How *America's Funniest Home Videos* Tore Down Our Wall

(ABC: 1990–Present)

The first surprise hit of the 1990s actually premiered as a special, over the last Thanksgiving holiday of the 1980s, to less-than-resounding critical acclaim. "'Funniest Home Videos' Is Oddly Unpleasant," read the headline in the *Los Angeles Times,* though that first show was typical of what was to follow—camcorder tapes, submitted by "ordinary" Americans, which showed a singer's teeth falling out; a baby, being diapered, "spraying" his dad; a woman who got her head caught in a dishwasher—and so on. "[M]any of the vidbits are real people, many of them children, in differing degrees of pain and humiliation," complained that critic for the *Times.* But no matter: As the show's theme song would remind us every week, "America, America—this is you!"

ABC's *America's Funniest Home Videos* (*Home Videos*) shot almost to the top of the charts within weeks of its installation on the Sunday-night schedule in January 1990. Though it has never been a consistent Top Ten performer, it has been one of the more durably popular shows of the decade. Its rise also mirrored—if not triggered—a number of other televisual trends during the decade. Because it was a hit that was cheap to put together (all the producers had to do was review the tape submissions and give out a few prizes), *Home Videos* was the forerunner of a trend to staging the least-expensive show possible: Even if ratings were somewhat lower, profits were higher, and that was increasingly important as broadcasting became more competitive. Moreover, *Home Videos* was at the forefront of a movement which saw "real" camcorder recordings by ordinary citizens increasingly enter the broadcasting and cultural universe—from news shows to weather reporting, and on to the infamous tape of the Rodney King beating.

Such tapes would always be the right stuff, as the popularity of "reality programming" increased on shows like *Rescue 911* and *Inside Edi-*

tion. Yet, for a seemingly frivolous show, *America's Funniest Home Videos* also had important cultural implications. By making the audience at home the stars, and then giving the studio audience the power to decide the best video of the show, this series was the most democratic show on television—a populist rebellion packaged as programming. It was no accident that back when the Wall was being torn down in Berlin, and a virtually unprecedented number of voters were rejecting the two major parties for H. Ross Perot's independent effort, viewers from Pittsburgh to Portland were flocking to this show.

The program had its origins in not just one technical innovation—the video camcorder—but two others, also—the hand-held remote and the VCR. All three devices helped erode network control and empower viewers in the 1990s, encouraging them to skip around the dial and make their own viewing schedules. For its first 40 years, television had been largely hegemonic: Network executives dictated what Americans should watch. "We control the television set," the announcer had intoned at the beginning of *The Outer Limits* in the mid-sixties. *America's Funniest Home Videos* appeared to challenge that authority. Composed each week of dozens of home videos submitted by viewers, the clips often were badly produced, and featured a cast looking like it had just wandered away from Main Street—or at least out of a mall. Predictably, most of the "funny" shots were stupid, even if relatively wholesome—like those of people falling off swings, and toddlers running into trees. However, since "the people" supplied both the product and the critical audience, it was a hit. Roll over, Bill Paley, and tell Norman Lear the news.

For all its cultural currency, *Home Videos* was actually a Japanese import. The show's executive producer, Vin DiBona, on a trip to Japan, discovered that the most popular segment in a weekly variety show, *Fun With Ken and Kato Chan,* featured video clips. He purchased the U.S rights and sold them to ABC, which installed Bob Saget, a star of one of its sitcoms, *Full House,* as the MC. As it turned out *Home* outlasted the sitcom. Within weeks of its appearance in the Sunday-night lineup, the show was already receiving almost 100 videos for every one it broadcast. Tape screeners noticed regional differences in submissions: Californians went for stunts, and Midwesterners for families, while Southerners, according to one screener, often submitted "bizarre guys sitting around drinking beer while trying to produce a video."

Of course, movies shot by amateurs had been making headlines for years: Witness the 1963 Zapruder film of the Kennedy assassination. There had been many programming antecedents as well. Beginning in the 1940s, Allen Funt's *Candid Camera*—which had actually begun on radio as *Candid Microphone*—perfected the art of capturing real people in embarrassing situations, though the camera still rested in the hands of professionals. Similarly, Art Linkletter's *People Are Funny* had featured ordinary people being themselves, while *Ted Mack's Original Amateur Hour,* presenting average Americans as performers, encouraged viewers to vote by postcard for their favorite acts. Game and quiz shows had always featured "the hoi polloi," a fact which persuaded Chuck Barris in the mid-1970s to combine that concept with Mack's amateurism on *The Gong Show*—a program which invited amateurs on the air in order to humiliate them.

The modern seeds of *Home Videos* were planted in 1979 with NBC's *Real People,* a program which featured average Americans with odd talents or hobbies—like eating dirt and walking backwards. By the late 1980s, series like *Roseanne* and *Married . . . With Children* had even made the depiction of average, shlumpy Americans more commonplace on fictional TV. Yet those programs either showed average Americans on the fringes of culture, or were dramatizations. *America's Funniest Home Videos* made heroes of common men and women being themselves. If the camcorder had theatricalized daily life for millions, turning even a kindergarten graduation into a documentary film, this show was a kind of weekly Academy Awards for John and Jane Q. Public. "It's very hard for us to compete in our everyday lives with television," *M*A*S*H* coproducer Larry Gelbart once told an interviewer. "We're not as well made-up, we're not as in focus, we're not as glamorous." This show was a form of affirmative action, making a virtue of those liabilities.

The show was also helped by its position on the ABC schedule. With strong appeal to the elderly—not a particularly desirable demographic group because they don't buy many expensive products—*Home Videos* had an audience the mirror image of the one that watched *Saturday Night Live.* That might have killed the show in many time slots, but on

Sunday nights, families of several generations still watch TV together, just like they did in the old days when there was only one set per household. Thus, programming on that night still tends to be anachronistic: *America's Funniest Home Videos,* a kind of variety show on tape, succeeded as a 1990s, populist version of *The Ed Sullivan Show.*

The slapstick humor was cartoonish. Yet, given the show's slot in family viewing time, it was vaguely sadistic to focus so strongly on children continually humiliating and injuring themselves—something which did not go unnoticed by the critics. As Howard Rosenberg of the *Los Angeles Times* wrote in March 1990:

> As anyone who has been a parent knows, a small boy who walks head-first into a camera usually cries. A small boy getting hit in the face with a shovelful of snow usually cries. . . . But there is no sound of crying here because each video usually ends on impact with crunched bodies becoming the punch lines. . . . After all, we can't have crying ruining America's funniest home videos.
>
> Here's a thought that ABC and the producers of this program may not like, but is worth considering: "America's Funniest Home Videos" inadvertently encourages child abuse.

Thus the show was part of the same wave of "kids are a pain" sentiment that helped make *Roseanne* a success, and became an implicit theme in yuppie series like *Seinfeld* and *Friends,* both of which tended to denigrate children by often ignoring altogether the fact that they exist.

Almost immediately the show's success spread as ABC launched a clone, *America's Funniest People,* in the following season. Within months of the premiere of *Home Videos,* it was reported that KCBS, the local CBS news affiliate in Los Angeles, had begun encouraging viewers to send similar videos to them. "Shoot your family and friends . . . with the videocamera," went an ad, "and KCBS will air them during the 11 P.M. ACTION NEWS broadcast." Soon, the trend turned serious. CNN began including a "video hot line" number with some broadcasts, and the Weather Channel eventually began relying on similar ventures.

In March 1991, after a passing Los Angeles motorist, George Holliday, stopped to film the police beating of Rodney King, the home videotape entered a new dimension. "Orwell said video would give government a huge influence over people, and it has," said Art Levis, editor-in-chief of *Video* magazine, "but this shows how it might turn around." Home videos of Iraqi tanks in Kuwait were smuggled out by the underground after the invasion, and similar tapes played a key role in helping the FBI to investigate the 1996 bombing at the Olympics in Atlanta. In 1994, *Nightline* devoted an entire show to a documentary, shot with a small-format camera, chronicling life in a small Haitian town. "Ultimately," mused Levis, "you can imagine a world of people mailing tapes of rude shopkeepers to store bosses, or reformers taping workmen asleep on the job, or local activists armed with camcorders to deter the police."

It didn't turn out that way, though *America's Funniest Home Videos* would hardly be to blame. When the Iron Curtain collapsed at the turn of the decade, the Washington press corps had a field day bemoaning how the United States was sitting on the sidelines. "This country is going nowhere fast," wrote the *New York Times'* Maureen Dowd. "While the world celebrates American values, America is home watching the party on TV."

All this carping aside, in order to understand what was changing the world, you didn't have to be in Prague or Berlin; you could instead just watch ABC's postmodern embodiment of democracy in action. After all, popular culture is a primary outlet for political expression. We all know that, in the television age, the roads from Hollywood and Madison Avenue lead to the White House—as Ronald Reagan helped prove.

There is a subtler side to this link between culture and politics, however: Americans express their political feelings primarily as consumers of cultural products—records, films, and TV shows. We don't rally or protest much anymore; we watch, listen, and buy. Concerned about the health-care system? Watch *ER* or *Chicago Hope*. Upset about the problems of women in the workplace? Then *Murphy Brown* may be your answer. In the world television has created, you take your empowerment where you can find it—if not in the streets, then in front of the screen. The heck with Berlin: As the theme song says: "America, America, this is you."

55
Hill-Thomas and the
Congressional Hearing as Miniseries
(ALL MAJOR NETWORKS: 1991)

On October 3, 1995, more than 100 million people watched the O. J. Simpson criminal trial verdict on television. Even though the Simpson case and trial had dominated the nation's consciousness for over a year, however, the number of viewers who actually watched the legal proceedings live was usually fairly small: The proceedings were held on weekdays, during working hours. Except for infrequent moments, like at the time the verdict was announced, the three major networks didn't cover the daily legal proceedings line. They left all that to such cable networks as CNN and Court TV.

By contrast, there have been certain quasilegal proceedings, televised by the major networks for decades, which have regularly attracted mass audiences: congressional hearings. And the biggest congressional hearings of them all starred Clarence Thomas and Anita Hill, in October 1991. Those hearings were at the intersection of a number of televisual trends that changed the confirmation process, and even Congress itself. Moreover, because those sessions proved such a success on TV, they paved the way for a slew of televised trials in the 1990s that featured among other notables William Kennedy Smith, the Bobbitts, the Menendez brothers, and finally O. J.—and which changed the culture as well.

Television had in fact been drawn to Congressional hearings since its early days, beginning with the Kefauver hearings on organized crime in 1951 and continuing through the Army–McCarthy hearings of 1954, the Watergate drama in the 1970s, and the Iran–Contra hearings of the late 1980s. To be sure, Congress has conducted investigations since the 1790s, when it looked into the military misadventures of Maj. Gen. Arthur St. Clair. And no American-history book would be complete without mention of the congressional investigation of the Teapot Dome scandal in the 1920s, or that of the Truman commission that looked into military expenditures in the 1940s.

Yet it is undeniable that such investigations have flourished in the television age, providing most of the memorable moments of the past five decades in Congress. After all, unlike the typical slow, back-room lawmaking processes that are hardly conducive to good TV-watching, these hearings offer the networks high drama and compelling characters featured in a stately setting. They also present a steady stream of stories—much like a regular television series.

And yet, as Daniel Boorstin pointed out almost 40 years ago in his book *The Image,* the real purpose of these investigations is often difficult to discern. "In many cases," he wrote, "these committees have virtually no legislative impulse, and sometimes no legislative assignment." Moreover, if such hearings aren't trampling over witnesses' rights (as they did during the Army–McCarthy hearings), or ultimately allowing lawbreakers to go free because of congressional grants of immunity (which is what happened with the Iran–Contra investigation), they do tend to set up a system whereby the entertainment values of television control who triumphs. Just ask Ollie North, who used his Iran–Contra appearances to remake himself into a national hero; or Sam Ervin, who ended up making commercials for American Express after he left both the Senate and the Watergate investigation behind.

In other words, smart witnesses and legislators now speak to the *living* room, not the *hearing* room—advice which Carter budget director Bert Lance should have followed when he was investigated by the Senate in the late 1970s. Rather than deal with the abstractions television abhors, savvy TV-conscious participants in such goings-on attempt to turn their testimony into good personal stories, as North did during his hearings and John Dean did during Watergate. Good guys gradually let loose some memorable sound bites: "Have you no sense of decency, sir, at long last?" made Joseph Welch a household name during the McCarthy hearings; and people are still mimicking Senator Howard Baker's "What did he know, and when did he know it?" during Watergate. Finally, like all regular media performers, the parties realize that a television picture is worth a thousand words. That's the reason why North insisted on wearing his military uniform when he appeared at his 1987 hearings where, sitting below dozens of over-eager congressmen, he came across as a lone crusader.

A similar phenomenon has occurred in recent years with regard to the process of confirming political appointees. Confirmation fights are also part of our history, but sensationalized confirmation *hearings* are a media-age phenomenon. Here, too, the consensus is that the cameras have indeed contorted the process into great TV drama, but also into something of a legislative travesty. Many nominees now just refuse to answer substantive questions, giving the committee instead a political version of *This Is Your Life*. After all, where else could serious commentators suggest that Robert Bork might have been confirmed for the Supreme Court in 1987, if only he had shaved his 19th-century-style beard and acted a little nicer?

And, what other country could have played host to a miniseries like Hill-Thomas? The initial confirmation hearings for Thomas's Supreme Court nomination in September 1991 were uneventful. Yet, shortly before a final vote on the nomination, when Anita Hill—one of Thomas's assistants when he had been at the Equal Employment Opportunity Commission—charged that he had asked her out on numerous occasions, and had sexually harassed her, TV had found its adversarial drama. On the morning of Friday, October 11, Thomas appeared first before the committee. "I cannot imagine anything that I said or did to Anita Hill that could be mistaken for sexual harassment," he began; and he concluded by defiantly telling the committee that he would answer no questions as to "what goes on in the most intimate parts of my private life or the sanctity of my bedroom." "I will not," he said, "provide the rope for my own lynching."

Then came Hill, whose shocking allegations were delivered in a serious, even voice. She told of conversations with Thomas in which he had talked about pornographic films he had seen that starred Long Dong Silver. She described another incident whereupon Thomas suddenly asked, "Who has put pubic hair on my Coke?" She was cross-examined until 7:40 that Friday night, ensuring that viewers returning home and tuning in for their regular programming saw at least some of the proceedings. Thomas then returned to the witness table and, under prodding by Senator Orrin Hatch, exploded. In prime time, Thomas denied the charges and called the hearings a "high-tech lynching for uppity blacks." Hill's charges that he had bragged about his own anatomy, he said, "play into the worst stereotypes about black men in our society." "And I have no way of changing it, and no way of refuting these charges," he added.

On the following morning, the committee reconvened and heard from Thomas again—and then spent the day investigating wild rumors that Hill was either a spurned woman or a crazy zealot (or both). At one point, the senators examined whether some of her story had been lifted from *The Exorcist*. All Sunday, as the networks continued to preempt or break into their regular programming, character witnesses for the two appeared. By then, however, Thomas had turned the tide back in his favor. He was confirmed less than a week later, by a 52–48 vote.

According to many commentators of that time, Thomas triumphed because governmental institutions and the public alike are sexist: After all, the senators never questioned him nearly as rigorously as they did Hill, and few other witnesses were called to support her testimony, even though they apparently existed. Still, the main reason why Thomas prevailed was that his supporters understood better than his opponents that confirmation fights were now political struggles cast in the form of TV shows.

Whereas Anita Hill used distinguished lawyers to prepare a legal case against Thomas, he approached the hearings from a public-relations standpoint, using rhetorical flourishes. She testified during a weekday, when the TV audience was relatively small; Thomas made sure his appearances were on a Friday night and Saturday, when the potential audiences were much larger. Her supporting witnesses, though credible, tended to be Yale Law School colleagues, and thus could have been yuppie extras on *thirtysomething;* Thomas's supporters often looked as though they had just stepped off the set of the more popular and earthy *Roseanne*. Hill's senatorial supporters acted as judges, hardly endearing pop-culture icons; Thomas's allies on the committee played Perry Mason as they attempted to tear Hill's allegations apart.

In fact, the story of Hill and Thomas seemed straight out of the daytime talk shows of Sally Jessy Raphael and Maury Povich, on which the political was always personal. The hearings legitimately were high drama which some critics compared to Kurosawa's classic *Rashomon* and others called a reality drama which resembled the then-popular film *Fatal Attraction*. They also triggered a national debate about sexual harassment which ended up increasing exponentially the number of harassment claims filed in the years ahead.

The hearings' effect on television itself was equally as great. In the wake of Hill-Thomas, the networks programmed even more prime-time, made-for-TV docudramas about women abused by their spouses or associates. More importantly, the hearings escalated a trend which had begun in the decade before this confrontation, when an increasing number of courts had been allowing cameras to televise their proceedings live. After Hill-Thomas, there was a push by cable executives to televise even more trials, beginning with the William Kennedy Smith rape case several months later. Soon, such proceedings began appearing on air frequently—especially as segments on the local news. Not only were such hearings exciting and inexpensive ("You don't even have to pay Judge Wapner!"), but they also conformed to the trend in the 1990s of "reality tabloid" programming—with an emphasis on celebrities, scandal, crime, and carnality.

There were strong arguments for opening the nation's courtrooms to cameras: In a free society, people should be able to watch what they want, even if they want racy trials. Theoretically, publicity could encourage court officers, lawyers, and juries to do their jobs better. Yet it soon became apparent that TV cameras, by their very presence, changed behavior in the courtroom—which meant that the judicial system began to become infected by the entertainment values of television in much the same way that politics and sports had been. In the early nineties, it might have seemed farfetched to suggest that, if the trend continued, trials would one day be moved to meet the demands of prime-time television; and that courts would be refashioned as TV studios; and that judges and lawyers would use courtrooms as TV forums; and that the public would become accustomed to the idea that a trial is not a search for truth, but rather the ultimate game show or sporting contest.

Then came the Simpson trial, and it all began to come true.

As George Gerbner, the former dean of the Annenberg School, warned long before O. J., the great show trials of the 20th century—Joe McCarthy's "investigations" and Iranian TV trials—have often been the product of totalitarian regimes or witch hunts. Presented partly as entertainment, these show trials often exploited public prejudice in order to rally support for the status quo and suppress the truth that fair legal proceedings are designed to disclose. The O. J. trial showed that the values of entertainment and truth could clash here too, as the "not guilty" verdict in that case undermined confidence in trial judge Lance Ito in particular, and the legal system generally. Within weeks of that verdict, judges began closing their courtrooms to cameras—especially if a case had "tabloid" potential. The Simpson criminal trial, hailed as the dawn of a new type of TV programming, was actually the end of a very short era.

Yet by its very presence, television had changed Congress too—and that institution could hardly pull the plug on the cameras. Commentators and political scientists had been writing for years about how a different kind of congressional persona tends to flourish in the television age. As Michael J. Robinson, a professor at Catholic University, once wrote: "The increasingly greater reliance on the media for nomination, election, status in the Congress, and reelection is one sign of a new congressional character—one more dynamic, egocentric, immoderate, and perhaps intemperate." These telegenic figures, according to one source Robinson cited, were often more concerned with getting on television than with legislative mechanics—one reason for the lack of consensus and results that voters often say bothers them about Congress.

Network television also subtly changed how the public perceived Congress by focusing its news coverage on what the audience wanted from any regular series. (C-Span began televising Congress in the eighties, but its audience still is very small.) Because television is drawn to strong characters, it elevates the importance of the President and the Speaker of the House *vis-à-vis* the institution of Congress. Because the medium is drawn to conflict, it denigrates the value of compromise upon which legislatures depend, and exaggerates scandal and contentiousness. A study by S. Robert Lichter and Daniel R. Amundson of the Center for Media and Public Affairs found that, from 1972 to 1992, the proportion of network news stories concerning ethical lapses in Congress more than quadrupled, and the proportion of those portraying conflict between members nearly tripled from 1987 to 1992.

Television is wedded to the dramatic gesture, and deliberative legislative bodies rarely are theatrical. What's more, the legislative process is often messy and difficult; its abstruse methods and rambling monotony violate the spirit of scripted entertainment that has come to dominate the culture. The workings of Congress are complex and esoteric, and time to explain is something that network television cannot afford. "This is a slow-moving body in a fast-moving world," former representative Al Swift once said. "And it's in trouble because of it."

Thus, with Congress increasingly ignored or denigrated by the culture of television in its mission to legislate, it's no surprise that its members increasingly undertook other tasks nurtured by television, like holding hearings. Nor is it surprising that those hearings soon reflected the unreal, tabloid programming then in vogue on the small screen. Everything that television touches it transforms into a popular "show"—even Congress and the courts. That's a fact Anita Hill and Clarence Thomas will undoubtedly never forget.

56

The Oprah Winfrey Show
and the Talk-Show Furor
(SYNDICATION: 1986–PRESENT)

Start with these two basic premises:

1. Oprah Winfrey is probably the most celebrated and powerful black woman in U.S. history.
2. Oprah Winfrey is the undisputed leader of a television genre which has been more vehemently attacked by the Establishment than any other in television history.

You don't have to be an Albert Einstein to recognize that these two propositions are related.

The modern daytime talk show—created by Phil Donahue in the late 1960s, revolutionized by Oprah in the 1980s, and then transmogrified in the 1990s by everyone from Ricki Lake to Jenny Jones—is the newest genre to sweep television. On an average mid-nineties weekday, *The Oprah Winfrey Show* was watched by around ten million Americans, mostly women, and the 20 or so other daytime talk shows in 1995 had a combined daily audience of around 50 million viewers—though many people undoubtedly watched a whole slew of these shows each day. Though these numbers were high, they pale when compared to those of the combined audiences that watch the violence of prime-time action shows or the local news.

Yet the talk-show genre was absolutely vilified by critics—blamed for everything from the culture's preoccupation with victimization to the general decline of civic discourse. Daytime talk generated a well-publicized crusade (led by two U.S. senators and former Secretary of Education William Bennett) to purify the medium, not to mention a dozen or so critical books and hundreds of negative articles which joined these Washington officials in calling the new genre a "case study of rot" and "the pollution of the human environment."

Admittedly daytime talk shows are not for the squeamish or children—though one hopes that Bennett and his minions were as concerned about the millions who live full-time in economic and so-cial surroundings far more squalid than anything on *The Maury Povich Show.* The shows typically involve from two to six guests talking about their personal experiences, followed by boos, applause, tears, questions, and shouts from a studio audience modeled roughly on Howdy Doody's Peanut Gallery. A typical week of mid-nineties programming on these shows was likely to include such topics as:

> Leathermen Love Triangles
> Bisexuals
> Abusive Boyfriends
> Men Engaged to Three Pregnant Women
> Clueless Men
> Women Who Marry Their Rapists
> Runaway Teens
> Secret Crushes

This was the genre where a man was surprisingly "confronted" with a secret admirer on *Jenny Jones,* found the admirer was a man, and killed him after the show for humiliating him on national television. (The show was never broadcast due to the shooting.) "Rather than being mortified, ashamed, or trying to hide their stigma," two sociologists wrote of this genre, "guests willingly and eagerly discuss their child-molesting, sexual quirks, and criminal records in an effort to seek 'understanding' for their particular disease."

These shows obviously offer a distorted vision of America, thrive on feeling rather than thought, and worship the sound-bite rather than the art of conversation. Yet it's not like television hasn't been walking down these same paths in other forms every day for the past 50 years. If daytime talk has been preoccupied with sex, race, and family dysfunction, it may be because there is still so little discussion of those rather significant topics elsewhere on television, even in the nineties. All movements have their crazies. Yet when Oprah Winfrey can rank in a poll as the celebrity Americans believe to be most qualified to be president (far more than Bill Bennett, by the way), something significant is going on.

Just as vaudeville was the root of much early American television, the circus and carnival with their freak shows influenced talk shows. Like any new television genre, these talk shows were a mixture of old programming types—many of which once dominated the daytime. Morning and afternoon talk, geared mostly to women, has a long TV history, beginning with Arthur Godfrey and with Art Linkletter's *People Are Funny*. From the soap opera, these new shows borrowed a feminine style of disclosure and a focus on issues considered to be of particular relevance to women, like family and relationships. Game shows were a rich source: From programs like *The Price Is Right* the new talk shows learned how to involve an audience of ordinary people. From games like *Strike It Rich* and *Queen for a Day* they learned about the entertainment value of debasing "contestants" who will tell their sob story for money or fleeting fame. And from *Family Feud* they learned that conflict sells in the daytime. Throw in a smattering of TV religion (the televised confession and revelation so prominent on these shows), melodrama (Will the runaway teenager's father take her back?), and the news sensibility of Barbara Walters, once an early-morning mainstay on *Today,* and the pieces were in place for a profitable genre—especially because daytime talk shows are so inexpensive to stage.

Like other popular forms of programming, these shows also mirrored their times. Phil Donahue created the genre because network television wasn't reflecting the serious concerns of many of its women viewers. It began in 1967, at the dawn of the women's movement, when this Midwestern Catholic started a new type of daytime talk show in Dayton, Ohio, hosting for that first show atheist Madalyn Murray O'Hair. Donahue's theory was simple: "The average housewife is bright and inquisitive," he said, "but television treats her like a mental midget." His approach was to take TV talk out of its preoccupation with entertainment celebrities, and tackle instead (often with only one guest an hour) "difficult" women's issues that television wasn't addressing—sexism, artificial insemination, impotence, and homosexuality—combined with more-traditional topics, like bathroom fixtures. "He flies in the face of TV tradition, which used to be that you didn't risk offending anyone," Steve Allen, former host of *The Tonight Show,* said. Donahue also brilliantly added an active studio audience, usually composed almost entirely of women (though not by design—they're just the ones who showed up), which not only served as a kind of Greek chorus for the guests, but also asked many of the show's most penetrating questions.

For his part, Donahue the rebel frequently bounced about the crowd, microphone in hand, smashing the barrier between host and audience. It didn't hurt the show's populist appeal that it came to stations independently through syndication, rather than from a paternalistic network. In its heyday, *Donahue* also originated from Chicago—in the nation's heartland—rather than among the elites in New York. The more the women's movement progressed, however, the more well-educated women left home for the workplace, and found other outlets for their interests. That left Donahue and his imitators with a growing audience of less-affluent, homebound women who often were full of anger and confusion, ignored as they were by more-elite media. The women's movement first made Donahue, and then took away the cream of his audience who were interested in more serious topics.

Still, for over a decade he had the field to himself before along came a certain Oprah Winfrey in 1984. She was an empathetic black woman and former coanchor of the local news in Baltimore. Oprah's advantage over Donahue was that, seeming to resemble her audience, she used that similarity to create a talk show which made the political more personal. Her program was infused with a therapeutic sensibility: Though Oprah did some politics, like her celebrated show in Forsyth County, Georgia, in 1987 (when white racists were on the march), she was more likely to do a show on abusive boyfriends, recovering alcoholics, or competitive sisters. The cause of many of the problems discussed on her show was not so much men, but the so-called rigid confines of the traditional family. "What we are witnessing with the proliferating talk show is a social revolution which has at its core the demystification of the family," Michael Arlen, former TV critic for the *New Yorker*, would tell a reporter much later. Say goodbye to Ozzie and Harriet!

Oprah's style was different, too. If Donahue was, at heart, a journalist exposing issues, Oprah ran what she called a "ministry"—the "church" being a branch of pop psychology which held that revealing problems, improving self-esteem, and receiving empathy could cure just about anything, and empower women besides. Oprah hugged her guests, wept openly, and personally said good-bye to each member of the studio audience after a show. Even in 1996, Oprah spoke far more often on her shows than hosts on others did. She confessed on the air that she had been sexually abused by relatives as a child, and in later years that she had smoked cocaine. On a show about dieting, she told the audience about the night she ate hot-dog buns drowned in syrup.

Oprah's race and street sass ("Hey, Girl!") also made her more authentically hip, at least to her audience, than almost anyone else on television. Oprah would call her success an alternative to the "Twinkies and Barbie and Ken dolls" that make up so much of television. "Racism remains the most difficult subject in America, and it is only really on the talk show that the raw hatred and suspicion that the races feel for each other is vented," Arlen had told that reporter. As a host who could walk the narrow line between the races, Oprah offered reassurance which others couldn't hope to match. That cultural bilingualism also allowed her to put together an audience coalition of the sort that Jesse Jackson could only dream about.

With rock-and-roll in the 1950s, black artists had been swept aside so that more-acceptable white singers could "cover" their songs. With daytime talk, the opposite occurred: Oprah's show soon wiped out

Donahue in the ratings—and everyone else, too. By 1994, *Working Woman* put Oprah's net worth at over $250 million. By then the show itself was grossing almost $200 million a year, had 55 percent more viewers than *Donahue* (its closest competitor), and enjoyed higher ratings on many days than *Today, Good Morning America,* and the *CBS Morning News* combined.

Understandably, Oprah's success bred imitators. Since other hosts couldn't hope to match her in identifying with the audience personally (Ricki Lake was a notable exception, as she went after younger viewers), they tried to win viewers by topping her with their list of sensationalistic topics and revelations. As TV news became ever more tabloid, these shows pushed the envelope even further. By 1992, even Donahue was tackling topics like "Safe Sex Orgies" and "What Happens When Strippers Get Old?" Other shows borrowed from the confrontational style of talk shows once run by Mort Downey Jr. and turned Oprah's group hug into a daily talk riot with topics like "Wives Confront the Other Woman."

By the mid-1990s, an average day on these other shows revealed subjects like "Married Men Who Have Relationships With Their Next-Door Neighbors," "Mothers Who Ran Off With Their Daughter's Fiancé," and "Drag Queens Who Got Makeovers." A 1995 study of these programs, done by a team of researchers at Michigan State University, found that a typical one-hour show had:

> four sexual-activity disclosures, one sexual-orientation disclosure, three abuse disclosures, two embarrassing-situation disclosures, two criminal-activity disclosures and four personal-attribute disclosures, for a total of 16 personal disclosures. . . .

These entertainments programs were selling more, however, than just their guests' disclosures or the "hot" topics which seemed to come straight out of the supermarket tabloids. They also purported to offer group therapy for the masses, at a price everyone could afford. As psychotherapist Murray Nossel once told a reporter, America is "the country that popularized psychoanalysis. Freud's theory of the psyche is that repression brings depression, whereas expression is liberating. Emotionally to cathart in America, to reveal one's darkest secrets, is a desired social good in and of itself." Critics would have a field day pointing out the dangers of trying to provide such "therapy" on television, but that played right into the notion that elites were trying to keep the masses away from something that had once exclusively been available only to the well-to-do. After all, if daytime talk shows thrived on the violation of taboos, that was, in part, to stick a finger in the eye of those members of the Establishment who looked down on a television pursuit favored by the downscale.

The supporters of these shows also felt that they regularly received too little credit for tackling issues which mainstream television had traditionally ignored, like race and family dysfunction. "If people didn't get up there and talk about incest," Lee Fryd, director of media relations for the *Sally Jessy Raphael* show once told a reporter, "it would never come to light." If these shows often presented what many considered a freak parade, others would argue that they had helped bring nonconformists further into the mainstream. Joshua Gamson, a cultural critic, once wrote:

> The story here is not about commercial exploitation but just about how effective the prohibition on asking and telling is in the United States, how stiff the penalties are, how unsafe this place is for people of atypical sexual and gender identities. You know you're in trouble when Sally Jessy Raphael (strained smile and forced tear behind red glasses) seems your best bet for being heard, understood, respected, and protected. That for some of us the loopy, hollow light of talk shows seems a safe, shielding haven should give us all pause.

On the other hand, the values of these talk shows were oddly traditional—one reason why they posted such strong ratings with Bible Belt females who considered themselves conservative. The parade of guests was almost always hooted down by the studio audience, which embodied a rather conventional view of morality (albeit one heavily tempered by empathy for victims). The parade of "trash," to use one critic's words, was also a way for those at home to feel better about themselves, since their lives were rarely as hopeless as what they could find here on the screen. Like so much else on TV, what these shows offered was a form of reassurance.

If these talk shows had a larger political consequence, it came with the administration of Bill Clinton, who accomplished little but empathized with everybody. He ran a kind of talk-show presidency—forged in the 1992 campaign with his appearance on *Donahue,* and continuing in that year into a second debate with George Bush and H. Ross Perot which did away with journalist-questioners and substituted an inquiring studio audience like Oprah's. One of Clinton's principal contributions to our culture was to take the language and zeitgeist of the talk show and bring it into mainstream politics. After all, the "I feel your pain" trademark of his presidency first gained cultural prominence as a talk-show staple: The whole point of talk shows like Oprah's is to encourage "audience-victims" to "feel their pain" as a way of empowering themselves to strike back against those who seem more powerful.

Such a stance was undoubtedly a big reason why women, over time, supported Clinton so strongly. In fact, by 1996, the talk-show style and its celebration of victims was on display throughout both political conventions: There was Liddy Dole's Winfreyesque "among the delegates" talk to the Republican convention, Al Gore's speech recounting his dying sister's final moments, and the endless parade of the disease-afflicted. Our politics had been Opracized.

Yet if the nineties has been a decade tending to elevate feeling over thought and encourage a no-fault approach to behavior, the talk shows were hardly the only culprit, no matter what Bill Bennett thought. Few cultural movements of this magnitude proceed from the bottom up rather than the other way around. As Michiko Kakutani would point out in another context in the *New York Times,* the cult of subjectivity enveloping America came as much from Oliver Stone, with his fantasies about JFK, and from "inventive" biographers like Joe McGinniss, as they came from Ricki Lake. Invective was as much a calling card of CNN's *Crossfire* as it was of Montel and Jerry Springer.

By late 1995, however, in response to criticisms by Bennett and others (and as ratings for the "confrontational" shows dropped by as much as a third), Oprah changed her mix of guests and topics too, moving away from tabloid psychology and toward less-conventional, more-"educational" subjects like anorexia, and planning for old age. "She said to us that after 10 years and 2,000 shows of mostly dysfunctional people, she felt it was time to start focusing on solutions," said Tim Bennett, Oprah's production-company president. At the same time, *The Rosie O'Donnell Show* rose to daytime prominence by essentially taking the old fifties' upbeat variety formula, popularized by Arthur Godfrey, and repackaging it with a likable female host, celebrity guests, and a nineties' zeitgeist.

But were even these small shifts something of a betrayal of a large portion of the talk show audience? What was always most striking about this form of "entertainment"—and what made it so different from anything else on television—was its never-ending portrait of despair and alienation. If the downtrodden who populated these shows popularized deviancy or celebrated the cheap confessional, they did it mostly as a plaintive cry for help. Yet Oprah had been there to bless them at the end of every weekday. "They are the people you'd ignore if you saw them in line at the supermarket instead of on TV," Wendy Kaminer, a cultural analyst, once wrote, but that was precisely the point. Talk television was yet another step in the 1990s' trend to democratization of the medium—this time to include the real havenots. That may be why the elites responded with their usual rejoinder to let them eat cake.

57
A Tale of Two Sitcoms
(*Home Improvement* [ABC]: 1991–Present)
(*Seinfeld* [NBC]: 1990–Present)

The popular shows of a decade are usually a lot alike. In many ways *Dallas* and *Dynasty* were indistinguishable, and it would take Wyatt Earp himself to discern great differences between *Wagon Train* and *Gunsmoke*. In the late seventies *Happy Days, Laverne and Shirley,* and *Three's Company* often seemed to form one long seamless web.

Yet sometimes, in eras of cultural conflict or confusion, no one type of show can accurately capture the public mood. In the early 1970s, for example, *All in the Family* made a hero of a conservative traditionalist while *The Mary Tyler Moore Show* romanticized the life of a single career woman blazing new ground. In their own ways, both shows reflected their times and both were popular—often with the same viewers.

In much the same fashion, popular programming in the nineties offered a contrast, as it struggled with an emerging question which had no clear answer: What does it mean to be a man in a postfeminist age? Two very different situation comedies which hit Number 1 in that decade tried to provide an answer. On the one hand, there was ABC's *Home Improvement*—the top-rated show for the 1993–94 season. And then, there was NBC's *Seinfeld*—which hit Number 1 the following season.

Even the reaction to both shows provided a sharp contrast. Critics regularly lavished *Seinfeld* with praise for its postmodern plots; its technical innovations were hailed as breakthroughs; and the show was always an Emmy contender in several categories. Novelist Jay McInerney went so far in a 1996 issue of *TV Guide* to ask, "Is Seinfeld the Best Comedy Ever?" By comparison, *Home Improvement* was perhaps the quietest Number 1 in TV history, eliciting few critical comments and winning little more than a slew of (what else?) People's Choice awards, in which the public does the voting.

There were indeed surface similarities between the two shows. Both starred male comedians, who took their standup nightclub acts and transformed them for television. Both comedians wrote best-selling books once they hit it big, and both shows featured subplots about television itself. Both presented memorable supporting players, like Kramer of *Seinfeld,* or next-door neighbor Wilson of *Home Improvement,* whose full face is never shown over his fence. Both ran in prime time and in syndication over roughly the same period with similar ratings—though the one time *Seinfeld* was matched directly against *Home Improvement* in 1992-93, *Seinfeld* got plastered in the ratings.

Yet the differences between the shows were more revealing. *Home Improvement* was set in suburban Detroit, in the white-bread heartland. Though actually filmed in L.A., *Seinfeld* was a New York show which roughly approximated the lifestyles of influential New York critics and

Madison Avenue types. *Home Improvement* was solidly suburban middle class; *Seinfeld* was a portrait of life in yuppie Upper Manhattan.

Home Improvement was a rather traditional family sitcom about a
wife, three kids, and a bumbling Dad; the *Seinfeld* family of friends featured no children and no workplace either, at least in the traditional
sense. With its "morality tale" quality, *Home Improvement* was a cousin
of *Leave It to Beaver* and *My Three Sons*—an anachronism in an era
when wisecracking shows like *Friends* or *Murphy Brown* dispensed
with nuclear families altogether.

By contrast, *Seinfeld* was closer to Jack Benny, or even Milton Berle.
That was a remarkable turnaround for a medium which for much of
its bland and homogeneous entertainment life took single Jews like
Seinfeld, changed their names, converted them to Christianity, married them off to attractive WASP housewives, and moved the m to the
suburbs. New York *Newsday* once called *Seinfeld* "the most fully realized schlemiel in the history of television."

What encouraged programmers to take these chances was the way
that cable television had atomized the viewing audience. Because of
cable competition, network television was not the mass medium in
1995 that it was in 1975; it took far fewer viewers to make a hit. *Seinfeld* won the 1994-95 ratings race with a rating that two decades earlier wouldn't have even placed the show in the Top Twenty-five. Such
a disintegration of the network audience meant that the networks no
longer had to program for as large a mass to make money, and shows
like *Seinfeld*—which appealed to upscale viewers—often were the result. By 1995, half the sitcoms on TV seemed to feature singles living
in cities like New York, if only because these series appealed to viewers similarly situated who, in turn, appealed to advertisers because they
have lots of discretionary income.

Yet even though television was finally acknowledging the nation's
diversity, that didn't mean that shows like *Seinfeld* were realistic national self-portraits either. After all, the more that television sitcoms
have moved in the direction of "realism," the less authentic they have
often become. For all the praise that *All in the Family* received, Archie
Bunker was a parody; even the witty comedy of *Mary Tyler Moore*
hardly reflected a workplace anyone could recognize with honest as-
surance. Similarly, no one—not even an Upper East Sider—has hours

every day to spend chatting with friends in a diner. Yet critics were fond of praising the realism of *Seinfeld*. "Men probably laughed louder than women at the episode in which Elaine discovered that her nipple was exposed on her Christmas card photo," wrote McInerney. "This stuff happens to all of us." Oh, really?

Seinfeld did have considerable strengths, however. The show was genuinely funny, a rare treat on prime-time television. Some of the series episodes, like the one on the "soup Nazi" or on losing a car in a parking lot, were inspired, and the supporting cast of Elaine, Kramer, and George was exceptional. "It's about nothing, everything else is about something; this, it's about nothing," said George in pitching his and Jerry's sitcom proposal to a network, as *Seinfeld* became a show within a show. Already, some of its lines have become pop culture classics: "I'm Cosmo Kramer, the Assman!"; "Not that there's anything wrong with that"; and "Master of your Domain."

Seinfeld was also a hit because it appealed to men more than did many other sitcoms, as it reflected a new adolescent sensibility sweeping America in the 1990s. Along with the comedy of David Letterman, the cartoon series *Beavis and Butt-Head,* megamovies like *Jurassic Park,* and syndicated radio talkmeisters Howard Stern and Don Imus, *Seinfeld* often echoed the world of 11-to-15-year-old boys. The radio style of Stern and Imus, for example, was that of the narcissistic class cutup in seventh grade: Both sat in a playhouse-like radio studio with a bunch of guys and horsed around for hours talking about sex, sports, and politics, all the while laughing at their own loutish, subversive jokes.

Seinfeld shared a similar sensibility, albeit softened somewhat for television. Like a group of 14-year-olds, the men on *Seinfeld* seemed not to hold real regular jobs, the better to devote time to "the gang." (One woman, Elaine, was allowed to tag along with the boys, much like those younger sisters who are permitted to hang out with their brothers.) Not only was every man in Seinfeld's gang unmarried and pushing fortysomething, but it also was difficult to imagine any having a real relationship with any woman but his mother. Note how much more often parents of adult children appeared here than on other shows.

Or compare *Seinfeld* to its predecessor in its NBC Thursday night time slot, *Cheers*. If the men on that show didn't spend much time at work either, they did hang out in a traditional domain of adults—the tavern—and the hero, Sam Malone, spent many of his waking hours chasing women. Seinfeld, by contrast, was better known for sitting in a restaurant eating french fries with his pals. One of the most celebrated risqué *Seinfeld* episodes was about (what else?) masturbation, while others dealt with urinating in the shower or on couches. That's usually big stuff in the seventh grade, but not much beyond.

The *Seinfeld* evocation of early male adolescence did reflect deeper cultural strains. This country has always venerated "bad boys," from Huck Finn to Holden Caulfield. Moreover, many psychologists consider that preteen stage of life, when one is acutely aware of being powerless, as the time when individuals are most subversive of the society at-large. That sentiment fit a nineties cultural mood, as America became full of the defiant, oppositional anger that often characterizes the early adolescent—witness the tearing down of public figures with the ready help of the tabloid press, and the flocking to antiestablishment talk radio whereon the humor grew more derisive by the day. In a similar vein, one could imagine the whole *Seinfeld* cast of perpetual adolescents on the Clinton White House staff working with George Stephanopoulos or Craig Livingstone. Yet boys will be boys: Maybe that's why much of the country viewed the Clinton administration's missteps as benignly as they viewed George Costanza's.

Because this country has always had tendencies that remind observers of a 14-year-old boy, no one would blame *Seinfeld* alone for society's failure to grow up and take care of its real children; its current ambivalence about paternal authority; or its vulgarity and exhibitionist inclinations. Yet the show definitely played a role, along with its cultural cousins. In much the same way that *Roseanne* had domesticated tabloid television for the masses, *Seinfeld* did the same for sophomoric talk radio, as embodied by fellow Manhattanites Stern and Imus.

By contrast, *Home Improvement* had the gentle ring of mainstream truth. It's no accident that 14-to-30-year-olds in a *TV Guide* poll voted Jill and Tim the TV parents most like their own. Naturally, that state of affairs sometimes drew the critics' ire. "'Home Improvement' is a reactionary return, after 'Roseanne' and 'Married With Children' and all those Census Bureau reports, to the semi-extinct idea of a nuclear family whose members actually like each other," wrote Chuck Eddy in a review of the show for *millennium pop.*

Unlike *Seinfeld, Home Improvement* was about grown-ups. Take the premiere episode: Tim (the Toolman) Taylor, host of a cable show called *Tool Time,* wants to rewire his dishwasher to make it more powerful but ends up breaking it. When he tries to comfort his wife after she doesn't get a job, he inadvertently ends up making her feel worse. In just such a fashion *Home Improvement* was built around that preoccupation central to the zeitgeist of the nineties: If television once told us *Father Knows Best,* this show probed what it meant to be the best father and husband in an age of feminism and embattled male identity.

When Matt Williams and David McFadzean were developing the idea for this show, they were both reading the work of noted linguist Deborah Tannen on male-female communication. "Her book deals with the fact that men and women speak different languages," Williams once remembered. "That right there is the piston that drives this television series. Jill and Tim will never do the same thing the same way, and both sides are valid." On another occasion, Williams noted:

> The biggest challenge for us is to take absurd situations, or extreme points of view or actions, and root them in some kind of truth. . . . If we do our job correctly, those are the things the audience will never think twice about, because we've rooted them in some kind of behavioral truth.

And so the show went in the 1990s, quietly drawing better in rural than urban areas yet still doing well among professionals. Like Jerry Seinfeld, Tim Allen's persona became a new cultural icon—the postfeminist handyman. His was a sitcom prototype with the qualities that many Americans in the 1990s held dear—low-key, predictable, intelligent but not particularly well-educated, with a little dirt under his fingernails. If he'd been a politician in the nineties, he would have had little in common with Bill Clinton or Newt Gingrich—Washington insiders and policy preachers to the core. (Colin Powell would be another story.) For different reasons, Taylor also would have had little to talk about with Seinfeld, who never would have tuned in to *Tool Time,* much less own a hammer. (Like many Manhattanites, Seinfeld always seemed to prefer the movies to television anyway.)

Here, then, were two conflicting strains in the American character: *Seinfeld,* a popular urban show about eccentric individualism and the flight from adulthood, versus *Home Improvement,* a popular suburban show about commitment and ultimately about family. The forces which create "the buzz" in this country—the press, the public relations establishment, and Madison Avenue—simply loved *Seinfeld,* which tells us as much about their makeup and tastes as about the show itself. We also had our Seinfeld-esque White House.

The guess here, however, is that *Home Improvement* was still a better reflection of who we are, despite major social changes over decades. In the not-so-grand tradition of television, viewers still feel more comfortable with the Cleavers, the Andersons, and the Bradys than they do with the *Seinfeld* alternative. Viewers want happy, traditional families, even when they realize that a TV family and setting is idealized—or perhaps *especially* when they realize it. The perfect man for the nineties? It's OK to have that fling with the "bad boy"—who, after all, has always been part of the greater American family. But when it's time to settle down, he isn't the guy you're going to want to bring into your living rooms and bedrooms, night after night.

58

Home Shopping: Commercialism as Salvation
(QVC: 1986–PRESENT)

Cable television helped bring influential ventures like MTV and CNN to the public. Its most significant contribution to programming in the long run, however, may be the way it has made the world safe for home shopping. Home shopping is usually ignored by television critics, who would no more review an offering on one of these channels than a low-budget commercial. Yet home shopping shows and networks are proliferating, and half-hour infomercials—their televisual cousins—are the lifeblood of many cable networks, particularly late at night. Networks like Lifetime and the Nashville Network have been known to run hours of these shows a week, and other networks, like the Family Channel and USA, aren't far behind. Even networks such as the Sci-Fi Channel and MTV have already begun to ape home shopping, with programs offering items such as rock-tour T-shirts.

Home shopping began, in the early 1980s, with the somewhat downscale Home Shopping Club—which became the Home Shopping Network. QVC (the initials stand for Quality, Value, and Convenience) started in 1986, offering more-upscale products and a laid-back approach, with structured programs which mimic the regular fare of television programming. A typical routine on these networks involves the hostess breathlessly describing the value and beauty of a bracelet, a jumpsuit, skin cream, and so on. Viewers then have a few minutes to call in to order the item while the hostess continues to sing its praises. Then the buying opportunity of a lifetime is over, and the nonstop hostess relentlessly moves on to the next product, effervescing anew.

By the mid-nineties, the largest home shopping network, QVC, was said to be drawing audiences somewhere in the neighborhood of the average audiences for the far more celebrated MTV and CNN. It has been estimated that around 9 percent of the viewers who watch QVC's shows are regular buyers spending about $300 each per year. By the mid-nineties, the Home Shopping Network and QVC each had sales of over a billion dollars a year and QVC alone now logs well over 50 million calls a year. Around 70 percent of the audience for home shopping is women, meaning that both the programming and the merchandising tend to reflect their tastes. According to one 1994 account, jewelry accounts for 42 percent of QVC's sales, with apparel second at 18 percent, though the real markets to be tapped, everyone agrees, are in anything big that can be demonstrated, such as exercise machines. In 1997, QVC even broke into politics, with special shows selling Clinton inaugural memorabilia.

Viewers tuning in to all these around-the-clock shopping offerings often aren't there just to browse or buy. They're also watching a TV performance, just as much as is anyone tuning in to *Homicide* or *Masterpiece Theatre*. What they generally find are one or two amiable emcees—something like Regis and Kathie Lee—soothingly but glowingly describing the kind of women's clothing or jewelry one might find at a glorified Kmart. Models usually display most or all of the items. These shows frequently feature celebrities, too—some regulars, like a Joan Rivers, and at times a special guest, such as a Willie Nelson. In fact, the special appearances often are indistinguishable from those on the usual TV talk show. Instead of hawking a movie or a book, as on *The Tonight Show,* however, these celebrities sell their own consumer products.

Infomercials often involve the same type of celebrity, though they differ from home shopping networks in at least one important way. Viewers actively tune in to the home shopping experience, whereas infomercials—which often run in the middle of the night and without advance publicity—tend to ensnare viewers who are channel surfing. That's why they're often made to resemble real programming.

On one level, this is all part of a deeply rooted American tradition: There's not much here that door-to-door salesmen and the Sears catalogue haven't tried for at least a century. Yet, like other forms of television programming, home shopping and infomercials have their roots in other kinds of television entertainment that go beyond the commercials to which they are often compared—game shows, religious series, fundraising telethons, even sitcoms. The line between "Live Aid," *Queen for a Day, Oral Roberts,* and QVC is faint indeed.

As theorists like Mimi White have pointed out, the fare on home shopping networks differs from commercials in a key respect: The goal of home shopping is not to deliver audiences to advertisers, but to attract its own audiences, who will spend money on the spot by calling a telephone number. Thus home shopping probably had its earliest broadcasting roots in the pre-TV fundraising efforts to conquer polio or sell war bonds. It was there, after all, that broadcasting first developed the techniques of "the sell." Even Kate Smith was a pioneer in raising money over the radio, using an 18-hour marathon in 1943 to extract pledges of almost $40 million for war bonds.

In April 1949, television staged its first "telethon" (a combination of the words *television* and *marathon* which entered the language during the following year), when Dean Martin and Jerry Lewis joined Milton Berle and a host of other celebrities during a 16-hour stint designed to raise money for the Damon Runyon Memorial Fund, which fought cancer. The Muscular Dystrophy Association held its first telethon in the early 1950s, though it wasn't until 1966 that it began staging its annual Labor Day event, modeled on the old variety shows and starring Jerry Lewis—who is to this form of programming what Walter Cronkite was to the news.

Over the years, other charities and causes would (with varying degrees of success) attempt to replicate that telethon's impact. Viewers would eventually see telethons to benefit everything from the fight against Cerebral Palsy, the struggle against world hunger ("Live Aid"), or the Democratic National Committee, to the Argentinian government, which staged a telethon in its country in order to help finance its brief unsuccessful war against Great Britain in the Falklands. Joining the trend was Richard Nixon, who held a telethon on the eve of his 1968 election, and an indicted California sheriff who once held a two-day TV fest to try to raise money for his legal-defense fund. The most pervasive and poorly produced televised telethons today occur as pledge drives on—where else?—public television, where many PBS stations would probably be better off just running ads, and forgetting about "giving" us the personalized umbrella, should we respond favorably to the pitch.

To a casual television observer, the network telethon is a striking event: It is really the only time—other than during a major news or sports event—when television is willing to suspend its regular programming. Though telethons have changed over time, they consistently retain characteristics which can be seen today on their descendant home shopping channels. They are almost always live. Appearances by celebrities are a calling card, as is the persistent theme of expectant optimism tempered by fatigue. Dramatizing the plight of the victim is *de rigueur* as well. Many critics have charged that Lewis's Muscular Dystrophy telethons have a way of "dehumanizing the sick, reducing them to pitiable objects"—though a similar process went on daily for years on *Queen for a Day,* the oft-ridiculed yet popular 1950s "game" show, hosted by Jack Bailey, that featured women describing to a studio audience how pitiful their lives were. The contestant garnering the loudest response on the applause meter got the queenly crown and went home with a prize.

Viewers contribute to these televisual causes, a fundraising consultant once explained, because "the average American doesn't have power. He is looking for ways to make a difference, to feel significant, to get self-esteem; and what better way for him to get that than to be significantly involved in an organization which is meeting human needs?" A similar pitch thus soon found its way into both of the nation's political conventions: In 1996, both Democrats and Republicans put a group of disabled Americans on display in prime time to tell us their tales of despair and struggle. The goal here was to gain votes, not money—but the approach was the same.

What's odd is how closely the mood on home shopping shows conforms to this air of commiseration: Without a strong implicit sense of self-absorption, these networks would fail. It's as if the self-pitying viewer and buyer making the "contribution" to QVC and receiving merchandise in return is as much a victim worthy of a broadcast as the winner of *Queen for a Day*, the starving child in Africa, and the arthritic patient in Texas. If the daytime talk shows of the nineties helped create a national sense of victimization, then most assuredly these networks were there to reap the profits.

It is here, too, that these shows cross paths with televised religious programs, which have perfected not only the art of the pitch, but also the notion that givers will inherit the earth. Writers like Elizabeth Kaye have noted how the QVC message is constantly infused with similar protestations of love—for products, the host, and even the network itself. Too, the pitches on home shopping shows often include "testimonials" from satisfied customers who attest to the ability of the product to transform one's life. It's worth recalling that a founder of an original home shopping network went on to start a not-for-profit religious channel.

The Grade-B celebrities one tends to see on the telethons are also the sort of folks one finds in infomercials: Fran Tarkenton, Meredith Baxter, Victoria Principal, *et al.* (Once upon a time, these personalities populated the cubical compartments of *Hollywood Squares* or made guest appearances on *The Love Boat*.) On the infomercial, these icons are dispatched to sell everything from irons to beauty products to oldies collections. Those infomercials that invoke the spirit of telethons the most are the multitude that push self-improvement products. Bearing such titles as "Inside Secrets" and "Amazing Discoveries," these shows deal with everything from weight control and "personal power" to "Laugh Your Way to Success." In the same ways that telethons often promise to cure what appear to be insoluble problems (say, hunger in Africa), the infomercials pledge to help viewers deal with seemingly insurmountable physical and personal problems—all by dialing a number and spending money.

We are still in the early days of these new genres. Yet it already seems clear that home shopping will further accelerate the trend to encourage Americans to stay at home—with a resulting loss of community involvement. Moreover, commercial television has always tried to blur the line between advertising and program, the better to make the ads unobtrusive. Indeed, in the early days of television, Ricky and Lucy would hawk cigarettes during breaks which seemed to be parts of the show. Even more than MTV videos, home shopping obliterates those differences, making its innovations extremely enticing to the people who control the industry. Thus, no matter how well home shopping does—and it seems destined to do exceedingly well—it will always emphasize a fundamental truth about American television: No matter how you look at it, it's always going to be *commercial* broadcasting.

59

The Innovations of *ER* and the Fight for Health-Care Reform
(NBC: 1994–PRESENT)

There has always been a place for medicine on television. There was NBC's *Medic* in the 1950s, starring Richard Boone; *Dr. Kildare* and

Ben Casey in the 1960s; *Marcus Welby, M.D.* and *Medical Center* in the 1970s; and *St. Elsewhere* and *Trapper John, M.D.* in the 1980s. *General Hospital* has been one of daytime's most consistent hits for decades.

Still, it took almost everyone by surprise when *ER* shot to second in the ratings for the 1994–95 season in which it premiered, and then took over the top spot a year later. After all, critics had been declaring prime-time drama dead for several years—a victim of shorter attention spans in an MTV age. "Fans need not be told that the form is in trouble," wrote Marc Gunther for the Knight-Ridder Newspapers group in 1993. Moreover, the fact that Bill Clinton was making health-care reform the centerpiece of his first two years in office seemed to signal something of a disenchantment with medicine in general, and doctors in particular.

Yet *ER* shattered all the preconceptions. It brilliantly took a number of trends in programming—the push to realism, the focus on dysfunction, and the emphasis on shorter segments—and combined them to create a synthesis of an early-evening "reality" show, a daytime talk fest, and *Hill Street Blues.* It played into a growing national obsession with health, as the baby boomers got older. Most important, it had Bill and Hillary Rodham Clinton to thank: In trying to reform American medicine, they had inadvertently caused the public once again to focus on how much it admired doctors—our traditional broadcast heroes—and *ER* was the beneficiary.

If television has always been drawn to the medical profession, it's because medical dramas take place in a controlled setting that's easy to film. Doctor stories also present dramatic "life and death" crises, an opportunity to show blood, and an array of characters of both sexes. (By contrast, adventure or crime shows tend to be male-dominated.) "Grownups, like children, like to be frightened," James Brolin, costar of the early 1970s hit *Marcus Welby,* once told *TV Guide.* "Kids go for monsters and horror creatures. Adults go for cancer and brain tumors."

Marcus Welby, M.D. was the father of *ER*—claiming the Number 1 slot for doctors 25 years earlier, during the 1970–71 season. As the sixties became the seventies, TV had turned to doctor shows because the television industry was undergoing one of its periodic attacks from Congress for violent programming. Unwilling to produce the usual spate of shoot-'em-up Westerns, and anxious to tap risqué topics like drug use and teen pregnancy in a way that would keep conservative critics happy, the networks turned out an unusual number of medical shows. These included *The Bold Ones, Medical Center,* and *Welby*—the travails of a general practitioner who worked out of his home.

Yet there was more to the trend than that. "We don't treat fingers or skins or skulls or bones or lungs," Dr. Welby said in the show's first episode, which featured the unusual story of a young teacher who was terminally ill. "We treat people." The lead was played by Robert Young, who had starred in the 1950s sitcom *Father Knows Best,* and he embodied virtually the same role here—leading critics to dub the show "Doctor Knows Best."

Welby shared a number of characteristics with other television heroes of that era, like *Owen Marshall: Counsellor at Law,* whose show had the same executive producer. Welby was a good listener. He also was an older and warmer kind of family man (even though he didn't have much of a family), who spent much of each week solving his patients' problems—which often had less to do with medicine than with the existential travails of modern living, such as unhappy marriages, ungrateful children, and terrible jobs. "What we do are stories about people—people who have something wrong," David Victor, who developed the show, once said. "The guy who can fix it just happens to be a doctor."

Welby's reassuring manner helped quell the outcry that normally would have greeted a show which tackled everything from impotence and homosexuality to drug addiction. While *All in the Family* in the same era drew the headlines and controversy because of its outspoken style, *Welby* was dealing with many of the same issues, albeit in a way which usually strongly reinforced "traditional values": Drug use was condemned, homosexuality was treated as an illness that needs to be cured, and so on.

ER, which hit the hospital floor running on Thursdays at 10:00 P.M. on NBC, was Welby plus a gaggle of other medicos passed on to the next generation, as doctor shows continued to deal with controversial topics in an uncontroversial manner. Yet, instead of following the traditional formula whereby an older doctor imparts wisdom to his junior associates, the younger Kildares and Kileys were in control on *ER.* Now the doctors themselves—self-absorbed baby boomers—had to deal with the existential problems that Welby had once detected in his patients.

The dramatic formula was also updated for the 1990s. Between 1981 and 1990, Hill Street Blues and St. Elsewhere had changed the definition of drama on television—introducing soap-opera-like, multiple plots and characters, cinema vérité techniques, and a more-complex, often downbeat ethos which attracted an upscale audience. Yet these more-cosmopolitan dramas didn't attract especially large audiences: Between 1984 and 1994, despite their more-sophisticated techniques, the number of prime-time, hour-long dramas on the networks dropped from 37 to 23, while the number of reality-based, action-packed tabloid shows, such as Rescue 911 and COPS (which took viewers on actual ambulance or police chases), went from 4 to 11.

The chief ER innovation was to combine the upscale drama and reality genres. The most popular aspects of Hill Street and St. Elsewhere were still there—the serial plots, the big-city locale, the focus on the workplace, the odd lighting, the tremulous hand-held cameras, the chaos, and a cast of more than a dozen regulars. In its day, which had only been a decade earlier, all of this was supposed to give viewers a taste of realism. Yet St. Elsewhere, like Welby before it, was somewhat removed from the hectic world of emergency-room medicine. "Medicine is the byproduct," Tom Fontana, coproducer of St. Elsewhere, once said. "We want to make good stories about human beings who happen to be doctors and nurses and patients."

By contrast, ER upped the ante as creator Michael Crichton—a medical doctor and the author of (among other hit novels) Jurassic Park—based ER on his own experiences in an emergency room. The language on ER was so "inside" that average Americans could now discern a "Tox Screen" from an "O Negative." The show employed six real nurses, performing as extras, to ensure that scenarios were accurately portrayed. The premiere had 87 speaking parts, and viewers simply lost count of the stories as bodies were quickly wheeled in and out of the emergency room.

"The pace of TV has been artificially slowed," Crichton had told a reporter. "I wanted to crank it up to something resembling reality." One can quibble with his definition of "reality," but this acceleration drew men back to a genre which had traditionally appealed more to women. This was a soap opera on speed; *Newsweek* called the show's pacing "channel surfing without the remote."

A focus on violence and disorder didn't hurt, either. *ER* was something of a police and tabloid-news show masquerading as a doctor show, as the preoccupation with social dissolution which had once been the province of reality-based cop shows and the news now migrated into Cook County General. Death was a constant, often by bloody stabbings or drug overdoses—as were unhappy endings. Yet all of the above just made this show blend more seamlessly into the local news that followed it on the schedule, thus pleasing the local affiliates. "Almost everything in television is a cop show. It just is," *Hill Street* creator Steven Bochco had once told an interviewer, and this show proved his point. One of the highest-rated segments of the second season revolved around pediatrician Doug Ross's efforts to save a boy trapped in a flooding storm drain. On another, a drug smuggler from Bolivia swallowed a condom full of cocaine: Would it burst?

Like the tabloid shows it aped, the message of *ER* was that things weren't working the way television had once taught us they should. "People see the U.S. as a grittier place," said David Westin, president of ABC Television Networks Group. "Good entertainment has to reflect how people are feeling." That "grittiness" was the credo of a number of drama shows that defined the mid-1990s—*Homicide, NYPD Blue,* and *Law and Order* among them. Yet few ever asked: Was life in the nineties really grittier, or had television simply gotten that way so it could acceptably increase the level of blood and violence that has always attracted audiences?

ER also had an obvious health angle, which tied into the boomers' increasing obsession with sickness and aging. "Who knows?" asked one critic, who added that in 20 years "[a]rthritis could replace murder as the most dramatic storyline on television." Like daytime talk shows, with their appeal to women, ER was also a show as obsessed with dysfunction as any *Sally Jessy Raphael* segment—and not simply because everyone in the hospital was suffering from a severe case of sleep deprivation. In a typical second season conundrum, the doctors had to deal with child abuse, Ross was a womanizer, Dr. Greene's marriage was failing, Nurse Hathaway was a pill-popper, and Jeanie Boulet was worried that her estranged husband might have given her AIDS. (It turned out he did in one of the show's more celebrated plot twists.) Meanwhile Dr. Susan Lewis wanted to adopt the baby that her sister abandoned, which raised the question: Since the show takes place in Chicago, why didn't she just travel across town and go on The Oprah Winfrey Show so someone could help her?

Yet the bottom line was that doctors were again among our most venerated TV heroes—even if they were younger, more ambivalent about their role, and less respectful of their elders than before. "Guardian of Birth . . . Healer of the Sick . . . Comforter of the Aged" was the way *Medic* described the medical profession in the 1950s, ascribing to it qualities such as "the eye of an eagle, the heart of a lion, and the hand of a woman." Though such images were up-dated over four decades to account for the women's movement and a baby-boom sensibility, they would never waver much. Even in adver-tising, doctors would always lead a charmed TV life ("I'm not a doc-tor, but I do look like one, and I'm here to tell you . . ."). The heroes of *M★A★S★H* were doctors, and Cliff Huxtable of *The Cosby Show* was, too. With few exceptions, doctors have always gotten even better treatment on television than do religious figures, which tells you who have become our new priests in a high-tech, secular age. Ever wonder why they called it "*Saint* Elsewhere"?

ER also reinforced the traditionally positive TV image of doctors as interns or residents in public hospitals, projecting an image of selfless service: TV doctors will treat anybody, anywhere, anytime. House calls? On TV, doctors have been known to drive patients home—and even clean their houses. After all, the biggest cliché line in medical dramas has never been "Let's hit the golf course!" or "Get these hypochondriacs out of my office!" but "You've been working for two days straight. Go home and get some rest." As for the claims of real-ism, ever see an episode on a medical show about filling out health-insurance forms?

Little wonder, then, that Bill and Hillary had a problem with their health-care plan—which frightened Americans so much that they flocked to *ER* in response. In reality, the TV image of doctors had never existed in a vacuum; it became part of our national conscious-ness. Thus even though Americans might sense that something was amiss in our health-care system, their idealized vision of the medical profession would always get in the way of significant reform—particularly if doctors themselves went to work to oppose those efforts (which they almost always did). It's difficult to tamper with national myths: Just as no one would think of passing a law saying that Mr. Smith can't go to Washington, it would always be impossible to directly target the medical profession. Face it: There have been many great doctors on TV, but it's hard to remember many great politicians. In a cultural clash between Clinton and the whole panoply of doctors from Kildare and Casey to the gang at Cook County General, it was invariably wise to put your money on Welby and his children. After all, the doctor always knows best.

60

How *Wheel of Fortune* Won the Cold War
(NBC, CBS, SYNDICATION: 1975–PRESENT)

For a time in the 1990s, Paul Gilbert may well have been the world's foremost expert on television's monster hit, *Wheel of Fortune*. During a span of almost two decades, Gilbert viewed well over 6,000 episodes of the popular syndicated game show, which ran five times a week—usually at around 6:30 P.M. or 7:00 P.M., between the news and the start of prime-time programming. This means that Gilbert, who worked on the show's premiere in the mid-1970s with creator Merv Griffin, saw the wheel turn well over 100,000 times, the hangman-like puzzle solved on more than 15,000 occasions, and a contestant scream maybe 5,000 times. He probably witnessed the giveaway of a fleet of cars, not to mention countless mantel clocks, serving carts, and whatever else might be thrown in for good measure. After almost 20 years, he could probably recite the show's disembodied opening call ("WHEEL OF FORTUNE!") backwards, and flip letters on the game board with an aplomb worthy of hostess Vanna White.

As the Director of International Program Development and International Projects for King World Productions, the company that distributes *Wheel of Fortune* to over 50 countries, however, Gilbert became more than just a game-show sage. He was at the center of an enormous corporate effort which in turn was part of a far larger movement that saw American television and its popular culture literally engulf the planet. The products of Hollywood have become one of our more influential—if not economically vital—exports, ranking just behind agriculture. *Beverly Hills 90210* was a hit in Australia, Italy, and Brazil; *The Cosby Show* drew high ratings in South Africa, even during apartheid; *Dynasty* rose to near the top of the charts in China; and Tom & Jerry cartoons became a TV hit in, of all places, Lebanon. As Marshall McLuhan predicted, the world has become a global village—and, throughout that village, the natives all drink Coke, eat Big Macs, wear Mickey Mouse watches, buy Barbie dolls, and follow the career of Arnold Schwarzenegger, film by film. As Gore Vidal has said, the capital of the world is no longer Washington, but Hollywood—whose pervasive global role and influence have been compared to that of the Church in medieval times.

One of the sacred rites of today's "church" has been *Wheel of Fortune,* one of the most consistent American television hits abroad in the 1990s. Since going international in Australia in the mid-1980s, the show was often watched by over 100 million people each week in places like Turkey, Hungary, and Croatia—which launched its show in the middle of a war in the early nineties and saw it go directly to Number 1. Whether the country was Finland, Belgium, Israel, or Denmark, the show tended to dominate its time slot; *Kolo Fortuny* was the most popular program in Poland for a time in the mid-1990s, where it was watched by an astounding 70 percent of the nation's households. One night, the show asked viewers to turn off their lights if they were watching—and whole neighborhoods went black. In France, long diffident to any American pop culture product not starring Jerry Lewis, there were near-riots when *La Roue de la Fortune* held its contestant tryouts.

One reason for *Wheel's* success was that the international versions were often custom-made for countries, in their own language. "If I tried to do an American game in Germany, people wouldn't watch it,"

Fred Cohen, president of King World Productions, once said. "The idioms wouldn't work and it wouldn't be their show." Thus about half the foreign editions had their own version of Pat Sajak, their own Vanna, their own prizes, and their own distinctive puzzles.

Game shows, of course, were traditionally designed as daytime fare for housewives, and still bear some of the earmarks of their origin: good-looking male hosts; mostly women in the studio audience and as contestants; and household goods as prizes. Merv Griffin modeled *Wheel* on the old childhood game of "hangman." The premise was unnervingly simple: Three contestants each spin the wheel in turn. If the wheel stops on an amount of money, the player gets credit for that money, and a chance to guess a letter in the mystery phrase, which can run the gamut from "MEDIUM RARE" to "BETTER LUCK NEXT TIME" to "SATURDAY MORNING CARTOONS." If a contestant guesses a letter which appears in the phrase, the contestant gets to go again—otherwise, play passes to the next player. Each goes in turn until someone guesses the phrase, winning the money he or she has accumulated and additional prizes. At the end of the show, the contestant with the most money has a chance to compete in the bonus round and win a really big prize, like a cruise.

Trying to describe the popularity and mystique of *Wheel of Fortune* simply by reciting its rules, however, is like trying to do the same with baseball. There's a lot more to it—and many of those subtleties evolved as the kinks in the game were worked out in daytime obscurity in the seventies. At one point, contestants were given clues to the puzzle by a telephone, which rang on a table. That took too long. Originally, the all-important wheel lay flat, and so couldn't really be seen by home viewers enough to engage them. (The installation of an overhead camera made it more visible to the home viewer.) Winning contestants used to go shopping onstage with their winnings, a segment that was ended once cable channels began offering home viewers a similar experience. In the beginning, there was also only one host—the traditional male—and the board was run electronically.

The key changes began to come in 1983, after eight years on NBC's daytime schedule, when Griffin took the then-unusual route of offering his game show in syndication to local stations looking for an evening program to fill the niche between the news and prime time.

With far more men and people with daytime jobs watching at that hour, the show changed and went upscale: The set got glitzier, the prizes got better, the puzzles got harder, and Vanna White's newly created role as letter-turner was glamorized. The shrewd result, which neatly coincided with the rise of the Reagan era's celebration of conspicuous consumption, was the biggest syndication success in television history until then, as *Wheel* drew ratings higher than those of many prime-time shows.

Over the years, as the show retained its hold on the viewing audience far longer than the typical program, other changes were added. The show has thus raised to an art form the process of everything from how to lay out the merchandise on the set to how to pick contestants. (First you have to take a written test. Then you're put through a practice round with other *Wheel* wannabees, to see if you get excited, smile, are outgoing, and like to have fun. Only a very small percentage of those who try out make it.)

Why this rather simple show so consistently captivated America became a source of speculation for everyone from writers for *People* to left-wing social theorists. The simple explanation was that the game "plays well" at home, while appealing to both genders and all ages. Like Monopoly, the country's most beloved board game, *Wheel* combined in roughly equal measures elements of gambling (the wheel), intellect (guessing the puzzle), and money (winning prizes). Critics such as Alexander Cockburn found in *Wheel* an "idealized representation of the proper motions of the economy"—contestants didn't so much compete with one another for material rewards as against the wheel and their own intellectual capabilities. Vanna White's appeal came in for some heavy analysis, too, with one Yale psychologist reasoning, in an academic journal, that what contestants are really playing for is not money, but Vanna herself. "No matter how many letters Ms. White turns over," he wrote, "the message is always the same: 'Take it off, Vanna!'"

In any event, the show was a virtual gold mine for King World, not only because it was popular but because it was cheaper and easier to produce than the average dramatic show. Many sponsors donated the prizes for publicity value, and there was little of the usual high costs for actors, new sets, or scores of writers that plague other shows. That meant *Wheel* was made to order for a world market which often can't afford the extravagant overhead of a Hollywood production.

Wheel had the advantage of hitting the international market at a time when many countries were allowing private broadcasters to compete with state-run television for the first time. The Iron Curtain was also crumbling, opening up a vast new territory for commercial television. Those events created a ready-made market for the kind of cookie-cutter programming that a game show offers, and particularly one produced locally in the native language. "In most of the world, television was designed to be an information or propaganda medium," Ellen Politi, an executive who worked on *Wheel* once said. "In the United States, it was designed to be an entertainment medium, and we understand better than anyone else how to do that."

There were some problems. Though Western Europe had a history of game shows, Eastern Europe did not, and the production values there were far different, at least in the beginning. Some audiences had to be taught when to clap, and contestants when to scream or even smile. "You couldn't give away big products like refrigerators in some of these countries because the winners couldn't afford to pay the taxes on them without selling the prize," said Cohen.

Some programmers at King World had originally thought that *Jeopardy!* (their other syndicated game-show hit) would be a better fit for the world. "But the problem we ran into is that a lot of people elsewhere don't understand the concept of receiving an answer to a question and then having to guess the question," explained Cohen. "You give them the answer and they think that's the end of it." *Jeopardy!* was also more expensive to produce because of the complicated electronic set that has to feature all those answers.

The puzzles of *Wheel of Fortune* were also a little different abroad, even after translation into Flemish, Hungarian, or Turkish. American pop culture does rule the world, which is why Elvis Presley could be a puzzle answer in Germany, or Donald Duck in Belgium. Once you got away from music and movies, however, foreign puzzles tended to be harder—a tribute, perhaps, to the dumbing down of America, or at least to the concept that viewers here would rather beat the TV contestants than admire them.

There were also some regional distinctions. In several countries, laws prevented shows from giving away money, so contestants just played for prizes. Finland filmed its shows on board a cruise ship. A children's version of the game was introduced in—where else?—Denmark, the home of Hans Christian Andersen. In some places, new categories were added to the traditional phrases or names of celebrities. In Holland, for example, there was a category entitled "Canals." Eastern-bloc countries differed a bit from those in the West, too. That's less because of the production values, which tended to be surprisingly high, and more because the prizes (at least in the beginning) sometimes didn't quite measure up to the standards of the West.

The larger question, of course, is why this particular show was able to grip the rest of the world as firmly as it did the United States. Through a combination of shrewdness and luck, *Wheel* had found itself at the center of a number of hot trends in America. Its emphasis on the gambling wheel resonated in a culture where state lotteries and legalized gambling were proliferating. Even the mystical metaphor of "the wheel of fortune" itself was bound to strike a chord in a culture where half the books on the nonfiction best-seller list usually deal with spirituality and the other half with how to make more money. Yet those gambling and spiritual metaphors also carried currency worldwide, as did the show's preoccupation with conspicuous consumption and material success. With its mingling of prizes and the game—or advertising and programming—*Wheel* was as good an introduction as any to the Brave Old World of commercial programming.

Wheel's success abroad, however, was also due to the way it presented key elements of American folklore and values to the globe daily, in some places for the first time. Take the Horatio Alger myth— the appealing idea that on the level playing-field that is America, anyone can advance to the top through hard work. At home or abroad, most *Wheel* contestants appeared to be about the same height, and dressed in the same way. The capriciousness of the wheel (or life) aside, they had an equal opportunity to advance based on intellectual—though not academic—skills. Unlike the old quiz shows like *The $64,000 Question,* Wheel required street-smart knowledge, not an arcane ability to recall the tiniest details of a subject.

In its own way, *Wheel* also reflected a true understanding of the nature of television—which Americans, after all, do comprehend better than anyone else. When asked about the success of their show abroad, the producers of *Wheel* cited its simplicity. "It's the kind of show you can leave for a few minutes and come back and grasp immediately," said Paul Gilbert, who left King World in 1996 to become vice-president of international project development at Columbia Tri-Star. Hardly fighting words, but there is a profound lesson there about the nature of our television—if not our pop culture—and why it is so appealing and exportable. Other nations developed their popular culture with specific goals in mind: In Britain, the purpose was to uplift the populace; in the Soviet Union, it was to propagandize. By contrast, driven by the impulses of the market, American popular culture just wanted to entertain its audience, and therefore developed a much better sense of what sells than elsewhere.

What's more, America is a nation of immigrants. As Todd Gitlin has written, any pop-culture product that has succeeded here has already been test-marketed in a multicultural environment which best resembles the world market. That fact has a historical counterpart, too: Our popular culture had its origins in the rowdiness of turn-of-the-century vaudeville. In that setting, before an audience where many couldn't speak good English, it was necessary to create entertainment that could be grasped quickly, without knowing much of the language.

That intrinsic search for the simplicity that appeals universally is the secret of the success of American popular culture abroad. It also contains an intuitive understanding of the way people actually watch TV. Throughout its history, television has been criticized frequently for its failure to educate and to present better programming. Those are criteria better applied to other art forms, however. In its purest form, television is a user-friendly medium. It is designed for viewers in the home, often tired or just back from work, watching halfheartedly. Presenting what scholar Robert Thompson once called "the aesthetic of the anaesthetic," American television knows how to appeal to viewers who aren't paying full attention and just want to be entertained. It's no small feat to create that type of programming, and if Americans have mastered the art better than most, *Wheel*'s creators did it better than most Americans.

This show's genius, of course, was that it delivered the world its daily dose of Americana in the guise of a game show—often in each country's own language, no less. Today, for better or worse, the rush to modernity is largely identified in American terms: By buying our programs, these cultures not only buy our know-how and products; they buy our values. In the half-century "twilight struggle" between our ideology and communism, we won. Or, better yet—if television is any guide—*Wheel of Fortune* did.

Appendix: How I Came Up with the 60 Shows

When I began writing this book, I interviewed a number of TV fans and even appeared on a radio talk show or two, to see which 60 shows the public thought should make my list. I found surprising agreement among respondents about—oh—40 of the shows they thought were TV's most notable, influential, or revealing. Harold Bloom would be proud: There's an accepted "canon" of great TV shows, and it includes *All in the Family, The Ed Sullivan Show, I Love Lucy,* and—yes—even *The Brady Bunch*.

Still, any list of 60 is going to be arbitrary at least to some extent. Here's how I came up with mine: I began with a presumption that any show that hit Number 1 for a season would receive strong consideration, on the theory that any program that popular had obviously struck a chord with viewers. Even then, I eliminated nine of those 23 shows on various grounds, and came up with these initial 14:

> *Texaco Star Theater* (with Milton Berle)
> *I Love Lucy*
> *Twenty-One* (substituted for *The $64,000 Question*)
> *Gunsmoke*
> *The Beverly Hillbillies*
> *Rowan and Martin's Laugh-In*
> *All in the Family*
> *60 Minutes*
> *Dallas*
> *The Cosby Show*
> *Roseanne*
> *Home Improvement*
> *Seinfeld*
> *ER*

What got eliminated? *Arthur Godfrey's Talent Scouts* was Number 1 for the 1951–52 season, but its influence was limited. I wouldn't quite say that if you've seen one Western you've seen them all, but there was nothing to write about *Wagon Train* (1961–62 season) which couldn't be covered while discussing *Gunsmoke*. Leaving *Bonanza* off the list was harder (it was Number 1 for three seasons in the mid-1960s), but it, too, gets discussed in the *Gunsmoke* chapter. *The Andy Griffith Show* hit the top spot for the 1967–68 season, but its success was really a continuation of the trend to "rural sitcoms" that was best exemplified by *The Beverly Hillbillies,* and so gets dealt with there.

Marcus Welby, M.D. was Number 1 for the 1970–71 season. With its dramatic focus on doctors, I chose to handle that series by contrasting it with *ER* at the end of the book. *Happy Days* (1976–77) and *Laverne & Shirley* (1977–79) were Number 1 hits in the late 1970s, but they were set in the

1950s, and thus are part of the nostalgia craze I write about in the *Leave It to Beaver* chapter. In the 1980s, *Dynasty* was a one-season wonder (1984–85), but again, there was nothing there that *Dallas* hadn't done first or better. *Cheers,* a terrific show, claimed the top spot for the 1990–91 season, but it was more the embodiment of previous innovations (like the workplace comedy), than a trend-setter itself. Finally, I combined *Home Improvement* (1993–94) and *Seinfeld* (1994–95) into one chapter—on the supposition that they were two sides of a similar coin.

Using my theory about public response and importance, I then added to my initial 13 selections three shows whose episodes produced some of the highest ratings in the history of the medium:

Roots
The Super Bowl
M★A★S★H (the final episode)

Then came the shows that forced their way into the book on almost the opposite theory: Not terribly popular in their own time, these shows remained icons of their age, or of strong cultural sentiments long after they left prime-time TV:

Leave It to Beaver
The Twilight Zone
The Brady Bunch

I then added to these 19 a number of popular shows representative of television genres which hadn't been covered by previous shows. I included these on the theory that any genre persistent and popular enough to continually attract large audiences on TV told us a lot about both the medium's influence and ourselves as a people.

Soap Opera: *All My Children*
Game Show: *The Dating Game*
Religion: *Life Is Worth Living*
Teen Show: *American Bandstand*
Early morning: *Today*
Late night: *The Tonight Show*
Talk: *The Oprah Winfrey Show*
Children's: *Howdy Doody*
PBS: *Masterpiece Theatre*

It's true some might quarrel with the specific choices here: A case could be made for *General Hospital* or *The Guiding Light* instead of *All My Children,* and certainly the choice of *Howdy Doody* is arbitrary, given that most children's programming which followed was of the cartoon variety, not puppetry. Yet most, I think, would agree with the general thrust of the choices.

Three influential cable networks also made the list, as they tried—at least initially—to replace the concept of a show with a kind of seamless telecast devoted to a discrete subject:

CNN
MTV
QVC (home shopping)

That makes 31. Because of their coverage of current affairs, innovative news shows can often mold public sentiment and perceptions more easily than other programming. Thus four such shows made the list:

Meet the Press
The *CBS Evening News* (with Walter Cronkite)
The Local News
Entertainment Tonight

Moreover, because television changes everything into a show (even breaking news), most of the great "events" of the past 50 years have each become a kind of TV event. Thus, these six "shows" made the book:

The Presidential Press Conference
The Kennedy Assassination
The Space Program
The Hostage Crisis
The Ronald Reagan Show
The Hill-Thomas Hearings

Yes, I left out O. J. While he dominated the nation's attention for almost three years and a majority of the country saw at least some aspect of the infamous chase, few watched much of the criminal trial (except for the verdict) because it occurred during the week, when most viewers were at work. By contrast, the Hill-Thomas hearings—a kind of forerunner to our 1990s obsession with televised trials—attracted huge audiences.

Added to these 41 were 8 shows that almost everyone agrees had a key impact on the medium—because of either their critical success or their role as a harbinger in changing television's dramatic conventions and structure:

Dragnet
Disneyland
The Ed Sullivan Show
The Dick Van Dyke Show
Sesame Street
The Mary Tyler Moore Show

Hill Street Blues
Star Trek

Finally, there are two shows which almost everyone puts on his or her list of influence but which I found to be among television's most overrated (if only in terms of influence), and thus worthy of discussion for that reason:

See It Now (with Edward R. Murrow)
Saturday Night Live

That leaves us with but nine shows—and it's here, really, that the choices get to be controversial. For what it's worth, I tried to select these final shows with an eye to programs which, though not as popular as some other series, had captured their times:

The Lawrence Welk Show ('50s)
Mister Ed ('60s)
The Smothers Brothers Comedy Hour ('60s)
The Monkees ('60s)
Mission: Impossible ('60s)
America's Funniest Home Videos ('90s)
Wheel of Fortune ('80s and '90s)

That leaves two shows. For these, I picked two series often overlooked even by television aficionados. Drama shows don't usually do that well in syndication, but *Perry Mason* has been so popular for so long that its success tells us a lot about television, if not our cultural attitude toward lawyers. Finally, Bob Newhart's string of shows are the kind of series, featuring the kind of performer, that consistently do well on television, but few ever notice. It seemed to me worth examining why.

In constructing this book, I positioned most shows in the era in which they premiered. Yet, in the case of some long-lasting series, I put the show in the decade in which I thought it first had a strong influence on the culture. Thus, *The Tonight Show* appears in the 1970s, when it moved from New York to Burbank; The Super Bowl in the 1970s, when "Super Sunday" really became a national holiday; and *Star Trek* in the 1980s, when the whole cult surrounding the series took off.

In my radio-related conversational exchanges, the shows that tended to attract the most attention for being left out of the book were *The Honeymooners* and *The Simpsons*. Though both were excellent series, neither proved popular enough to be included on that account, nor influential enough that many other shows attempted to copy their approaches. On the news side, many viewers mentioned the Kennedy-Nixon debates during 1960. True, those four debates helped to decide an election, but I thought that the institution of the live televised presidential press conference—which began as a result of those debates—had a more far-reaching impact. In a longer book, I might have included the above "shows," plus some of the Number 1's I left out, as well as *The Ernie Kovacs Show, Your Show of Shows, Playhouse 90, The Miss America Pageant, Wide World of Sports,* and *The Red Skelton Show*—which ran for 20 years on NBC and CBS. But alas, television fan that I am, I couldn't include everything.

Bibliography

In the first short section of the bibliography, I've listed those invaluable works upon which I relied frequently throughout the book. (If one of these books was used in detail in a particular chapter, it is usually listed there as well.) A more detailed chapter by chapter bibliography follows of major sources. For each chapter, I've listed books first, then articles. In the case of listings on the World Wide Web, I've often listed only the fact that a show has websites, since the addresses tend to change often, and sites often present duplicate information. For those interested, the best way to find those sites and others is by going to the Ultimate TV Show List on the World Wide Web at http://www.tvnet.com/UTVL/utvl.html.

PRINCIPAL SOURCES USED THROUGHOUT

Brooks and Marsh, *The Complete Directory to Prime Time Network and Cable TV Shows,* Ballantine, 1995.

Castleman and Podrazik, *Watching TV: Four Decades of American Television,* McGraw-Hill, 1982.

Greenfield, *Television: The First Fifty Years,* Crescent Books, 1981.

Javna, *Cult TV,* St. Martin's Press, 1985.

Marc, *Comic Visions: Television Comedy and American Culture,* Unwin Hyman, 1989.

Marc and Thompson, *Prime Time, Prime Movers,* Little, Brown, 1992.

McNeil, *Total Television: The Comprehensive Guide to Programming from 1948 to the Present,* Penguin Books, 1996.

Sackett, *Prime-Time Hits,* Billboard Books, 1993.

Steinberg, *TV Facts,* Facts on File, 1980.

Stempel, *Storytellers to the Nation: A History of Television Writing,* Continuum, 1992.

Stern and Stern, *Encyclopedia of Pop Culture,* Harper Perennial, 1992.

Weiner and eds., *The TV Guide TV Book,* Harper Perennial, 1992.

TV Guide 2000th Issue, 1991.

1. MILTON BERLE AND *THE TEXACO STAR THEATER*

Baughman, *The Republic of Mass Culture: Journalism, Filmmaking and Broadcasting in America since 1941,* Johns Hopkins University Press, 1992.

Berle, *B.S. I Love You: Sixty Funny Years with the Famous and Infamous,* McGraw-Hill, 1988.

Berle and Frankel, *Milton Berle: An Autobiography,* Delacorte Press, 1974.

Brooks and Marsh, *The Complete Directory to Prime Time Network and Cable TV Shows,* Ballantine, 1995.

Greenfield, *Television: The First Fifty Years,* Crescent Books, 1981.

Kisseloff, *The Box: An Oral History of Television,* Viking, 1995.

MacDonald, *One Nation Under Television: The Rise and Decline of Network TV,* Pantheon, 1990.

McNeil, *Total Television: The Comprehensive Guide to Programming from 1948 to the Present,* Penguin Books, 1996.

Snyder, *The Voice of the City: Vaudeville and Popular Culture in New York,* Oxford University Press, 1989.

Spigel, *Make Room for TV: Television and the Family Ideal in Postwar America,* University of Chicago Press, 1992.

Stein (ed.), *American Vaudeville As Seen by Its Contemporaries,* Knopf, 1984.

"New Ratings Show Filmed TV Programs in Audience Hypo." *Variety,* 2/7/51.

"Tele Followup Comment." *Variety,* 2/7/51.

"Television's Top," *Newsweek,* 5/16/49.

"The Child Wonder," *Time,* 5/16/49.

"'Toast of Town' Tape Comparable to Live Shows," *Variety,* 12/21/48.

"Variety Shows Cop Top Hooper Laurels," *Variety,* 12/28/49.

Berle, "A Week's Work," *The New Republic,* 8/25/47.

Cohen, "'Vaudeo' Comes of Age in Texaco Show; Seen Outlet to Vast Talent Pool," *Variety,* 6/16/48.

Gould, "Ed Wynn on TV," *New York Times,* 10/16/49.

Gross, "Milton Berle: Can Miltie, the Man Who Turned America on to Television, Make the Nation Cry 'Uncle' Again?," *People,* 1/25/88.

Hamburger, "Television," *New Yorker,* 10/29/49.

Kaplan, "Milton Berle Honored by Broadcast Museum," *New York Times,* 4/6/85.

Millstein, "TV's Comics Went Thataway," *New York Times,* 2/2/58.

O'Connor, "Milton Berle—Mr. Television," *New York Times,* 3/15/94.

Powers, "A Short Opinionated History of Television," in *TV Guide 2000th Issue,* 1991.

Rosen, "Texaco TV Show Hits Milestone," *Variety,* 6/9/48.

Rosen, "TV Stars Play 'Hospital Tune,'" *Variety,* 12/24/52.

Rosen, "Danger—TV Comics at Work," *Variety,* 12/15/54.

Setlowe, "Comedic Couple Pioneers 'Vaudeo' TV," *Variety,* 1/16/96.

Shayon, "An Old Star with New Tricks," *Saturday Review,* 10/4/52.

Wertheim, "The Rise and Fall of Milton Berle," in O'Connor (ed.), *American History/American Television,* Frederick Ungar Publishing, 1983.

2. *HOWDY DOODY*

Davis, *Say Kids! What Time Is It?,* Little, Brown, 1987.

Eliot, *American Television: The Official Art of the Unofficial,* Doubleday, 1981.

Fischer, *Kids' TV: The First 25 Years,* Facts on File, 1983.

Glut and Harmon, *The Great Television Heroes,* Doubleday, 1975.

MacDonald, *One Nation Under Television: The Rise and Decline of Network TV,* Pantheon, 1990.

Palmer, *Children in the Cradle of Television,* Lexington Books, 1987.

Smith and McCrohan, *Howdy and Me: Buffalo Bob's Own Story,* Plume, 1990.

Spigel, *Make Room for TV: Television and the Family Ideal in Postwar America,* University of Chicago Press, 1992.

Stern and Stern, *Encyclopedia of Pop Culture,* Harper Perennial, 1992.

Tichi, *Electronic Hearth: Creating an American Television Culture,* Oxford University Press, 1991.

TV Guide 2000th Issue, 1991.

"Six-Foot Baby Sitter," *Time,* 3/27/50.

"Who Looks Like Howdy Doody?," *Life,* 5/10/50.

Brown, "Hey Kids! What Time Is It?," *Washington Post,* 2/9/83.

Cuthbert, "It's Howdy Doody Time . . . All Over Again," *New Orleans Times Picayune,* 5/27/95.

McDonough, "Down the Tube," *Chicago Tribune,* 12/17/89.

Powers, "A Short Opinionated History of Television," in *TV Guide 2000th Issue,* 1991.

3. *MEET THE PRESS*

Kurtz, *Hot Air! All Talk, All of the Time,* Times Books, 1996.

"Meet the President," *Economist,* 11/15/75.

"Obituary for Lawrence Spivak," *Cleveland Plain Dealer,* 3/11/94.

"Question Man," *Newsweek,* 9/3/62.

"SEP Meets Television," *Newsweek,* 6/25/51.

Transcript of *Larry King Live* on CNN, 5/15/96.

Ebbitt, "Television," *New Republic,* 1/23/56.

Marek, "The Talk Circuit," *Chicago Tribune,* 5/29/94.

McDonough, "Down the Tube," *Chicago Tribune,* 12/17/89.

Mifflin, "Officials Try to Save TV Crime Show," *New York Times,* 9/7/96.

Moore, "Bloopers," *Washington Post,* 1/9/77.

Rosenstiel, "The Media: Bush Plays it Cozy," *Los Angeles Times,* 12/9/89.

Ross, "Meet the Press," *Reader's Digest,* 9/51.

Smith, "Spivak Obituary," *Washington Post,* 3/10/94.

Smith, "What Makes Russert Run," *New York,* 12/7/92.

NBC information sheet on *Meet the Press,* WWW site.

4. *I LOVE LUCY*

Andrews and Watson, *Loving Lucy: An Illustrated Tribute to Lucille Ball,* St. Martin's Press, 1980.

Arnaz, *A Book,* Morrow, 1976.

Baughman, *The Republic of Mass Culture: Journalism, Filmmaking and Broadcasting in America since 1941,* Johns Hopkins University Press, 1992.

Harris, *Lucy & Desi: The Legendary Story of Television's Most Famous Couple,* Simon & Schuster, 1991.

Higham, *Lucy,* St. Martin's Press, 1986.

Jones, *Honey I'm Home!: Sitcoms, Selling the American Dream,* Grove Weidenfeld, 1992.

Marc, *Comic Visions: Television Comedy and American Culture,* Unwin Hyman, 1989.

Marc and Thompson, *Prime Time, Prime Movers,* Little, Brown, 1992.

Newcomb, *TV: The Most Popular Art,* Doubleday, 1974.

Spigel, *Make Room for TV: Television and the Family Ideal in Postwar America,* University of Chicago Press, 1992.

Winship, *Television,* Random House, 1988.

TV Guide 2000th Issue, 1991.

"Desilu Formula for Top TV: Brains, Beauty, Now a Baby," *Newsweek,* 1/19/53.

"Sassafrassa, the Queen," *Time,* 5/26/52.

Arnold, "Lucille Ball Dies; TV's Comic Genius Was 77," *Los Angeles Times,* 4/27/89.

Champlin, "Everybody Loved Lucy: Lucille Ball Made It All Look Spontaneous," *Los Angeles Times,* 4/27/89.

Haithman, "The Industry's Debt to Lucy," *Los Angeles Times,* 4/30/89.

Mendoza, "Having a Ball," *Dallas Morning News,* 11/5/95.

Miller, "Deride and Conquer," in Gitlin (ed.), *Watching Television,* Pantheon, 1986.

Rosenberg, "Everybody Loved Lucy: She Set the Standard for Television Comedy," *Los Angeles Times,* 4/27/89.

5. *DRAGNET*

Barnouw, *Tube of Plenty: The Evolution of American Television,* Oxford University Press, 1975.

Carlson, *Prime Time Law Enforcement: Crime Show Viewing and Attitudes Toward the Criminal Justice System,* Praeger, 1985.

Castleman and Podrazik, *Watching TV: Four Decades of American Television,* McGraw-Hill, 1982.

Gitlin, *Inside Prime Time,* Pantheon, 1983.

Greenfield, *Television: The First Fifty Years,* Crescent Books, 1981.

Harris, *TV Guide: The First 25 Years,* 1978.

MacDonald, *Don't Touch That Dial: Radio Programming in American Life,* Nelson-Hall, 1979.

Marc, *Comic Visions: Television Comedy and American Culture,* Unwin Hyman, 1989.

Mellinkoff, *The Language of the Law,* Little, Brown, 1976.

Newcomb, *TV: The Most Popular Art,* Doubleday, 1974.

Porter, *The Pursuit of Crime: Art and Ideology in Detective Fiction,* Yale University Press, 1981.

Sackett, *Prime-Time Hits,* Billboard Books, 1993.

Stern and Stern, *Encyclopedia of Pop Culture,* Harper Perennial, 1992.

Weiner and eds., *The TV Guide TV Book.* Harper Perennial, 1992.

Williams, *TV: The Casual Art,* Oxford University Press, 1982.

"Dead on Arrival," *Time,* 1/25/54.

Gallup Report, 8/15/85.

"Jack Be Nimble!," *Time,* 3/15/54.

"The Case of the Unhappy DA," *TV Guide,* 4/26/58.

"These Gunns for Hire," *Time,* 10/26/59.

Daley, "Police Report on Cop Shows," *New York Times,* 11/19/72.

Efron, "What Makes a Hit?," *TV Guide,* 4/27/74.

Gerbner, "Trial by Television: Are We at the Point of No Return?," *Judicature* 63, 1980.

Gerbner and Gross, "The Scary World of TV's Heavy Viewer," *Psychology Today,* 4/76.

Haney and Manzolati, "Television Criminology: Network Illusions of Criminal Justice Realities," in Aronson (ed.), *Readings About the Social Animal,* 1981.

Hennigan, Heath et al., "Impact of the Introduction of Television on Crime in the United States, *Journal of Personality & Social Psychology,* 1982.

Jorgensen, "The Permanence of Dragnet," *Film Quarterly,* Fall 1958.

Katsch, "Is Television Anti-Law?," *ALSA Forum,* 7/83.

Miller, "Off the Prigs," *New Republic,* 7/18/81.

Morton, "Accent on Living," *Atlantic Monthly,* 9/51.

Peek, Alston, and Loew, "Comparative Evaluation of the Local Police," *Public Opinion Quarterly* 42, 1978.

Prial, "Jack Webb, Laconic Sgt. Friday on TV 'Dragnet' is Dead," *New York Times,* 12/24/82.

Rothenberg, "Yesterday's Boob Tube Is Today's High Art," *New York Times,* 10/7/90.

Shaw, "Onetime Allies: Press and LAPD," *Los Angeles Times,* 5/24/92.

Vancheri and Weiskind, "Arresting Television," *Pittsburgh Post-Gazette,* 10/9/94.

Zuckerman, "The Year of the Cop," *Rolling Stone,* 4/21/77.

Dragnet description on America Online Nickelodeon site.

6. BISHOP SHEEN AND *LIFE IS WORTH LIVING*

Brooks and Marsh, *The Complete Directory to Prime Time Network and Cable TV Shows,* Ballantine, 1995.

Himmelstein, *Television Myth and the American Mind,* Praeger, 1984.

Hoover, *Mass Media Religion: The Social Sources of the Electronic Church,* Sage Publications, 1988.

Horsfield, *Religious Television: The American Experience,* Longman, 1984.

Lichter, Lichter, and Rothman, *Watching America,* Prentice-Hall, 1991.

McKibben, *The Age of Missing Information,* Random House, 1992.

Postman, *Amusing Ourselves to Death: Public Discourse in the Age of Show Business,* Viking, 1985.

Schwartz, *Media: The Second God,* Doubleday, 1983.

"Great Medium for Messages," *Time,* 6/17/57.

"Microphone Missionary," *Time,* 4/14/52.

PR Newswire, 8/27/85.

"Reality and Television: An Interview with Dr. Edmund Carpenter,"
  Television Quarterly, Fall 1972.

"Video Debut," *Time,* 2/4/52.

Alley, "The Television Church," in Rose, *TV Genres: A Handbook and
  Reference Guide,* Greenwood Press, 1985.

Friend, "Sitcoms Seriously: Popularity of Situation TV Comedies," *Esquire,*
  3/93.

Holston, "Where Angels Go, Networks Fear to Follow," *Minneapolis Star
  Tribune,* 12/24/95.

Roddy, "A Talk with Bishop Sheen," *Look,* 1/27/53.

Simon, "DuMont Awards Range from Chevy's Ego to Cheers Hype,"
  Buffalo News, 1/9/94.

Steinfels and Steinfels, "The New Awakening," *Channels,* 1-2/83.

Watson, "And They Said 'Uncle Fultie' Didn't Have a Prayer," *Television
  Quarterly,* Winter 1993.

7. EDWARD R. MURROW AND *SEE IT NOW*

Bedell, *In All His Glory: The Life of William S. Paley, the Legendary Tycoon and
  His Broadcast Circle,* Simon & Schuster, 1990.

Boyer, *Who Killed CBS?: The Undoing of America's Number One Network,*
  Random House, 1988.

Brooks and Marsh, *The Complete Directory to Prime Time Network and Cable
  TV Shows,* Ballantine, 1995.

Greenfield, *Television: The First Fifty Years,* Crescent Books, 1981.

Halberstam, *The Powers That Be,* Knopf, 1979.

Kendrick, *Prime Time: The Life of Edward R. Murrow,* Little, Brown, 1969.

Kisseloff, *The Box: An Oral History of Television,* Viking, 1995.

Kurtz, *Hot Air! All Talk, All of the Time,* Times Books, 1996.

McLuhan, *Understanding Media: The Extensions of Man,* Signet Books, 1964.

McNeil, *Total Television: The Comprehensive Guide to Programming from 1948 to
  the Present,* Penguin Books, 1996.

Persico, *Edward R. Murrow, An American Original,* McGraw-Hill, 1988.

Ritchie, *Please Stand By: The Prehistory of Television,* Overlook Press, 1994.

Sperber, *Murrow: His Life and Times,* Freundlich Books, 1986.

"Edward R. Murrow of CBS: Diplomat, Poet, Preacher," *Newsweek,*
  3/9/53.

"See It Now," *Time,* 11/26/51.

"Television in Controversy," *Newsweek,* 3/29/54.

"The Whole World Is Watching," *Chicago Tribune,* 4/23/89.

Bliss, "Remembering Edward R. Murrow," *Saturday Review,* 5/31/75.

Clark, "Murrow—Person to Person," *Chicago Tribune,* 11/29/85.

Farni, "Showdown with a Senator," *Washington Post,* 6/15/94.

Howe, "The Rise and Fall of the Radio Commentator," *Saturday Review,* 10/26/57.

Leab, "See It Now: A Legend Reassessed," in O'Connor (ed.), *American History/American Television,* Frederick Ungar Publishing, 1983.

Miller, "The Night Ed Murrow Struck Back," *Esquire,* 12/83.

Phillips, "See It Now? Not Likely in Today's Television," *Bergen Record,* 7/29/90.

Rosenberg, "The Beacon That Was Murrow," *Los Angeles Times,* 7/30/90.

Saunders, "'See It Now' TV's Infant Tobacco Expose," *Rocky Mountain News,* 11/19/95.

Schorr, "Harvest of Sham," *Channels,* 3/86.

Seldes, "At Home with Edward Murrow," *Saturday Review,* 11/7/53.

Walsh, "When Television Took on Joe McCarthy," *Washington Post,* 3/11/94.

Whitworth, "An Accident of Casting," *New Yorker,* 8/3/68.

Wisehart, "Murrow's Legacy: A Tale of Two Eras," *Sacramento Bee,* 3/16/94.

8. TODAY

Davis, *"The Today Show": An Anecdotal History,* Morrow, 1987.

Kessler, *Inside Today: The Battle for the Morning,* Villard Books, 1992.

Kisseloff, *The Box: An Oral History of Television.* Viking, 1995.

Metz, *"The Today Show": An Inside Look at 25 Tumultuous Years and the Colorful and Controversial People Behind the Scenes,* Playboy Press, 1977.

Oppenheimer, *Barbara Walters: An Unauthorized Biography,* St. Martin's Press, 1990.

Weaver, *The Best Seat in the House: The Golden Years of Radio and Television,* Knopf, 1994.

Weiner and eds., *The TV Guide TV Book,* Harper Perennial, 1992.

"New Star," *Time,* 4/20/53.

"The 100 Most Memorable Moments in TV History," *TV Guide,* 6/29/96.

"Today," *Life,* 12/20/71.

"Today's Nice People," *Newsweek,* 5/9/66.

Boedeker, "Walters Changed News for Better and Worse," *Pittsburgh Post-Gazette,* 5/1/96.

Bumiller, "So Famous, Such Clout, She Could Interview Herself," *New York Times,* 4/21/96.

Carter, "Tender Trap," *New York Times,* 8/23/92.

Clark, "Later Today at 40, The Show Tries to Recover Its Early Made-In-Chicago Zest," *Chicago Tribune,* 1/12/92.

Greenfield, "The Showdown at ABC News," *New York Times,* 2/13/77.

James, "Barbara Walters Recalls 20 Years of Confessions, Digressions, and Tears," *New York Times,* 5/1/96.

Krolik, "Indestructible Today," *Television Quarterly,* 2/92.

Kruger, "Remote Control," *Artforum,* 1/88.

Layne, "After 40 Years of Evolution, the Date's Still 'Today' on NBC," *Hollywood Reporter,* 1/14/92.

Miller, "Sex Lives and Videotape," *Savvy Woman,* 10/89.

Waters, "The Troubles of 'Today,'" *Newsweek,* 9/1/80.
Weaver, "Television's Prime Time," *Advertising Age,* 6/18/90.

9. DISNEYLAND

Anderson, *Hollywood TV: The Studio System in the Fifties,* University of Texas
    Press, 1994.
Engelhardt, *The End of Victory Culture: Cold War America and the Disillusioning
    of a Generation,* Basic Books, 1995.
Goldenson, *Beating the Odds: The Untold Story Behind the Rise of ABC,*
    Scribners, 1991.
Jackson, *Walt Disney: A Bio-Bibliography,* Greenwood Press, 1993.
Jones, *Great Expectations: America and the Baby Boom Generation,* Coward,
    McCann & Geoghegan, 1980.
MacDonald, *Who Shot the Sheriff?: The Rise and Fall of the Television Western,*
    Praeger, 1987.
Schickel, *The Disney Version: The Life, Times, Art, and Commerce of Walt Disney,*
    Simon & Schuster, 1985.
TV Guide 2000th Issue, 1991.
"Disney on the Dial," *Newsweek,* 11/8/54.
"Tidal Wave," *New Yorker,* 4/9/55.
Ellis-Simons, "The Disney Channel," *Channels,* 10/87.
Freeman, "'Disney' Magic There, If a Wee Bit Overdone," *San Diego Union
    Tribune,* 12/9/94.
Joyner, "Revisiting the 50's Disney with 90's Children in Tow," *New York
    Times,* 7/28/96.
Warsh, "When Spin Met Marty . . . and What Happened Next," *Boston
    Globe,* 8/6/95.

10. THE LAWRENCE WELK SHOW

Weiner and eds., *The TV Guide TV Book,* Harper Perennial, 1992.
Welk, *Wunnerful, Wunnerful,* Prentice-Hall, 1971.
"Champagne with Welk," *Newsweek,* 5/21/56.
"Some Champagne for the Folks," *Life,* 5/6/57.
"Success Sneaks Up on Lawrence Welk," *Look,* 5/29/56.
"The Big Corn Crop," *Time,* 5/14/56.
Corry, "'Lawrence Welk' on 13," *New York Times,* 3/19/87.
Davidson, "Nobody Likes Him but the Public," *Look,* 6/25/57.
Goldsborough, "America's 'Champagne Music' Maker Was a Rare Blend
    Himself," *Advertising Age,* 5/26/86.
Gorman, "Lawrence Welk, Popular TV Bandleader Dies at 89," *Los Angeles
    Times,* 5/19/92.

11. *THE ED SULLIVAN SHOW*

Bowles, *A Thousand Sundays: The Story of the "Ed Sullivan Show,"* Putnam, 1980.

Gabler, *Winchell: Gossip, Power, and the Culture of Celebrity,* Vintage, 1994.

Weiner and eds., *The TV Guide TV Book,* Harper Perennial, 1992.

TV Guide 2000th Issue, 1991.

"20 Years of Ed Sullivan," *Life,* 10/20/67.

"The Toast of the Town," *Time,* 6/24/57.

"Why Ed Rates High," *Newsweek,* 12/21/53.

Brennan, "How Big Is Really Big?" *Washington Post,* 2/17/91.

King, "Sunday Night Is Ed's Again," *Los Angeles Times,* 2/17/91.

Moore, "Bloopers," *Washington Post,* 1/9/77.

Walker, "Rockin' the Tube," *Arizona Republic,* 8/8/94.

The Ed Sullivan Show WWW sites.

12. *GUNSMOKE*

Barabas and Barabas, *Gunsmoke: A Complete History and Analysis . . . ,* McFarland, 1990.

Brauer and Brauer, *The Horse, The Gun, and the Piece of Property: Changing Images of the TV Western,* Bowling Green University Popular Press, 1975.

Essoe, *The Book of TV Lists,* Arlington House Publishers, 1981.

Greenfield, *Television: The First Fifty Years,* Crescent Books, 1981.

Kirkley, *A Descriptive Study of the Network Television Western During the Seasons 1955-56* and *1962-63,* Arno Press, 1979.

MacDonald, *Who Shot the Sheriff?: The Rise and Fall of the Television Western,* Praeger, 1987.

McCrohan, *Prime Time, Our Time,* Prima Publishing & Communications, 1990.

Newcomb, *TV: The Most Popular Art,* Doubleday, 1974.

Sackett, *Prime-Time Hits,* Billboard Books, 1993.

Weiner and eds., *The TV Guide TV Book,* Harper Perennial, 1992.

"Hot as a Pistol," *Newsweek,* 11/20/67.

"Just Wild About Westerns," *Newsweek,* 7/22/57.

"The Six-Gun Galahad," *Time,* 3/30/59.

"TV Goes Wild over Westerns," *Life,* 10/28/57.

Eells, "How Long Will the Western Craze Last?," *Look,* 6/24/58.

Flanagan, "Horses Galore! Recalling the Golden Age of the TV Western," *Chicago Tribune,* 6/21/87.

Kuhns, "Bonanza," and "Gunsmoke," in *Why We Watch Them: Interpreting TV Shows,* Benziger, 1970.

Lemon, "The Last Showdown," *Entertainment Weekly,* 9/1/95.

Millstein, "TV's Comics Went Thataway," *New York Times,* 2/2/58.

Poppy, "The Worldwide Lure of Bonanza," *Look,* 12/1/64.

Shayon, "Togetherness on the Range," *Saturday Review,* 10/4/58.

Walstad, "Trotting Out a Saddle Bag of Television's Legendary Western Heroes for One Video," *Los Angeles Times,* 7/10/94.

13. *AMERICAN BANDSTAND*

Belz, *The Story of Rock,* Harper Colophon Books, 1969.

Brooks and Marsh, *The Complete Directory to Prime Time Network and Cable TV Shows,* Ballantine, 1995.

Essoe, *The Book of TV Lists,* Arlington House Publishers, 1981.

Kisseloff, *The Box: An Oral History of Television.* Viking, 1995.

Shore with Clark, *The History of "American Bandstand,"* Ballantine, 1985.

Shore, *The Rolling Stone Book of Rock Video,* Rolling Stone Press, 1984.

Stern and Stern, *Encyclopedia of Pop Culture,* Harper Perennial, 1992.

Stokes, Ward, and Tucker, *Rock of Ages: The Rolling Stone History of Rock and Roll,* Summit Books, 1986.

"'Lover' Breaks Wide Open After Studio 1," *Billboard,* 11/27/54.

"See TV as Most Potent Plug Medium with Phenom Overnight Click of 'Lover,'" *Variety,* 11/24/54.

"Tall, That's All," *Time,* 4/1/58.

"TV Top Medium For Launching New Platters," *Variety,* 11/24/54.

Bangs, "Screwing the System with Dick Clark," in Marcus (ed.), *Psychotic Reactions,* Knopf, 1987.

Devlin, "Fan Clubs: Stairways to the Stars," *Allentown Morning Call,* 10/2/94.

Fong-Torres, "Dick Clark: Twenty Years of Clearasil Rock," *Rolling Stone,* 8/16/73.

King, "Dick Clark: Rockin' Man," *Los Angeles Times,* 12/31/95.

Leo, "All Awards TV, All the Time," *US News and World Report,* 4/17/95.

Martin, "I Call on Dick Clark," *Saturday Evening Post,* 3/10/59.

McDonough, "Down the Tube," *Chicago Tribune,* 12/17/89.

Morthland, "The Payola Scandal," in Miller (ed.), *Rolling Stone Illustrated History of Rock and Roll,* Random House, 1992.

Perkins, "A True Genius: Dick Clark Gets His Due—and Shows His Class," *Chicago Tribune,* 6/24/94.

Raddatz, "From 'Crazy Daddy-O' to 'Right On,'" *TV Guide,* 6/13/73.

Shaw, "The Teen Idols," in DeCurtis and Henke (eds.), *The Rolling Stone Illustrated History of Rock and Roll,* Random House, 1992.

Snyder, "Dick Clark Grows Up," *Channels,* 5/87.

14. *TWENTY-ONE* AND THE QUIZ SHOW SCANDAL

Anderson, *Television Fraud: The History and Implications of the Quiz Show Scandal,* Greenwood Press, 1978.

Barnouw, *Tube of Plenty: The Evolution of American Television,* Oxford University Press, 1975.

Steinberg, *TV Facts,* Facts on File, 1980.

"Purity Kick," *Time,* 11/2/59.

"Special TV Report," *Newsweek,* 10/26/59.

"Special TV Report," *Newsweek,* 11/16/59.

"The Enormity of It," *Time,* 9/19/55.

"The $64,000 Question," *Newsweek,* 9/5/55.

"The Wizard of Quiz," *Time*, 2/11/57.

Brogen, "Television," *New Republic*, 8/8/55.

Brownen, "They Conned America," *Los Angeles Times*, 8/28/94.

Gould, "Quiz for TV," *New York Times*, 10/25/59.

Lardner, "Life Around the Booths," *New Yorker*, 1/30/57.

Popkin, "The Trouble with Quiz Shows," *New Republic*, 10/13/58.

Whitfield, "The 1950's: The Era of No Hard Feelings," *South Atlantic Quarterly*, Autumn 1977.

15. *LEAVE IT TO BEAVER*

Applebaum, *The World According to Beaver*, Bantam Books, 1984.

Elliott, *The Day Before Yesterday: Reconsidering America's Past, Rediscovering the Present*, Simon & Schuster, 1996.

Javna, *Cult TV*, St. Martin's Press, 1985.

Kisseloff, *The Box: An Oral History of Television*. Viking, 1995.

Marc, *Comic Visions: Television Comedy and American Culture*, Unwin Hyman, 1989.

Weiner and eds., *The TV Guide TV Book*, Harper Perennial, 1992.

"Television," *Saturday Review*, 2/1/58.

"TV's Eager Beaver," *Look*, 5/27/58.

Brown, "Where Are They Now? Beaver's Old Image Still Cleaves," *Washington Post*, 6/11/82.

Catlin, "The Beav's Career Takes a Natural Turn," *Hartford Courant*, 4/8/93.

Freeman, "It's Not Hip to Say So, But the Beave's OK," *San Diego Union-Tribune*, 7/26/93.

Kakutani, "Second Childhood," *New York Times*, 4/28/96.

King, "'Gosh, Beav, We're Still a Hit,'" *Los Angeles Times*, 2/23/92.

Saunders, "Observers Try to Fathom Baby Boomer Nostalgia for TV Shows," *Rocky Mountain News*, 12/31/95.

Scott, "UPI Dispatch," 5/12/95.

Simon, "The Eternal Rerun: Oldies, But Goodies," *Television Quarterly*, Spring 1986.

Stengel, "When Eden Was in Suburbia," *Time*, 8/9/82.

Terry, "The Beav Is Back, and It's Time-Warp Time," *Chicago Tribune*, 9/8/86.

16. *THE TWILIGHT ZONE*

Castleman and Podrazik, *Harry and Wally's Favorite TV Shows*, Prentice-Hall, 1989.

Engelhardt, *The End of Victory Culture: Cold War America and the Disillusioning of a Generation*, Basic Books, 1995.

Javna, *Cult TV*, St. Martin's Press, 1985.

Marc and Thompson, *Prime Time, Prime Movers*, Little, Brown, 1992.

Panati, *Panati's Parade of Fads, Follies, and Manias*, Harper Perennial, 1991.

Sackett, *Prime-Time Hits,* Billboard Books, 1993.

Steinberg, *TV Facts,* Facts on File, 1980.

Stern and Stern, *Encyclopedia of Pop Culture,* Harper Perennial, 1992.

Weiner and eds., *The TV Guide TV Book,* Harper Perennial, 1992.

Zicree, *The Twilight Zone Companion,* Bantam Books, 1982.

TV Guide 2000th Issue, 1991.

"The Weary Young Man," *Newsweek,* 9/28/59.

Gay, "Serling Silver," *Newsday,* 11/26/95.

Rothenberg, "Synergy of Surrealism and 'The Twilight Zone,'" *New York Times,* 4/2/91.

Sarris, "Viewed from Beyond the Twilight Zone," *Television Quarterly,* Fall, 1984.

17. THE PRESIDENTIAL PRESS CONFERENCE

Atherton, *The Presidential Press Conference: Its History and Role in the American Political System,* University Press of America, 1982.

Kernell, *Going Public: New Strategies of Presidential Leadership,* CQ Press, 1993.

Kisseloff, *The Box: An Oral History of Television.* Viking, 1995.

Morgan, *The Presidency and the Press Conference,* American Enterprise Institute, 1971.

Ritchie, *Please Stand By: The Prehistory of Television,* Overlook Press, 1994.

TV Guide 2000th Issue, 1991.

Winship, *Television,* Random House, 1988.

Corry, "The President's Impressive Use of the Camera," *New York Times,* 5/7/83.

Henry, "Just Bray It Again, Sam," *Time,* 4/11/83.

King, "The TV News Conference at 25," *New York Times,* 1/25/86.

Lear and Bennet, "The Flak Pack," *Washington Monthly,* 11/91.

Phillips, "Q & A on the Press Conference," *New York Times,* 2/13/55.

Rosenstiel, "The Media: Bush Plays it Cozy," *Los Angeles Times,* 12/9/89

18. *PERRY MASON*

Harris, *TV Guide: The First 25 Years,* Simon & Schuster, 1978.

Kelleher and Merrill, *The Perry Mason TV Show Book: The Complete Story of America's Favorite Television Lawyer,* St. Martin's Press, 1987.

Newcomb, *TV: The Most Popular Art,* Doubleday, 1974.

Weiner and eds., *The TV Guide TV Book,* Harper Perennial, 1992.

"Bette for Burr," *Newsweek,* 1/28/63.

"The Snoopers," *Time,* 5/26/58.

Holsopple, "Viewers Embrace the Lawyer Who Ruled Courtroom," *Phoenix Gazette,* 10/22/93.

Johnson, "TV's Make-Believe Lawyer," *Saturday Evening Post,* 10/3/59.

Kendall, "If Perry Mason Lost a Case," *New York Times,* 1/21/62.

King, "Re-runs to Re-watch: Popular Perry," *Los Angeles Times,* 3/31/91.

Margolick, "Perry Mason Was Fictional, But He Was Surely Relevant and, Oh So Competent," *New York Times*, 9/24/93.

Pisetzner, "Burr Tells All about Perry Mason," *Bergen Record*, 5/25/86.

Rosenberg, " 'I Confess! I Confess!' I Did Watch Perry Mason," *Los Angeles Times*, 9/15/93.

Shayon, "Exit Perry Mason," *Saturday Review*, 6/11/65.

Shayon, "Transmogrification," *Saturday Review*, 3/22/58.

Perry Mason WWW sites.

19. *THE DICK VAN DYKE SHOW*

Javna, *Cult TV*, St. Martin's Press, 1985.

Jones, *Honey I'm Home!: Sitcoms, Selling the American Dream*, Grove Weidenfeld, 1992.

Marc, *Comic Visions: Television Comedy and American Culture*, Unwin Hyman, 1989.

Moore, *After All*, Putnam, 1995.

Sackett, *Prime-Time Hits*, Billboard Books, 1993.

Stempel, *Storytellers to the Nation: A History of Television Writing*, Continuum, 1992.

Taylor, *Prime-Time Families: Television Culture in Postwar America*, University of California Press, 1989.

Weissman and Sanders, *"The Dick Van Dyke Show:" Anatomy of a Classic*, St. Martin's Press, 1983.

"Howlier Than Thou," *Newsweek*, 1/1/62.

Ferrer, "A Good Show Quits While It's Ahead," *Life*, 6/3/66.

Inman, "Classic Sitcom Turns 30, Moves Back to Prime Time," *Louisville Courier-Journal*, 10/1/91.

Zuckerman, "Gentiles in Paradise" from WWW, a site on *The Dick Van Dyke Show*.

Dick Van Dyke description on America Online Nickelodeon website.

20. THE SPACE PROGRAM

Barnouw, *Tube of Plenty: The Evolution of American Television*, Oxford University Press, 1975.

Bliss, *Now the News: The Story of Broadcast Journalism*, Columbia University Press, 1991.

Dayan and Katz, *Media Events: The Live Broadcasting of History*, Harvard University Press, 1992.

James, *Walter Cronkite: His Life and Times*, JM Press, 1991.

Matusow, *The Evening Stars: The Making of the Network News Anchor*, Houghton Mifflin, 1983.

Wolfe, *The Right Stuff*, Farrar, Straus, Giroux, 1979.

"Chronicling the Voyage," *Time*, 7/25/69.

"Pad 19," *New Yorker*, 4/3/65.

Arlen, "The Air," *New Yorker*, 1/26/66.

Lapham, "The Secret Life of Walter (Mitty) Cronkite," *Saturday Review,*
    3/16/63.
Mendoza, "Moonstruck," *Dallas Morning News,* 7/10/94.
Rathbun and Wussler, "All the Moon's a Stage," *Broadcasting & Cable,*
    6/27/94.
Shayon, "The Telenauts," *Saturday Review,* 5/26/62.
Shayon, "Cosmic Nielsen," *Saturday Review,* 8/9/69.

21. *THE BEVERLY HILLBILLIES*

Barnouw, *Tube of Plenty: The Evolution of American Television,* Oxford
    University Press, 1975.
Cox, "*The Beverly Hillbillies,*" Harper Perennial, 1993.
Douglas, *Where the Girls Are: Growing Up Female in the Mass Media,* Times
    Books, 1994.
Essoe, *The Book of TV Lists,* Arlington House Publishers, 1981.
Himmelstein, *Television Myth and the American Mind,* Praeger, 1984.
Marc, *Comic Visions: Television Comedy and American Culture,* Unwin Hyman,
    1989.
Marc and Thompson, *Prime Time, Prime Movers,* Little, Brown, 1992.
McCrohan, *Prime Time, Our Time,* Prima Publishing & Communications,
    1990.
Sackett, *Prime-Time Hits,* Billboard Books, 1993.
"On the Cob," *Time,* 11/30/62.
"The Corn Is Green," *Newsweek,* 12/3/62.
"The Country Slicker," *Newsweek,* 12/6/65.
Funk, "TV's Southern Exposure," *Orlando Sentinel Tribune,* 10/10/91.
Hano, "The G.A.P. Loves the Hillbillies," *New York Times,* 11/17/63.
Johnston, "Why 30 Million Are Mad about Mary," *New York Times,*
    4/7/74.
Kloer, "Hillbilly Trivia, Fun Facts, and Theme Song Lyrics," *Atlanta Journal-*
    Constitution, 10/15/93.
Kuhns, "Beverly Hillbillies," in *Why We Watch Them: Interpreting TV Shows,*
    Benziger, 1970.

22. ASSASSINATION TELEVISION

Barnouw, *Tube of Plenty: The Evolution of American Television,* Oxford
    University Press, 1975.
Bliss, *Now the News: The Story of Broadcast Journalism,* Columbia University
    Press, 1991.
Brinkley, *David Brinkley,* Knopf, 1995.
Castleman and Podrazik, *Watching TV: Four Decades of American Television,*
    McGraw-Hill, 1982.
Dayan and Katz, *Media Events: The Live Broadcasting of History,* Harvard
    University Press, 1992.
James, *Walter Cronkite: His Life and Times,* JM Press, 1991.

Matusow, *The Evening Stars: The Making of the Network News Anchor,*
Houghton Mifflin, 1983.

Posner, *Case Closed: Lee Harvey Oswald and the Assassination of JFK,* Random
House, 1993.

Zelizer, *Covering the Body: The Kennedy Assassination, the Media, and the
Shaping of Collective Memory,* University of Chicago Press, 1992.

"The Sight and the Sound," *Time,* 12/20/63.

David, "The TV Image," *The Nation,* 12/14/63.

Friedman, "JFK 25 Years Later," *Newsday,* 11/22/88.

Miller, "Views of a Death," *New Yorker,* 12/28/63.

Taves, "Walter Cronkite: Why Won't He Be Himself on TV?" *Look,*
8/25/64.

23. *MISTER ED* AND TV'S ESCAPIST COMEDIES

Castleman and Podrazik, *Harry and Wally's Favorite TV Shows,* Prentice-Hall,
1989.

Javna, *Cult TV,* St. Martin's Press, 1985.

Jones, *Honey I'm Home!: Sitcoms, Selling the American Dream,* Grove
Weidenfeld, 1992.

Marc, *Comic Visions: Television Comedy and American Culture,* Unwin Hyman,
1989.

Marc and Thompson, *Prime Time, Prime Movers,* Little, Brown, 1992.

Nalven, *The Famous "Mr. Ed": The Unbridled Truth about America's Favorite
Talking Horse,* Warner, 1991.

Stempel, *Storytellers to the Nation: A History of Television Writing,* Continuum,
1992.

Friend, "Sitcoms Seriously: Popularity of Situation TV Comedies," *Esquire,*
3/93.

Henry, "Another Season, Another Reason, for Making Sitcoms," *Channels,*
9/10/83.

Selleck, "Alan Young Talks Tonight about the Horse He Rode to Fame on
'Mr. Ed,'" *Los Angeles Times,* 10/28/86.

Smyth, "Hollywood Thinking about 'Mr. Ed' Movie, of Course," *Toronto
Star,* 8/21/94.

Viets, "Ed Heads," *Houston Chronicle,* 8/25/92.

24. *THE DATING GAME*

Barris, *The Game Show King: A Confession,* Carroll and Graf, 1993.

Elliott, *The Day Before Yesterday: Reconsidering America's Past, Rediscovering the
Present,* Simon & Schuster, 1996.

Marc and Thompson, *Prime Time, Prime Movers,* Little, Brown, 1992.

Winship, *Television,* Random House, 1988.

Barris appearance on *Larry King Live,* CNN, 10/29/93.

"Games Pretty People Play," *Newsweek,* 7/31/67.

"Theatre of Humiliation," *Newsweek,* 12/4/78.

Buckley, "Game Shows—TV's Glittering Gold Mine," *New York Times,* 11/18/79.

Cyclops, "Nausea in the Afternoon," *Life,* 9/8/72.

Gay, "Playing for Keeps," *Newsday,* 1/19/90.

Jacobs, "Games People Play," *Entertainment Weekly,* 5/24/96.

Lovese, "You've Come a Long Way, Bachelorette No. 3," *Newsday,* 6/4/95.

Mahler, "Game Shows as American as Apple Pie," *Electronic Media,* 8/88.

Malko, "I Want a Deal," *Harper's,* 8/72.

Merwin, "The King of Schlock," *Forbes,* 11/27/78.

Pollan, "Defendant for a Day," *Channels,* 4–5/82.

Shales, "The Gong Show," *Washington Post,* 1/7/77.

Waters, "Game Shows: The Nut Glut," *Newsweek,* 7/7/75.

The Newlywed Game WWW sites.

25. WALTER CRONKITE AND THE *CBS EVENING NEWS*

Alterman, *Sound and Fury: The Washington Punditocracy and the Collapse of American Politics,* HarperCollins, 1992.

Bliss, *Now the News: The Story of Broadcast Journalism,* Columbia University Press, 1991.

Halberstam, *The Powers That Be,* Knopf, 1979.

Himmelstein, *Television Myth and the American Mind,* Praeger, 1984.

Hodgson, *America in Our Time,* Doubleday, 1976.

James, *Walter Cronkite: His Life and Times,* JM Press, 1991.

Matusow, *The Evening Stars: The Making of the Network News Anchor,* Houghton Mifflin, 1983.

Ritchie, *Please Stand By: The Prehistory of Television,* Overlook Press, 1994.

TV Guide 2000th Issue, 1991.

Weiner and eds., *The TV Guide TV Book,* Harper Perennial, 1992.

"Cronkite Takes a Stand," *Newsweek,* 3/11/68.

"How Have We Changed?," *American Heritage,* 12/94.

"The Most Intimate Medium," *Time,* 10/14/66.

"You Want Uncle Walter," *Esquire,* 4/73.

Gans, "How Well Does TV Present the News?," *New York Times,* 1/11/70.

Goodman, "40 Years Holding Forth Before a Nation," *New York Times,* 5/23/96.

Hall, "The Man Who Winds the Clock," *Los Angeles Times,* 1/13/91.

Hodgson, "The Box, Seen by Itself," *Financial Times,* 3/20/85.

Lapham, "The Secret Life of Walter (Mitty) Cronkite," *Saturday Review,* 3/16/63.

Mayer, "How Television News Covers the World (in 4000 Words or Less)," *Esquire,* 1/71.

Menaker, "Art and Artifice in Television News," in Newcomb (ed.), *Television: The Critical View,* Oxford University Press, 1982.

Oulahan, "His Curse was Playing It Straight," *Life,* 8/28/64.

Smith, "TV News Did Not Just Happen—It Had to Invent Itself," *Smithsonian,* 6/89.

Snow, "He Was There," *American Heritage,* 12/94.

Strout, "Cronkite Steps Down," *Christian Science Monitor,* 3/5/81.

Taves, "Walter Cronkite: Why Won't He Be Himself on TV?" *Look,* 8/25/64.

Whitworth, "An Accident of Casting," *New Yorker,* 8/3/68.

26. *THE MONKEES*

"Monkee Do," *Time,* 11/1/66.

"Romp! Romp!," *Newsweek,* 10/24/66.

"TV's Swinging Monkees," *Look,* 12/27/66.

Kenny, "Simian's Rainbow," *Entertainment Weekly,* 9/29/95.

Monkees WWW sites (both the TV show and the group).

27. *MISSION: IMPOSSIBLE*

Barnouw, *Tube of Plenty: The Evolution of American Television,* Oxford University Press, 1975.

Brown, *Les Brown's Encyclopedia of Television,* Visible Ink, 1992.

Javna, *Cult TV,* St. Martin's Press, 1985.

Lichter, Lichter, and Rothman, *Watching America,* Prentice-Hall, 1991.

MacDonald, *Television and the Red Menace: The Video Road to Vietnam,* Praeger, 1985.

Stempel, *Storytellers to the Nation: A History of Television Writing,* Continuum, 1992.

"Mission Possible," *Time,* 3/1/68.

Gaitskill, "Requiem for a Moose," *Channels,* 7-8/83.

King, "Nothing was Impossible," *Los Angeles Times,* 3/14/93.

Kuhns, "Mission Impossible," in *Why We Watch: Interpreting TV Shows,* Benziger, 1970.

Mission: Impossible WWW sites.

28. *THE SMOTHERS BROTHERS COMEDY HOUR*

Brooks and Marsh, *The Complete Directory to Prime Time Network and Cable TV Shows,* Ballantine, 1995.

Castleman and Podrazik, *Watching TV: Four Decades of American Television,* McGraw-Hill, 1982.

Hill and Weingrad, *Saturday Night: A Backstage History of Saturday Night,* Beech Tree Books, 1986.

Javna, *Cult TV,* St. Martin's Press, 1985.

Marc, *Comic Visions: Television Comedy and American Culture,* Unwin Hyman, 1989.

McNeil, *Total Television: The Comprehensive Guide to Programming from 1948 to the Present,* Penguin Books, 1996.

Letter from Lyndon Johnson Library, Austin, Texas.

"The Brothers Smothered," *Newsweek,* 4/14/69.

"Verrry Interesting . . . But Wild," *Time,* 4/11/68.

Bednarski, "The Year Television Grew Up," *Electronic Media,* 4/18/88.

Dempsey, "Social Comment and TV Censorship," *Saturday Review,* 7/12/69.

Ferrer, "Courage at Last . . . Or Just Bleeps," *Life,* 4/12/68.

Hentoff, "The Smothers Brothers: Who Controls TV?" *Look,* 6/24/69.

Kaufman, "Censors Beware! 20 Years After They were Banned by CBS, the Smothers Brothers are Back in a Breakthrough Special," *Time,* 2/8/88.

Meisler, "The Smothers Brothers Redux," *New York Times,* 1/31/88.

Redicliffe, "The Brothers Come in from the Cold," *Rolling Stone,* 2/11/88.

Richmond, "Bane of the Censors," *Los Angeles Daily News,* 1/1/93.

Shayon, "Smothering the Brothers," *Saturday Review,* 4/5/69.

Spector, "A Clash of Cultures: The Smothers Brothers vs. CBS Television," in O'Connor (ed.), *American History/American Television,* Frederick Ungar Publishing, 1983.

The Smothers Brothers and Pat Paulsen WWW sites.

29. *ROWAN AND MARTIN'S LAUGH-IN*

Castleman and Podrazik, *Watching TV: Four Decades of American Television,* McGraw-Hill, 1982.

Javna, *Cult TV,* St. Martin's Press, 1985.

Marc, *Comic Visions: Television Comedy and American Culture,* Unwin Hyman, 1989.

McCrohan, *Prime Time, Our Time,* Prima Publishing & Communications, 1990.

McNeil, *Total Television: The Comprehensive Guide to Programming from 1948 to the Present,* Penguin Books, 1996.

Postman, *Amusing Ourselves to Death: Public Discourse in the Age of Show Business,* Viking, 1985.

Sackett, *Prime-Time Hits,* Billboard Books, 1993.

Stempel, *Storytellers to the Nation: A History of Television Writing,* Continuum, 1992.

Stern and Stern, *Encyclopedia of Pop Culture,* Harper Perennial, 1992.

"Sock It to 'Em, Judy," *Look,* 10/1/68.

"Verrry Interesting . . . But Wild," *Time,* 4/11/68.

Arkush, "Television: Sock It to 'Em!" *Los Angeles Times,* 2/7/93.

Barthel, "Hilarious, Brash, Flat, Peppery, Repetitious, Topical, and in Borderline Taste," *New York Times,* 10/6/68.

Dempsey, "Social Comment and TV Censorship," *Saturday Review,* 7/12/69.

Dietz, "Where TV Comedy Is At," *Saturday Evening Post,* 11/30/68.

Ferrer, "Courage at Last—or Just Bleeps?" *Life,* 4/12/68.

Lipton, "Sock It to Us—Again," *People,* 2/8/93.

Pollan, "The 'Vice' Look," *Channels,* 7-8/85.

Shales, "America's Love-In with Laugh-In," *Washington Post,* 2/7/93.

Werts, "You Bet Your Bippy That 'Laugh-In' Is Back Again," *Newsday,* 2/7/93.

30. *SESAME STREET*

Cook, Appleton, Conner, Shaffer, Tamkin, and Weber, *"Sesame Street" Revisited*, Sage Foundation, 1975.

Day, *The Vanishing Vision: The Inside Story of Public Television*, University of California Press, 1995.

Steinberg, *TV Facts*, Facts on File, 1980.

"Is 'Sesame' Authoritarian?" *Newsweek*, 9/20/71.

"Sesame Street: The Acceptable Face of Political Correctness," *The Economist*, 1/18/92.

"The Children's Hour," *Newsweek*, 12/22/69.

"TV's Switched-On School," *Newsweek*, 6/1/70.

Adler, "Cookie, Oscar, Grover, Henry, Ernie, and Company," *New Yorker*, 6/3/72.

Arlen, "Some Problems," *New Yorker*, 10/29/66.

Baer, "The Secrets of Sesame Street," *Look*, 9/22/70.

Blau, "'Sesame Street' Girds for Bumpy Times," *New York Times*, 3/23/86.

Bowman, "The Myth of Educational Television," *The Weekly Standard*, 1/1/96.

Butler and Pickering, "Big Bird of 'Sesame Street': An Interview," *Antioch Review*, Fall '79.

Culhane, "Report Card on 'Sesame Street,'" *New York Times*, 5/24/70.

Fox, "Preschool Five Still the Cornerstone of CTW Empire," *Variety*, 11/29/93.

Gates, "Henson's Son Builds on Muppet Tradition," *New York Times*, 12/25/95.

Gerard, "'Sesame Street' Talking about Race, from A to Z," *New York Times*, 11/21/90.

Goldberg, "Media Kids," *Artforum*, 2/90.

Holt, "Big Bird Meet Dick and Jane," *Atlantic Monthly*, 5/71.

Jarvik, "Public Broadcasting Can Flourish Without Government Subsidies," *Policy Review*, 4/1/95.

Lystad, "20 Years on 'Sesame Street.'" *Children Today*, 9/89.

Rainie, "Now, Who Can Tell Us How to Get to 'Sesame Street'?," *U.S. News & World Report*, 5/28/90.

Rosenthal, "Sunny Days on Sesame Street," *Newsday*, 7/17/88.

Seligmann, "Jim Henson: 1936–1990," *Newsweek*, 5/28/90.

Sharbutt, "'Sesame Street' Begins Third Decade of Bringing Laughs, Lessons to Kids," *Los Angeles Times*, 11/13/89.

Sesame Street WWW sites.

31. THE SUPER BOWL

Barnouw, *Tube of Plenty: The Evolution of American Television*, Oxford University Press, 1975.

Lipsyte, *Sportsworld: An American Dreamland*, Quadrangle, 1975.

Weiss, *Latitudes and Attitudes: An Atlas of American Tastes, Trends, Politics, and Passion*, Little, Brown, 1994.

Winship, *Television,* Random House, 1988.
"Super Sunday: A Shared American Experience," *Washington Post,* 1/29/92.
"Tune In to the History of Sports TV," *USA Today,* 12/3/91.
Arledge with Rogin, "It's Sport . . . It's Money . . . It's TV," *Sports Illustrated,* 4/25/66.
Buckley, "Reflections on the Phenomenon," *Esquire,* 10/74.
Caesar, "Friday No. 2 in Olympic TV History," *St. Louis Post-Dispatch,* 2/27/94.
Carter, "Confessions of a TV Wrestling Fan," *Television Quarterly,* 2/89.
Deford, National Public Radio Commentary, 4/13/94.
Klein, "Believe It or Not: The NFL Once Saw TV as a Bad Idea," *Wall Street Journal,* 1/19/96.
Lipsyte, "NFL's Remote Control," *New York Times,* 12/26/93.
Rushin, "The Titan of Television," *Sports Illustrated,* 8/15/94.
Rushin, "Time Tunnel on the Tube," *Sports Illustrated,* 10/26/92.
Sandomir, "Sports through the Cozy Prism of Television," *New York Times,* 12/1/91.
Schecter, "Why It's Better to Watch the Game on TV," *New York Times,* 3/3/68.

32. *THE BRADY BUNCH*

Marc and Thompson, *Prime Time, Prime Movers,* Little, Brown, 1992.
Stern and Stern, *Encyclopedia of Pop Culture,* Harper Perennial, 1992.
"Go On, Take the Brady Quiz," *Cincinnati Enquirer,* 9/29/94.
PR Newswire, "Creator of the Brady Bunch," 7/20/94.
Briller, "Will the Real Live Brady Bunch Stand Up?," *TV Quarterly* 1/92.
Carter, "Brady Mania," *Cincinnati Enquirer,* 9/19/94.
Gliatto, "An Actor's Last Wish," *People,* 5/25/92.
Gliatto, "Here's the Story," *People,* 6/1/92.
Shales, "Return of the Bradys," *Washington Post,* 2/9/90.
Thomas and Farquhar, "Brady by the Bunch," *Washington Post,* 4/12/92.
The Brady Bunch WWW sites.

33. *ALL IN THE FAMILY*

Adler (ed.), *"All in the Family": A Critical Appraisal,* Praeger, 1979.
Barnouw, *Tube of Plenty: The Evolution of American Television,* Oxford University Press, 1975.
Gitlin, *Inside Prime Time,* Pantheon, 1983.
Hamamoto, *Nervous Laughter: Television Situation Comedy and Liberal Democratic Ideology,* Praeger, 1989.
Himmelstein, *Television Myth and the American Mind,* Praeger, 1984.
Javna, *Cult TV,* St. Martin's Press, 1985.
Jones, *Honey I'm Home!: Sitcoms, Selling the American Dream,* Grove Weidenfeld, 1992.

MacDonald, *One Nation Under Television: The Rise and Decline of Network TV,* Pantheon, 1990.

Marc, *Comic Visions: Television Comedy and American Culture,* Unwin Hyman, 1989.

Marc and Thompson, *Prime Time, Prime Movers,* Little, Brown, 1992.

McCrohan, *Prime Time, Our Time,* Prima Publishing & Communications, 1990.

Panati, *Panati's Parade of Fads, Follies, and Manias,* Harper Perennial, 1991.

Stempel, *Storytellers to the Nation: A History of Television Writing,* Continuum, 1992.

Stern and Stern, *Encyclopedia of Pop Culture,* Harper Perennial, 1992.

Taylor, *Prime-Time Families: Television Culture in Postwar America,* University of California Press, 1989.

"The Team Behind Archie Bunker & Co.," *Time,* 9/25/72.

"TV: Speaking about the Unspeakable," *Newsweek,* 11/29/71.

Dawson, "Homage to Mettle and a Meathead," *The Record,* 1/20/91.

Frady, "It's 'All in the Family,' Too," *Life,* 11/9/71.

Johnston, "Why 30 Million Are Mad about Mary," *New York Times,* 4/7/74.

Levy, "In Defense of Prejudice," *New Republic,* 8/5/72.

Rabinowitz, "Watching the Sit-Coms," *Commentary,* 10/75.

Rosenberg, "Remembering the Lenny Bruce of TV Sitcoms," *Los Angeles Times,* 12/2/90.

Wolff, "Shortcuts to the Heart," *Esquire,* 8/81.

Woods, "Bunkerism," *New Republic,* 12/22/73.

All in the Family WWW sites.

34. *THE MARY TYLER MOORE SHOW*

Alley and Brown, *Love Is All Around: The Making of "The Mary Tyler Moore Show,"* Delta, 1989.

Elliott, *The Day Before Yesterday: Reconsidering America's Past, Rediscovering the Present,* Simon & Schuster, 1996.

Feuer, Kerr, and Vahimagi, eds., *MTM Quality Television,* BFI Publishing, 1984.

Javna, *Cult TV,* St. Martin's Press, 1985.

Jones, *Honey I'm Home!: Sitcoms, Selling the American Dream,* Grove Weidenfeld, 1992.

Marc, *Comic Visions: Television Comedy and American Culture,* Unwin Hyman, 1989.

Marc and Thompson, *Prime Time, Prime Movers,* Little, Brown, 1992.

Moore, *After All,* Putnam, 1995.

Sackett, *Prime-Time Hits,* Billboard Books, 1993.

Stern and Stern, *Encyclopedia of Pop Culture,* Harper Perennial, 1992.

Taylor, *Prime-Time Families: Television Culture in Postwar America,* University of California Press, 1989.

"100 Most Memorable Moments in TV History," *TV Guide,* 6/29/96.

"Serious Comedy," *Channels,* 10/22/90.

"Victorious Loser," *Time,* 9/3/73.

Corliss, "Happy Days Are Here Again," *Film Quarterly,* 8/79.

Edsall, "TV Tattered Nation's Social Fabric, Political Scientist Contends," *Washington Post,* 9/3/95.

Ephron, "A Fond Farewell to the Finest, Funniest Show on Television," *Esquire,* 2/77.

Friend, "Sitcoms Seriously; Popularity of Situation TV Comedies," *Esquire,* 3/93.

Johnston, "Why 30 Million are Mad about Mary," *New York Times,* 4/7/74.

Marc, "MTM's Past and Future," *The Atlantic,* 11/84.

Williams, "It's Not So Much, You've Come a Long Way Baby—as You're Gonna Make It after All," in Newcomb (ed.), *Television: The Critical View,* Oxford University Press, 1979.

Zoglin, "The Trouble with Mary," *Television Quarterly,* Summer-Fall '77.

Zurawik, "TV Season Sets Young Adults Free to Work and Play in the Big City: A New Circle of Friends," *Baltimore Sun,* 9/3/95.

The Mary Tyler Moore Show WWW sites.

35. *MASTERPIECE THEATRE*

Twenty Seasons of Mobil "Masterpiece Theatre" 1971–1991, Acme Printing, 1991.

Baughman, *The Republic of Mass Culture: Journalism, Filmmaking and Broadcasting in America since 1941,* Johns Hopkins University Press, 1992.

Bogart, *Commercial Culture: The Media System and the Public Interest,* Oxford University Press, 1995.

Castleman and Podrazik. *Watching TV: Four Decades of American Television,* McGraw-Hill, 1982.

Cooke, *Masterpieces: A Decade of "Masterpiece Theatre" Masterpieces,* Knopf, 1981.

Day, *The Vanishing Vision: The Inside Story of Public Television,* University of California Press, 1995.

O'Flaherty, *"Masterpiece Theatre:" A Celebration of 25 Years of Outstanding Television,* KQED Books, 1996.

"As the Victorian World Turns," *Time,* 10/3/69.

Bawer, "How Cool is PBS?" *New Republic,* 3/27/95.

Burgess, "Seen any Good Galsworthy Lately?," *New York Times,* 11/16/69.

Dawson, "British TV: King of Quality," *Orlando Sentinel Tribune,* 7/6/91.

Gay, "Once the Jewel in PBS' Crown, 'Masterpiece Theatre' Faces an Uncertain Future," *Newsday,* 10/8/95.

Howe, "Have You Hugged a Brit Today?," *Washington Post,* 11/7/85.

King, "Master Strokes," *Los Angeles Times,* 1/13/91.

Kitman, "Masterpiece de Resistance," *Newsday,* 3/24/91.

Kitman, "The Disquiet over Public TV," *Newsday,* 6/4/92.

Kowet, "PBS: Still Television's Best?," *Washington Times,* 10/7/91.

Lapham, "Adieu, Big Bird," *Harper's,* December 1993.

Lipsyte, "On Baseball: In Memoriam," *New York Times,* 9/15/94.

Marin, "20 Years of Television for Armchair Anglophiles," *Washington Times,* 1/10/91.

McMillan, "A 10th Birthday for 'Masterpiece Theatre,'" *New York Times,* 9/21/80.

O'Connor, "A Very Model of a Modern Major Mini-Series," *New York Times,* 1/13/91.

Sedulus, "Forward with Forsyte," *New Republic,* 11/7/70.

Siegel, "'Quality' and the Single Sponsor," *Boston Globe,* 3/31/91.

Wallach, "Cooke's Last Tour," *Newsday,* 11/29/92.

Zurawik, "America Wants Good Old Elitism, Insists PBS Boss," *Baltimore Sun,* 7/29/94.

36. THE LOCAL NEWS

Bliss, *Now the News: The Story of Broadcast Journalism,* Columbia University Press, 1991.

Bogart, *Commercial Culture: The Media System and the Public Interest,* Oxford University Press, 1995.

Day, *The Vanishing Vision: The Inside Story of Public Television,* University of California Press, 1995.

Diamond, *The Tin Kazoo: Politics, Television, and the News,* MIT Press, 1975.

Gans, *Deciding What's News: A Study of CBS Evening News, NBC Nightly News, Newsweek, and Time,* Pantheon Books, 1979.

Greenfield, *Television: The First Fifty Years,* Crescent Books, 1981.

Kaniss, *Making Local News,* University of Chicago Press, 1991.

Powers, *The Newscasters,* St. Martin's Press, 1977.

Stephens, *A History of News: From the Drum to the Satellite,* Viking, 1988.

"A Day in the Life of Local TV News in America," *Rocky Mountain Media Watch,* 1/11/95.

"Happy News," *Time,* 2/8/71.

"Local TV News: Nipping at the Heels of the Networks," *Broadcasting,* 5/5/86.

Press Release of Center for Media and Public Affairs, 3/4/96.

"State of the Art Journalism; Growing Importance of Local News," *Broadcasting,* 12/3/84.

Cohen and Solomon, "TV's Penchant for News That Bleeds," *Seattle Times,* 2/6/93.

Crossen, "Why Truly Terrible Weather Makes for Terrific TV," *Wall Street Journal,* 10/3/96.

Frankel, "More on TV Mayhem," *New York Times,* 1/28/96.

Frankel, "Word & Image: Body Bags at 11," *New York Times,* 4/2/95.

Grove, "The Bland Leading the Bland," *Washington Post,* 11/6/83.

James, "Killer Sleepwalkers? Scary Squid? That's News?," *New York Times,* 5/23/96.

Kaniss, "A Victory for Local News," *New York Times,* 12/5/92.

Kurtz, "Murder! Mayhem! Ratings!," *Washington Post,* 7/4/93.

Lightman, "Local Media, National Message," *Hartford Courant,* 9/24/92.

Malone, "Clinton Set to Highlight His Outreach Campaign for Cities Participating in TV Town Meeting," *Atlanta Journal and Constitution,* 2/9/93.

Matlack, "Target Television," *National Journal,* 2/1/92.

Mifflin, "A Generation Gap in News Viewership is Suddenly Wider," *New York Times,* 5/13/96.

Morrow, "The Wonderful Art of Weathercasting," *Time,* 3/17/80.

Rosenstiel, "The Myth of CNN," *New Republic,* 8/22/94.

Sanello, "Eyewitness Sleaze: It's TV Sweeps Time in Los Angeles," *Chicago Tribune,* 11/11/88.

Walker, "TV News: Emperor Has No Clothes, Show Says," *Arizona Republic,* 7/23/95.

Waters, "TV News: The Rapid Rise of Home Rule," *Newsweek,* 10/17/88.

Yardley, "News? I Thought it was a Sitcom," *Washington Post,* 2/24/86.

37. *THE TONIGHT SHOW*

Carter, *The Late Shift: Letterman, Leno and the Network Battle for the Night,* Hyperion, 1994.

McNeil, *Total Television: The Comprehensive Guide to Programming From 1948 to the Present,* Penguin Books, 1996.

Metz, "*The Tonight Show,*" Playboy Press, 1980.

"Late Night Affair," *Time,* 8/18/58.

Johnson, "Seeing TV with '20/20' Vision," *Chicago Tribune,* 5/15/95.

Weaver, "The 50's: Television's Prime Time, *Advertising Age,* 6/18/90.

38. *60 MINUTES*

Bliss, *Now the News: The Story of Broadcast Journalism,* Columbia University Press, 1991.

Boyer, *Who Killed CBS?: The Undoing of America's Number One Network,* Random House, 1988.

Campbell, *"60 Minutes" and the News: A Mythology for Middle America,* University of Illinois Press, 1991.

Castleman and Podrazik, *Watching TV: Four Decades of American Television,* McGraw-Hill, 1982.

Hewitt, *Minute by Minute,* Random House, 1985.

Madsden, *"60 Minutes": The Power and the Politics of America's Most Popular TV News Show,* Dodd, Mead, 1984.

Sackett, *Prime-Time Hits,* Billboard Books, 1993.

"Sons of '60 Minutes,'" *Newsweek,* 5/16/77.

"The Merry Magazines," *Time,* 4/1/69.

"Turning the Tables on '60 Minutes,'" *Newsweek,* 3/16/81.

Bianculli, "'60 Minutes' Adopting a Hard News Vision," *Calgary Herald,* 5/14/95.

Campbell, "Don Hewitt's Durable Hour," *Columbia Journalism Review,* 9/93.

Carter, "'60 Minutes' to Add Breaking News, Commentary," *New York Times,* 2/15/96.

Endrst, "CBS's '60 Minutes' Celebrates Silver Anniversary Atop the Ratings," *Hartford Courant,* 11/12/93.

Frank, "Brand Name News," *New Leader,* 3/14/94.

Funt, "Seeing Isn't Believing," *Saturday Review,* 11/80.

Gay, "The Comeback," *TV Guide,* 4/27/96.

Goodman, "How '60 Minutes' Holds Its Viewers' Attention, *New York Times,* 9/22/93.

Hall, "The Man Who Winds the Clock," *Los Angeles Times,* 1/13/91.

Jerome, "Don Hewitt," *People,* 4/24/95.

Johnson, "Hour That Shaped TV," *USA Today,* 11/12/93.

Kahn, "The Candy Factory," *New Yorker,* 7/19–26/82.

Kitman, "A Show that Makes the Bad Guys Sweat," *Newsday,* 11/14/93

Lubasch, "Court Throws Out Libel Suit Filed Against CBS By Colonel," *New York Times,* 1/16/86.

McFarlin, "Networks Cut Back on Magazines as Credibility and Ratings Go South," *Detroit News,* 6/14/95.

Pope, "ABC Network Loses Libel Suit Over '20/20,'" *Wall Street Journal,* 12/19/96.

Reibstein, "The Battle of the TV News Magazine Shows," *Newsweek,* 4/11/94.

Rich, "Smoking Guns at '60 Minutes,'" *New York Times,* 2/3/96.

Rosenthal, "25 and Still Ticking," *St. Louis Post-Dispatch,* 11/14/93.

Salerno, "The Interview That Didn't Happen," *Wall Street Journal,* 7/29/96.

Shales, "Still Ticking at 25; The Granddaddy of Magazine Shows," *Washington Post,* 11/13/93.

Zimmerman, "'60 Minutes' 25th Anniversary," *Variety,* 11/8/93.

39. *SATURDAY NIGHT LIVE*

Bianculli, *Teleliteracy: Taking Television Seriously,* Continuum, 1992.

Castleman and Podrazik, *Watching TV: Four Decades of American Television,* McGraw-Hill, 1982.

Hill and Weingrad, *Saturday Night: A Backstage History of Saturday Night,* Beech Tree Books, 1986.

Marc, *Comic Visions: Television Comedy and American Culture,* Unwin Hyman, 1989.

Stempel, *Storytellers to the Nation: A History of Television Writing,* Continuum, 1992.

Stern and Stern, *Encyclopedia of Pop Culture,* Harper Perennial, 1992.

"Flakiest Night of the Week," *Time,* 2/2/76.

"'SNL' by the numbers," *TV Guide,* 11/25/95.

Arlen, "A Crack in the Greasepaint," *New Yorker,* 11/24/75.

Barol and Foote, "'Saturday Night Live' Lives!" *Newsweek,* 9/25/89.

Greenfield, "Live from New York," *New York,* 4/19/93.

Hirschorn, "It's a Wayne's Wayne's Wayne's Wayne's World," *Esquire,* 3/92.

Kushman, "Never Mind," *Sacramento Bee,* 10/21/94.
Lubell, "There Was Nothing Like It," *Newsday,* 9/22/89.
Rich, "Saturday Night," *New Republic,* 7/28/86.
Schindhette, "15th Annniversary: 'Saturday Night Live,'" 9/25/89.
Schwartz, "College Humor Comes Back," *Newsweek,* 10/23/78.
Zoglin, "At 15, 'Saturday Night Live' Lives," *Time,* 9/25/89.
Saturday Night Live WWW sites.

40. *ROOTS*

Carroll, *It Seemed Like Nothing Happened: The Tragedy and Promise of America in the 70's,* Holt, Rinehart, and Winston, 1982.
Castleman and Podrazik, *Watching TV: Four Decades of American Television,* McGraw-Hill, 1982.
Gitlin, *Inside Prime Time,* Pantheon, 1983.
Lichter, Lichter, and Rothman, *Watching America,* Prentice-Hall, 1991.
Marc and Thompson, *Prime Time, Prime Movers,* Little, Brown, 1992.
Marill, *Movies Made for Television: The Telefeature and the Mini-Series* 1964–1979, Arlington House Publishers, 1980.
Stempel, *Storytellers to the Nation: A History of Television Writing,* Continuum, 1992.
Winship, *Television,* Random House, 1988.
"'Roots': Eight Points of View" in Newcomb (ed.), *Television: The Critical View,* Oxford University Press, 1979.
"'Roots' Grows into a Winner," *Time,* 2/7/77.
"'Roots' Takes Hold in America," *Newsweek,* 2/7/77.
"Why 'Roots' Hit Home," *Time,* 2/14/77.
Bianculli, "The Roots of the Problem," *Channels,* 1/87.
Carveth, "Amy Fisher and the Ethics of 'Headline' Docudramas," *Journal of Popular Film & Television,* 9/1/93.
Daley, "'Roots' Entrenched in Television's Soul," *Chicago Tribune,* 1/29/87.
Farber, "Making Book on TV," *Film Comment,* 11–12/82.
Greider, "Shared Legacy: Why Whites Watched 'Roots,'" *Washington Post,* 2/3/77.
Kriegsman, "America's Passage into the 'Then' Generation," *Washington Post,* 2/6/77.
Vanocur, "Dramatic 'Roots' of America," *Washington Post,* 1/23/77.
Waters, "After Haley's Comet," *Newsweek,* 2/14/77.
Waters, "The Black Experience," *Newsweek,* 1/24/77.
Weinstein, "A Quarter-Century of Television Movies," *Los Angeles Times,* 4/23/89.
Wood, "Roots of Victory, Roots of Defeat," *New Republic,* 3/12/77.

41. *ALL MY CHILDREN*

Allen, *Speaking of Soap Operas,* University of North Carolina Press, 1985.
Greenfield, *Television: The First Fifty Years,* Crescent Books, 1981.

Kaminsky with Mahan, *American Television Genres,* Nelson-Hall, 1985.

LaGuardia, *Soap World,* Arbor House, 1983.

MacDonald, *One Nation Under Television: The Rise and Decline of Network TV,* Pantheon, 1990.

Marc and Thompson, *Prime Time, Prime Movers,* Little, Brown, 1992.

Newcomb, *TV: The Most Popular Art,* Doubleday, 1974.

Stern and Stern, *Encyclopedia of Pop Culture,* Harper Perennial, 1992.

Wakefield, *All Her Children,* Doubleday, 1976.

Warner. *All My Children—The Complete Family Scrapbook,* General Publishers' Group, 1994.

TV Guide 2000th Issue, 1991.

"ABC Mounts a Threat in the Daytime," *Broadcasting,* 8/19/85.

"Hall of Fame," *Broadcasting,* 12/9/91.

Adler, "Afternoon Television: Unhappiness Enough and Time," in Newcomb (ed.), *Television: The Critical View,* Oxford University Press, 1976.

Allen, "'The Guiding Light': Soap Opera as Economic Product and Cultural Document," in O'Connor (ed.), *American History/American Television,* Frederick Ungar Publishing, 1983.

Bellos, "The Scientists of Sudsville," *The Guardian,* 10/22/94.

Garrel, "Soaps Take an Entertaining Look at their History," *Indianapolis News,* 10/27/94.

Grant, "The Mother of all Soaps," *Los Angeles Times,* 8/25/91.

Hart, "A Rut in the Afternoon," *Chicago Tribune,* 2/22/96.

Karp, "The Soaps du Jour," *Channels* 7–8/85.

Kuntz, "Word for Word," *New York Times,* 9/25/94.

Laurence, "Suds Are De-sudsed by O.J. Trial Coverage," *San Diego Union-Tribune,* 8/28/95.

Maynard, "Simpson vs. the Soaps," *Washington Post,* 7/31/95.

O'Connor, "Soaps' New Sophistication," *Houston Chronicle,* 8/2/92.

Passalacqua, "20-Year-Old 'Children' Celebrates on ABC," *Newsday,* 1/5/90.

Passalacqua, "Will 'All My Children' Search for Tomorrow?" *New York Times,* 6/23/91.

Porter, "Soap Time: Thoughts on a Commodity Art Form," in Newcomb (ed.), *Television: The Critical View,* Oxford University Press, 1981.

Rosen, "Search for Yesterday," in Gitlin (ed.), *Watching Television,* Pantheon, 1986.

Spate, "Oh 'My Children,'" *Los Angeles Times,* 1/15/95.

42. M*A*S*H

Alda, *The Last Days of "MASH,"* Unicorn Publishing House, 1983.

Barone, *Our Country: The Story of America from Roosevelt to Reagan,* Free Press, 1990.

Carroll, *It Seemed Like Nothing Happened: The Tragedy and Promise of America in the 70's,* Holt, Rinehart, and Winston, 1982.

Javna, *Cult TV,* St. Martin's Press, 1985.

Kalter, *The Complete Book of "M★A★S★H,"* Abrams, 1984.

Reiss, *"M★A★S★H": The Exclusive Inside Story of TV's Most Popular Show,* Bobbs-Merrill, 1980.

Sackett, *Prime-Time Hits,* Billboard Books, 1993.

Stempel, *Storytellers to the Nation: A History of Television Writing,* Continuum, 1992.

Corliss, "'M★A★S★H,' You were a Smash," *Time,* 2/28/83.

Darrach, "M★A★S★H," *People,* 3/7/83.

Friend, "Sitcoms Seriously: Popularity of Situation TV Comedies," *Esquire,* 3/93.

Gelbart, "Its Creator Says Hail and Farewell to 'M★A★S★H,'" *New York Times,* 2/27/83.

Haithman, "What's In Store for TV Dramedies," *Los Angeles Times,* 4/27/88.

Hoffeldt, "Cultural Bias in M★A★S★H," in Newcomb (ed.), *Television: The Critical View,* Oxford University Press, 1982.

Jahr, "Alan Alda—Life Since 'M★A★S★H,'" *Ladies Home Journal,* 3/85.

O'Connor, "Hawkeye and Company in a 'M★A★S★H' Salute, *New York Times,* 11/25/91.

O'Connor, "TV: 'M★A★S★H' Ends on a Sentimental Note," *New York Times,* 3/2/83.

Rosenberg, "A Closer Glance at Emmys Outing," *Los Angeles Times,* 9/22/87.

Shales, "A Farewell to 'M★A★S★H,'" *Washington Post,* 2/28/83.

Waters, "Farewell to the 'M★A★S★H' Gang," *Newsweek,* 2/28/83.

*M★A★S★H★*WWW sites.

43. THE HOSTAGE CRISIS

Barone, *Our Country: The Story of America from Roosevelt to Reagan,* Free Press, 1990.

Hammond, "Hostage Crisis Gave Birth to 'Nightline,'" *The San Diego Union-Tribune,* 11/7/89.

Hill, "Illusion Still Easily Carries the Day in Gulf War Coverage," *Baltimore Sun,* 8/2/92.

Kurtz, "The Night Stalker," *Columbia Journalism Review,* 5-6/96.

Leo, "Lessons from a Sanitized War," *U.S. News & World Report,* 3/18/91.

Mueller, "Will America Stand a Stalemate in Iraq?," *New York Times,* 8/27/90.

Valeriani, "Talking Back to the Tube; Covering the Gulf War," *Columbia Journalism Review,* 3/91.

44. *DALLAS*

Ang, *Watching "Dallas": Soap Opera and the Melodramatic Imagination,* Routledge, 1989.

Brooks and Marsh, *The Complete Directory to Prime Time Network and Cable TV Shows,* Ballantine, 1995.

Castleman and Podrazik, *Harry and Wally's Favorite TV Shows,* Prentice-Hall, 1989.

Castleman and Podrazik, *Watching TV: Four Decades of American Television,* McGraw-Hill, 1982.

Himmelstein, *Television Myth and the American Mind,* Praeger, 1984.

Lichter, Lichter, and Rothman, *Watching America,* Prentice-Hall, 1991.

Liebes and Katz, *The Export of Meaning: Cross-Cultural Readings of "Dallas,"* Oxford University Press, 1993.

MacDonald, *One Nation Under Television: The Rise and Decline of Network TV,* Pantheon, 1990.

Marc and Thompson, *Prime Time, Prime Movers,* Little, Brown, 1992.

Sackett, *Prime-Time Hits,* Billboard Books, 1993.

Carter, "So 'Dallas' Is Finally Over. Or Is It?," *New York Times,* 5/6/91.

Carter, "Sunset at Southfork," *New York Times,* 5/5/91.

Corliss, "Goodbye to Gaud Almighty," *Time,* 4/29/91.

Corliss, "The 'Dallas' Shot That Was Heard Round the World," *Los Angeles Times,* 11/23/90.

Feuer, "Melodrama, Serial Form and Television Today," in Vande Berg and Wenner, *Television Criticism,* Longman, 1991.

Margulies, "Facing Up to Life Without 'Dallas'," *Los Angeles Times,* 5/3/91.

Newcomb, "Texas: A Giant State of Mind," in Newcomb (ed.), *Television: The Critical View,* Oxford University Press, 1982.

Waters, "Who Shot That Nice Mr. Ewing?" *Newsweek,* 11/17/80.

45. THE RONALD REAGAN SHOW

McCrohan, *Prime Time, Our Time,* Prima Publishing & Communications, 1990.

Reagan, *An American Life,* Simon & Schuster, 1990.

Wills, *Reagan's America: Innocents at Home,* Doubleday, 1987.

Cannon, "President Recycles a Story," *Washington Post,* 10/23/84.

Cannon, "The Problem Was Reagan," *Washington Post,* 10/15/84.

Corry, "A Look at the Debate Between Reagan and Mondale," *New York Times,* 10/9/84.

Gabler, "Now Playing: Real Life, the Movie," *New York Times,* 10/20/91.

Henry, "The President, Biggest Host of the TV Season," *Channels,* 1–2/85.

Safire, "Reagan Comes Back," *New York Times,* 10/22/84.

Tuchman, "Ladies and Gentlemen, the Next President of the United States," *Film Quarterly,* 7/8/80.

46. CNN

Bliss, *Now the News: The Story of Broadcast Journalism,* Columbia University Press, 1991.

Boorstin, *The Image: A Guide to Pseudo-Events in America,* Atheneum, 1985.

Goldberg and Goldberg, *Citizen Turner: The Wild Rise of an American Tycoon,* Harcourt Brace, 1995.

Whittemore, *CNN, The Inside Story,* Little, Brown, 1990.

"Monarch of the Lens," *Sunday Telegraph,* 10/9/94.

"Too Much News?," Transcript of *The Newshour with Jim Lehrer,* 10/8/96.

Bennett, "Polling Provoking Debate in News Media About Its Use," *New York Times,* 10/4/96.

Boorstin, "A History of the Image," *New Perspectives Quarterly,* 6/22/94.

Cloud, "A King Who Can Listen," *Time,* 10/5/92.

Duff, "The Television Picture," *Wall Street Journal,* 8/14/96.

Finkel, "Hello, What's Your Question?" *Orlando Sentinel Tribune,* 3/24/91.

Freedland, "All Mouth and No Rousers," *The Guardian,* 1/3/94.

Fund, "It'll Be Close," *Wall Street Journal,* 11/1/96.

Kurtz, "A Pundit Among Pundits," *Washington Post Weekly,* 2/26/96.

Matusow, "Twinkle, Twinkle, Little Stars," *Washingtonian,* 5/93.

McGrory, "Larry King Close Up," *Boston Globe,* 12/5/95.

Meyer, "The Maestro of Chin Music," *New York Times,* 5/26/91.

Robins, "The Soul of a News Machine," *Channels,* 3/90.

Rosenstiel, "Dead Air: How CNN Wrecked Television News," *New Republic,* 8/22/94.

47. *HILL STREET BLUES*

Germond and Witcover, *Whose Broad Stripes and Bright Stars,* Warner, 1989.

Gitlin, *Inside Prime Time,* Pantheon, 1983.

Marc and Thompson, *Prime Time, Prime Movers,* Little, Brown, 1992.

Stempel, *Storytellers to the Nation: A History of Television Writing,* Continuum, 1992.

"100 Most Memorable Moments in TV History," *TV Guide,* 6/29/96.

Buckley, "'Hill Street Blues,' New NBC Police Series, *New York Times,* 1/17/81.

Coe, "Quality TV: Hollywood's Elusive Illusions," *Broadcasting,* 11/18/91.

Corliss, "Too Good for Television? 'Hill Street Blues' Has Everything Going for It—Except Ratings," *Time,* 9/14/81.

Cramer and Blumental, "The *Playboy* Interview—'Hill Street Blues,'" *Playboy,* 10/83.

Daley, "Despite the Predictions, 'Blues' Remains the Same," *Chicago Tribune,* 9/26/85.

Grimes, "Welcome to 'Twin Peaks' and Valleys," *New York Times,* 5/5/91.

Gunther, "Adult Dramas: Dying Breed on TV?," *Boston Globe,* 10/12/93.

Henry, "The Best New Programming Trend in Years," *Channels,* 1-2/84.

Jacobs, "Tales of the Gritty," *Entertainment Weekly,* 11/4/91.

Jarvis, "'Hill Street Blues,' The Show That Arrested the Decline of TV, Finally Fades to Black," *People,* 5/4/87.

Kiesenwetter, "A Decade Later, The 'Hill' Influences Nightly Television," Gannett News Service, 1/3/91.

Kiesenwetter, "The Best-Ever 'Hill-Street' Episode," Gannett News Service, 1/3/91.

Lindsey, "From 'Hill Street' to 'LA Law,'" *New York Times,* 8/24/86.

Miller, "Off the Prigs," in Miller, *Boxed In,* Northwestern University Press, 1988.

O'Connor, "'Hill Street Blues'—A Hit with Problems," *New York Times,* 5/10/81.

O'Connor, "The 'Hill Street Blues' Lesson," *New York Times,* 12/13/81.

Pollan, "Can 'Hill Street Blues' Save NBC?," *Channels,* 3–4/83.

Rosenberg, "Requiem for Best TV 'Blues,'" *Los Angeles Times,* 4/15/87.

Terry, "'Hill Street' Finale: It's Time to Go; Television's Beloved Cops Turn in Their Badges," *Chicago Tribune,* 5/12/87.

Shales, "Hill & Renko Being Careful Out There," *Washington Post,* 4/28/83.

Shales, "'Hill Street,' Back on the Beat," *Washington Post,* 9/26/85.

Shales, "'Hill Street,' Hail and Farewell," *Washington Post,* 5/12/87.

Shales, "The Hill Street Zanies and the Boys in Blue," *Washington Post,* 1/15/81.

Siegel, "TV's Endangered Species," *Boston Globe,* 3/21/93.

Zoglin, "Changing the Face of Prime Time," *Time,* 5/2/88.

Zoglin, "'Hill Street,' Hail and Farewell; A Groundbreaking Show Heads for Its Final Roll Call," *Time,* 4/27/87.

48. MTV

Denisoff, *Tarnished Gold: The Record Industry Revisited,* Transaction Books, 1986.

Kaplan, *Rocking Around the Clock: Music Television, Postmodernism, and Consumer Culture,* Methuen, 1987.

Marcus, *Ranters & Crowd Pleasers: Punk in Pop Music,* Doubleday, 1993.

Stern and Stern, *Encyclopedia of Pop Culture,* Harper Perennial, 1992.

Ainslie, "Confronting a Nation of Grazers," *Channels,* 9/88.

Aufderheide, "The Look of the Sound," in Gitlin (ed.), *Watching Television,* Pantheon, 1986.

Bravin, "Why You Want Your MTV," *Los Angeles Times,* 7/22/90.

Cleland, "The MTV Touch," *Advertising Age,* 2/28/95.

Cook, "The Infobeast Turns 15," *Boston Phoenix,* 7/26/96.

Dollar, "10 Years of MTV," *Atlanta Journal and Constitution,* 7/28/91.

Gabler, "Now Playing: Real Life, the Movie," *New York Times,* 10/20/91.

Harrington, "Rock Around the Clock," *Washington Post,* 11/28/91.

Hughes, "We Have Met the Future—and it is MTV," Gannett News Service, 7/29/91.

Landler, "Now on MTV: Madonna, Nirvana—and Newt Gingrich," *Business Week,* 9/21/92.

Landler, "They Want Their MTV," *Business Week,* 12/14/92.

Leland, "A Salute to 'America's Most Wasted,'" *Newsweek,* 7/19/93.

Leland, "Do You Still Want Your MTV?" *Newsweek,* 8/5/91.

McKenna, "A Decade of Art—Yes Art—On MTV," *Los Angeles Times,* 8/1/91.

Miller, "Deride and Conquer," in Gitlin (ed.), *Watching Television,* Pantheon, 1986.

Owen, "The MTV Decade," *Newsday,* 7/31/91.

Pareles, "Pop Goes the World," *New York Times,* 7/7/91.

Pendleton, "Chalk Up Another Victory for Trend-Setting Rock'n Roll,"
    Advertising Age, 11/9/88.

Pittman, "The Man Behind the Monster," *Los Angeles Times Magazine,*
    7/28/91.

Reilly, "MTV Changes Its Tune to Boost Ratings," *Wall Street Journal,*
    11/27/96.

Shales, "The Pop Network That's Dim & Ditzy to Decor," *Washington Post,*
    8/1/85.

Shales, "Video Nouveau," *Washington Post,* 4/12/87.

Siegel, "Remote Control," *Boston Globe,* 7/21/91.

Smith, "New TV Technologies Alter Viewing Habits," *New York Times,*
    10/9/85.

Strauss, "The 'M' in MTV Loses a Little of Its Standing," *New York Times,*
    8/13/95.

Williams, Brown, and Gaillard, "MTV as Pathfinder for Entertainment,"
    Washington Post, 12/13/89.

49. BOB NEWHART

Novak, "Same to you Fella!" *People,* 5/9/83.

Pollan, "Newhart," *Channels,* 9–10/85.

50. *ENTERTAINMENT TONIGHT*

Boorstin, *The Image: A Guide to Pseudo-Events in America,* Atheneum, 1985.

Gamson, *Claims to Fame: Celebrity in American Culture,* University of
    California Press, 1994.

Postman, *Amusing Ourselves to Death: Public Discourse in the Age of Show
    Business,* Viking, 1985.

Tannen, *You Just Don't Understand: Women and Men in Conversation,* Morrow,
    1990.

Weiner and eds., *The TV Guide TV Book,* Harper Perennial, 1992.

Weiss, *Latitudes and Attitudes: An Atlas of American Tastes, Trends, Politics, and
    Passion,* Little, Brown, 1994.

"Inside Edition Has Emerged As the Top-ranked Syndicated News
    Magazine," *Broadcasting & Cable,* 5/17/93.

"More Entertainment for 'Entertainment Tonight,'" *Broadcasting,* 2/17/86.

Bertram, "'ET' Still Seeking New Frontiers as It Turns 10," *Electronic Media,*
    9/16/91.

Carter, "Now It Can Be Told: Tabloid TV is Booming," *New York Times,*
    12/23/91.

Edmundson, "TV's Celebration of Itself," *Channels,* 9–10/85.

Foltz, "The Stars of the Bottom Line," *Newsweek,* 8/26/85.

Fretts, "Hard Copy," *Entertainment Weekly,* 8/18/95.

James, "E-Shows: All Fluff, All the Time," *New York Times,* 7/28/91.

Klinghoffer, "Dateline: Hollywood," *Washington Times,* 9/13/91.

Kogan, "Celebrity Journalism Done Right," *Chicago Tribune,* 3/27/91.

Kurtz, "A Current Affair's Strip-Sleaze Act," *Washington Post,* 9/20/95.

Kurtz, "The Press Bypass," *Washington Post,* 1/22/93.

Marin, "The Teshing of America," *Newsweek,* 4/3/95.

Rosenberg, "Fox's 'E.D.J.' Nips at Heels of Show Business Lap Dog," *Los Angeles Times,* 7/22/91.

Shaw, "Obsessed with Flash and Trash, *Los Angeles Times,* 2/16/94.

Thomas, "Show Biz Values Tainting TV News," *St. Petersburg Times,* 2/4/90.

Tobenkin, "Fifteen and Still Entertaining," *Broadcasting and Cable,* 7/10/95.

Watson, "'ET' Enters its Blue Period," *Entertainment Weekly,* 8/11/95.

Weinstein, "A Brush with Celebrity," *Los Angeles Times,* 9/11/91.

Zoglin, "E.T. Gets a New Challenger, and Show-Biz Fluff Triumphs Again," *Time,* 10/3/94.

Entertainment Tonight WWW sites.

51. *THE COSBY SHOW*

Jones, *Honey I'm Home!: Sitcoms, Selling the American Dream,* Grove Weidenfeld, 1992.

MacDonald, *Blacks and White TV: African-Americans in Television Since 1948,* Nelson-Hall Publishers, 1992.

Sackett, *Prime-Time Hits,* Billboard Books, 1993.

"100 Most Memorable Moments in TV History," *TV Guide,* 6/29/96.

Braxton, "'Color Adjustment': A Bittersweet Look at Black TV Roles," *Los Angeles Times,* 6/15/92.

Carter, "In the Huxtable World, Parents Knew Best," *New York Times,* 4/26/92.

Du Brow, "Breaking Color Barriers," *Los Angeles Times,* 6/6/92.

Hodges, "Saying Farewell to 'Cosby,'" *Houston Chronicle,* 4/26/92.

Gates, "TV's Black World Turns—But Stays Unreal," *New York Times,* 11/12/89.

Grimes, "Make It Real. Make It Funny. But Don't Tell a Joke," *New York Times,* 6/8/96.

Littlefield, "It's Not All Black and White," *News Tribune,* 3/9/94.

Malone, ". . . And Gracie Begat Lucy Who Begat Laverne," *Channels,* 10-11/81.

Meyers, "Cosby's Last Show," *Entertainment Weekly,* 5/3/96.

Miller, "Deride and Conquer," in Gitlin (ed.), *Watching Television,* Pantheon, 1986.

O'Connor, "Cosby Leads the Way, But TV Still Stumbles in Depicting Blacks," *New York Times,* 3/30/86.

Seitz, "Black and White Television," *Minneapolis Star Tribune,* 4/25/96.

Waters, "Bill Cosby Comes Home," *Newsweek,* 11/5/84.

Waters, "Cosby's Fast Track," *Newsweek,* 9/2/85.

Weber, "Eventually All Things End, Even a Big Hit Like 'Cosby,'" *New York Times,* 3/7/92.

Whitman, "Watching Ourselves: Black and White in Color," *U.S. News & World Report,* 5/11/92.

Zoglin, "Prime Time's New First Family," *Time,* 5/6/85.

52. *STAR TREK*

Engelhardt, *The End of Victory Culture: Cold War America and the Disillusioning of a Generation,* Basic Books, 1995.

"100 Most Memorable Moments in TV History," *TV Guide,* 6/29/96.

"Preview," *TV Guide,* 9/10/66.

Daley, "Staying Power," *Chicago Tribune,* 1/4/87.

Justman and Solow, "Shaky Launch," *TV Guide,* 8/24/96.

Logan, "Endless Voyage," *TV Guide,* 8/24/96.

Logan, "'Star Trek' XXV," *TV Guide,* 8/31/91.

Siegel, "Science Fiction and Fantasy TV," in Rose, *Television Genres: A Handbook and Reference Guide,* Greenwood Press, 1985.

Werts, "'Star Trek: The Next Generation' Logs Its Last Stardate on TV," *Newsday,* 5/19/94.

Star Trek WWW sites.

53. *ROSEANNE*

Castleman and Podrazik, *Harry and Wally's Favorite TV Shows,* Prentice-Hall, 1989.

Lichter, Lichter, and Rothman, *Watching America,* Prentice-Hall, 1991.

Marc and Thompson, *Prime Time, Prime Movers,* Little, Brown 1992.

McNeil, *Total Television: The Comprehensive Guide to Programming from 1948 to the Present,* Penguin Books, 1996.

Sackett, *Prime-Time Hits,* Billboard Books, 1993.

Stern and Stern, *Encyclopedia of Pop Culture,* Harper Perennial, 1992.

Weiss, *Latitudes and Attitudes: An Atlas of American Tastes, Trends, Politics, and Passion,* Little, Brown, 1994.

Cole, "Roseanne," *Nation,* 6/21/93.

Freed, "The Gripes of Wrath," *TV Quarterly,* Winter '96.

Friend, "Sitcoms Seriously: Popularity of Situation TV Comedies," *Esquire,* 3/93.

Jeffries, "The Yabba Dabba Guy," *The Guardian,* 7/21/94.

Lahr, "Dealing with Roseanne," *New Yorker,* 7/17/95.

Laurence, "Rosie Reality," *San Diego Union-Tribune,* 11/22/92.

Miller, "Deride and Conquer," in Gitlin (ed.), *Watching Television,* Pantheon, 1986.

Murphy, "Roseanne's Positive New Attitude," *TV Guide,* 4/6/96.

Robins, "Here Come the News Punks," *Channels,* 9/88.

Rowe, "Roseanne: Unruly Woman as Domestic Goddess," in Newcomb (ed.), *Television: The Critical View,* Oxford University Press, 1994.

54. *AMERICA'S FUNNIEST HOME VIDEOS*

Sackett, *Prime-Time Hits,* Billboard Books, 1993.

Weiss, *Latitudes and Attitudes: An Atlas of American Tastes, Trends, Politics, and Passion,* Little, Brown, 1994.

Winship, *Television,* Random House, 1988.

Aufderheide, "In the Growing Genre of Camcorder Journalism Nothing Is Too Personal," *Columbia Journalism Review,* 1/95.

Carter, "ABC's 'Home Videos' Pays Off Big," *New York Times,* 2/19/90.

Cerone, "The Candid Camcorder," *Los Angeles Times,* 2/14/90.

DuBrow, "KCBS May Add Home Videos to News Show," *Los Angeles Times,* 4/26/90.

Fore, "America This Is You," *Journal of Popular Film & Television,* 4/1/93.

Gunther, "News Has a Million New Eyes," *Orlando Sentinel Tribune,* 4/9/91.

Letofsky, "'Funniest Home Videos' Is Oddly Unpleasant," *Los Angeles Times,* 11/25/89.

Muro, "The Videocam Caper," *Boston Globe,* 3/14/91.

O'Connor, "A Prime-Time Ratings Runaway With Low Costs," *New York Times,* 3/1/90.

Rabiner, "Zombies, Freaks, Crackpots & Other Real People," *Channels,* 8-9/91.

Rosenberg, "The Sadness Behind Funniest Home Videos," *Los Angeles Times,* 3/21/90.

Waters, "Revenge of the Couch Potatoes," *Newsweek,* 3/5/90.

Zoglin, "The Bride Is, Er, Excused; Life's Embarrassing Moments Add Up to a Homegrown Hit," *Time,* 3/5/90.

55. THE HILL-THOMAS HEARINGS

Mayer and Abramson, *Strange Justice: The Selling of Clarence Thomas,* Houghton Mifflin, 1994.

Meyrowitz, *No Sense of Place: The Impact of Electronic Media on Social Behavior,* Oxford University Press, 1985.

Baldwin, "Is it Fact? Or is it Fiction?," *Common Cause,* 1/1/93.

Du Brow, "Thomas-Hill Docudrama Couldn't Do the Real Drama Justice," *Los Angeles Times,* 10/19/91.

Hall, "Thomas-Hill Hearings Help PBS Stations Garner High Ratings," *Los Angeles Times,* 10/16/91.

Huff, "100M Found Verdict a Turn On," *New York Daily News,* 10/5/95.

Leroux, "Thomas vs. Hill—America Hates a Fight Without a Clear-Cut Winner," *Chicago Tribune,* 10/20/91.

Moeller, "From Islamabad to Issaquah—How Turner's CNN Changed the World," *Seattle Times,* 1/5/92.

Rosenbaum, "Congress May Inquire to Its Heart's Desire," *New York Times,* 7/31/94.

Zoglin, "The Networks Court Woman Viewers with a Parade of Heroines Who Are Betrayed, Battered, and Bewildered," *Time,* 11/11/91.

56. *THE OPRAH WINFREY SHOW*

Weiss, *Latitudes and Attitudes: An Atlas of American Tastes, Trends, Politics, and Passion*, Little, Brown, 1994.

"Harper's Index," *Harper's*, 12/95.

"The Sordid World of Daytime Television Talk Shows," *NPR Morning Edition*, 11/9/95.

"The Talk of Television," *Newsweek*, 10/29/79.

Alter, "Next: 'The Revolt of the Revolted,'" *Newsweek*, 11/6/95.

Biddle, "The Silencing of Ambush-Style Talk Shows," *Boston Globe*, 11/15/96.

Biddle, "TV's New Shocker: The Talk Turns Tame," *Boston Globe*, 1/5/96.

Brown, "Oprah Well Ahead of Others in Ratings," *Cleveland Plain Dealer*, 2/25/96.

Chidley, "Taking in the Trash," *Maclean's*, 2/19/96.

Cohen, "Real Lives: True Confessions," *The Guardian*, 7/16/94.

Crabtree, "Trash TV Pulls America Down the Tubes," *Washington Times*, 12/4/95.

Dougary, "Soul Queen," *The London Times*, 3/4/95.

Gabler, "Audience Stays Superior to the Exploitalk Shows," *Los Angeles Times*, 3/19/95.

Gamson, "Freak Talk on TV," *American Prospect*, Fall '95.

Grimes, "The Deconstruction of Jenny and Jerry, Maury and Montel," *New York Times*, 12/10/95.

Harrison, "The Importance of Being Oprah," *New York Times*, 6/11/89.

Jones, "On TV, Talk Is Cheap," *Chicago Tribune*, 12/25/94.

Kakutani, "Howard Stern and the Highbrows," *New York Times*, 1/28/96.

Kaminer, "Private Practices, Public Confessionals," *Chicago Tribune*, 6/14/92.

Lavin, "It's All Going Oprah's Way," *Chicago Tribune*, 12/19/85.

Littleton, "Talk Shows: Talk's Veterans Hang Tough," *Broadcasting & Cable*, 12/11/95.

Littleton, "TV Talk Toughs It Out," *Broadcasting & Cable*, 1/15/96.

Lovece, "Mixed Signals," *Newsday*, 11/4/92.

Nelson, "Talk Is Cheap," *The Nation*, 6/5/95.

Noglows, "Oprah: The Year of Living Dangerously," *Working Woman*, 5/94.

Oliver, "Freak Parade," *Reason*, 4/95.

Reynolds, "Oprah Unbound," *Chicago Magazine*, 11/93.

Roan, "Next! When Abnormal Becomes Normal!" *Los Angeles Times*, 9/6/94.

Shah, "Heeere's . . . Phil Donahue!" *Newsweek*, 3/13/78.

Stasio, "When Talk Shows Become Horror Shows," *Cosmopolitan*, 10/95.

Strauss, "Why Is Everybody Talking?," *Los Angeles Times*, 10/1/95.

Zoglin, "'People Sense the Realness,'" *Time*, 9/15/86.

Zoglin, "Talking Trash," *Time*, 1/30/95.

57. *HOME IMPROVEMENT* AND *SEINFELD*

Buena Vista Television Information Sheet.
Home Improvement Production Notes provided from Touchstone Television.
Carter, "After Being No. 1, What? Ask Tim Allen," *New York Times,*
    9/14/95.
Carter, "Too Popular for its Own Good," *New York Times,* 12/5/95.
Davis, "Seinfeld," *The Atlantic,* 12/92.
Eddy, "All Thumbs," *Millennium Pop,* Fall '94.
Gabriel, "In Touch with the Tool-Belt Chromosome," *New York Times,*
    9/22/91.
Hirshey, "Dressed to Drill," *GQ,* 3/94.
Littlefield, "Pick Your Favorite TV Dad," *Calgary Herald,* 6/18/95.
McInerney, "Is 'Seinfeld' the Best Comedy Ever?," *TV Guide,* 6/1/95.
Millman, "Seinfeld: Back on the Laugh Track," *Salon,* 12/30/95.
Mink, "Tim Allen, Your Show Needs Improvement," *New York Daily News,*
    9/19/95.
Sharkey, "Family Life (Arrgh!) in the Comfort Zone," *New York Times,*
    9/18/94.
Zoglin, "Prime-Time Power Trip," *Time,* 5/3/93.
Zoglin, "Tim at the Top," *Time,* 12/12/94.
Zurawik, "TV Season Sets Young Adults Free to Work and Play in the Big
    City," *Baltimore Sun,* 9/3/95.

58. QVC

Billiteri, "A TV Church Called Worship," *St. Petersburg Times,* 10/17/92.
Carlin, "The Jackpot in Television's Future," *New York Times,* 2/28/93.
Johnston and Leonard, "TV Charities: Let the Giver Beware," *Los Angeles
    Times,* 1/20/85.
Kaye, "The New Phone Sex," *Esquire,* 5/94.
Klassen, "Channel Surfing the TV Shopping Shows," *Kiplinger's Personal
    Finance Magazine,* 8/1/94.
Koepp, "Can You Believe This Price?" *Time,* 10/20/86.
Landler, "Barry Diller Used to Work Here?" *New York Times,* 5/20/96.
Miller, "Sickness on TV," in *Boxed In,* Northwestern University Press,
    1988.
More, "Is Home Shopping the Future of Television?," Gannett News
    Service, 3/26/93.
Olcott, "The Roots of Fund Raising," *Fund Raising Management,* 4/89.
Passalacqua, "Talking & Hawking," *Newsday,* 2/6/94.
Saltzman, "Infomercials—Television's Newest Success," *USA Today
    Magazine,* 9/94.
Seplow, "Sell-evision," *The Sunday Patriot-News,* 9/25/94.
Shales, "Hamming It Up, But Good," *Washington Post,* 9/2/80.
Shearer, "Telethon," *Film Comment,* 3-4/79.
White, "Ideological Analysis and Television," in Allen (ed.), *Channels of
    Discourse,* University of North Carolina Press, 1992.

Whitford, "TV or not TV," *Inc.*, 6/94.

Winzenburg, "Infomercials Flowering on Cable TV," *Advertising Age,*
2/22/93.

59. *ER*

Castleman and Podrazik, *Watching TV: Four Decades of American Television,*
McGraw-Hill, 1982.

Kuhns, *Why We Watch Them: Interpreting TV Shows,* Benziger, 1970.

Newcomb, *TV: the Most Popular Art,* Doubleday, 1974.

Sackett, *Prime-Time Hits,* Billboard Books, 1993.

Winship, *Television,* Random House, 1988.

"Back to the Future," *The Scotsman,* 1/26/95.

Biddle, "The Script Doctors of ER," *Boston Globe,* 5/16/96.

Bonko, " 'ER': Ensemble Cast Just What the Doctor Ordered," *The
Virginian-Pilot,* 3/7/96.

Caldwell, "TV Viewers Love Gritty Realism, Fast-Talking Close-Ups and
Life-and-Death Stories," *The Boston Globe,* 11/20/94.

Canin, "Code-Blue Chaos vs. Medical Utopia," *New York Times,* 9/11/94.

Dientsfrey, "Doctors, Lawyers & Other TV Heroes," in Newcomb (ed.),
Television: The Critical View, Oxford University Press, 1976.

Dunkin, "A Doctor in the Living Room," *Arthritis Today,* 5/91.

Jacobs, "Tales of the Gritty," *Entertainment Weekly,* 11/4/94.

James, "TV Doctors: An Image Made Too Well," *New York Times,* 3/25/89.

Korman, "Are Those Fictional Doctors Bad for the Viewer's Health," *New
York Times,* 12/15/85.

Laschever, "Not so PC After All," *Millennium Pop,* 10/95.

Lovece, " 'ER' Delivers Strong Medicine," *Newsday,* 10/16/94.

Marin, "S★M★A★S★H," *Newsweek,* 10/31/94.

McGrath, "The Triumph of the Prime-Time Novel," *New York Times,*
10/22/95.

Moser, "The Medicine Shows," *Hippocrates,* 1/88.

Pennington, "Hospital Dramas Fight to Make Cut," *St. Louis Post-Dispatch,*
9/18/94.

Siegel, "TV's Endangered Species," *Boston Globe,* 3/21/93.

Turow, "Now's the Right Time for 'Dr. Kildare' and 'Ben Casey,' " *Los
Angeles Times,* 12/18/93.

ER WWW sites.

60. *WHEEL OF FORTUNE*

Interview with Paul Gilbert, Fall, 1993, and Fall, 1996.

Interview with Fred Cohen, Fall, 1993.

Interview with Ellen Politi, Fall, 1993.

"Channel Surfing Through U.S. Culture in 20 Lands," *New York Times,*
1/30/94.

"The Controversy about Popular Culture," *American Enterprise,* 5-6/92.

"What a Deal," *Newsweek,* 2/9/87.

Ecenbarger, "There's No Escaping Us," *Chicago Tribune,* 2/13/94.

Giniger, "J.R. Ewing and Captain Furillo in Paris," *New York Times,* 11/21/87.

Gitlin, "Who Are the World?" Conference Paper, American Enterprise Institute, 3/10/92.

Hall, "Wheel of Fortune," *People,* 4/1/85.

Huey, "America's Hottest Export: Pop Culture," *Fortune,* 12/31/90.

Iyer, "Why 'Made in America' Still Sells," Conference Paper, American Enterprise Institute, 3/10/92.

Logan, "'Wheel of Fortune' Sends in the Clones," *TV Guide,* 10/26/91.

Mindich, "Wheel of Fortunski!" *Buzz,* 3/94.

Pollan, "Jackpot!" *Channels,* 6/86.

Tempest, "Tuning in the Global Village," *Los Angeles Times,* 10/20/92.

Tempest, "We Are the World," *TV Guide,* 7/3/93.

Terry, "Why 'Wheel' Is Such a Big Deal," *Chicago Tribune,* 5/14/86.

Index

ABC Evening News, The, 67
Ace, Goodman, 107
Adams, Don, 181
Addams Family, The, 154, 157
Admiral Broadway Revue, The, 13
Ailes, Roger, 308
Aladdin, 77
Alda, Alan, 279–84
ALF, 351
Alger, Horatio, 400
Ali, Muhammad, 188
Allen, Fred, 11, 14, 63, 81, 341
Allen, Steve, 93, 243, 373
Allen, Tim, 245, 383
Allen, Woody, 248, 353
All in the Family, 38, 147, 183,
            216–24, 275, 280, 281, 296,
            297, 340, 342, 354, 379, 380,
            391
All My Children, 270–78
All-Star Revue, 12
Alpert, Herb, 162
Altman, Robert, 180, 279

Amanpour, Christiane, 258, 312
American Bandstand, 92–98
American Experience, The, 234
America's Funniest Home Videos,
            359–63
America's Most Wanted, 30, 221
Ames, Ed, 246
Amory, Cleveland, 213
Amos and Andy Show, The, 111, 340
Amsterdam, Morey, 11, 125, 136
Amundson, Daniel R., 369
Andersen, Hans Christian, 400
Anderson, Christopher, 71
Anderson, Jack, 254
Anderson, John, 305–306
Anderson, Kent, 99
Andy Griffith Show, The, 145–46
Annie Oakley, 88
Antoine, Tex, 241
Anybody Can Play, 104
Apple, R. W., Jr., 27
Archie Bunker's Place, 222
Archies, 175

Arledge, Roone, 173, 206, 208, 209
Arlen, Michael, 262, 374
Armstrong, Neil, 139, 141
Arnaz, Desi, 36–39, 41, 227, 263
Arness, James, 85
Arnett, Peter, 312
Arnie, 218
Asher, Bill, 158
Asner, Ed, 225, 267
As the World Turns, 150, 271, 272
Atwater, Lee, 339
Aubrey, James, 137, 167
Augustine, Saint, 56
Austen, Jane, 233
Author Meets the Critics, 11, 28
Autry, Gene, 87, 89
Avalon, Frankie, 95
Avengers, The, 177, 181
Axelrod, Jonathan, 48–49
Aykroyd, Dan, 260–63

Bachelor Father, 111, 137
Baez, Joan, 187, 191
Bailey, F. Lee, 130
Bailey, Jack, 387
Bailey, Pearl, 11
Bain, Barbara, 180
Baker, Howard, 304, 365
Baker, Jim, 308
Baker, Russell, 231, 233–34, 331
Ball, Lucille, 35–42, 54, 63, 67, 214,
   226, 227, 340–41
Bangs, Lester, 98
Barber, Benjamin, 328
Barthels, Joan, 193
Barkley, Alben, 28
Barnaby Jones, 48
Barney Miller, 319
Barnouw, Eric, 88, 107, 146–47,
   208–10
Barr, Rosanne, 35, 38, 351–56
Barris, Chuck, 160–65, 361
Barry, Gene, 85
Barry, Jack, 102, 103, 105
Bates, Alan, 232

Batman, 48, 132, 194
Baxter, Meredith, 388
Beast, The, 240
Beatles, 78, 79, 81, 82, 146, 174, 175,
   184
Beat the Clock, 159
Beaumont, Hugh, 110
Beavis and Butt-Head, 330, 381
Begin, Menachem, 124, 172
Belafonte, Harry, 186
Bell, Daniel, 100
Bell, Jack, 27
Belushi, John, 259–62
Ben Casey, 390
Bennett, Tim, 378
Bennett, William, 371, 372, 377
Benny, Jack, 11, 39, 107, 137, 184,
   246, 380
Benny Hill, 233
Bergman, Ingrid, 67
Berle, Milton, 9–17, 19–20, 23, 51,
   52, 54, 93, 135, 136, 192, 263,
   332, 380, 387
Berlin, Meredith, 323
Bernstein, Carl, 252, 255
Berry, Chuck, 94, 95, 96
Bettag, Tom, 240
Beverly Hillbillies, The, 9, 137, 143–48,
   217, 344
Beverly Hills 90210, 350, 396
Bewitched, 41, 154, 158
Bid 'n' Buy, 104
Big Beat, 94
Big Chill, 322
Big Valley, The, 89
Billingsley, Barbara, 110
Bishop, Joey, 243
Bixby, Bill, 337
Blackstone Rangers, 184
Blair, Frank, 65
Blake, Amanda, 85, 86
Blind Date, 161
Bloodworth-Thomason, Linda,
   146
Blue, Linda Bell, 338

Bobbitt, John Wayne, 312, 364
Bob Newhart Show, The, 332
Bochco, Steven, 318–23, 393
Boesky, Ivan, 295
Bogart, Humphrey, 27
Bold and the Beautiful, The, 277
Bold Ones, The, 391
Bonanza, 16, 21, 89, 155, 170, 174, 183–84
Bono, Sonny, 176
Boone, Pat, 62
Boone, Richard, 389
Boorstin, Daniel, 315, 317, 340, 365
Borge, Victor, 81
Bork, Robert, 366
Bormann, Ernest, 291
Borowitz, Susan, 56
Boston Pops, 234
Bowie, David, 175
Boyer, Peter, 57
Boylan, Barbara, 77
Bradley, Ed, 255
Bradley, Tom, 345
Brady Bunch, The, 113, 212–15
Braudy, Leo, 340
Brauer, Ralph and Donna, 88
Breen, Jon, 304
Brennan, William, 129
Brian's Song, 266
Brinkley, David, 28–29, 108, 140, 166, 168, 170
Broadway Open House, 249
Broder, David, 27, 30, 316
Brokaw, Tom, 65
Brolin, James, 390
Brooks, Albert, 262
Brooks, James, 224, 227
Brothers, Joyce, 101
Brown, H. Rap, 174
Brown, Les, 218
Bruce, Lenny, 249
Bryan, William Jennings, 51
Buccaneers, The, 231
Buchanan, Pat, 148, 220, 314–15, 316

Buchwald, Art, 251
Buckley, William F., Jr., 191, 194, 206, 299, 302–303
Burgess, Anthony, 232
Burgess, Bobby, 77
Burnett, Carol, 261, 275
Burning Bed, The, 266
Burns, Allan, 224
Burns, George, 155, 156, 184, 246
Burns, Ken, 229
Burns and Allen Show, The, 39
Burr, Raymond, 85, 130–31
Burton, LeVar, 267
Bush, George, 126, 128, 187, 241, 263, 297, 299, 304–305, 309, 315, 333, 377
Buttons, Red, 106
Buzzi, Ruth, 192–93

Caesar, Sid, 13, 77, 135–36, 259
Cagney and Lacey, 50
Camel News Caravan, The, 165–66
Campbell, Glen, 184
Campbell, Richard, 252–54, 256
Candid Camera, 301
Cannon, Lou, 300, 304, 307
Cantor, Eddie, 10
Capital Gang, 27, 314
Capote, Truman, 67
Capp, Al, 147
Capra, Frank, 72
Captain Kangaroo, 19, 201, 205
Car 54, Where Are You?, 48, 132
Carlin, George, 261
Carlson, James, 49
Carmichael, Stokely, 174
Carne, Judy, 192, 194
Caroline in the City, 223, 227
Carpenter, Edmund, 247
Carpenter, Scott, 139, 141
Carson, Johnny, 69, 136, 160, 164, 244–47, 249–50, 260
Carter, Amy, 306
Carter, Bill, 248
Carter, Jack, 11

Carter, Jimmy, 68, 124, 125–26, 128, 148, 188, 221, 244, 267–68, 284, 289, 296–97, 299, 305–309, 313, 333, 365

Carter, Rosalynn, 68

Carvey, Dana, 260, 263–64

Casals, Pablo, 94

"Case Against Milo Radulovich, The," 59

Cash, Johnny, 96

Castleman, Harry, 116, 333

Castro, Fidel, 68

Catholic Hour, The, 52

Cavett, Dick, 243, 249

CBS Evening News, 165–73, 240, 289, 335

CBS Morning News, 338, 375

Chamberlain, Richard, 334

Chamberlain, Wilt, 191

Chambers, Whittaker, 30

Chancellor, John, 65

Channing, Carol, 217

Chaplin, Charlie, 353

Charlie's Angels, 181

Chase, Chevy, 243, 260–62

Chayefsky, Paddy, 229

Cheers, 21, 382

Cher, 176

Chesterfield Sound Off Time, 44

Chicago Hope, 363

Chung, Connie, 170, 257, 338

Civilization, 230

Civil War, 229

Civil Wars, 323

Clark, Dick, 92–98

Clark, Ramsey, 251

Clay, Cassius, 188

Cleaver, Eldridge, 254

Clinton, Bill, 91, 125, 126, 143, 146, 189, 241, 245, 255, 314–16, 334, 338, 377, 382, 383, 390, 395

Clinton, Hillary Rodham, 68, 146, 200, 390

CNN, 310–17, 384

Coca, Imogene, 13, 38, 259

Cockburn, Alexander, 398

Cohen, Fred, 397, 399

Cohen, Myron, 81

Cohen, Richard, 127

Cole, Nat "King," 96, 340

Collingwood, Charles, 57, 150, 168

Collins, Joan, 348

Colt .45, 89

Combat, 177, 180, 280

Como, Perry, 13, 54, 61–62, 95, 130, 137

Connell, Paul, 200

Connelly, Joe, 111–12

Connors, Chuck, 85, 89

Conrad, Michael, 322

Conrad, William, 85

Cooke, Alistair, 230–31, 234

Coolidge, Calvin, 124

Cooney, Joan Ganz, 199–205

Cooper, Gary, 87, 139, 299

Cop Rock, 323

COPS, 45, 50, 392

Corliss, Richard, 224, 297

Cosby, Bill, 17, 181, 246, 331, 340–46

Cosby Show, The, 38, 41, 266, 340–46, 351, 353, 394, 396

Cosell, Howard, 188–89, 207, 245

Couric, Katie, 65

Cowan, Lou, 100

Crabbe, Buster, 142

Craig, May, 27

Crane, Les, 243

Crawford, Broderick, 47

Crichton, Michael, 392

Crime and Punishment, 232

Crockett, Davy, 73, 96

Cronin, A. J., 231

Cronkite, Walter, 28–29, 61, 63, 66, 78, 79, 83, 108, 139–42, 150, 159–60, 165–73, 187, 244, 252, 255, 289, 338, 387

Crosby, John, 22, 64, 72, 80

Crossfire, 29, 220, 310, 313, 314, 377

Crossroads, 54

Cruise, Tom, 177
Crystal, Billy, 260, 263
Cullen, Bill, 159
Culp, Robert, 341
Cuomo, Mario, 248, 333
Current Affair, A, 336, 337, 356
Curtin, Jane, 260, 262

Daley, Richard, 172
Dallas, 91, 265, 275, 276, 292–97, 318, 319, 324, 378
Daly, John Charles, 25, 168
Dana, Bill, 243
Dann, Mike, 89
Dateline, 257
Dating Game, The, 159–63
Davis, Bette, 131
Davis, Ossie, 266
Davis, Sammy, Jr., 194
Davy Crockett, 70, 73, 96, 145
Day, James, 200, 202
Dayan, Daniel, 139
Dayan, Moshe, 194
Days and Nights of Molly Dodd, The, 283
Dean, Jimmy, 202
Dean, John, 365
Death Valley Days, 15, 113, 299
Deaver, Michael, 306
de Cordova, Fred, 246
Dee, Ruby, 266
Defenders, The, 132
Defoe, Daniel, 232
Dennis the Menace, 112
Designing Women, 146
Devine, Andy, 88
Dewey, Thomas E., 11
Diamond, Edwin, 170, 300
Diamond, Mel, 15, 94
DiBona, Vin, 360
Dichter, Ernest, 87
Dickens, Charles, 270
Dick Van Dyke Show, The, 16, 134–38, 216, 220, 224, 226, 227, 296
Diddley, Bo, 93

Different World, A, 351
Diff'rent Strokes, 343
Diller, Phyllis, 38, 195
Ding Dong School, 18
Dione Lucas Cooking Show, 23
Dire Straits, 327
Disney, Walt, 23–24, 70–75, 81, 96
Disney Channel, 75
Disneyland, 70–74
Dr. Kildare, 389–90
Dodge Dancing Party, The, 76
Dole, Bob, 26, 27, 91, 114, 304, 315
Dole, Elizabeth, 68, 189, 377
Dolenz, Mickey, 174–75
Domino, Fats, 94
Donahue, 53, 373–77
Donahue, Phil, 20, 284, 370, 373–75
Donaldson, Sam, 27, 29, 124, 126–28
Donna Reed Show, The, 40, 97, 112
Doors, 81, 96, 184, 214
Dotto, 104–105
Dow, Tony, 110
Dowd, Maureen, 363
Downey, Mort, Jr., 351, 375
Downey, Tim, 259
Downs, Hugh, 64, 65, 67, 244, 257, 332
Do You Trust Your Wife?, 101
Dragnet, 42–50, 131, 132, 253
Dreiser, Theodore, 270
Dubrow, Burt, 18
Dukakis, Michael, 315, 324, 333
Duran, Duran, 327
Durante, Jimmy, 12, 54
Dylan, Bob, 81, 174
Dynasty, 91, 275, 293, 324, 378, 396
Dzienza, Denny, 94

E!, 336
Early Prime, 310
Eastwood, Clint, 85
Ebbitt, David, 26
Ebersol, Dick, 262
Ebsen, Buddy, 145
Edge of Night, The, 272

Ed Sullivan Show, The, 184, 259, 298
Edwards, Douglas, 165–67
Ed Wynn Show, The, 13
Eight Is Enough, 294
Eisenhower, Dwight D., 18, 88, 99, 124, 166, 333
Eisenhower, Mamie, 67
Eliot, T. S., 283
Elizabeth R, 232
Ellington, Duke, 81, 141
Elliott, Michael, 113
Enright, Dan, 102
Entertainment Daily Journal, 336
Entertainment Tonight, 27, 66, 314, 334–40
Ephron, Nora, 224
ER, 55, 77, 206, 270, 276, 293, 331, 353, 363, 389–95
Ervin, Sam, 365
Everly Brothers, 94
Eyes on the Prize, 266

Fabares, Shelley, 97
Fabian, 95
Face the Nation, 28, 29
Fahri, Paul, 58
Falcon Crest, 293
Falwell, Jerry, 51
Family Feud, 164, 372
Family Ties, 146, 225, 355
Farley, James, 25
Farmer's Daughter, The, 16
Farrell, Mike, 279, 282
Fat Albert and the Cosby Kids, 342
Father Knows Best, 16, 37, 89, 111, 135, 147, 218, 383, 391
Fawlty Towers, 233
FBI, The, 48
Feit, Ben, 101
Feliciano, José, 80
Fickett, Mary, 276
Field, Sally, 54
Fine, Marlene, 274
Finkel, Bob, 195
Firing Line, 302

First Churchills, The, 231
Fisher, Amy, 266, 269
Fisher, Stan, 11
Fitzgerald, Ella, 81
Fleetwood Mac, 75
Flintstones, The, 23, 147, 353, 355
Flip Wilson Show, The, 342
Floren, Myren, 77
Flowers, Gennifer, 314, 338
Flying Nun, The, 54
Fonda, Henry, 214
Fonda, Jane, 27
Fontana, Tom, 392
Ford, Gerald, 172, 188, 261, 333
Ford, Tennessee Ernie, 54, 162
For Love or Money, 104
Forsyte Saga, The, 230, 231
Fort Apache, the Bronx, 319
48 Hours, 313
Franchi, Sergio, 80
Francis, Arlene, 161
Frank, Reuven, 312
Frankel, Max, 240
Franken, Al, 263
Frank's Place, 283, 284
Freed, Alan, 94
Fretts, Bruce, 337
Freud, Sigmund, 375
Friedan, Betty, 37
Friendly, Fred, 60, 125, 252
Friendly Fire, 266
Friends, 134, 223, 353, 380
Frontline, 234
Frost, Robert, 27
Fryd, Lee, 376
F Troop, 177
Fugitive, The, 132
Fuller, Buckminster, 141–42
Full House, 360
Funt, Allen, 361

Gabor, Zsa Zsa, 60, 249
Gamson, Joshua, 376
Gans, Herbert, 170
Garagiola, Joe, 65

Garbo, Greta, 35
Gardner, Erle Stanley, 129–30
Garland, Judy, 61
Garner, James, 85, 331
Garroway, Dave, 63–65, 104, 106, 154
Garroway at Large, 64
G. E. College Bowl, 26
Gelbart, Larry, 35, 269–70, 279–83, 361
Geller, Bruce, 178, 180
General Electric Theater, 107, 113, 298
General Hospital, 271, 294, 390
Geraldo, 353
Gerber, David, 48
Gerbner, George, 49, 56, 368
Gergen, David, 300, 305, 307
Get Smart, 177, 181, 200
Gibson, Henry, 192, 194
G. I. Joe, 19, 23, 74
Gifford, Kathie Lee, 386
Gilbert, Paul, 395–96, 401
Gilligan, Carol, 41, 274
Gilligan's Island, 144, 145, 154, 157, 214, 223
Gingrich, Newt, 316, 383
Giordano, Frani, 94–95
Girl from U.N.C.L.E., The, 181
Gitlin, Todd, 268, 320, 401
Gleason, Jackie, 13, 52, 54, 77
Glenn, John, 79, 139, 141
Gobel, George, 217
Godfrey, Arthur, 23, 54, 82, 300, 372, 378
Going My Way, 54
Goldberg, Gary David, 225
Goldbergs, The, 15
Golden Girls, The, 351
Goldenson, Leonard, 71, 72, 94
Goldwater, Barry, 299
Gomer Pyle, U.S.M.C., 177, 186, 348
Gong Show, The, 160, 164, 361
Goode, Chester, 85
Goodman, John, 353
Goodman, Walter, 258

Good Morning America, 65, 375
Goodson, Mark, 106, 159
Good Times, 222
Gore, Al, 316, 377
Gould, Elliott, 279
Gould, Jack, 89, 153, 225
Goulet, Robert, 191
Graham, Billy, 51, 53, 54, 191
Grant, Hugh, 233, 338
Grass Roots, 174
Graves, Peter, 178, 179
Gray, Bill, 242
Green, Gerald, 67
Green Acres, 144, 146, 174, 195, 217
Greenfield, Jeff, 18, 258, 259, 289
Greider, William, 268
Griffin, Merv, 164, 243, 395, 397
Griffith, Andy, 145–46, 331
Griffith, D. W., 317
Grissom, Gus, 141
Gross, Ben, 300
Guiding Light, The, 271, 272
Guillory, Ferrel, 328
Gumbel, Bryant, 65
Gunsmoke, 9, 16, 25, 84, 170, 192, 340, 378
Gunther, Marc, 390

Hackman, Gene, 213
Haggis Baggis, 104
Hagman, Larry, 293
Hailey, Arthur, 319
Halberstam, David, 62, 69
Hale, Barbara, 130
Haley, Alex, 246, 265–67
Hall, Arsenio, 243
Hammerstein, Oscar, 80
Happy Days, 113, 378
Harbor Command, 47
Hard Copy, 329, 337–38, 340, 356
Harding, Tonya, 207, 257, 337
Harding, Warren G., 124
Harper, Valerie, 225
Harrison, Albertis, 153
Hart, Gary, 143

Hart, Lois, 310

Hart, Mary, 335, 337

Hart, William S., 87

Hartford, John, 184

Hartman, Phil, 260

Hartz, Jim, 65, 67, 239

"Harvest of Shame," 59, 61, 108

Hatch, Orrin, 366

Have Gun Will Travel, 84, 85, 89

Hawaii Five-O, 48

Hawn, Goldie, 192, 193

Hayes, Helen, 256

Hazel, 41

HBO, 62

Hear It Now, 61

Hecht, Ben, 248

Hee Haw, 78, 187, 191, 195, 217

Heidi, 207

Hemingway, Ernest, 231

Henderson, Skitch, 243

Hendrix, Jimi, 175

Henning, Paul, 145–47

Henry, William, 320

Henson, Jim, 202, 261

Hepburn, Katharine, 36, 69

Herbert, Col. Anthony, 256

Here's Lucy, 192

Hesse, Hermann, 116

Heston, Charlton, 263

Hewitt, Don, 62, 166, 169, 239,
    251–57

Hickok, Wild Bill, 88

Highway Patrol, 47

Highway to Heaven, 16, 56

Hill, Anita, 139, 341, 364–70

Hill, Stephen, 178

Hill Street Blues, 49–50, 227, 276,
    318–24, 390, 392, 393

Hiss, Alger, 30

Hoffman, Alice, 356

Hoffman, Dustin, 131

Hoffman, Nicholas von, 254

Hogan's Heroes, 177, 280, 348

Holliday, George, 362–63

Holly, Buddy, 95, 96

Hollywood Beat, 329

Hollywood Squares, 388

Hollywood Television Theatre, 230

Holocaust, 268

Holt, John, 204

Home Improvement, 25, 70, 75, 207,
    220, 284, 378–84

Home Shopping Network, 55

Homicide, 50, 293, 318, 386, 393

Homicide Squad, 44

Honeymooners, The, 9, 110, 218, 219,
    353

Hooper, Larry, 77

Hooperman, 283

Hoover, Herbert, 124

Hopalong Cassidy, 88

Hope, Bob, 12, 15, 81, 106

Horn, Bob, 93

Horne, Lena, 81

Horowitz, Myrna, 94

Horton, Willie, 324

Hour of Power, 55

House of Cards, 229

Howdy Doody, 18–24, 199

Howe, Quincy, 61

How Green Was My Valley, 231

Hughes, Howard, 254

Humbard, Rex, 51

Humphrey, Hubert H., 27, 185, 191,
    251

Huntley, Chet, 108, 140, 166,
    168–69, 170, 172

Huntley-Brinkley Report, The, 166

Hurt, John, 232

Hussein, Saddam, 292

I, Claudius, 229, 232

Ian, Janis, 261

I Dream of Jeannie, 154, 158, 180

I Love Lucy, 9, 13, 35–42, 110, 113,
    135, 147, 192, 220, 223, 298,
    340–41, 346, 351

Imus, Don, 30, 256, 381

Inside Edition, 221, 329, 336–38,
    359–60

Ionesco, Eugene, 304
Iran Crisis: America Held Hostage, 289
Ironside, 48
Irving, Clifford, 254
I Spy, 177, 181, 341
Ito, Lance, 369
It's News to Me, 160, 168
"It's Not Easy Being Green," 203
I've Got a Secret, 25, 104, 106

Jack Benny Program, The, 39
Jackson, Glenda, 232
Jackson, Jesse, 204, 256
Jackson, Michael, 338, 352
Jacobi, Derek, 232
Jake and the Fatman, 85
Jakes, John, 268
James, Henry, 230
Jamieson, Kathleen Hall, 316
Javna, John, 178
Jefferson Airplane, 96, 174
Jeffersons, The, 222, 340
Jenny Jones, 161, 371–72
Jeopardy!, 23, 337, 399
Jetsons, The, 19
Jewel in the Crown, 229
Jewell, Richard, 315
Jimenez, Carmen, 94
Joffe, Gerald, 318
Johnson, Arte, 192
Johnson, Don, 246, 329
Johnson, Lady Bird, 67
Johnson, Lyndon B., 84, 124, 125, 151, 171–72, 184, 186, 230
Johnson, Nicholas, 187
Jones, Davy, 174–75, 214
Jones, Gerald, 40, 110, 158
Jones, James Earl, 141
Jones, Jenny, 371
Jones, Paula, 338
Joplin, Janis, 78, 252
Jordan, Will, 81
Judd for the Defense, 188
Julia, 340

Kadaffi, Muammar, 292
Kahn, E. J., 255
Kakutani, Michiko, 114, 377
Kaltenborn, H.V., 61
Kaminer, Wendy, 378
Kaniss, Phyllis, 237
Karloff, Boris, 349
Karp, Walter, 274
Kate & Allie, 260, 342
Katz, Elihu, 139, 295–96
Katz, Jon, 30
Kaye, Elizabeth, 388
Keeshan, Bob, 20
Kefauver, Estes, 362
Kennedy, David, 114
Kennedy, Edward, 143, 172
Kennedy, Jacqueline, 60, 113, 151, 153, 312
Kennedy, John F., 24, 25–26, 51, 60, 79, 86, 90, 109, 123–27, 139, 144, 146, 148–54, 155, 165, 249, 309, 317, 334, 361, 377
Kennedy, Joseph, 135
Kennedy, Robert F., 299, 301–303
Kent, Arthur, 212
Kerrigan, Nancy, 207
Keystone Cops, 44
Khomeini, Ayatollah Ruhollah, 255
Khrushchev, Nikita, 86, 167
Kilgallen, Dorothy, 244
Kilpatrick, James J., 254
King, Billie Jean, 207, 215, 254
King, Larry, 20, 30, 66, 310, 315–17
King, Martin Luther, Jr., 51, 268, 347
King, Martin Luther, Sr., 268
King, Rodney, 50, 363
Kinsley, Michael, 220
Kirkpatrick, Jeane, 306
Kirshner, Don, 175
Kisseloff, Jeff, 15, 94, 125
Knots Landing, 293
Kojak, 49, 182, 253
Koppel, Ted, 289
Koresh, David, 266
Kovacs, Ernie, 192, 247, 259

Kozoll, Michael, 318–19
Kraft Television Theatre, 117
Kroft, Steve, 255
Kukla, Fran, and Ollie, 18, 64
Kuralt, Charles, 168
Kurtz, Howard, 57
Kyle, Crystal, 215

Lahr, John, 352, 356
Lake, Ricki, 371, 375, 377
L.A. Law, 77, 276, 318, 322, 329, 355
Lance, Bert, 365
Landau, Martin, 180
Landis, John, 259
Landon, Michael, 16, 56, 85, 89, 331, 337
Lange, Jim, 162
Lansbury, Bruce, 180
Laramie, 137
Lardner, John, 102
Larry King Live, 310, 313, 315–17
Lassie, 155, 217
Last of the Mohicans, The, 231
Late Night With David Letterman, 191, 247–48, 253, 329
Laugh-In, 23, 175, 190–96, 200, 218, 260, 262
Laughton, Charles, 82
Laverne and Shirley, 35, 113, 378
Law and Order, 270, 393
Lawford, Peter, 135
Lawrence Welk Show, The, 76–79, 148, 229
Layne, Rickie, 81
Lear, Norman, 217–72, 264
Leary, Timothy, 158, 174
Leave It to Beaver, 16, 37, 92, 147, 215, 283, 344, 353, 380
Lee, Will, 203
Leland, John, 327
Lennon, John, 175
Lennon Sisters, 77, 78
Leno, Jay, 69, 176, 247–50
Leonard, John, 219, 223, 329

Leonard, Sheldon, 135–37
Lerner, Max, 101
Lescoulie, Jack, 64, 66–67
Let's Make a Deal, 159, 161
Letterman, David, 67, 69, 108, 176, 247–50, 253, 259, 330, 344, 381
Levis, Art, 363
Lewis, Jerry, 12, 79, 80, 195, 217, 387, 396
Lewis, Jerry Lee, 94
Lewis, Warren, 144
Liar's Club, 160
Liberace, 60
Lichter, S. Robert, 188, 369
Liebes, Tamar, 295–96
Life Is Worth Living, 51–57
Life of Riley, The, 354
Life with Luigi, 15
Linkletter, Art, 71, 82, 361, 372
Lippmann, Walter, 69, 314
Lipsyte, Robert, 210, 234
Lisagor, Peter, 27
Littlefield, Warren, 192
Little Richard, 92
Livingstone, Jay, 155
Loder, Kurt, 328
Logan, Michael, 350
Lombard, Carole, 36
Lon, Alice, 77
Lone Ranger, The, 84, 87, 88, 113
Lonesome Dove, 232, 269
Long, Huey, 101, 331
Lou Grant, 227
Louis-Dreyfuss, Julia, 260
Love Boat, The, 319, 388
Lovitz, Jon, 263
Lubin, Arthur, 155
Lucci, Susan, 276
Lucky Partners, 104
Lucy-Desi Comedy Hour, 39
Lupus, Peter, 180
Lutz, Sam, 78
Lymon, Frankie, 94
Lynch, David, 323

McCaffrey, John K.M., 28
McCarthy, Joseph, 57–63, 100,
    364–65, 368
McCartney, Paul, 175
MacDonald, J. Fred, 180, 182, 272
McFadzean, David, 383
McGee, Frank, 65, 67, 140, 239
McGinniss, Joe, 377
McGovern, George, 279
McGrory, Mary, 304
McHale's Navy, 180
McInerney, Jay, 379
Mack, Ted, 361
McKay, Jim, 207
McKibben, Bill, 213
McKuen, Rod, 141
MacLachlan, Kyle, 323
MacLaine, Shirley, 334
McLaughlin Group, The, 26, 27, 29,
    220, 233
McLuhan, Marshall, 61, 80, 291,
    396
McMahon, Ed, 97, 245
MacMurray, Fred, 130
McNeil, Alex, 187
MacNeil, Robert, 149
MacNeil-Lehrer Report, The, 230
McQueen, Steve, 85, 89
Mad About You, 134, 220, 331
Madden, John, 212
Madonna, 35, 327, 330
Madsden, Axel, 253, 255
Maglie, Sal, 67
Magnum, P.I., 324
Make Room for Daddy, 111, 135
Man from U.N.C.L.E., The, 177, 181,
    192
Mankiewicz, Frank, 301–302
Mankiewicz, Herman J., 248
Mann, Michael, 329
Man of the Week, 28–29
Manson, Charles, 257
Mantley, John, 86
Marc, David, 111, 135, 144, 154, 225,
    246, 294

March, Hal, 101
Marcus, Greil, 328
Marcus Welby, M.D., 254, 280, 293,
    390, 392
Margulies, Stan, 267
Marinaro, Ed, 322
Markus, John, 344
Married . . . With Children, 343, 361,
    382
Martin, Billy, 263
Martin, Dean, 12, 79, 80, 184, 192,
    387
Martin, Dick, 192–95
Martin, Quinn, 48, 266
Martin, Steve, 185, 263
Marx Brothers, 72, 175
Mary Hartman, Mary Hartman, 222
Mary Tyler Moore Show, The, 41, 111,
    158, 183, 217, 223–28, 275,
    280, 281, 296, 297, 318, 321,
    332, 342, 343, 344, 379, 380
*M*A*S*H,* 38, 111, 174, 178, 265,
    270, 278–85, 295, 296, 321,
    342, 361, 394
Mason, Jackie, 81
Masterpiece Theatre, 228–35, 266, 276,
    320, 386
Mathers, Jerry, 110
Matthews, Larry, 136
Matusow, Barbara, 83, 167
Maude, 222
Maury Povich Show, The, 161, 371
Maverick, 84, 85
Mayberry RFD, 217
Mayor of Casterbridge, The, 232
Mazursky, Paul, 175
Medic, 389, 394
Medical Center, 390, 391
Meet the Press, 14, 25–31
Menaker, Daniel, 225
Meriwether, Lee Ann, 65
Metcalfe, Burt, 281
Miami Vice, 292, 328–29
Michaels, Al, 207
Michaels, Lorne, 259–64

Mickey Mouse Club, The, 23, 70, 73–74

Miller, Dennis, 263, 332

Miller, Jonathan, 152

Miller, Mark Crispin, 69, 71, 334, 336

Milli Vanilli, 174

Minnelli, Liza, 81

Minow, Newton, 153, 249

Miranda, Carmen, 12

Mission: Impossible, 113, 177–82

Mission to the World, 51

Mr. District Attorney, 47, 96

Mister Ed, 55, 154–58

Mister Rogers, 19, 23, 51, 230

Mitchell, Martha, 191

Mix, Tom, 87

Mod Squad, The, 133, 181, 188, 340

Molloy, Paul, 66

Mondale, Walter, 307–309, 333

Monday Night Football, 207, 210, 282

Monkees, The, 173–76, 330

Monroe, Marilyn, 27, 60

Monty Python's Flying Circus, 261

Moonlighting, 175, 318, 322–23, 329

Moore, Garry, 332

Moore, Mary Tyler, 136, 174, 223–28

Moore, Tom, 87

Morgan, Harry, 282

Mork and Mindy, 146

Morris, Garrett, 262

Morris, Greg, 180, 181

Morrison, Jim, 81

Morton, Charles, 43

Mosher, Bob, 111–12

Moss, Frank, 132–33

Moyers, Bill, 30, 314, 335

MTV, 55, 98, 310, 325–31, 384–85

Mudd, Roger, 168

Muggs, J. Fred, 64

Munsters, The, 154, 157

Murder, She Wrote, 253

Murphy, Eddie, 260, 263, 264

Murphy Brown, 30, 134, 147, 183, 206, 223, 363, 380

Murray, Bill, 260, 262–64

Murrow, Edward R., 14, 27, 54, 57–63, 67, 68, 125, 165, 167, 188, 244, 252, 316

Myers, Mike, 260, 263–64

My Favorite Husband, 36

My Favorite Martian, 144, 146, 154, 157–58

My Mother the Car, 154

My So-Called Life, 92

Mystery, 233

My Three Sons, 112, 218, 343, 380

Naked City, 47

Namath, Joe, 214

Name That Tune, 99

Nash, Joey, 118

Nature, 233

Nature of Things, The, 11

Nealon, Kevin, 263

Nelson, Lindsay, 209

Nelson, Ozzie, 111

Nelson, Ricky, 175

Nelson, Willie, 386

Nesmith, Michael, 174–75

Ness, Eliot, 47

N.E.T. Playhouse, 230

Newcomb, Horace, 283

Newhart, Bob, 331–34

Newlywed Game, The, 160, 162–63

Newman, Edwin, 309

Newman, Laraine, 262

Nichols, Nichelle, 347

Nightline, 243, 289, 291, 363

Nimoy, Leonard, 180

Nixon, Agnes, 272–75

Nixon, Richard M., 24, 26, 79, 100, 113, 123–26, 128, 139, 147, 166, 185, 191, 221–22, 244, 251, 254, 279, 312, 387

Nochimson, Martha, 274

"Noon on Doomsday," 118

North, Oliver, 365

North and South, 269
Northern Exposure, 323
Nossel, Murray, 375
NOVA, 230
Novak, Robert, 29
Nussbaum, Hedda, 356
NYPD Blue, 50, 318, 331, 393

O'Connor, Carroll, 217–18
O'Connor, Sinead, 263
O'Donoghue, Michael, 261
O'Hair, Madalyn Murray, 373
Omnibus, 230–31
O'Neill, Eugene, 28
O'Neill, Tip, 84
One Life to Live, 275
$1.98 Beauty Contest, The, 160, 165
Oprah Winfrey Show, The, 24, 42, 53,
　　66, 370–78
Oral Roberts, 386
Orlean, Susan, 262
Orwell, George, 363
Oswald, Lee Harvey, 149–52,
　　208–209
Our Miss Brooks, 13, 111, 224
Outer Limits, The, 360
Owen Marshall: Counsellor at Law, 391
Ozzie and Harriet, 40, 111, 136, 175,
　　227

Paar, Jack, 164, 167, 243–44, 245,
　　249, 250
Painted Dreams, 272
Paley, William, 90, 157
Palmer, Betsy, 65
Palmer, John, 239
Pappas, Ike, 152
Parker, Fess, 73, 145
Partridge Family, The, 213
Password, 159
Patty Duke Show, The, 16, 21
Pauley, Jane, 65
Paulsen, Pat, 184–86
Paul Whiteman's TV Teen Club, 93
Pavarotti, Luciano, 234

PBS, 23, 199–200, 205, 228–35,
　　387
Peale, Norman Vincent, 53, 101
Peckinpah, Sam, 85
Peewee's Playhouse, 329
Pendergrass, Teddy, 69
People Are Funny, 361, 372
People's Court, The, 164
Perlman, Itzhak, 81
Perot, H. Ross, 30, 79, 148, 316, 360,
　　377
Perrin, Nat, 157
Perry Mason, 129–33, 179–80, 329,
　　353
Person to Person, 27, 42, 60, 107
Petticoat Junction, 144, 145
Philbin, Regis, 386
Phillips, Irna, 270–72
Phillips, Stone, 257
Piccolo, Brian, 266
Picket Fences, 56, 276, 318
Pierpont, Robert, 126
Pinter, Harold, 304
Piscopo, Joe, 263, 264
Pittman, Bob, 326
Playhouse 90, 117, 118
Play Your Hunch, 104
Podrazik, Walter, 116, 333
Poe, Edgar Allan, 44
Poldark, 231
Police Story, 48
Police Woman, 181
Politi, Ellen, 399
Politically Incorrect, 188
Pollan, Michael, 332
Porter, Dennis, 273
Posner, Gerald, 149
Postman, Neil, 335–36
Pot O'Gold, 100
Povich, Maury, 367
Powell, Colin, 383
Power of Positive Thinking, The, 53
Powers, Ron, 238, 242, 338
Presley, Elvis, 79, 81–82, 93–95, 399
Pressman, Gabe, 239

Preston, Billy, 261
Price Is Right, The, 159, 160, 372
Prime Time Live, 66, 313
Principal, Victoria, 388
Prisoner, The, 349
Pryor, Richard, 81
Putnam, Robert, 228
Pyne, Joe, 243

Quayle, Dan, 30, 315
Queen for a Day, 372, 386–88
QVC, 385–86, 388

Rabinowitz, Dorothy, 221
Radner, Gilda, 260, 261, 262
Rafelson, Bob, 175
Raphael, Sally Jessy, 221, 367, 376, 393
Rather, Dan, 30, 124, 125, 127, 168, 170, 172, 240, 253–55, 311
Rat Patrol, The, 177
Rawhide, 89
Rayburn, Gene, 243
Raye, Martha, 64
Reagan, Nancy, 298
Reagan, Ronald, 26, 51, 61, 71, 78, 79, 83, 113–14, 124, 126–28, 148, 172, 248, 250, 297–309, 317, 328, 330, 333, 334
Real McCoys, The, 92, 145
Real People, 361
Reasoner, Harry, 150, 251, 254, 255
Redding, Otis, 96
Redford, Robert, 99, 102, 104, 131
Reed, Robert, 213
Reeve, Christopher, 189
Reeves, Jimmie, 245
Reiner, Carl, 16, 135–38, 164, 226
Reiner, Rob, 185, 219, 222
"Requiem for a Heavyweight," 118
Rescue 911, 30, 45, 50, 359, 392
Restless Gun, The, 89
Reston, James, 99, 123
Reynolds, Burt, 85, 162, 334
Reynolds, Gene, 279–82

Rhine, Larry, 156
Rich, Lee, 294
Richard Diamond, Private Detective, 136
Rich Man, Poor Man, 232, 266
Rickover, Hyman, 256
Rifleman, The, 84, 89
Riggs, Bobby, 207, 215
Rin Tin Tin, 155
Rivera, Geraldo, 292, 351
Rivers, Joan, 38, 243, 245, 386
Road Rules, 331
Roberts, Oral, 51
Roberts, Julia, 275
Roberts, Pernell, 90
Robertson, Pat, 51, 55
Robinson, Bill "Bojangles," 11
Robinson, Hubbell, 85, 87
Robinson, Jackie, 27
Robinson, Michael J., 369
Robinson, Smokey, 200
Rocca, Antonio (Argentino), 208
Rockefeller, Nelson, 248
Rocky and His Friends, 23, 180
Roddenberry, Gene, 348
Rodgers, "Nature Boy" Buddy, 208
Rolling Stones, 81, 262
Romance of Helen Trent, The, 272
Romper Room, 19, 23
Room 222, 188
Rooney, Andy, 255–56
Rooney, Mickey, 218
Roosevelt, Eleanor, 68, 249
Roosevelt, Franklin D., 124
Roosevelt, Teddy, 124
Rootie Kazootie, 18
Roots, 62, 70, 232, 265–70, 319, 340, 342
Roseanne, 35, 351–56, 361, 362, 367, 382–83
Rose, Brian, 244
Rose Marie, 136
Rosenberg, Howard, 133, 318, 335, 362
Rosenstiel, Tom, 312, 313–14
Rosenthal, A. M., 314–15

Rosie O'Donnell Show, The, 378

Roundtree, Martha, 25

Rowan, Dan, 190–95

Rowan and Martin's Laugh-In, 190–96

Rowe, James, 125

Roy Rogers, 88

Rozelle, Pete, 207

Rubin, Jerry, 262

Ruby, Jack, 152

Russert, Tim, 27, 30

Rydell, Bobby, 95

Sadat, Anwar, 172, 255

Sadr, Bani, 290

Safer, Morley, 67, 253–56

Sagan, Carl, 246

Saget, Bob, 360

Sahl, Mort, 249

St. Clair, Gen. Arthur, 364

St. Elsewhere, 318, 321, 322, 390, 392,
    394

Salant, Richard, 240

Salisbury, Harrison, 172–73

Sally Jessy Raphael, 277, 376

Sammartino, Bruno, 208

Sandler, Adam, 263

Sanford and Son, 222, 340

Sarnoff, David, 71

Sarson, Christopher, 231

Saturday Night Live, 17, 83, 183, 188,
    192, 201, 249, 253, 258–65,
    361

Savio, Mario, 174

Sawyer, Diane, 255, 257

Sayers, Gale, 266

Scheffler, Phil, 166

Schickel, Richard, 171

Schieffer, Bob, 29, 57

Schlatter, George, 192–93

Schneider, Bert, 174

Schorr, Daniel, 62

Schuller, Robert, 55

Schultz, John, 61

Schwartz, Sherwood, 213–15

Schwartz, Tony, 56

Schwarzenegger, Arnold, 334, 396

Schwarzkopf, Gen. Norman, 53

Schweitzer, Albert, 80, 249

Scott, Willard, 65, 241

Sears, John, 304

Secret Agent, 21, 181

Seeger, Pete, 184, 186, 191

See It Now, 57–63, 251

Seinfeld, 24, 39, 134, 191, 206, 260,
    296, 344, 362, 378–84

Selleck, Tom, 162

Serling, Rod, 116–20, 130, 160, 229

Serpas, Frank, 262

Sesame Street, 19, 23, 191, 195,
    199–205, 230, 249

Sevareid, Eric, 168, 184, 314

77 Sunset Strip, 92

Severinsen, Doc, 245

Shales, Tom, 319, 327–28

Shalit, Gene, 65

Shandling, Garry, 259

Sharpe, Don, 38

Shatner, William, 30

Shaw, Irwin, 266

Shayon, Robert Lewis, 9, 139, 184

Sheen, Rt. Rev. Fulton J., 51–57

Shepard, Alan, 139

Shepherd, Cybill, 323

Shields, Mark, 29

Shirer, William L., 165

Shore, Dinah, 13, 61, 81, 89–90

Short, Martin, 263, 264

Silver, Edward, 133

Silverman, Fred, 43, 266–68, 319

Silvers, Phil, 12

Simon, Paul, 263

Simon, Ron, 113

Simpson, O. J., 50, 56, 83, 119, 133,
    139, 240, 267, 292, 296, 310,
    312, 317, 331, 337, 341,
    345–46, 364, 368

Simpsons, The, 23, 181, 277, 350

Sinatra, Frank, 12, 52, 61

Singing Nun, 81

Singled Out, 331

Sisterhood Is Powerful, 158
$64,000 Question, 99–104, 208, 400
60 Minutes, 62, 69, 142, 169, 239, 251–58, 313, 329
"Slap" Maxwell Story, The, 283
Smith, "Buffalo Bob," 19, 20, 24
Smith, Cecil, 84
Smith, Kate, 386
Smith, Susan, 338
Smith, William Kennedy, 312, 364, 368
Smothers Brothers, 183–90, 191, 195, 207, 259, 262, 281
Smothers Brothers Comedy Hour, The, 90, 183–89, 220
Snyder, Tom, 262
Something About Amelia, 266
Sons & Lovers, 231
Soren, Tabitha, 330
Soul Train, 97
Spencer, Stuart, 299
Spigel, Lynn, 38
Spin City, 225
Spinney, Carroll, 202, 204
Spivak, Lawrence, 27–29
Spock, Benjamin, 186
Stahl, Lesley, 255
Stalin, Joseph, 53
Stanton, Frank, 107
Stanwyck, Barbara, 299
Stapleton, Jean, 218
Star Trek, 119, 234, 340, 346–50
Steel, Danielle, 232
Steele, Bob, 87
Steffans, Lincoln, 252
Stein, Benjamin, 16
Steinbeck, John, 106
Steinberg, David, 186, 187
Steinem, Gloria, 174
Steirs, David Ogden, 282
Stempel, Herbert, 102–106
Stern, Bill, 208
Stern, Howard, 381
Stevenson, Adlai, 106, 244
Stevenson, McLean, 282

Stewart, Jimmy, 299
Stiles, Martin, 200
Stills, Stephen, 174
Stockman, David, 305–307
Stone, Chuck, 268
Stone, Jon, 204
Stone, Milburn, 85
Stone, Oliver, 377
Stone, Sharon, 316
Stone, Sid, 12
Storefront Lawyers, 133
Streets of San Francisco, The, 48
Streisand, Barbra, 68, 255
Strike It Rich, 372
Struthers, Sally, 219
Stuart, Charles, 269
Studio One, 96, 118
Sullivan, Arlene, 94
Sullivan, Barry, 85
Sullivan, Ed, 12, 77, 79–84, 93, 142, 202, 208, 341, 362
Sunday Morning News, 29
Super Bowl, 205–12
Sutherland, Donald, 279
S.W.A.T., 182
Swayze, John Cameron, 165–66
Swift, Al, 370

Tales of Wells-Fargo, 84
Talman, William, 130
Tannen, Deborah, 41, 274, 383
Tarkenton, Fran, 388
Tartikoff, Brandon, 284
Taxi, 134, 223
Taylor, Clyde, 268
Taylor, Elizabeth, 275, 337
Taylor, Ella, 226
Ted Mack's Original Amateur Hour, 164, 361
Teely, Peter, 304–305
Temple, Shirley, 356
Terkel, Studs, 64
Tesh, John, 335
Texaco Star Theater, The, 9–17, 54, 107
That Girl, 158, 224

thirtysomething, 318, 322, 324, 329, 352, 355, 367

This Is Your Life, 76, 366

This Week with David Brinkley, 26–29

Thomas, Clarence, 139, 341, 364–70

Thomas, Danny, 135

Thomas, Marlo, 158, 224

Thomas, Phillip Michael, 329

Thompson, Robert, 144, 294, 401

Thorburn, David, 45

Thorn Birds, The, 70, 266, 269

Three's Company, 378

Till, Emmett, 118

Till Death Do Us Part, 217

Tinker, Grant, 133, 227

Tiny Tim, 192, 246

Toast of the Town, 13, 80–84

Tocqueville, Alexis de, 83, 339

Today, 63–70, 104, 106, 164, 167, 257, 272, 316, 335, 372, 375

Todman, Bill, 106

Tomlin, Lily, 192–93

Tonight Show, The, 17, 63, 145, 164, 183, 243–50, 272, 341, 344, 373, 386

Topo Gigio, 81

Tork, Peter, 174–75

Toscanini, Arturo, 21

Touched by an Angel, 56

Town Meeting of the Air, 28

Tracy, Spencer, 304

Treasury Agent, 44

Treasury Men in Action, 47

Trial of Anne Boleyn, The, 231

Truman, Harry S, 11, 364

Tuchman, Barbara, 172

Tucker, Sophie, 15

Turner, Lana, 334

Turner, Ted, 311–13

Turn-On, 218

Twentieth Century, The, 167

Twenty-One, 99, 102–106

20/20, 68, 257

Twilight Zone, The, 115–20, 157, 349

Twin Peaks, 323–24, 331

Tyson, Cicely, 267

Tyson, Mike, 68

Uggams, Leslie, 267

Untouchables, The, 47

Upstairs, Downstairs, 229, 232

Vance, Vivian, 38

Van Doren, Charles, 99, 102–108

Van Dyke, Dick, 136, 137, 224–26

Victor, David, 391

Vidal, Gore, 396

Vieira, Meredith, 255

Village Barn, The, 11

Von Bulow, Claus, 312

Vonnegut, Kurt, 116

Wagon Train, 84, 378

Wallace, George, 78, 147, 185

Wallace, Mike, 61, 118, 160, 167, 251–57, 313

Wall Street Week, 230

Walston, Ray, 157–58

Walters, Barbara, 27, 60, 65, 67–69, 170, 245, 255, 257, 316, 372

Waltons, The, 294, 297

Wanted—Dead or Alive, 89

War and Remembrance, 269

Warhol, Andy, 332

Warner, William, 87

Warner Brothers Presents, 87

Warren, Earl, 129, 133

Washington, Desiree, 68

Washington Week in Review, 29, 230, 234

Waters, Harry, 267, 294, 343

Watson, Mary Ann, 54

Wayne, John, 78, 85, 87, 91, 191, 299

Wayne and Shuster, 81

Weaver, Dennis, 85

Weaver, Sylvester "Pat," 63, 66, 164, 243, 248–49, 272

Webb, Jack, 43–46, 48, 50

Weisman, Michael, 206

Welch, Joseph, 58, 365

Welk, Lawrence, 76–79, 332
Wences, Señor, 11
Wershba, Joseph, 62
Wertheim, Arthur Frank, 14, 15
"We Shall Overcome," 268
West 57th Street, 329, 330
Westin, David, 393
Wharton, Edith, 231
What's My Line?, 25, 104, 106, 168
Wheel of Fortune, 160, 337, 395–402
White, Mimi, 386
White, Vanna, 160, 395, 398
Who, 184
Who Do You Trust?, 160, 246
Who Pays?, 160
Whorf, Richard, 145
"Who Shot J.R.?," 265, 295
Who's the Boss?, 351
Wide World of Sports, 207
Wigand, Jeffrey, 256
Wild, Wild West, The, 181
Will, George, 27, 29, 302, 306
Williams, Barry, 214
Williams, Martin, 44
Williams, Matt, 284, 344, 383
Williams, Robin, 200
Willis, Bruce, 232
Wills, Gary, 299
Wilson, Flip, 194
Wilson, Woodrow, 124, 317
Winchell, Walter, 9, 12, 47, 244, 317,
      335

Winds of War, The, 232, 291
Winfrey, Oprah, 370–78
Wister, Owen, 86
Wolper, David, 62, 266, 269
Wonder, Stevie, 78, 275
Wonderful World of Color, The, 74
Wonderful World of Disney, The, 254
Wonder Years, The, 283
Wood, Bob, 217, 218
Woodward, Bob, 252, 255
Wynn, Ed, 13, 63

X-Files, The, 119, 207, 332, 350

Yancy Derringer, 89
Yeltsin, Boris, 68
Yevtushenko, Yevgeny, 68–69
You Are There, 61, 167
Young, John, 141
Young, Loretta, 54
Young, Robert, 391
Young and the Restless, 271
Young Dr. Malone, 272
Young Lawyers, The, 133
Youngman, Henny, 11
Your Big Moment, 161
Your Show of Shows, 259

Zelizer, Barbie, 153
Zicree, Mark, 116
Zimmer, Norma, 77
Zoglin, Richard, 258, 336, 343